Globalization and Labor Markets

Globalization and Labor Markets

E. Kwan Choi and David Greenaway

Iowa State University and University of Nottingham

Copyright © Blackwell Publishers Ltd 2001

This edition first published 2001

Blackwell Publishers Ltd
108 Cowley Road
Oxford OX4 1JF, UK

Blackwell Publishers Inc.
350 Main Street
Malden, Massachusetts 02148, USA

All rights reserved. Except for the quotation of sort passages for the purposes of criticism and review, no part of this publication may be reproduced, stored in a retrieval system, or transmitted, in any form or by any means, electronic, mechanical, photocopying, recording or otherwise, without the prior permission of the publisher.

Except in the United States of America, this book is sold subject to the condition that it shall not, by way of trade or otherwise, be lent, re-sold, hired out, or otherwise circulated without the publisher's prior consent in any form of binding or cover other than that in which it is published and without a similar condition including this condition being imposed on the subsequent purchaser.

British Library Cataloguing in Publication Data has been applied for

Library of Congress Cataloging in Publication Data has been applied for

ISBN   0-631-022410-6 (pbk)

Typeset by Best-set Typesetter Ltd., Hong Kong
Printed and bound in Great Britain
by MPG Books Ltd, Bodmin, Cornwall

This book is printed on acid-free paper

Contents

Introduction   vii

1. **Evolving Patterns of International Trade**
   James Proudman and Stephen Redding   1

2. **Trade and Labor Approaches to Wage Inequality**
   Jonathan E. Haskel   25

3. **Trade Liberalization and Technology Choice**
   Rod Falvey and Geoff Reed   37

4. **Dynamics of Intraindustry Trade and Labor-Market Adjustment**
   Marius Brülhart   48

5. **Marginal Intraindustry Trade and Labor Adjustment**
   Mary E. Lovely and Douglas R. Nelson   64

6. **Swedish Multinationals and Competition from High- and Low-Wage Locations**
   Henrik Braconier and Karolina Ekholm   76

7. **The Choice of Structural Model in Trade–Wages Decompositions**
   Lisandro Abrego and John Whalley   90

8. **Policy Implications of the Trade and Wages Debate**
   Alan V. Deardorff   106

9. **Technical Progress, Price Adjustments, and Wages**
   Ronald W. Jones   125

10. **The Effect of International Trade on Labor-Demand Elasticities: Intersectoral Matters**
    Sébastien Jean   132

11. **Smooth and Sticky Adjustment: A Comparative Analysis of the US and UK**
    Michelle Haynes, Richard Upward, and Peter Wright   145

12. **Relative Demand for Skills in Swedish Manufacturing Technology or Trade?**
    Pär Hansson   161

13 **Trade and Wages When the Trade Regime is Determined Endogenously**
    Robin Naylor 184

14 **Structural Change, Competition, and Job Turnover in Swedish Manufacturing, 1964–96**
    Linda Andersson, Ola Gustafsson, and Lars Lundberg 194

Index 211

Introduction

E. Kwan Choi and David Greenaway

Over the last twenty years there have been some significant changes in OECD labor markets. In the US, and to a lesser extent in the UK, there has been a marked growth in wage inequality, with the gap between skilled and unskilled workers becoming ever larger. In continental Europe, the divergence is nothing like as marked, though there have been growing inequalities in employment opportunities between skilled and unskilled workers.

These developments have initiated a major research programme which has largely focused on two key suspects: globalization and technological change. The former starts from the continued growth in trade and cross-border investment and in particular North-South linkages. If there is growing integration between low wage and high wage economies, so the reasoning goes, this will naturally drive down the relative wages of the unskilled in industrialized countries and increase the premium to being skilled. The alternative hypothesis is that rapid technological development, as seen most obviously in the proliferation of information technology, has increased demand for skilled labor and driven up the return to skills.

A great deal of research effort has been invested in laying the theoretical foundations to these explanations, testing them empirically, through time and across countries and exploring their policy implications. The papers in this volume embrace all three of these dimensions. On theory, Ron Jones and Rod Falvey/Geoffrey Reed focus on trade and technology; Jonathan Haskel's subject is the contrasting approaches which trade and labor economists take to analysing wage inequality; Doug Nelson and Mary Lovely address the links between intra-industry trade and labor market adjustment; and Robin Naylor investigates wage determination when the trade regime is endogenous.

Our empirical contributions are varied both in terms of the methodological approaches deployed and the countries on which they focus. James Proudman and Stephen Redding set the scene with a comprehensive analysis of evolving patterns of international trade; Lisandro Abrego/John Whalley and Sébastien Jean apply computable general equilibrium methods to the UK and France respectively; Marius Brülhart and Michelle Haynes/Richard Upward/Peter Wright focus on the issue of whether adjustment will be smoother in a setting of intra-industry trade; Pär Hansson investigates the role of trade and technology and Linda Andersson, Ola Gustafsson and Lars Lundberg the role of structural change and competition in Sweden. Finally, Henrik Braconier and Karolina Ekholm report on Swedish multinational activity and its links to wages. Policy issues feature prominently in a number of the chapters but are picked up specifically in Alan Deardorff's overview paper.

The volume offers a comprehensive collection of papers on the key issues in the trade, technology and labor market adjustment literature. We are grateful to the authors for providing such a high quality collection and trust they will be of value to researchers and analysts of international trade. First drafts of the papers were presented at a Conference on 'Globalization and Labor Markets' held at the University of Nottingham in March 1999. Financial support from the Leverhulme Trust under Programme Grant F114/BF is gratefully acknowledged.

1
Evolving Patterns of International Trade

James Proudman and Stephen Redding

1. Introduction

Much of the existing empirical trade literature is concerned with patterns of international trade at a point in time. This focus of empirical work stands in marked contrast with the theoretical literature on growth and trade, which emphasizes that comparative advantage is dynamic and evolves endogenously over time. This chapter proposes an empirical framework for analyzing the evolution of patterns of international trade over time, which consists of two main components. First, the extent of a country's specialization in an individual industry is measured by a modified index of revealed comparative advantage (RCA). A country's pattern of international specialization at a point in time is then fully characterized by the distribution of RCA across industries. Second, the dynamics of international specialization correspond to the evolution of this *entire* cross-section distribution over time. We employ a model of distribution dynamics from the cross-country growth literature, that is explicitly suited to the analysis of the evolution of an entire distribution.

Within this empirical framework, it is possible to address a variety of issues relating to international trade dynamics. In particular, we examine changes in countries' overall degree of specialization (the evolution of the *external shape* of the distribution of RCA) and the extent to which initial patterns of international specialization persist over time (an issue of *intra-distribution dynamics*). The theoretical literature on trade and growth typically yields ambiguous conclusions concerning both these issues. One strand of the theoretical literature emphasizes the role of factor accumulation in determining the evolution of international trade flows over time (see, e.g., Findlay, 1970, 1995; Deardorff, 1974). A second strand of research stresses the endogeneity of technological change (e.g., Grossman and Helpman, 1991; Krugman, 1987; Lucas, 1988; Redding, 1999). A third body of work concerned with economic geography underlines the importance of agglomeration economies (see in particular Krugman, 1991; Fujita et al., 1999). Each of these strands of theoretical research identifies some forces that lead to persistence in patterns of international trade and others that engender mobility. For example, within the literature on endogenous technological change, sector-specific learning-by-doing is typically a force for persistence, while knowledge spillovers or technology transfer give rise to mobility. Therefore, whether international trade flows persist or exhibit mobility over time (and whether there is increasing or decreasing specialization over time) is an empirical question.

The objective of this chapter is to propose an empirical framework for modeling international trade dynamics, within which it is possible to address issues such as persistence versus mobility and changes in the degree of international specialization. The chapter is structured as follows. Section 2 presents a theoretical model of international trade and endogenous technological change, that combines elements from Dornbusch et al. (1977), Krugman (1987), and Bernard and Jones (1994, 1996). The objective of this section is to illustrate how a precisely specified economic model yields ambiguous conclusions concerning whether international trade flows exhibit persistence or mobility over time. As such, it provides direct motivation for the empirical analysis that follows. Section 3 introduces the empirical framework: a country's pattern of international specialization is thought of as a distribution across sectors, and international trade dynamics correspond to the evolution of the entire distribution over time. This very general specification is consistent with a wide range of possible international trade dynamics, and allows us to determine the degree of persistence versus mobility in patterns of international specialization from the observed data. Later sections implement the empirical framework using industry-level manufacturing data from the G-5 economies.

The dynamics of patterns of international trade are analyzed in two stages. First, section 4 undertakes the preliminary data analysis. Measures of *RCA* are presented for the manufacturing sectors of France, Germany, Japan, the United Kingdom, and the United States. The evolution of patterns of international trade over time is analyzed graphically. Second, the model of distribution dynamics is estimated econometrically in section 5. Transition probability matrices are presented for each of the G-5 economies and for the sample formed by pooling observations across economies. The extent of persistence and mobility in patterns of international trade is quantified using formal indices of mobility. We find evidence of significant differences in international trade dynamics among the G-5 economies. France exhibits the most mobility and Japan the least. Japan is the only G-5 economy to experience an increase in the degree of international specialization over time. Section 6 summarizes our conclusions.

2. Theoretical Modeling of Trade Dynamics

This section presents a simple theoretical model of international trade and endogenous technological change. The model uncovers some forces that lead to persistence in patterns of international trade and other conflicting influences that tend to induce mobility. Static equilibrium is determined exactly as in the standard Ricardian model with a continuum of goods (Dornbusch et al., 1977). There are two economies (home and foreign) and A_{ij} denotes the productivity of labour in sector j of economy $i \in \{H, F\}$. Each economy may produce any of a fixed number of goods indexed by $j \in [0, n]$. An individual good j will be produced in home (H) if and only if the unit cost of producing that good in home is below or equal to that in foreign (F):

$$\frac{w_H(t)}{w_F(t)} \le \frac{A_{Hj}(t)}{A_{Fj}(t)} \tag{1}$$

where w_H and w_F are the home and foreign wage rates, respectively. If we denote home productivity relative to foreign by $B_j \equiv A_{Hj}/A_{Fj}$, and index goods so that higher values of j correspond to lower values of home productivity relative to foreign (B_j), then the right-side of (1) may be illustrated diagrammatically by the downward-sloping curve in Figure 1. Given a value for the home relative wage w_H/w_F, all goods $j \le \hat{j}$ in Figure 1 are produced in home and all goods $j > \hat{j}$ *are* produced in foreign. $\hat{j}$ denotes the limit good such that home's relative wage is exactly equal to home productivity relative to foreign's.

In static equilibrium, home's relative wage is pinned down by the additional requirement that home income equals world expenditure on home goods (or alternatively that trade is balanced). Under the assumption that instantaneous utility is a symmetric Cobb–Douglas function of the consumption of each good j (with the elasticity of instantaneous utility with respect to the consumption of each good equal to β), a constant fraction β of world income is spent on each good produced in home. Therefore, if the range of goods $[0,\hat{j}]$ is produced in home, the requirement that home income equals world expenditure on home goods is given by

$$w_H \cdot \overline{L}_H = \hat{j}\beta \cdot [w_H \overline{L}_H + w_F \overline{L}_F].$$

This condition may be re-expressed as

$$\frac{w_H}{w_F} = D_{\hat{j}}, \quad \text{where} \quad D_{\hat{j}} \equiv \frac{\hat{j} \cdot \beta}{1 - \hat{j} \cdot \beta} \cdot \frac{\overline{L}_F}{\overline{L}_H}, \tag{2}$$

where $\overline{L}_H$ and $\overline{L}_F$ are the home and foreign supplies of labor, respectively. The right-hand side of equation (2) ($D_{\hat{j}}$) is monotonically increasing in $\hat{j}$, and provides a demand-side relationship between the range of goods produced in home and home's relative wage (w_H/w_F). $D_{\hat{j}}$ is illustrated diagrammatically by the upward-sloping curve in Figure 1. Static equilibrium is defined by the intersection of the two curves, where both (1) and (2) are satisfied.

Within this framework, the evolution of patterns of international trade over time is determined by rates of technological progress in each sector of the two economies. In general, rates of technological change will themselves be endogenous, and are determined in part by the existing pattern of international trade. The existing empirical literature suggests a variety of determinants of endogenous technological change; the analysis here focuses on three sets of influences. First, a wide range of empirical evidence exists that learning-by-doing is an important source of productivity improvement (see, e.g., Lucas, 1993). We follow Krugman (1987) in introducing sector-specific learning-by-doing into the Ricardian model with a continuum of goods. The rate of learning is assumed to depend upon economy i's allocation of labor (the sole factor of production) to sector j (L_{ij}) and a parameter (ψ_j) that may vary across sectors.

Second, a variety of case study and econometric evidence suggests that transfers of technology or knowledge spillovers are an important source of technological change (e.g., Rosenberg, 1982; Coe and Helpman, 1995; Keller, 1999). Therefore, we also allow

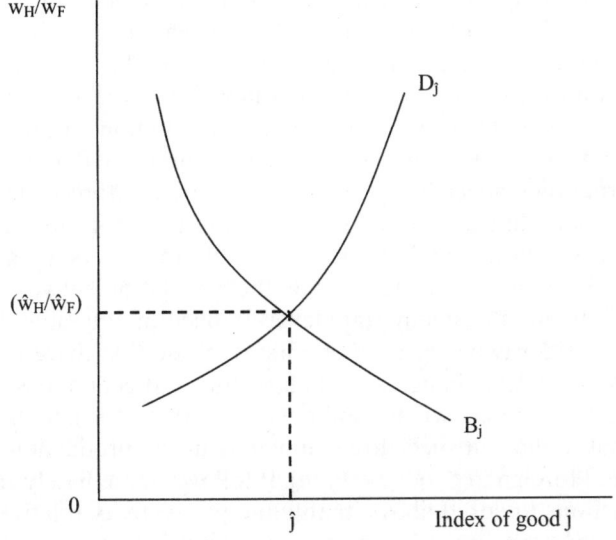

Figure 1. Static Equilibrium and International Specialization

for spillovers of production knowledge across economies. In particular, following Bernard and Jones (1994, 1996), we assume that technology in each sector may be transferred from a leading to a follower economy. Technology transfer is assumed to occur at a constant proportional rate (λ_j), so that economy i's rate of productivity growth in sector j is increasing in the distance between its level of productivity in sector j and the corresponding level in the economy that is the technological leader in sector j.

Third, it is plausible that the rate of productivity growth in sector j of economy i depends upon a variety of other observed and unobserved characteristics. We parameterize these observed and unobserved characteristics by a constant (γ_{ij}), that varies across economies and sectors (a "fixed effect"). Combining all three sets of influences, the rate of productivity growth in sector j of economy i is given by

$$\ln\left(\frac{A_{ij}(t)}{A_{ij}(t-1)}\right) = \gamma_{ij} + \psi_j \ln(1 + L_{ij}(t-1)) + \lambda_j \ln\left(\frac{A_{Xj}(t-1)}{A_{ij}(t-1)}\right),$$

$$\gamma_{ij}, \psi_{ij}, \lambda_{ij} \geq 0 \quad \forall i, j \tag{3}$$

where A_{Xj} denotes productivity in sector j in whichever of the two economies $i \in \{H, F\}$ is the world's technological leader. If economy H is the technological leader in sector j, $A_{Hj} = A_{Xj}$ and the third term on the right-hand side of equation (3) is zero. In this case, sector-specific learning-by-doing and the country–industry characteristics embodied in the fixed effect provide the sole potential sources of productivity growth. Throughout the analysis, technological change is modeled as a pure externality of current production and is therefore consistent with the assumption of perfect competition in the Ricardian model. Equation (3) implies that, in each sector j of the two economies i, the evolution of productivity relative to the world technological leader may be expressed as

$$\Delta \ln\left(\frac{A_{ij}(t)}{A_{Xj}(t)}\right) = (\gamma_{ij} - \gamma_{Xj}) + \psi_j \ln\left(\frac{1 + L_{ij}(t-1)}{1 + L_{Xj}(t-1)}\right) - \lambda_j \cdot \ln\left(\frac{A_{ij}(t-1)}{A_{Xj}(t-1)}\right). \tag{4}$$

The dynamics of international trade patterns are fully characterized by the static equilibrium conditions (1) and (2), together with the specification of productivity growth in equations (3) and (4). Initial levels of productivity determine the pattern of comparative advantage and international specialization. The pattern of international specialization (with its associated allocation of labor across sectors) then affects rates of productivity growth and hence the evolution of international trade flows over time.

On the one hand, the presence of sector-specific learning-by-doing means that initial patterns of international specialization will tend to be reinforced over time. On the other hand, technological transfer and differences in the exogenous rates of productivity growth across sectors may both be responsible for reversing initial patterns of international specialization—depending upon the correlation between initial levels of relative productivity and the steady-state levels implicit in equation (4).

For example, consider two special cases. First, suppose that there is a common rate of exogenous technological change across all sectors and economies ($\gamma_{Hj} = \gamma_{Fj} = \gamma$ for all j) and no international knowledge spillovers ($\lambda_j = 0$ for all j). Static equilibrium at time t implies that home will specialize completely in the production of the range of goods $j \in [0, \hat{j}]$ and foreign in goods $j \in (\hat{j}, n]$. It follows immediately, from (3) and the parameter restrictions imposed above, that home productivity relative to foreign will rise in the sectors where home initially specializes and fall in the sectors where home does not initially specialize. As a result, initial patterns of international specialization persist and will become increasingly locked-in over time (as in Krugman, 1987).

Second, suppose that there is no sector-specific learning-by-doing ($\psi_j = 0$ for all j); nonetheless, exogenous technological progress occurs at varying rates across sectors and economies ($\gamma_{ij} > 0$ for all i, j; $\gamma_{Hj} \neq \gamma_{Fj}$ for all j) and is accompanied by knowledge spillovers ($\lambda_j > 0$ for all j). Suppose also that those sectors in which home productivity is initially less than foreign are the same sectors in which $\gamma_H > \gamma_F$, and that the converse is also true. Then, from equation (4), sectors where home productivity is initially less than foreign will become, in the steady-state, sectors in which home productivity exceeds foreign. This is sufficient (though not necessary) for initial patterns of international specialization to be reversed over time.

Thus, this model of international trade and endogenous technological change identifies some forces that lead to persistence in patterns of international trade and others that give rise to mobility. Similar results may be obtained within theoretical frameworks that emphasize either factor accumulation (see, e.g., Deardorff, 1974; Findlay, 1970, 1995) or economic geography (e.g., Krugman, 1991; Fujita et al., 1999). Whether international trade flows persist or exhibit mobility over time is ultimately an empirical question, and we require an empirical framework sufficiently general as to encompass both possibilities. This chapter proposes such an empirical framework.

3. Empirical Modeling of Trade Dynamics

This section introduces the empirical framework for analyzing the dynamics of international trade flows. The extent of an economy's specialization in an individual sector is characterized using a modified version of Balassa's (1965) index of revealed comparative advantage (*RCA*).[1] An economy i's *RCA* in sector j is given by the ratio of its share of exports in sector j to its average export share in all sectors:[2]

$$RCA_{ij} = \frac{Z_{ij}/\sum_i Z_{ij}}{\frac{1}{N}\sum_j (Z_{ij}/\sum_i Z_{ij})}, \qquad (5)$$

where Z_{ij} denotes the value of economy i's exports in sector j.

RCA yields information about the pattern of international specialization insofar as it evaluates an economy's export share in an individual sector relative to some benchmark—namely, the economy's average export share in all sectors. The pattern of international specialization at any one point in time t is characterized by the distribution of *RCA* across sectors. A value of RCA_{ij} above unity indicates an industry in which economy i's share of exports exceeds its average share in all industries: that is, an industry in which economy i *specializes*.

Evaluating the dynamics of patterns of international specialization over time involves an analysis of the evolution of the entire cross-section distribution of *RCA*. Issues such as persistence versus mobility in international trade flows correspond to questions of *intra-distribution dynamics*. What is the probability that a sector moves from one quartile of the *RCA* distribution to another? Are the sectors in which $RCA_{ij} > 1$ at time $t + k$ ($k \geq 1$) the same sectors as at time t? Changes in the overall degree of international specialization may be evaluated by analyzing the evolution of the *external shape* of the *RCA* distribution. Do we observe an increasing specialization in a limited subset of industries (a polarization of the *RCA* distribution towards extreme values), or has the degree of international specialization remained broadly unchanged?

The evolution of the *RCA* distribution over time may be modeled formally, employing techniques already used in the cross-country growth literature to analyze income convergence (see Quah, 1993, 1996a,c). Thus, denote *RCA* by the measure x and its distribution across sectors at time t by $F_t(x)$. Corresponding to F_t, we may define a probability measure λ_t where $\forall x \in \Re$, $\lambda_t((-\infty, x)) = F_t(x)$. Following Quah *op cit.*, the evolution of the distribution of *RCA* over time is then modeled in terms of a stochastic difference equation:

$$\lambda_t = P^*(\lambda_{t-1}, u_t), \quad \text{integer } t, \tag{6}$$

where $\{u_t: \text{integer } t\}$ is a sequence of disturbances and P^* is an operator that maps disturbances and probability measures into probability measures. For simplicity, we assume that this stochastic difference equation is first-order and that the operator P^* is time-invariant. Even so, equation (6) is intractable and cannot be estimated directly. However, setting the disturbances u to zero and iterating the stochastic difference equation forwards, we obtain

$$\lambda_{t+s} = P^*(\lambda_{t+s-1}, 0) = P^*(P^*(\lambda_{t+s-2}, 0), 0)$$
$$\vdots$$
$$= P^*(P^*(P^*\ldots(P^*(\lambda_t, 0), 0)\ldots 0), 0)$$
$$= (P^*)^s \lambda_t. \tag{7}$$

If the space of possible values of *RCA* is divided into a number of distinct, discrete cells, P^* becomes a matrix of transition probabilities which may be estimated by counting the number of transitions out of and into each cell.[3] From these transition probabilities, one is able to characterize the extent of mobility between different segments of the *RCA* distribution. Furthermore, by taking the limit $s \to \infty$ in equation (7), one obtains the implied ergodic or stationary *RCA* distribution. This is simply the eigenvector associated with the largest eigenvalue of the transition probability matrix (see, e.g., Karlin and Taylor, 1975), and provides information concerning the evolution of the external shape of the *RCA* distribution.

4. Preliminary Data Analysis

The empirical methodology outlined above is used in the remainder of this chapter to analyze the evolution of patterns of international specialization in the manufacturing sectors of the G-5. The techniques used enable a wide range of issues concerning international trade dynamics to be addressed. We consider the extent to which there are changes in patterns of specialization over time and at what levels of specialization the greatest degree of mobility is observed. It is possible to examine whether international trade dynamics are different in the US from Japan or the major European economies. We evaluate the degree to which each economy is increasingly specializing in small subsets of manufacturing sectors.

This section presents the *RCA* data on patterns of specialization in the G-5 economies, and looks informally at changes in international specialization over time. The following section estimates the formal model of distribution dynamics econometrically. The source for all the data is the OECD's *Bilateral Trade Database* (BTD). This provides consistent information on exports to the OECD and 15 trade partners for 22 manufacturing industries for the period 1970–93.[4] We begin by characterizing the distribution of *RCA* at any one point in time in the United Kingdom and the United States, before widening the analysis to encompass the other three members of the G-5. Table 1 presents measures of *RCA* for the United Kingdom in each of the 22 manufacturing industries in the sample for the period 1970–93. For ease of exposition, the data are presented in the form of five-year averages.

Exactly the same analysis may be undertaken for each of the other four members of the G-5. Tables 2 and 3 list the industries in which *RCA* exceeds one in either or both of the periods 1970–74 and 1990–93 for each of the G-5 economies.[5] While the G-5 economies' patterns of international specialization show some similarities, there are also important differences. For example, during the period 1970–74, industries in which the UK had an *RCA* and the United States did not were petroleum refining, metal products, nonferrous metals, pharmaceuticals, and other manufacturing. During the same period, industries in which the US had an *RCA*, but the UK did not, were motor vehicles and communication. Table 2 and 3 also make clear that the identity of industries in which an economy has an *RCA* changes over time; industries in which an *RCA* is either acquired or lost during the sample period are denoted by italics.

Comparing the periods 1970–74 and 1990–93, the UK lost its *RCA* in electrical machinery, nonelectrical machinery, metal products and nonferrous metals, but gained an *RCA* in industrial chemicals and communication. Comparing the same two periods, the US lost an *RCA* in motor vehicles, but acquired an *RCA* in food and drink, and

Table 1. RCA in the United Kingdom

Industry	1970–74	1975–79	1980–84	1985–89	1990–93
Food and drink	0.71	0.80	0.87	0.84	0.93
Textiles and clothing	0.93	0.90	0.84	0.78	0.79
Timber and furniture	0.22	0.35	0.32	0.28	0.29
Paper and printing	0.54	0.58	0.62	0.62	0.80
Industrial chemicals	0.96	1.04	1.16	1.16	1.17
Pharmaceuticals	1.46	1.44	1.54	1.51	1.61
Petroleum refining	1.10	1.18	1.27	1.27	1.36
Rubber and plastic	0.96	0.98	1.02	0.91	0.95
Nonmetallic minerals	0.98	0.94	0.84	0.79	0.81
Ferrous metals	0.58	0.50	0.51	0.69	0.89
Nonferrous metals	1.27	1.13	1.21	0.96	0.98
Metal products	1.12	0.98	0.96	0.83	0.82
Nonelectrical machinery	1.12	1.07	1.12	0.97	0.93
Computers	1.08	1.21	1.19	1.33	1.53
Electrical machinery	1.03	0.96	0.99	0.86	0.84
Communication	0.72	0.77	0.72	0.77	1.02
Shipbuilding	0.59	0.61	0.52	1.85	0.94
Other transport	0.72	0.61	0.61	0.42	0.40
Motor vehicles	0.94	0.78	0.62	0.48	0.67
Aerospace	1.49	1.68	1.98	1.74	1.63
Instruments	1.00	0.97	1.15	1.09	1.07
Other manufacturing	2.48	2.50	1.93	1.85	1.57
Mean	1.00	1.00	1.00	1.00	1.00

Table 2. RCA in the United Kingdom and United States

Country	Industry	1970–74	1990–93
UK	Industrial chemicals	×	✓
	Instruments	✓	✓
	Electrical machinery	✓	×
	Computers	✓	✓
	Petroleum refining	✓	✓
	Nonelectrical machinery	✓	×
	Metal products	✓	×
	Nonferrous metals	✓	×
	Pharmaceuticals	✓	✓
	Aerospace	✓	✓
	Other manufacturing	✓	✓
	Communication	×	✓
US	Electrical machinery	✓	✓
	Motor vehicles	✓	×
	Communication	✓	✓
	Industrial chemicals	✓	✓
	Instruments	✓	✓
	Nonelectrical machinery	✓	✓
	Computers	✓	✓
	Aeropsace	✓	✓
	Food and drink	×	✓
	Paper and printing	×	✓

Note: ✓ indicates $RCA_{ij} \geq 1$, × indicates $RCA_{ij} < 1$.

chapter and printing. Changes in patterns of international specialization are observed in each of the remaining G-5 economies. The case of Japan is particularly worthy of note, where an *RCA* is lost in rubber and plastic, textiles and clothing, and other manufacturing, and an *RCA* is acquired in nonelectrical machinery, electrical machinery, motor vehicles and computers. From these two tables alone, patterns of international specialization in France and Germany appear to be less mobile than those in Japan and the United Kingdom.

While Tables 2 and 3 provide one means of analyzing the dynamics of international specialization and yield some interesting information, the conclusions that may be drawn are necessarily limited. First, the analysis is concerned with only two of the five-year periods. Second and more importantly, by restricting attention to movements of *RCA* above or below the value of one, one loses a vast amount of information on changes in the degree of specialization in individual industries. Movements between other segments of the *RCA* distribution are also of interest. For example, between 1970–74 and 1980–84, *RCA* in the US textiles and clothing industry rose to 173% of its original value, while that in the US ferrous metals industry fell to 64% of its initial value. Neither of these substantial changes in patterns of international specialization enters into Table 2.

The econometric techniques employed in this chapter analyze the evolution of the entire distribution of *RCA* over time, and therefore overcome both limitations. Before

Table 3. RCA in France, Germany, and Japan

Country	Industry	1970–74	1990–93
France	Metal products	✓	✓
	Industrial chemicals	✓	✓
	Electrical machinery	✓	✓
	Motor vehicles	✓	×
	Pharmaceuticals	✓	✓
	Ferrous metals	✓	✓
	Nonmetallic minerals	✓	✓
	Textiles and clothing	✓	✓
	Food and drink	✓	✓
	Other transport	✓	×
	Rubber and plastic	✓	✓
	Aerospace	×	✓
Germany	Rubber and plastic	✓	✓
	Computers	✓	×
	Pharmaceuticals	✓	✓
	Ferrous metals	✓	✓
	Nonmetallic minerals	✓	✓
	Instruments	✓	✓
	Industrial chemicals	✓	✓
	Metal products	✓	✓
	Motor vehicles	✓	✓
	Electrical machinery	✓	✓
	Nonelectrical machinery	✓	✓
	Textiles and clothing	×	✓
Japan	*Rubber and plastic*	✓	×
	Textiles and clothing	✓	×
	Other manufacturing	✓	×
	Instruments	✓	✓
	Ferrous metals	✓	✓
	Communication	✓	✓
	Shipbuilding	✓	✓
	Other transport	✓	✓
	Nonelectrical machinery	×	✓
	Electrical machinery	×	✓
	Motor vehicles	×	✓
	Computers	×	✓

Note: ✓ indicates $RCA_{ij} \geq 1$, × indicates $RCA_{ij} < 1$.

proceeding to the econometric estimation, we present the results of an informal graphical analysis of the evolution of the entire distribution of *RCA*. This is undertaken for the UK in Figures 2–7. In Figure 2, UK industries are ordered in terms of increasing five-year averaged *RCA* for the period 1970–74, and deviations of *RCA* from the value of 1 are graphed. A value of zero on the *y*-axis therefore corresponds to an *RCA* of 1, while industries in which the UK specializes are shown by positive deviations of *RCA* from the value 1. Figure 2 simply presents the information in Table 1 graphically, and corresponds to the cross-section distribution of *RCA* during 1970–74. Figures 3, 4, 5 and 6 preserve the same ordering of industries and graph deviations of *RCA* from 1

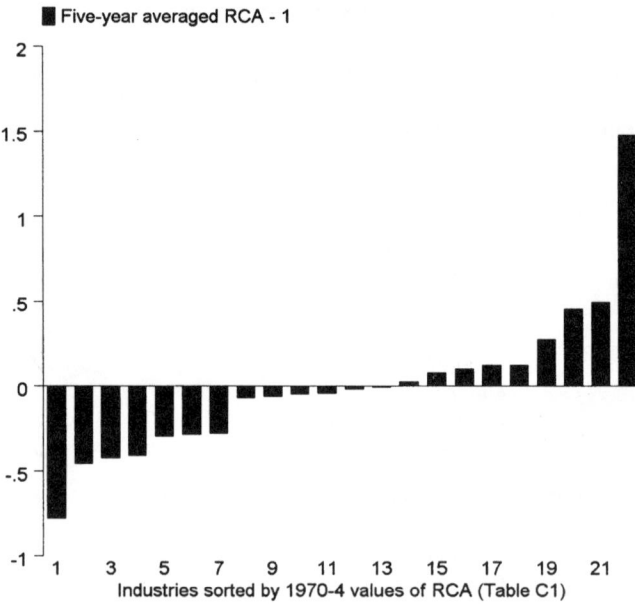

Figure 2. Deviations of RCA from 1, UK 1970–74

for the periods 1975–79, 1980–84, 1985–89 and 1990–93, respectively. Figure 7 re-orders industries in terms of increasing *RCA* for the period 1990–93, and again graphs the cross-section distribution of *RCA* in the form of deviations from a value of 1.

Taken together, Figures 2–6 yield information concerning *intra-distribution dynamics*. If patterns of international specialization in the UK exhibited persistence, one would expect the distribution of *RCA* to remain similar across successive time periods. Industries with high values of *RCA* in 1970–74 would also have high values of *RCA* in 1990–93. In fact, what one observes, as one moves between the figures, is considerable mobility in the UK's pattern of international specialization. This is particularly true in the middle of the distribution. For example, between 1970–74 and 1985–89, the UK's *RCA* in motor vehicles fell from 0.94 to 0.48, before rising to 0.67 in 1990–93. The same exercise can be undertaken for each of the G-5 economies: industries are ordered in terms of increasing *RCA* for the period 1970–74, and the cross-section distribution of *RCA* in successive time periods is graphed. In each case, we find evidence of changes in the distribution of *RCA* over time—a finding that will be confirmed in the econometric analysis to follow.

We also examine changes in countries' overall degree of international specialization (the evolution of the *external shape* of the *RCA* distribution). One way of addressing this issue is to analyze the evolution of the sample standard deviation of *RCA* over time.[6] Table 4 presents sample standard deviations of five-year averaged *RCA* data across industries for each of the G-5 economies and the pooled sample. A complete absence of specialization corresponds to an equal share of exports in all sectors: that is, an *RCA* of 1 in all sectors with zero standard deviation. In four of the five G-5 economies and the pooled sample, we observe a decline in the sample standard deviation of *RCA* over time, while the latter remains roughly constant in France. In itself, this suggests there was a decline in the degree of international specialization during

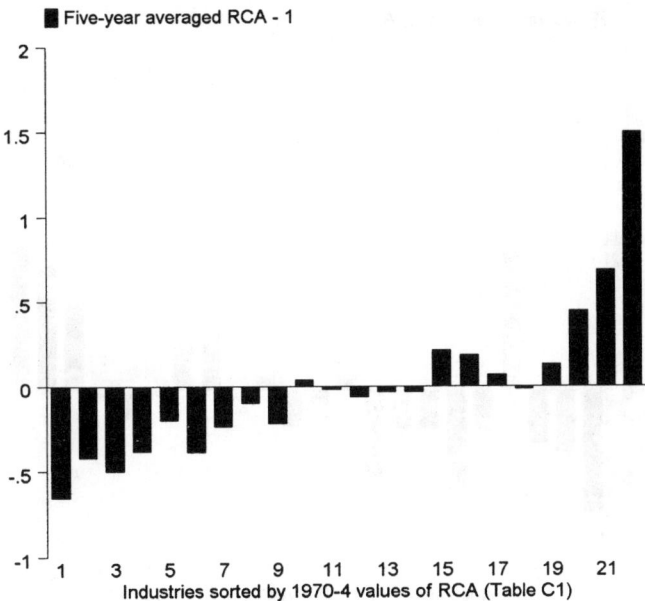

Figure 3. Deviations of RCA from 1, UK 1975–79

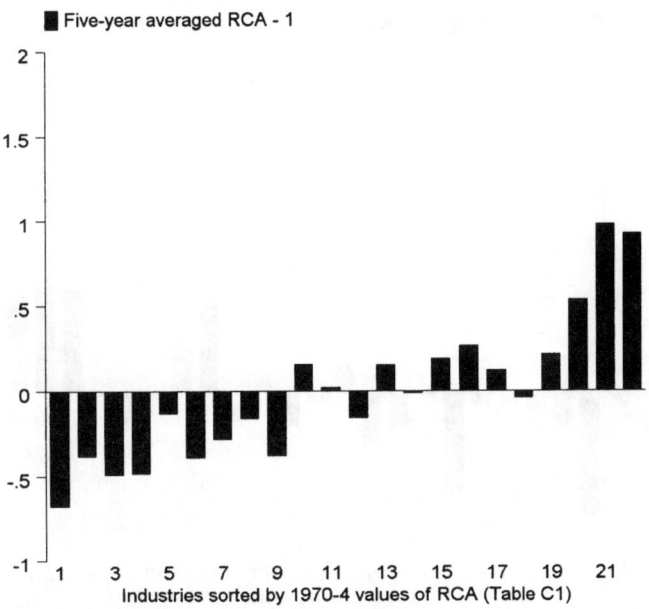

Figure 4. Deviations of RCA from 1, UK 1980–84

the sample period. However, the sample standard deviation of *RCA* is not, in general, a summary statistic for the external shape of the entire distribution. An analysis of the evolution of the sample standard deviation of *RCA* over time may therefore yield misleading conclusions about changes in economies' overall degree of international specialization.

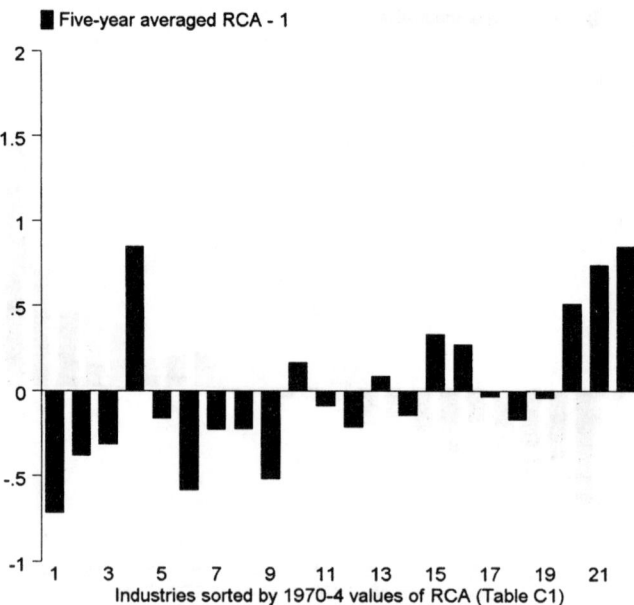

Figure 5. Deviations of RCA from 1, UK 1985–89

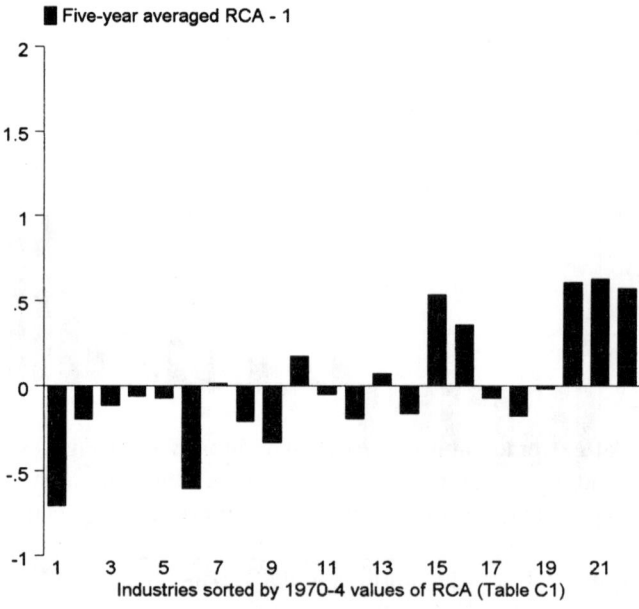

Figure 6. Deviations of RCA from 1, UK 1990–93

A more complete—although again informal—analysis may be carried out for the UK using Figures 2–7. If the UK were increasingly specializing in a subset of industries, one would observe *RCA* systematically increasing in specific sectors and systematically decreasing in others. The distribution of *RCA* would therefore exhibit an

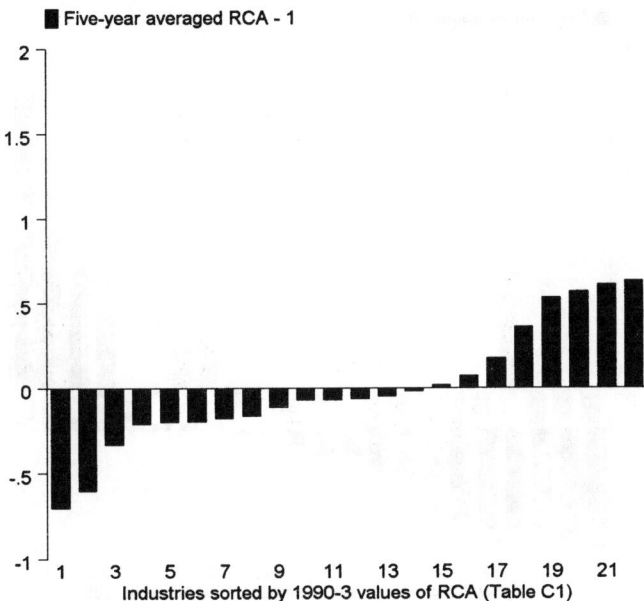

Figure 7. Deviations of RCA from 1, UK 1990–93 (resorted)

Table 4. *Sample Standard Deviations of Five-Year Averaged RCA*

	1970–74	1975–79	1980–84	1985–89	1990–93
Pooled sample	0.60	0.59	0.56	0.56	0.51
France	0.32	0.26	0.29	0.31	0.32
Germany	0.38	0.31	0.30	0.33	0.29
Japan	0.92	0.96	0.94	0.87	0.85
United Kingdom	0.45	0.43	0.43	0.44	0.36
United States	0.74	0.73	0.65	0.70	0.57

increasing mass at extreme values of *RCA*. A comparison of Figures 2 and 7 reveals that there is no evidence of an increase in the degree of international specialization in the UK. The same conclusion holds for each of the other G-5 economies, with the exception of Japan. Only in the latter do we find evidence of an increase in the overall degree of international specialization; an increase that was not revealed by the analysis of sample standard deviations in Table 4.

In Figure 8, Japanese industries are ordered in terms of increasing five-year averaged *RCA* for the period 1970–74, and deviations of *RCA* from the value of 1 are graphed. Figure 9 re-orders industries in terms of increasing *RCA* for the period 1990–93, and again graphs the cross-section distribution of *RCA* in the form of deviations from a value of 1. At the beginning of the sample period, there were a large number of Japanese industries with values of *RCA* close to 1. Thus, during 1970–74, there were eight industries with an *RCA* between 0.8 and 1.2, and only four industries with an *RCA* above 1.2.

14 *James Proudman and Stephen Redding*

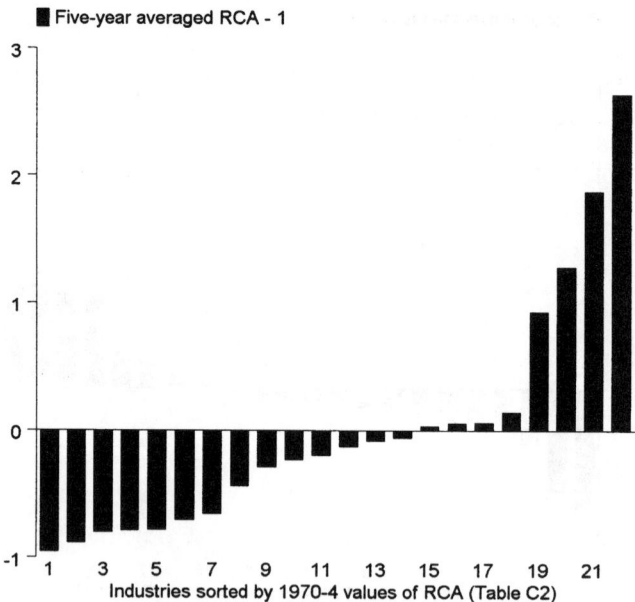

Figure 8. Deviations of RCA from 1, Japan 1970–74

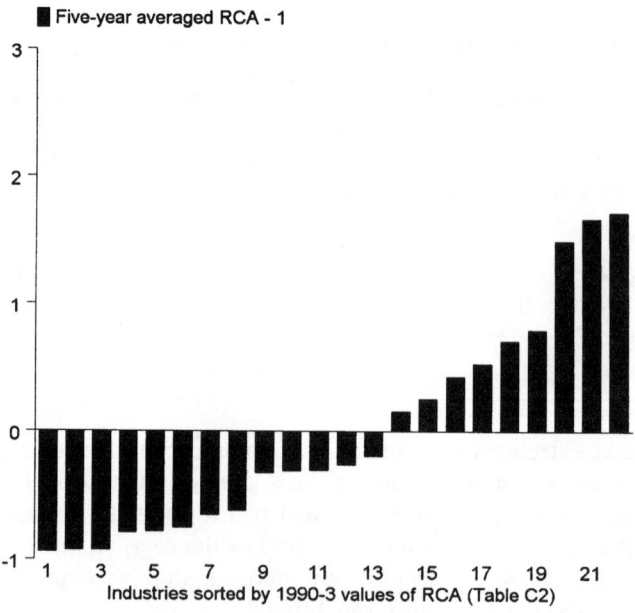

Figure 9. Deviations of RCA from 1, Japan 1990–93

Over time, *RCA* systematically moves away from values of 1, as Japan progressively specializes in one set of industries and reduces its specialization in another set of industries. Thus, during 1990–93, there were only two industries with an *RCA* between 0.8 and 1.2, and eight industries with an *RCA* above 1.2. This increase in Japan's degree of international specialization is seen in Figures 8 and 9 by a decrease in the mass of the distribution concentrated around the *x*-axis. This trend was obscured in the analysis of sample standard deviations by the decline in the value of *RCA* in the two industries where Japan had the highest levels of *RCA* in both 1970–74 and 1990–93: shipbuilding, and other transport equipment.

The next section conducts a more formal econometric analysis of both the degree to which initial patterns of international specialization persist over time and the extent to which we observe changes in economies' overall degree of international specialization over time.

5. Econometric Estimation

This section estimates the formal model of distribution dynamics econometrically. If the space of possible values of *RCA* is divided into *m* discrete cells, the operator P^* in equations (6) and (7) becomes an $m \times m$ matrix of transition probabilities:

$$\lambda_t = P^* \cdot \lambda_{t-1}. \tag{8}$$

The matrix P^* contains elements p_{kl}, each of which denotes the probability that an industry moves from cell *k* to cell *l* (where $k, l \in \{1, \ldots, m\}$) and which may be estimated by counting the number of transitions out of and into each cell. All empirical estimation was undertaken using Danny Quah's TSRF econometrics package.[7] In each case, the boundaries between cells were chosen such that industry–year observations are divided roughly equally between the grid cells.

In order to provide a benchmark against which to compare the results for individual economies, we begin by pooling observations across economies. In so doing, we assume that the stochastic process determining the evolution of *RCA* in each economy is the same—an assumption that will be relaxed below. Table 5 presents the estimated transition probability matrix for the pooled sample. The interpretation of this table is as follows. The numbers in parentheses in the first column are the total number of

Table 5. Transition Probabilities, One-Year Transitions

Pooled sample		Upper endpoint		
Number	0.670	0.915	1.223	∞
(609)	0.90	0.10	0.00	0.00
(604)	0.09	0.83	0.09	0.00
(607)	0.00	0.08	0.84	0.07
(600)	0.00	0.00	0.06	0.94
Ergodic	0.234	0.249	0.244	0.273
	\multicolumn{4}{c}{$1 \times$ transitions iterated $5 \times$}			
	0.6518	0.2928	0.0574	0.0049
	0.2635	0.4928	0.2320	0.0421
	0.0459	0.2062	0.4892	0.2271
	0.0033	0.0321	0.1946	0.7655

industry–year observations beginning in a particular cell, while the first row of numbers denotes the upper endpoint of the corresponding grid cell. Thereafter each row denotes the estimated probability of passing from one state into another. For example, the second row of numbers presents (reading across from the second to the fifth column) the probability of remaining in the lowest *RCA* state and then the probability of moving into the lower-intermediate, higher-intermediate and highest *RCA* states successively. The final row of the upper section of the table gives the implied ergodic distribution. In the lower section of the table, the one-year transition probability matrix is iterated five times.

Transition probability matrices are also estimated for each of the G-5 economies individually. Here, we allow the stochastic process shaping the evolution of *RCA* to vary across economies. The results of this estimation are presented in Table 6. The interpretation of the table is directly analogous, except that the one-year transition probability matrix iterated five times is now omitted. Since the boundaries between grid cells are chosen such that industry–year observations are divided roughly equally between the cells, each grid cell corresponds approximately to a quartile of the distribution of *RCA* across industries and over time. The values of estimated transition probabilities characterize the degree of mobility between different quartiles of this distribution. Estimated values of transition probabilities close to one along the diagonal are indicative of persistence in the *RCA* distribution, while large off-diagonal terms imply greater mobility.

In France, the probability of moving out of one grid cell after one year ranges from 11% to 27%, while in the United States the same probability varies from 10% to 21%. Iterating the one-year transition matrix five times (not shown in Table 7), the extent of mobility is brought out more strongly: for France, the probability of remaining in the same grid cell over a five-year period ranges from 64% to 37%. Thus, the estimates in Table 6 imply that, if an industry begins in the second quartile of the French *RCA* distribution, there is a 37% probability that the industry will remain in this quartile of the *RCA* distribution after five years. This provides evidence of mobility in patterns of international specialization and confirms the results of the informal analysis in the previous section.

Comparing the estimated transition probability matrices across countries and with the results of the pooled estimation provides a further way of evaluating the degree of mobility in international specialization patterns of individual G-5 countries. A comparison of the diagonal and off-diagonal terms in the six estimated transition probabilities reveals that France and the UK exhibit the greatest mobility, while Japan displays the least. This conclusion would not be drawn from Tables 2 and 3 alone, and confirms the limitations of the informal analysis that were pointed out earlier. By restricting attention solely to whether *RCA* rises above or falls below a value of one, one rules out of consideration a wide range of interesting international trade dynamics.

The finding that mobility is highest in France and the UK, and lowest in Japan, is confirmed with the use of formal indices of mobility (see, e.g., Bartholomew, 1973; Shorrocks, 1978; Geweke et al., 1986; Quah, 1996b). These seek to reduce information about mobility in the matrix of transition probabilities (P^*) to a single statistic, and Table 7 presents the values of three mobility indices for the pooled sample and the G-5 economies separately. The first of these mobility indices (M_1, following Shorrocks, 1978) evaluates the trace (tr) of the matrix; the second (M_2, after Bartholomew, 1973) presents information on the average number of class boundaries crossed by a sector originally in state k weighted by the corresponding proportions π_k

Table 6. Transition Probabilities, One-Year Transitions

	Upper endpoint			
France				
Number	0.743	1.047	1.245	∞
(114)	0.83	0.17	0.00	0.00
(116)	0.16	0.73	0.10	0.00
(118)	0.01	0.09	0.79	0.11
(114)	0.00	0.01	0.11	0.89
Ergodic	0.266	0.258	0.242	0.234
Germany				
Number	0.740	0.994	1.270	∞
(121)	0.86	0.14	0.00	0.00
(123)	0.14	0.80	0.07	0.00
(120)	0.00	0.06	0.88	0.07
(120)	0.00	0.00	0.07	0.93
Ergodic	0.233	0.237	0.265	0.265
Japan				
Number	0.222	0.768	1.446	∞
(122)	0.97	0.03	0.00	0.00
(119)	0.05	0.84	0.11	0.00
(124)	0.00	0.13	0.83	0.04
(119)	0.00	0.00	0.03	0.97
Ergodic	0.325	0.211	0.179	0.286
United Kingdom				
Number	0.739	0.942	1.176	∞
(123)	0.90	0.09	0.00	0.01
(119)	0.08	0.78	0.13	0.00
(123)	0.00	0.15	0.72	0.12
(119)	0.01	0.00	0.12	0.87
Ergodic	0.253	0.269	0.235	0.243
United States				
Number	0.608	0.878	1.143	∞
(118)	0.88	0.12	0.00	0.00
(114)	0.11	0.79	0.11	0.00
(115)	0.00	0.10	0.81	0.10
(115)	0.00	0.00	0.10	0.90
Ergodic	0.217	0.245	0.269	0.269

of the ergodic distribution; the third (M_3, following Shorrocks, 1978) evaluates the determinant (det).[8]

A key advantage of the present approach is that, by analyzing the evolution of the *entire* distribution of *RCA*, we are able to evaluate the degree of mobility through all possible values of *RCA*. Thus, it is not only the overall degree of mobility in a transition probability matrix that is interesting, but also the pattern. In each of the G-5 economies and in the pooled sample, the off-diagonal elements of the matrix are largest in the lower- and upper-intermediate grid cells, corresponding to greater mobility in the middle of the *RCA* distribution.

Table 7. Mobility Indices for the G-5

Country	M_1	M_2	M_3
Pooled	0.163	0.121	0.426
UK	0.243	0.187	0.590
US	0.207	0.161	0.518
France	0.253	0.196	0.607
Germany	0.177	0.135	0.460
Japan	0.130	0.083	0.360

$M_1 = \dfrac{m - tr[P]}{m-1}$, $M_2 = \Sigma_k \pi_k \Sigma_l p_{kl} |k - l|$, and $M_3 = 1 - |\det(P)|$.

The pattern of mobility is particularly important for understanding the evolution of international specialization in Japan. The estimated probabilities of moving out of the lower- and upper-intermediate grid cells in Japan (characterizing the degree of mobility in the middle of distribution) are not dissimilar to those estimated for the United States. What is noteworthy about Japan is the immobility in the lower and upper grid cells of the estimated transition probability matrix. Thus, mobility in the center of the distribution is combined with immobility at the extremes. There is a relatively high probability of industries moving out of the lower- and upper-intermediate grid cells; but, once industries move into the lower and upper grid cells, they are extremely likely to remain there. It is this combination of mobility in the center of the distribution and immobility at the extremes that is driving some of the movements in RCA above and below the value of one in Table 3. This is confirmed if one repeats for Japan the analysis undertaken earlier for the UK in Figures 2–6.

The empirical finding of mobility in patterns of international specialization contrasts with the results of a number of theoretical models of trade and growth. In the absence of international knowledge spillovers, models of endogenous technological progress through either sector-specific learning-by-doing (e.g., Krugman, 1987) or research and development (R&D) (e.g., Grossman and Helpman, 1991, ch. 8) predict that initial specialization patterns will become locked-in over time. This corresponds to no potential for technology transfer in the theoretical model of section 2 ($\lambda_j = 0$). However, the prediction of persistence in patterns of specialization is clearly at variance with the data. This suggests the importance of incorporating into theoretical models the economic forces capable of inducing changes in international specialization over time. These include knowledge spillovers, which correspond to $\lambda_j > 0$ in the theoretical model of section 2 (see also Grossman and Helpman, 1991, ch. 7). In models of international trade based on cross-sector differences in factor intensity and cross-country differences in factor abundance, factor accumulation provides an additional explanation for changes in international specialization over time (see, e.g., Findlay, 1970, 1995; Deardorff, 1974).

The econometric techniques implemented in this section also yield information about changes in economies' degree of international specialization over time (the evolution of the *external shape* of the RCA distribution). Iterating the estimated transition probability matrix forwards in time, and allowing the number of iterations to tend towards infinity, one obtains the implied ergodic or stationary RCA distribution towards which patterns of international specialization are evolving. This corresponds to the unconditional probability of an industry being in a particular grid cell. If economies are increasingly specializing in a subset of industries, this will be reflected in a polarization of *RCA* towards extreme values and the emergence of a bimodal distribution of *RCA*.

The final row of each panel of Tables 5–6 reports the ergodic distribution implied by each transition probability matrix. In the pooled sample and four of the five G-5 economies (France, Germany, the UK, and the US), the ergodic distribution is approximately uniform. For these economies, there is no evidence of an increase in the degree of international specialization over time. The exception to this pattern is Japan. The high persistence in the lower and upper grid cells noted above is responsible for a polarization of *RCA* towards extreme values and implies a bimodal ergodic distribution. The results of the econometric estimation therefore confirm the earlier informal analysis of the changing external shape of the *RCA* distribution in Figures 2–9. Formal and informal analyses of the evolution of the *entire* distribution of *RCA* only reveal evidence of an increase in the degree of international specialization in Japan.

The techniques implemented in this section may also be used to examine whether the stochastic process determining the evolution of *RCA* across industries is the same in each of the G-5 economies. Anderson and Goodman (1957) show that, for each state k, under the null hypothesis $p_{kl} = \tilde{p}_{kl}$:

$$\sum_{l=1}^{m} n_k^* \cdot \frac{(p_{kl} - \tilde{p}_{kl})^2}{\tilde{p}_{kl}} \sim \chi^2(m-1), \quad n_k^* \equiv \sum_{t=0}^{T-1} n_k(t), \tag{9}$$

where p_{kl} are the estimated transition probabilities, $\tilde{p}_{kl}$ are the probabilities of transition under the (known) null, and $n_k(t)$ denotes the number of sectors in cell k at time t.

The test statistic in equation (9) may be used to test the hypothesis that the transition probabilities estimated for an individual G-5 economy are the result of a Data Generation Process (DGP) given by the transition probabilities estimated for the pooled sample. From equation (9), this test may be undertaken for each state $k = 1, \ldots, m$. Furthermore, since the transition probabilities are independently distributed across states, we may sum over states and test the hypothesis that, for *all* states $k = 1, \ldots, m$, the estimated transition probabilities are equal to those under the null. The resulting test statistic is asymptotically distributed $\chi^2(m(m-1))$.

Implementing this test procedure for the G-5 economies, the null that the DGP is given by the matrix of transition probabilities estimated for the pooled sample is rejected at the 5% level in France and the UK (the two most mobile economies). The same hypothesis is not rejected at conventional levels of statistical significance in Germany, Japan, and US (though the hypothesis is close to rejection at the 10% level in Japan). These results suggest that, as well as there being considerable mobility in patterns of international specialization in each economy, there are significant differences in international trade dynamics across economies.[9]

Finally, we undertake a whole series of econometric robustness tests.[10] Our results are robust to all of these tests. First, the space of values of *RCA* was divided into five cells rather than four and transition probability matrices were re-estimated. Second, the transition probabilities were estimated allowing transitions to occur over five-year rather than one-year periods. The probabilities estimated over five-year transition periods exhibit some differences from the one-year transition probabilities iterated five times, suggesting that the evolution of *RCA* is not fully characterized by a first-order, time homogenous model. However, in both cases, the results suggested a broadly similar interpretation to that given above.

Third, we examine the stability of the econometric estimates over time. Transition probability matrices were estimated separately for the periods 1970–81 and 1982–93. For both the pooled sample and each of the G-5 economies, the null hypothesis that the matrix of transition probabilities estimated during either (a) 1970–81 or (b) 1982–93 is the result of a DGP given by the matrix of transition probabilities estimated for the full sample (1970–93) cannot be rejected at the 5% level. Fourth, we consider measurement error and the sensitivity of the results to observations from any single industry. An industry in all G-5 countries was sequentially excluded from the sample and transition probability matrices were re-estimated. For both the pooled sample and each of the G-5 economies, the sample mean of each element of the transition probability matrix across the 22 sets of estimation results lies close to the value estimated for the full sample in Tables 5–6. The sample standard deviation of each element of the transition probability matrix is an order of magnitude smaller than the estimated transition probabilities.

Fifth, to address the sensitivity of the results to the exact level of sectoral disaggregation employed, we aggregate the four-digit industries in the sample to the three-digit level. This yields 16 industries, compared with the 22 industries classification used in the analysis above (see Table A1 in the Appendix). For both the pooled sample and each of the G-5 economies, there is little change in the estimated transition probabilities. The null hypothesis that the matrix of transition probabilities estimated for the 16 industry classification is the result of a DGP given by the matrix estimated for the 22 industry classification cannot be rejected at the 5% level.

6. Conclusion

We have presented evidence of substantial mobility in patterns of international specialization, and the extent of mobility in individual G-5 countries has been quantified using formal indices of mobility. Overall, mobility was found to be highest in France and the United Kingdom and lowest in Japan.

The empirical finding of substantial mobility in patterns of international specialization contrasts with the results of a number of theoretical models of trade and growth. In the absence of international knowledge spillovers, models of endogenous technological progress through either sector-specific learning-by-doing or research and development (R&D) predict that initial specialization patterns will become locked-in over time. The fact that this prediction is at variance with the data suggests the importance of incorporating into theoretical models forces such as knowledge spillovers and factor accumulation, which are capable of generating changes in international specialization over time.

If countries are increasingly specializing in subsets of sectors, we would expect to observe the revealed comparative advantage (*RCA*) systematically increasing in some industries and systematically decreasing in others. That is, we would expect to observe a polarization of the *RCA* distribution towards extreme values. Both a formal and informal analysis of the evolution of the *entire* distribution of *RCA* has revealed no evidence of an increase in international specialization in France, Germany, the United Kingdom and the United States. Only in Japan is there evidence of an increase in international specialization over time, directly linked to the extreme immobility observed in the tails of the Japanese *RCA* distribution.

Appendix

Data

The data source for the indices of revealed comparative advantage is the OECD's *Bilateral Trade Database* (BTD). This provides information on the value of exports and imports between the 23 OECD countries and 15 partner economies. The partner countries are: Argentina, Brazil, China, Czech and Slovak Republics, Hong Kong, Hungary, India, Indonesia, Malaysia, Mexico, Philippines, Singapore, Korea (South), Taiwan, and Thailand. Although OECD imports from and OECD exports to these partner countries are included in the database, trade entirely outside the OECD area (e.g., from one partner country to another) is not. The OECD estimates that 90–95% of world trade in goods is included in the database. Information is available for the 22 industries listed in Table A1.

Table A1. Industrial Classification

Industry	ISIC classification	Industry	ISIC classification
1. Food, Drink and Tobacco	31	12. Metal Products	381
2. Textiles, Footwear and Leather	32	13. Non-electrical Machinery	382 – 3,825
		14. Computers and Office Machinery	3,825
3. Wood, Cork and Furniture	33	15. Electrical Machinery	383 – 3,832
4. Paper, Print and Publishing	34	16. Communication Equipment	3,832
5. Industrial Chemicals	351 + 352 – 3,522	17. Shipbuilding	3,841
		18. Other Transport Equipment	3,842 + 3,844 + 3,849
6. Pharmaceuticals	3,522	19. Motor Vehicles	3,843
7. Petroleum Refining	353 + 354	20. Aerospace	3,845
8. Rubber and Plastic Products	355 + 356	21. Instruments	385
9. Non-metallic Minerals	36	22. Other Manufacturing	39
10. Ferrous Metals	371		
11. Non-ferrous Metals	372		

Measuring RCA

Balassa (1965) defines an economy i's measure of "revealed comparative advantage" ($\widetilde{RCA}_{ij}$) in sector j as follows:

$$\widetilde{RCA}_{ij} = \frac{Z_{ij}/\sum_i Z_{ij}}{\sum_j Z_{ij}/\sum_i \sum_j Z_{ij}}. \tag{A1}$$

This suffers from the disadvantage that its arithmetic mean across sectors is not necessarily equal to one. The numerator in equation (A1) is unweighted by the proportion of total exports accounted for by a given sector, while the denominator is a weighted sum of export shares in all manufacturing sectors. Thus, if an economy's pattern of trade is characterized by high export shares in a few sectors, each of which accounts for a small share of total world exports (as is generally true for small economies), this implies high values for the numerator and low values for the denominator. As a result, the economy will be characterized by a mean value of $\widetilde{RCA}$ of above one.[11] Furthermore, mean values of $\widetilde{RCA}$ may change over time, so that, as measured by $\widetilde{RCA}$, an economy exhibits changes in its average extent of specialization over time.

This chapter adopts an alternative measure of revealed comparative advantage in which an economy's export share in a given sector is evaluated relative to its *average* export share in all manufacturing sectors. By construction, the mean value of RCA is constant and equal to one. It is straightforward to show that $RCA_{ij} = \widetilde{RCA}_{ij}/\frac{1}{N}\Sigma_j\widetilde{RCA}_{ij}$. Thus, an alternative interpretation of the present analysis is that, at each point in time, we normalize Balassa's measure by its cross-section mean in order to abstract from the changes in the average extent of specialization that this measure is subject to.

References

Amiti, M., "Specialisation Patterns in Europe," CEP discussion chapter 363, London School of Economics (1997).

Balassa, B., "Trade Liberalisation and Revealed Comparative Advantage," *Manchester School of Economic and Social Studies* 33 (1965):99–123.

Bartholomew, D., *Stochastic Models for Social Processes*, 2nd edn. Chichester: John Wiley (1973).

Bernard, A. and C. Jones, "Comparing Apples to Oranges: Productivity, Convergence and Measurement across Industries and Countries," MIT working chapter 94-12 (1994).

———, "Productivity Across Industries and Countries: Time Series Theory and Evidence," *Review of Economics and Statistics* 78 (1996):135–46.

Coe, D. and E. Helpman, "International R&D Spillovers," *European Economic Review* 39 (1995):859–87.

Deardorff, A., "Factor Proportions and Comparative Advantage in the Long Run: Comment," *Journal of Political Economy* 82 (1974):829–33.

Dollar, D. and E. Wolff, *Competitiveness, Convergence, and International Specialization*. Cambridge, MA: MIT Press (1993).

Dornbusch, R., S. Fischer, and P. Samuelson, "Comparative Advantage, Trade and Payments in a Ricardian Model with a Continuum of Goods," *American Economic Review* 67 (1977):823–39.

Findlay, R., "Factor Proportions and Comparative Advantage in the Long Run," *Journal of Political Economy* 78 (1970):27–34.

———, *Factor Proportions, Trade, and Growth*. Cambridge, MA: MIT Press (1995).

Fujita, M., P. Krugman, and A. Venables, *"The Spatial Economy: Cities, Regions, and International Trade*. Cambridge, MA: MIT Press (1999).

Geweke, J., R. Marshall, and G. Zarkin, "Mobility Indices in Continuous Time Markov Chains," *Econometrica* 54 (1986):1407–23.

Grossman, G. and E. Helpman, *Innovation and Growth in the Global Economy*. Cambridge, MA: MIT Press (1991).

Karlin, S. and H. Taylor, *A First Course in Stochastic Processes*, 2nd edn. New York: Harwood Academic Press (1975).

Keller, W., "How Trade Patterns and Technology Flows Affect Productivity Growth," NBER working chapter 6990 (1999).
Krugman, P., "The Narrow Moving Band, the Dutch Disease and the Competitive Consequences of Mrs Thatcher: Notes on Trade in the Presence of Scale Economies," *Journal of Development Economics* 27 (1987):41–55.
———, *Geography and Trade*. Cambridge, MA: MIT Press (1991).
Lucas, R., "On the Mechanics of Economic Development," *Journal of Monetary Economics* 22 (1988):3–22.
———, "Making a Miracle," *Econometrica* 61 (1993):251–72.
Proudman, J. and S. Redding, "Persistence and Mobility in International Trade," Bank of England working chapter 64 (1997).
Quah, D., "Empirical Cross-Section Dynamics in Economic Growth," *European Economic Review* 37 (1993):426–34.
———, "Twin Peaks: Growth and Convergence in Models of Distribution Dynamics," *Economic Journal* 106 (1996a):1045–55.
———, "Aggregate and Regional Disaggregate Fluctuations," *Empirical Economics* 21 (1996b):137–59.
———, "Convergence Empirics Across Economies With (Some) Capital Mobility," *Journal of Economic Growth* 1 (1996c):95–124.
Redding, S., "Dynamic Comparative Advantage and the Welfare Effects of Trade," *Oxford Economic Papers* 51 (1999):15–39.
Rosenberg, N., *Inside the Black Box: Technology and Economics*. Cambridge: Cambridge University Press (1982).
Shorrocks, A., "The Measurement of Mobility," *Econometrica* 46 (1978):1013–24.

Notes

1. For a more recent application of Balassa's original index, see Dollar and Wolff (1993).
2. Balassa (1965)'s actual measure of *RCA* is the ratio of economy i's export share in sector j to its share of total exports of all sectors. This measure suffers from the disadvantage that its arithmetic mean is not necessarily equal to one, and may vary both across economies and over time. The measure used in this chapter is formally equivalent to normalizing Balassa's measure by its cross-sectional mean. See the Appendix for further discussion.
3. More generally, if we continue to treat *RCA* as a continuous variable, one may estimate the stochastic kernel associated with P^* (see, e.g., Quah, 1996c). However, in the present application, there are too few cross-sectional units to permit such estimation.
4. Further details concerning the data used, including an industrial classification, are contained in the Appendix.
5. In the interests of brevity, actual values of *RCA* are not reported. A data appendix containing this information is available from the authors on request.
6. See also Amiti (1997). Since the mean of *RCA* across industries is 1, the standard deviation equals the coefficient of variation.
7. Responsibility for any results, opinions and errors is, of course, solely the authors'.
8. For the exact relationship between these indices and the circumstances under which they yield transitive rankings of transition probability matrices, see Shorrocks (1978) and Geweke et al. (1986).
9. It is also possible to test the null hypothesis for one G-5 economy that the DGP is given by the matrix of transition probabilities estimated for another G-5 economy. For a more detailed analysis of international trade dynamics in Germany and the UK, see Proudman and Redding (1997).
10. Further details of the robustness tests are contained in an appendix available from the authors on request.

11. For example, suppose there are two economies (the UK and France) and two goods (beer and wine). The total value of the UK's exports is £500 (£400 beer and £100 wine) and the total value of France's is £10,100 (£100 beer and £10,000 wine). It is straighforward to show that the UK's mean *RCA* is considerably above one (it is in fact 8.59) and France's considerably below one (it is in fact 0.63).

2
Trade and Labor Approaches to Wage Inequality

Jonathan E. Haskel

1. Introduction

Much recent research on changes in wage inequality has been undertaken by two groups who can loosely be identified, by training and/or recent research, as labor economists or trade economists. The empirical research methods adopted by these two groups has been quite different. A good deal of the work by labor economists has documented evidence of skill-biased technical change (SBTC) within many industries (see, e.g., Berman et al., 1994). Much of the work of trade economists has focused on total factor productivity growth and product price changes across industries (see, e.g., Leamer, 1998a; Deardorff, 1999).

The purpose of this chapter is to try to set out a common framework to understand reasons for the different empirical strategies. I shall argue that most labor economists organize their data analysis, either explicitly or implicitly, from a one-sector model. But most trade economists organize their work, again either explicitly or implicitly, from a multisector model.[1] As set out below, these models give rise to very different empirical approaches. Labor economists tend to focus on the factor bias of technical change whereas trade economists look for the sector bias of technical change and/or of price changes.

Section 2 sets out two different models as simply as possible. Section 3 provides a short review of the evidence on sector bias, and section 4 concludes.

2. Understanding the Trade and Labor Approaches: A Simple Framework[2]

A standard empirical labor approach is to use industry data to estimate relative labor demand functions and see if there is evidence that technical progress is skill-biased. Typically such skill-biased technical change (SBTC) is found in many industries. With the supply/demand intuition the presence of SBTC in many sectors seems strong evidence that technology has caused a rise in the skill premium.

Standard trade theory suggests that this reasoning is not conclusive. Consider an industry[3] where there is no skill-biased or any other type of technical progress (or price change). At first pass, this sector would seem to have no change in relative wages since there is no SBTC occurring. But suppose another industry releases workers, perhaps owing to falling prices from increased trade competition or technical change. This creates a flow of potential workers willing to work in the first industry and so potentially drives down wages. Relative wages therefore depend on whether technical progress and output prices are changing by more in one sector *relative* to another. It is these *differences across* sectors, their "sector bias," that potentially cause wage adjustments. Put another way, the finding that there is technical progress *occurring within* many sectors, driven perhaps by computers, may not be informative about changes in wages, for it does not establish whether technical progress is changing more in some sectors than in others. This type of logic is a feature of the Heckscher–Ohlin model and so explains why trade economists typically look for sector bias.[4]

To see this formally, suppose there are two sectors in the economy producing goods i and j. Following Johnson (1997), suppose that output (Y) is produced by skilled and unskilled labor (N_s and N_u) according to a constant-returns CES production function $Y = A[(\alpha(\lambda_s N_s)^{1-1/\sigma} + (1 - \alpha)(\lambda_u N_u)^{1-1/\sigma}]^{\sigma/(\sigma-1)}$, where A is a neutral technical parameter, λ_s and λ_u are intensive skilled-labor and intensive unskilled-labor biased technical parameters, respectively, α is an extensive skill-biased technical parameter, and σ is the elasticity of substitution.[5] Ignoring the λ for the moment, total costs, C, for each sector are

$$C^i = \left((\alpha^i)^\sigma w_s^{1-\sigma} + (1-\alpha^i)^\sigma w_u^{1-\sigma}\right)^{1/(1-\sigma)} (A^i)^{-1} Y^i,$$

$$C^j = \left((\alpha^j)^\sigma w_s^{1-\sigma} + (1-\alpha^j)^\sigma w_u^{1-\sigma}\right)^{1/(1-\sigma)} (A^j)^{-1} Y^j, \quad (1)$$

where skilled and unskilled labor receive wages w_s and w_u. Without loss of generality, assume further that sector i is skill-intensive, defined by the wage-bill share of skilled workers in C being higher in sector i than in sector j. Using Shephard's lemma, the relative demand for skilled and unskilled labor in sector i is

$$\frac{N_s^i}{N_u^i} = \left(\frac{\alpha^i}{1-\alpha^i}\right)^\sigma \left(\frac{w_s^i}{w_u^i}\right)^{-\sigma}. \quad (2)$$

Equation (2), the relative labor demand curve, is uncontroversial. Only α, skill-biased TC, appears in these first-order conditions. A number of papers have estimated (2) (or more general translog versions of it; see, e.g., Berman et al. (1994) for the US, Haskel and Heden (1999) for the UK, and Machin and van Reenen (1998) for many countries). Typically the $\alpha/(1 - \alpha)$ term is specified as a constant or replaced with an assumed correlate such as computers, both of which usually attract a positive coefficient. This is consistent with technology being (extensively) skill-biased. Machin and van Reenen (1998) further add import penetration to (2) and find no relation, thereby arguing that imports have not contributed changes in the relative demand for skilled labor.

What are the implications for wage inequality that follow from this? Assuming one sector, or that workers cannot move between sectors, each sector faces its own upward-sloping supply, curve. Equating relative supply, denoted $(N_s^i/N_u^i)^S$, and demand, totally differentiating (2), and rearranging gives the change in relative wages as

$$\Delta \ln(w_s/w_u)^i = \Delta \ln(\alpha/1-\alpha)^i - \frac{1}{\sigma} \Delta \ln(N_s^i/N_u^i)^S. \quad (3)$$

Hence increases in relative wages occur owing to increases in demand from SBTC (net of changes in supply).[6] Since there is evidence for SBTC from the estimation of (2), this suggests that technology has raised the wage premium. Further, since imports are insignificant when added to (2), it is argued that trade has had no effect.

The alternative, favored by trade economists, is to assume that workers are mobile across sectors. Thus each sector faces a flat relative labor supply curve and so another condition is required to close the model. This then is the production side of the H–O model and it is conventionally assumed that each sector is competitive so that revenue equals costs:

$$p^i Y^i = C^i,$$

$$p^j Y^j = C^j, \quad (4)$$

where p^i and p^j are prices in each sector. Changes in (log) relative wages can be written:[7]

$$\Delta \ln(w_s/w_u) = \frac{1}{V_s^i - V_s^j}(\Delta \ln(p^i/p^j) + \Delta \ln(TFP^i/TFP^j)), \qquad (5)$$

where V_s^i and V_s^j are the shares of skilled labor in the total wage bill in each sector, w_s and w_u are not indexed by i since free mobility ensures workers can move across sectors, and TFP is total factor productivity. Recall too that, by assumption, $V_s^i > V_s^j$.

Equation (5) is standard in the trade literature. First, it shows Stolper–Samuelson type effects of changes in p^i/p^j on w_s/w_u. The effects depend on the sector bias of changes in prices. If prices fall in the skill-intensive sector ($\Delta \ln p^i < 0$), then w_s/w_u falls; and if prices fall in the unskilled-intensive sector ($\Delta \ln p^j < 0$), then w_s/w_u rises. The mechanism works via the zero-profit conditions in (4). If prices fall in any sector then that sector is now unprofitable. Relative wages must adjust to restore zero-profit equilibrium. Hence if prices fall in the skill-intensive sector, w_s/w_u must fall (if they rose that would further render the skill-intensive sector unprofitable). If prices fall in the unskilled-intensive sector, w_s/w_u must rise.[8]

Equation (5) also shows that the effect of technology depends on sector bias of changes in $\Delta \ln TFP$. The mechanism also works via the zero-profit conditions in (4) and has the same intuition as changes in prices. Technical progress reduces a sector's costs and so makes it relatively profitable. Hence, technical progress in a skilled-intensive sector ($\Delta \ln TFP^i > 0$) makes that sector more profitable, and hence w_s/w_u must rise; progress in an unskilled-intensive sector ($\Delta \ln TFP^j > 0$) means that w_s/w_u must fall. See Findlay and Grubert (1959) for a classic early theoretical analysis of this.

Sector Bias and Factor Bias

Concerning technology, (3) suggests that only factor-biased TC affects wages since it changes the relative productivity of factors *within* a sector. By contrast, (5) suggests that *all* types of technical change, as summarized in $\Delta \ln TFP$, and price changes, are important. The reason is that they change the *relative profitability of sectors*. This is why the typical labor focus is on factor bias and the trade focus on sector bias.

Skill-Biased Technical Change

In (3), SBTC is of course essential. In (5), SBTC does not appear directly. So what is the role of SBTC in the multisector model? SBTC is of course part of $\Delta \ln TFP$; since $\Delta \ln TFP$ is increases in output net of measured inputs, it includes any form of technical progress, be it biased or neutral (see, e.g., Berndt and Wood, 1982, and below). The focus on *TFP* is appropriate in a multisector model since *any* type of technical change, as long as it reduces costs, potentially raises sectoral profitability and so necessitates wage changes.

This argument suggests that SBTC affects relative wages in this model under two conditions: first, that it should have the appropriate sector bias, and second, that it should reduce costs. The latter effect depends on the form of SBTC. In (1), SBTC is represented by a rise in α, which raises the productivity of the skilled relative to the unskilled. This type of SBTC is what Johnson (1997) terms "extensive SBTC" (whereby the skilled become better at performing the tasks previously done by the unskilled—

typing this chapter for example) which from (2) raises the relative demand for the skilled regardless of σ. From (1), however, a rise in α does not necessarily lower unit cost. Differentiation of (1) shows that it only does so as long as $V_s > \alpha$ (and $\sigma > 1$). This is not surprising since this type of technical change is a productivity gain by one factor and a loss by another. Intensive SBTC, that makes each factor more productive at the tasks it already performs, by contrast will lower costs.[9]

In the light of this, it is worth noting that it is perfectly possible, in multisector models, for SBTC to *lower* relative skilled wages if it occurs in unskilled-intensive sectors and lowers costs there. The intuition is as follows. In one-sector models, SBTC raises relative skilled wages (with certain conditions on technology) to "absorb" the unskilled by pricing them back into work when the skilled become more productive. In multisector models, changes in wages have to be consistent with zero profits in all sectors. If SBTC in the unskilled-intensive sector were to raise w_s/w_u the relative profitability of the unskilled-intensive sector would rise further. How then are these unskilled "absorbed"? The answer is that in a multisector model output is endogenous. Hence output rises in unskilled-intensive sectors and this absorbs the "extra" unskilled workers.

Consider then the finding that many industries in many countries have had rising relative wages and rising relative skill levels (see, e.g., Machin and van Reenen, 1998). This has led many to argue that this shows evidence of SBTC and that such SBTC has raised relative wages. It is clear from (2) that the evidence is consistent with SBTC.[10] But without knowing the sector bias of SBTC one cannot say whether SBTC has raised relative wages. Indeed it is theoretically possible that SBTC has tended to lower wages, if for example it occurred in the unskilled-intensive sectors, and that skilled sector biased price changes are responsible for the growth in relative wages. So the multisector perspective suggests that one should treat the finding of widespread SBTC with caution.

To see all this formally, using the cost function in note 9 we can write

$$\Delta \ln TFP^i = \Delta \ln A^i + V_s^i \Delta \ln \lambda_s^i + V_u^i \Delta \ln \lambda_u^i + \left(\frac{\sigma}{\sigma-1}\right)\left(\frac{V_s^i - \alpha_i}{1-\alpha_i}\right)\Delta \ln \alpha^i, \qquad (6)$$

which shows that TFP rises if A, λ_s, λ_u, and α rise, the latter as long as $\sigma > 1$ and $V_s^i > \alpha^j$ (which is the same condition for a rise in α to reduce total costs). Substituting (6) into (5) gives

$$\Delta \ln(w_s/w_u) = \frac{1}{V_s^i - V_s^j} \left(\begin{array}{l} \Delta \ln(p^i/p^j) + \Delta \ln(A^i/A^j) \\ + (V_s^i \Delta \ln \lambda_s^i - V_s^j \Delta \ln \lambda_s^j) + (V_u^i \Delta \ln \lambda_u^i - V_u^j \Delta \ln \lambda_u^j) \\ + \frac{\sigma}{\sigma-1}\left\{\left(\frac{V_s^i - \alpha^i}{1-\alpha^i}\right)\Delta \ln \alpha^i - \left(\frac{V_s^j - \alpha^j}{1-\alpha^j}\right)\Delta \ln \alpha^j\right\} \end{array} \right). \qquad (7)$$

So, for example, intensive SBTC ($\Delta \ln \lambda_s$) would raise w_s/w_u as long as it was concentrated in the skilled-intensive sector (i.e., $\Delta \ln \lambda_s^i > \Delta \ln \lambda_s^j$), whilst the effect of extensive SBTC ($\Delta \ln \alpha$) depends on where it occurs and whether it reduces costs. Note that, with this functional form, equally intensive SBTC throughout all sectors ($\Delta \ln \lambda_s^i = \Delta \ln \lambda_s^j$) would raise w_s/w_u. The intuition is that although SBTC is equal, the assumption there are more skilled workers in the i sector means the cost reduction is greater in that sector and hence relative skilled wages rise. Haskel and Slaughter (1998) looked at the sector-bias of SBTC and found that over the 1970s (1980s) SBTC was concentrated in unskilled-intensive (skill-intensive) sectors.

Labor Supply

To see the impact of labor supply, Figure 1 draws (3) and (5) in $[w_s/w_u, N_s/N_u]$ space. The left panel shows the downward-sloping relative demand (RD) curve (2) and an assumed upward-sloping relative labor supply curve (RS). Increases in w_s/w_u arising from SBTC (i.e., increases in α) shift RD to RD^1. The right panel shows (5), labeled as an economy-wide relative labor demand curve and relative supply. The curve is horizontal since w_s/w_u is determined by $(p^i/p^j$ and $TFP^i/TFP^j)$. Hence increases in w_s/w_u arise from skilled-sector biased rises in prices or TFP ($\Delta \ln p^i > 0$, or $\Delta \ln TFP^i > 0$) which shift the curve upwards from RD to RD^1.

To see the intuition for the "flat" shape of the curve, consider a rise in relative skilled supply that traces out aggregate relative labor demand. In the left panel, relative wages must fall to absorb the extra skilled workers, and so RD slopes downwards. The right panel is the aggregate relative demand curve in a multisector model. With many sectors the extra skilled workers can potentially be absorbed by a rise in output in the skilled-intensive sector. The flat shape shows that in the 2×2 model this absorption is done entirely by changes in these output mixes with no change in relative wages; this is the so-called *Rybczynski effect* (Rybczynski, 1955). Davis (1998) criticises H–O theory on the empirical grounds that estimated labor demand curves are not flat. Note, however, that a downward-sloping *single-sector* relative demand curve such as (2) still holds; it is the *economy-wide* curve that is flat, as is clear algebraically from (5). Note, too, that although the aggregate RD curve is, in an accounting sense, a weighted average of the individual sectoral demand curves, in a multisector model the weights are endogenous. The above exercise of varying RS to trace out RD shows that the employment/output weights adjust rather then relative wages, giving a flat RD curve.

How then might labor supply affect relative wages in this model? First, it depends on the number of factors and products. In the above model, with two products there are two zero-profit conditions, and with two factors of production relative wages are completely determined. In general, if there are N traded goods being produced and M factors, as long as $N \geq M$ there are enough zero-profit conditions to determine factor prices without any effect from labor supply. However, if there is insufficient

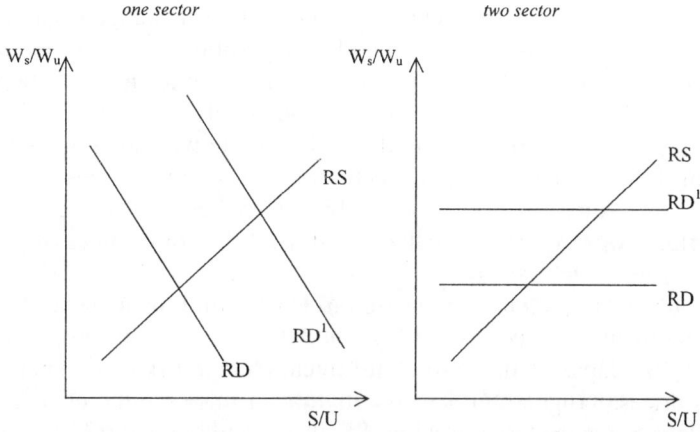

Figure 1. Aggregate Relative Demand and Supply of Labor Under the One-Sector and Two-Sector Models

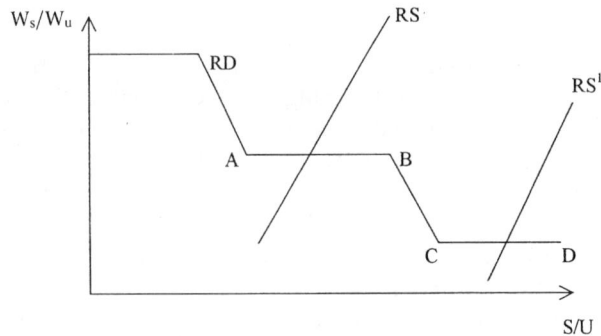

Figure 2. Aggregate Labor Demand in a Multisector Model with Changes in the Range of Goods

diversification in the economy such that there are more factors than products, then labor supply matters for relative wages since relative wages are not completely determined.[11] Second, as RS increases the economy might shift from producing N goods to N' goods. This gives a new set of zero-profit conditions in (4) and hence a new flat segment of the national relative demand curve. This is shown in Figure 2, where the increases in skilled labor supply mean the economy ceases to produce the most unskilled-intensive products and starts producing new, more skill-intensive products than before. Hence changes in supply affect relative wages as the economy moves from segment AB to CD. Third, if factors are immobile across sectors then each sector is a local labor market, in which case relative supply and demand will determine relative wages.

Prices

To say anything about trade, a convenient additional assumption is that the economy is small and open. Hence price changes can be due only to changes in world trading conditions. A number of recent papers have reconsidered the effects of technical progress when prices are endogenous, either because a country is large or because trading partners share the same technology and technical change is global.

When p^i/p^j is endogenous we have to add an equation to (5) whereby p^i/p^j is determined by goods' relative supply and relative demand. With homothetic preferences, relative demand does not depend on income, but solely on relative prices (and preference parameters).[12] Relative supply depends on relative wages and, crucially, technology. In this case, then, the effect of technology on relative wages depends on what one might call the "direct" effect of sector bias described by (5) at given p^i/p^j and the "indirect" effects working through changes in p^i/p^j due to changes in relative goods supply.

A number of recent papers, summarized in Haskel and Slaughter (1998), have considered the endogenous price case and reached different conclusions. Krugman (1995) and Davis (1997) consider the case of technical change (TC) in a single sector with endogenous prices. Krugman (1995) asserts that in this case the economy is analytically equivalent to being closed and that SBTC in either sector raises w_s/w_u. However, the above algebra suggests that the importance of sector bias arises from the assumption of two sectors, rather than the assumption that the economy is closed or open;

(5) still holds regardless of whether prices are endogenous or not. As Haskel and Slaughter (1998) show, Krugman's assertion is correct if one assumes Leontief technologies and ignores the direct effect. With general production functions, the direct and indirect effects offset each other and hence the overall impact of TC in one sector on w_s/w_u is ambiguous. If the direct effect exceeds the indirect effect, the results depend unambiguously on sector bias.

Berman et al. (1998) consider SBTC in *both* sectors when product prices are endogenous. They claim that relative wages rise in this case. Their model is a special case in two regards, however. They assume that SBTC lowers costs in both the skill-intensive and unskilled-intensive sectors and that these reductions in costs are exactly equal. Hence relative profitability does not change and so there is no direct effect on wages. The impact on relative wages comes entirely from the indirect effect of SBTC on relative supply and hence prices. Relative wages rise in this case, however, only if technology is Leontief. If there is any substitutability in production, relative wages depend on the sector bias of SBTC; see Haskel and Slaughter (1998) for more details.

The Definition of a Sector

The source of heterogeneity in this model derives from sectors (or industries) with different factor intensities ($V_s^i \neq V_s^j$). A number of points follow from this. First, working with a single-sector model is equivalent to assuming a representative firm. One would not like to argue that it is "wrong" to work with a representative firm, but representative-firm models usually do not have compositional effects which are key in the H–O model.[13] Second, empirical applications of the model are usually at the industry level, since an industry (hopefully) groups firms of like technology and hence skill intensity. If this assumption is incorrect, it is possible that an apparent sector bias is due to within-industry skill bias and suitable compositional effects. Third, the disappearance of a sector makes a big difference to the determinants of relative wages (in the two-sector case this would, for example, mean $N < M$ as discussed above). Whilst this means the model's results are knife-edged, it is to be expected in a model where wages are determined on the margin since a sector's disappearance is a substantial marginal change. Fourth, factor content analysis is an example of an empirical application that does assume differences in technologies across sectors; for a debate on this approach, see Deardorff (1997), Krugman (1995), and Leamer (1996).

Other Points

The effect of sector bias on relative wages is derived here for a 2×2 model. In models of even higher dimensions the effect of sector bias holds "on average": factors employed intensively in rising-price industries will experience relative price increases; see Ethier (1984).[14] Nontraded sectors can be added to the model, but as long as traded prices are exogenous the 2×2 traded sector determines relative wages which are the same throughout the economy owing to labor mobility (TC in the nontraded sector changes nontraded prices). Finally, a recent theoretical literature (e.g., Acemoglu, 1999) considers the case that trade might influence technology.

3. Empirical Analysis of the H–O Model

One statistical approach to examining the H–O model (Lawrence and Slaughter, 1993; Sachs and Shatz, 1994; Desjonques et al., 1997) has been to estimate

$$\Delta \ln p_{kt} = \alpha + \beta \left(\frac{N_s}{N_u} \right)_{kt} + \varepsilon_{kt}, \tag{8}$$

where ε_{kt} is a random error and (8) is estimated across k industries. However, (8) considers only the intensity of two factors. In addition, Stolper–Samuelson price effects arise from the assumption that each sector in the economy makes zero profits, so that, when prices change, relative wages have to change to restore zero-profit equilibrium. The zero-profit relation links the level of prices and levels of factor inputs. Yet (8) regresses the *change* in prices on the level of factor inputs.

Since the H–O model is based on zero-profit conditions, Leamer (1998a) proposes to estimate the N zero-profit conditions in (4) directly. Taking logs, totally differentiating, and using the definition of *TFP* above gives that, for each sector k:

$$\Delta \ln p^k + \Delta \ln TFP^k = (\Delta \ln w_s) V_s^k + (\Delta \ln w_u) V_u^k \tag{9}$$

(where note that (5) can be derived from writing (9) for sector i and j and subtracting the sector j equation from the sector i equation). This equation says that changes in p or *TFP* can be accompanied by changes in w_s and w_u and still be consistent with zero profits (note the changes in w_s and w_u are weighted by factor cost shares which gives the effect on profitability). In (9), we can use data on prices and outputs and inputs to construct Δp^k, ΔTFP^k, V_s^k, and V_u^k. The terms Δw_s and Δw_u are unknown since they are the changes in economy-wide factor prices required to maintain zero profits. To find them, Leamer (1998a) suggests running the regressions

$$\Delta \ln TFP^k = \beta_s V_s^k + \beta_u V_u^k + \varepsilon_1^k,$$
$$\Delta \ln p^k = \gamma_s V_s^k + \gamma_u V_u^k + \varepsilon_2^k, \tag{10}$$

where ε_1 and ε_2 are errors arising from measurement error, the failure of zero profits to hold exactly and the like (the capital share of total costs can be added into (10)). Comparing (10) and (9), β_s, β_u, γ_s, and γ_u are the changes in skilled and unskilled wages consistent with zero profits in response to changes in *TFP* when prices are constant and changes in prices when *TFP* is constant. These coefficients can be regarded as summarizing the sector bias of $\Delta \ln p_i$ and $\Delta \ln TFP_i$. If $\beta_s > \beta_u$ or $\gamma_s > \gamma_u$, then *TFP* or price changes are concentrated in skill-intensive sectors, in which case relative skilled wages rise. If $\beta_u > \beta_s$ or $\gamma_u > \gamma_s$, then *TFP* and price changes are concentrated in unskilled-intensive sectors and relative skilled wages fall. Finally, the estimates of $\Delta \ln w_s = \beta_s + \gamma_s$ and $\Delta \ln w_u = \beta_u + \gamma_u$ can of course be compared with actual changes to gauge the accuracy of the model.[15]

Table 1 reports Leamer's findings using 444 US industries, 1981–91. Consider the top cell in column 1. The figure of –2.11 shows that skilled (nonproduction) wages would have had to fall 211% to maintain zero profits in the face of changes in US *TFP* from 1981 to 1991. The cell beneath that shows the unskilled (production) wage would have had to fall 337%. So sector bias of $\Delta \ln TFP_{it}$ in the US over this period was in the skill-intensive sector, which would have tended to raise wage inequality. Column 5 shows analogous results for $\Delta \ln p_{it}$ and suggests that price changes were skilled-sector biased; again this would have tended to raise wage inequality.

The rest of the table sets out the results for the UK reported in Haskel and Slaughter (1999a) and Gregory and Zissimos (1998). Columns 2 and 6 use 123 three-digit manufacturing industries for 1979–86, drawn from the UK Census of

Table 1. Sector Bias of Prices and Technology for the US and UK in the 1980s: Estimates of Equation (10)

	$\Delta \ln TFP_{it}$				$\Delta \ln p_{it}$			
	(1)	(2)	(3)	(4)	(5)	(6)	(7)	(8)
Study	L	HS	HS	GZ	L	HS	HS	GZ
Years	1981–91	1979–86	1980–89	1981–91	1981–91	1979–86	1980–89	1981–91
Data	4 digit	3-digit	3-digit	IO	4 digit	3-digit	3-digit	IO
Country	US	UK	UK	UK	US	UK	UK	UK
V_s^k	−2.11	0.06	0.22	−0.47	5.82	0.92	0.77	2.50
	(1.65)	(0.13)	(0.41)	(0.16)	(4.61)	(2.11)	(1.40)	(5.38)
V_u^k	−3.37	0.49	0.29	3.65	4.89	−0.16	0.08	−0.31
	(3.00)	(3.18)	(1.47)	(1.37)	(4.45)	(0.96)	(0.40)	(0.74)
Observations	450	123	67	87	450	123	67	87

Notes: Dependent variables: $\Delta \log p_{it}$ and $\Delta \log TFP_{it}$ for each indicated year interval. Absolute *t*-statistics are in parentheses. Capital share of total costs included as a regressor: coefficients not reported. Studies are L (Leamer, 1998a, for the US); HS (Haskel and Slaughter, 1999a, for the UK, heteroskedastic-robust *t*-statistics reported); GZ (Gregory and Zissimos, 1998, for the UK) using, respectively, 4-digit, 3-digit industry and input/output data. V_s and V_u are shares in total costs of: non-production and production workers (L), nonmanual and manuals (HS), and highly and medium-educated workers (GZ). GZ also include the share of low-educated workers (not reported).

Sources: Leamer (1998a, Table 24), Gregory and Zissimos (1998, Table 3), Haskel and Slaughter (1999a, Table 5).

Production. Columns 3 and 7 use 67 three-digit industries for 1980–89, also drawn from the UK Census.[16] Both these datasets use nonmanuals/manuals as a measure of skill. Columns 4 and 8 use 87 sectors from the UK input/output tables, including the service sector and using fractions of highly, medium and low-educated workers (measured by matching educational attainment data to their industry categories) as skill measures.

Comparing the coefficients on V_s and V_u reveals a consistent picture for the UK. Growth in *TFP* is *not* concentrated in the skill-intensive sector. By this method, then, technology cannot have caused the rise in wage inequality. By contrast, relative price rises are concentrated in the skill-intensive sector, consistent with the idea that price changes have contributed to rising wage inequality.

The question this work raises is: What causes $\Delta \log TFP_{it}$ and $\Delta \log p_{it}$? This is taken up in three studies. For the US, Feenstra and Hanson (1999) investigate the causes of $(\Delta \ln TFP + \Delta \ln p)$ by regressing $(\Delta \ln TFP + \Delta \ln p)_{it}$ on computers and outsourcing. They find significant effects of computers and outsourcing in this regression and significant effects on wage inequality based on regressing the estimated contributions of computers and outsourcing to $(\Delta \ln TFP + \Delta \ln p)_{it}$ on the factor shares (as in (10)). For the UK, Haskel and Slaughter (1999a) look at $\Delta \ln p_{it}$ and $\Delta \ln TFP_{it}$ separately and the sector bias of the changes that foreign prices and competition induced. They find changes in foreign prices and trade barriers significantly raised 1980s wage inequality. Also, although foreign competition raised the UK's *TFP*, it did not do so in the skilled-intensive sectors and hence did not contribute (statistically significantly) to wage inequality. Finally, Haskel and Slaughter (1999b) find some effects of changes in US trade barriers on 1980s wage inequality via sector-biased changes in prices.

4. Conclusion

This chapter has tried to compare the "trade" and "labor" approaches to estimating the contributions of trade and technology to wage inequality. The labor approach looks for factor-biased technical change whilst the trade approach looks for sector-biased technical change and price change. We have presented a model to highlight why, and argued that the trade approach derives from an explicit model of heterogeneous firms across sectors. In the 1980s data, the US saw a skilled-sector bias to both prices and technology. The UK saw quite well-defined skilled-sector biased changes in prices with no strong sector bias for technology.

These issues raise two particular questions for future work. On the theory side, developing the H–O model to incorporate further the effects of labor supply would seem desirable. On the empirical side, we need a better understanding of what drives prices and technology and what explains the different sector bias of prices across countries.

References

Acemoglu, D., "Patterns of Skill Premia," NBER discussion chapter 7018 (1999).
Bernard, Andrew B. and J. Bradford Jensen, "Exporters, Skill Upgrading and the Wage Gap," *Journal of International Economics* 42 (1997):3–31.
Berman, Eli, John Bound, and Zvi Griliches, "Changes in the Demand for Skilled Labor within US Manufacturing: Evidence from the Annual Survey of Manufactures," *Quarterly Journal of Economics*, May (1994):367–97.
Berman, Eli, John Bound, and Stephen Machin, "Implications of Skill-Biased Technological Change: International Evidence," *Quarterly Journal of Economics*, November (1998):1245–80.
Berndt, Ernst R. and David O. Wood, "The Specification and Measurement of Technical Change in US Manufacturing," in *Advances in the Economics of Energy and Resources*, Vol. 4. JAI Press (1982):199–221.
Davis, Donald R., "Technology, Unemployment and Relative Wages in a Global Economy," *European Economic Review* 42 (1997):1613–33.
Davis, Stephen, J., "Comment on Leamer," in Susan Collins (ed.), *Imports, Exports and the American Worker*. Washington, DC: Brookings Institution (1998).
Deardorff, Alan V., "Overview of the Stolper–Samuelson Theorem," in Alan V. Deardorff and Robert M. Stern (eds.), *The Stolper–Samuelson Theorem: A Golden Jubilee*. Ann Arbor: University of Michigan Press (1994).
———, "Factor Prices and the Factor Content of Trade Revisited: What's the Use?" University of Michigan working chapter 409 (1997).
———, "Technology, Trade and Increasing Inequality: Does the Case Matter for the Cure?" University of Michigan working chapter 428 (1999).
Desjonqueres, Thibaut, Stephen Machin, and John van Reenen, "Another Nail in the Coffin? Or Can the Trade Based Explanation of Changing Skill Structures Be Resurrected?" Mimeograph, December (1997).
Ethier, Wilfred J., "Higher Dimensional Issues in Trade Theory," in R. Jones and P. Kenen (eds.), *Handbook of International Economics*, Vol. 1. Amsterdam: Elsevier Science (1984):131–84.
Feenstra, Robert C. and Gordon H. Hanson, "Productivity Measurement and the Impact of Trade and Technology on Wages: Estimates for the US, 1972–1990," *Quarterly Journal of Economics*, August (1999):907–40.
Findlay, Ronald and Harry Grubert, "Factor Intensities, Technological Progress, and the Terms of Trade," *Oxford Economic Papers* 11 (1959):111–21.
Freeman, Richard B., "Are Your Wages Set in Beijing," *Journal of Economic Perspectives*, Summer (1995):15–32.

Gregory, Mary and Ben Zissimos, "In Search of Stolper–Samuelson Effects: A Review of Methodological Issues and Some Illustrative Results using UK Wages," mimeograph (1998).

Haskel, Jonathan E. and Ylva Heden, "Computers and the Demand for Skilled Labour: Evidence from Establishment and Industry Panels," *Economic Journal* 109 (1999):C68–C79.

Haskel, Jonathan E. and Matthew J. Slaughter, "Does the Sector Bias of Skill-Biased Technical Change Explain Changing Wage Inequality?" NBER working chapter 6565 (1998); revised version available from www.qmw.ac.uk/~ugte153/.

———, "Trade, Technology and UK Wage Inequality," NBER working chapter 6978 (1999a); revised version available from www.qmw.ac.uk/~ugte153/.

———, "How Much Have Changing Trade Barriers Raised US Wage Inequality?" draft chapter (1999b).

Johnson, George, "Changes in Earnings Inequality: The Role of Demand Shifts," *Journal of Economic Perspectives* 11(2) (1997):41–54.

Johnson, George and Frank Stafford, "The Labour Market Implications of International Trade," in O. Ashenfelter and A. D. Card (eds.), *Handbook of Labor Economics*. Amsterdam: North-Holland (1998).

Johnson, Harry G., "Factor Market Distortions and the Shape of the Transformation Curve," *Econometrica* 34 (1966):690–8.

Jones, Ronald, "The Structure of Simple General Equilibrium Models," *Journal of Political Economy* 73 (1965):557–72.

Katz, Lawrence and David Autor, "Wage Inequality," in O. Ashenfelter and A. D. Card (eds.), *Handbook of Labor Economics*. Amsterdam: North-Holland (1999).

Krugman, Paul R., "Technology, Trade, and Factor Prices," NBER working chapter 5355 (1995).

Lawrence, Robert Z. and Matthew J. Slaughter, "International Trade and American Wages in the 1980s: Giant Sucking Sound or Small Hiccup?" in Martin Neil Baily and Clifford Winston (eds.), *Brookings Papers on Economic Activity: Microeconomics 2* (1993):161–211.

Leamer, Edward E., "What's the Use of Factor Content?" NBER working chapter 5448 (1996).

———, "In Search of Stolper–Samuelson Effects on US Wages," in Susan Collins (ed.), *Imports, Exports and the American Worker*. Washington, DC: Brookings Institution (1998a).

———, "Linking the Theory with the Data: That's the Core Problem of International Economics," chapter prepared for Handbook of Econometrics Conference, London (1998b).

Machin, Stephen and John van Reenen, "Technology and the Skill Structure: Evidence from Seven Countries," *Quarterly Journal of Economics* 113 (1998):1215–44.

Rybczynski, T. M., "Factor Endowments and Relative Commodity Prices," *Economica* 22 (1995):336–41.

Sachs, Jeffery D. and Howard Shatz, "Trade and Jobs in US Manufacturing," *Brookings Papers on Economic Activity* (1994):1–84.

Slaughter, Matthew J., "Globalisation and Wages: A Tale of Two Perspectives," *World Economy*, forthcoming (1999a).

———, "What are the Results of Product Price Studies and What can we Learn from their Differences?" in Robert C. Feenstra (ed.), *International Trade and Wages*. Cambridge, MA: National Bureau of Economic Research (1999b).

Wood, Adrian, "How Trade Hurt Unskilled Workers," *Journal of Economic Perspectives*, Summer (1995):57–80.

Notes

1. Another way of characterizing the contrast is that the labor approach is typically based on a representative firm or firms (all of whom have the same skill intensity), whereas the trade approach is based on technologically heterogenous firms who employ different skill intensities.

2. See Slaughter (1999a) for a similar perspective, and Johnson and Stafford (1998) and Wood (1995).

3. Defined as a collection of firms with like technology such that they employ workers at the same skill intensity.

4. Leamer (1998a), for example, emphasizes that an important message of the Heckscher–Ohlin model is that wages are determined on the margin.

5. Intensive-biased technical change (a rise in λ) makes each factor better at the tasks they perform and so raises the productivity of the relevant factor, *ceteris paribus*. Extensive-biased technical change (a rise in α) makes skilled workers better at performing the tasks of unskilled workers.

6. Indeed Johnson (1997) and Katz and Autor (1999) use aggregate data on changes in supply and relative wages to infer from (3) the change in aggregate relative demand. As both stress, when applied to aggregate data, changes in α are due to SBTC but also shifts in product demand from domestic or international sources.

7. This totally differentiates (1), uses Shephard's lemma and $-\partial \log C/\partial t = \Delta \ln TFP$. See Leamer (1998b).

8. In terms of flows of workers across sectors, a fall in prices in the skill-intensive sector (i) causes firms to move to the unskilled-intensive sector (j). Sector i contracts and, since it is skill-intensive, it releases comparatively more skilled workers. Hence w_s/w_u has to fall to re-employ them. See Deardorff (1994) for a statement of a number of different versions of the Stolper–Samuelson theorem. Note that (5) shows the Jones magnification effect (Jones, 1965), namely that $(\partial \ln(w_s/w_u)/\partial \ln(p^i/p^j)) > 1$ (since $[1/(V_s^i - V_s^j)] > 1$). If V_s^i is not too different from V_s^j, then large relative wage changes can result from small relative price or technology changes; Johnson (1966) finds this may be the case in some of his 2×2 simulations).

9. The cost function corresponding to the production function above (1) is $C = [(\alpha^\sigma(w_s/\lambda_s)^{1-\sigma} + (1-\alpha)^\sigma(w_u/\lambda_u)^{1-\sigma})]^{1/(1-\sigma)} A^{-1} Y$, differentiation of which shows that $\partial C/\partial \lambda < 0$. Johnson (1997) argues that the extensive-biased TC case is empirically relevant since it is consistent with computers causing SBTC but not raising *TFP*.

10. Depending on the extent to which the industry rises in skill-intensity are caused by between-firm averaging effects within-industries. Bernard and Jensen (1997) examine this using plant data for the US.

11. Freeman (1995) criticizes the knife-edge property of this model.

12. Krugman (1995) discusses the case where relative demand depends on income effects.

13. The aggregate relative labor demand curves shown in Figures 1 and 2 shift up as workers flow into the skill-intensive sector. This compositional effect cannot occur in a model with uniform skill intensity.

14. Deardorff (1994), quoted in Slaughter (1999b), states the correlation version of the Stolper–Samuelson theorem: "For any vector of goods price changes, the accompanying vector of factor price changes will be positively correlated with the factor-intensity-weighted averages of the goods price changes."

15. Leamer also considers the case where $\Delta \ln TFP$ passes through to prices, in which case the sum $(\Delta \ln TFP + \Delta \ln p)$ is regressed on the cost shares. See also Feenstra and Hanson (1999).

16. There was a major change in the UK Standard Industrial Classification (SIC) in 1980. The 1979 and 1986 data are matched to the 1968 SIC, necessitating substantial adjustment to the 1986 data. The 1980–89 data are based on the 1980 SIC and so are unadjusted.

3
Trade Liberalization and Technology Choice

Rod Falvey and Geoff Reed

1. Introduction

The search for explanations of the decline in the return to unskilled labor relative to skilled labor in developed countries has occupied the attention of both trade and labor economists over the last few years.[1] For trade economists the focus has been on the extent to which trade liberalization by relatively unskilled labor-abundant countries might have been responsible for the fall in the relative wage of unskilled workers in their trading partners, since this outcome is consistent with the predictions of the Heckscher–Ohlin and Stolper–Samuelson theorems.[2] The general conclusion that has emerged from this literature is that, while this trade liberalization might perhaps be directly responsible to some extent, skill-biased technology change has been a more significant factor.[3] But even accepting this conclusion, there remains the issue of what forces have given rise to changes in the utilized technology. In particular, might trade liberalization in the developing countries also be indirectly responsible for the shift in relative wages through its effects in inducing the adoption of new technologies in the developed countries.[4]

In this chapter we investigate the links between trade liberalization and technology choice in the nonliberalizing country. By changing relative product prices, trade liberalization directly induces changes in equilibrium relative wages. The corresponding changes in relative input costs may then lead producers to switch to alternative technologies, which will in turn induce a further, indirect change in equilibrium relative wages. We do not examine the actual development of the alternative technologies themselves, but take these as already in existence prior to the liberalization, and not in use because they would be unprofitable at the prevailing factor costs. One can then ask whether the indirect relative wage changes that are caused by the liberalization-induced changes in technology will exacerbate or ameliorate the direct liberalization-induced changes in relative wages. These are the two central questions investigated in this paper: What characterizes the input composition of any technology change in developed countries induced by trade liberalization in their developing trading partners? And, what effects might these induced technology changes be expected to have on relative factor returns, assuming no further change in product prices?

Most analyses in this area begin with a simple illustrative model that assumes two primary factors of production—skilled and unskilled labor. The conditions under which trade liberalization or technology change will increase the relative wage of skilled workers are then easily derived. In the next section we use this framework to illustrate how price changes can lead to the adoption of alternative extant technologies. If trade liberalization leads to a decline in the relative cost of unskilled labor, then it will encourage a switch to more unskilled-labor-intensive technologies. Whether this switch will exacerbate or ameliorate the direct effects of the trade liberalization on relative wages is ambiguous in general.

In applied analysis it is recognized that other primary factors (particularly capital) and also intermediate goods must be considered along with labor inputs. In section 3 we investigate the effects of including both of these in the illustrative model, under the simplifying, yet not unrealistic, assumption that capital is internationally mobile. In particular, we investigate the characteristics that product price changes and technology changes must exhibit in order to generate a further decline in the relative return to unskilled labor in this (slightly) more general framework.

Section 4 then looks at the characteristics of technology changes induced by a fall in the relative cost of unskilled labor, and its implications for relative wages. While our assumption of internationally mobile capital rules out changes in its return as a source of technology change, changes in the relative prices of intermediates may alter the optimal intermediate and primary factor input mixes. Section 5 presents a summary and some conclusions.

2. Trade-Induced Technological Change

The argument that changes in relative prices, possibly induced by trade liberalization, can lead to a switch in technology may be illustrated using Figure 1. For simplicity we assume that there are only two primary factors (skilled labor, S, and unskilled labor, U), that all technologies are Leontief,[5] that there is only one available technology for the unskilled-labor-intensive good 1, but two possible technologies for the skilled-labor-intensive good 2, and that these technologies differ in their skill intensities.

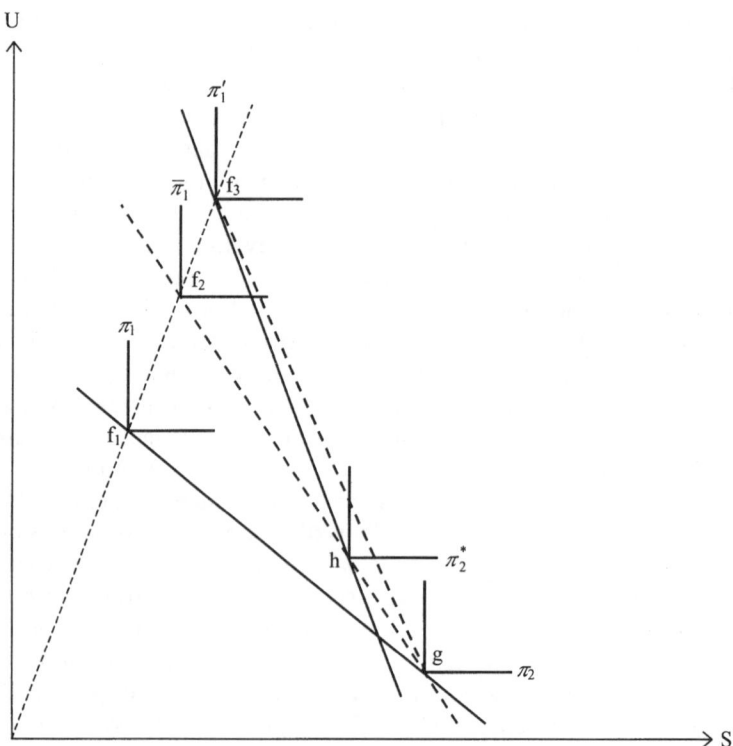

Figure 1. An Induced Switch in Technology

At given product prices both goods are produced in the initial equilibrium. Good 2 using the technology shown by the unit value-added isoquant π_2, with both π_2 and the unit value-added isoquant for good 1, π_1, tangential to the unit value isocost line f_1g (so that zero profits are made in both sectors). The alternative production technology for good 2, shown by the unit value-added isoquant π_2^*, will not be used, since the current price would not cover the unit production cost with that technology.

Now let the price of good 1 fall, so that its unit value-added isoquant is one further from the origin. In order to maintain equilibrium in factor markets, the relative price of unskilled labor must fall, so that the unit isocost line rotates clockwise around point g. For "small" decreases in the price of good 1, the original technology will continue to be used in production of good 2. But if the price of good 1 falls to the extent that its unit value-added isoquant becomes $\bar{\pi}_1$, producers of good 2 will be indifferent between using the two technologies available to them ($\bar{\pi}_1$, π_2, and π_2^* are all tangential to the unit isocost f_2hg). Further falls in the price of good 1, and consequent reductions in the relative cost of unskilled labor, will then result in the adoption of the alternative technology for good 2, as for example when the unit value-added isoquant for good 1 is π_1', so that the unit isocost line in the new equilibrium is f_3h, and the original good 2 technology is no longer least-cost. The change in the (relative) price of good 1 has thus induced a switch in technologies in the production of good 2. Note that the switch in the technology used to produce good 2 does not cause a "jump" in the relative wage rate for unskilled labor, but does cause a jump in the derivative of the relative wage rate with respect to the relative product prices (f_3h is steeper than f_2g).

The adoption of alternative technologies in the production of good 1 can be demonstrated in a similar fashion. Again we begin from an initial equilibrium where these alternative technologies are not profitable. A reduction in the price of good 1 shifts all such unit isoquants equi-proportionately away from the origin. The relative cost of unskilled labor falls and the isocost line becomes steeper. Given a sufficient change in relative input prices, it may become profitable to switch to an alternative technology in the production of good 1; and again, this alternative technology would be one more unskilled-labor-intensive than the original technology.

Figure 1 may also be used to illustrate another possible source of technology switching—changes in the prices of intermediate inputs. Suppose that production of good 1 requires the use of one intermediate (not good 2), which is also used in fixed proportions. A rise in the price of the intermediate would then reduce value-added in good 1, so leading to the same direction of movement of the good 1 unit value-added isoquants as would a fall in the price of good 1 itself, and with similar consequences.

In summary, if trade-liberalization-induced product price changes would lead to a fall in the relative cost of unskilled labor, then both sectors could be induced to switch to more unskilled-labor-intensive technologies. The implications that this has for relative factor returns are investigated in section 4 in a more general context.

3. Trade Liberalization or Technology Change?

We now extend the model to include internationally mobile capital and intermediate inputs,[6] and investigate the conditions that relative product price and technology changes must satisfy to generate a fall in the equilibrium relative return to unskilled labor. Consider a country currently producing two (composite) goods (1 and 2), using three factors of production (skilled labor S, unskilled labor U, and capital K) under the usual competitive assumptions. All inputs are used in fixed proportions in production under any given technology, but these proportions differ across technologies and sectors. Then if π_j is the domestic price of value-added in sector j ($j = 1, 2$), the competitive profit conditions imply that, in equilibrium

$$\pi_j = a_{Uj}w + a_{Sj}v + a_{Kj}r,$$

where r, w, are v the returns to capital, unskilled and skilled labor, respectively, and a_{ij} is the number of units of input i required to produce one unit of product j. The price of value-added in sector j depends on the output price (p_j) and the prices of the intermediate inputs (p_k; $k = 1, \ldots, n$) with

$$\pi_j = p_j - \sum_{k=1}^{n} a_{kj} p_k.$$

For convenience we assume that capital is freely tradable on an international market at given return r,[7] that sector 2 is the relatively more skill-intensive sector under all alternative technologies,[8] and that this country imports the relatively unskilled-labor-intensive good (1).

Trade Liberalization

Now suppose that, as a result of *trade liberalization* by this country's unskilled-labor-abundant trading partners, the value-added prices of these two goods change. With unchanged technologies, the changes in equilibrium factor returns (Δw and Δv, given $\Delta r = 0$) can be solved using the competitive profit conditions:

$$\Delta p_1 - \sum_{k=1}^{n} a_{k1} \Delta p_k = a_{U1} \Delta w + a_{S1} \Delta v + a_{K1} \cdot 0,$$

$$\Delta p_2 - \sum_{k=1}^{n} a_{k2} \Delta p_k = a_{U2} \Delta w + a_{S2} \Delta v + a_{K2} \cdot 0. \tag{1}$$

If $\hat{x}$ denotes the proportional change in any variable x, and θ_{ij} is the cost share of input i in sector j (e.g., $\theta_{Uj} = wa_{Uj}/p_j$) in the initial equilibrium, then these two equations can be solved for:

$$\hat{w} = \frac{\theta_{S2}[1-\theta_{I1}]\hat{\pi}_1 - \theta_{S1}[1-\theta_{I2}]\hat{\pi}_2}{|\theta|}; \quad \hat{v} = \frac{\theta_{U1}[1-\theta_{I2}]\hat{\pi}_2 - \theta_{U2}[1-\theta_{I1}]\hat{\pi}_1}{|\theta|}, \tag{2a}$$

so that

$$\hat{w} - \hat{v} = \frac{\theta_{L2}[1-\theta_{I1}]\hat{\pi}_1 - \theta_{L1}[1-\theta_{I2}]\hat{\pi}_2}{|\theta|}; \tag{2b}$$

where $|\theta| = \theta_{U1}\theta_{S2} - \theta_{U2}\theta_{S1}$ (and sign $|\theta|$ = sign $[s_2 - s_1] > 0$, since $s_2 > s_1$ by assumption), $\theta_{Ij} = \sum_{k=1}^{n}\theta_{kj}$ is the share of intermediates in unit costs in sector j, and $\theta_{Lj} = \theta_{Uj} + \theta_{Sj}$ is the total share of labor (skilled and unskilled) in the unit costs of sector j.

If relative product price changes are to induce a decline in the relative return to unskilled labor, we require that $\theta_{L2}[1 - \theta_{I1}]\hat{\pi}_1 < \theta_{L1}[1 - \theta_{I2}]\hat{\pi}_2$, which implies that

$$\hat{v} > \frac{[1-\theta_{I2}]\hat{\pi}_2}{\theta_{L2}} > \frac{[1-\theta_{I1}]\hat{\pi}_1}{\theta_{L1}} > \hat{w}.$$

There are three sources of bias that can generate this outcome. (a) First, trade liberalization by unskilled-labor-abundant countries can tend to reduce the relative value-added price of the unskilled-labor-intensive product in their trading partners (i.e., $\hat{\pi}_1 < \hat{\pi}_2$). With unchanged technology there are two channels through which trade liberalization can change value-added prices—through changes in the prices of the final output or through changes in the prices of intermediates. A fall in the relative value-added price of the unskilled-labor-intensive product could be due to a fall in its output price or an increase in the price of its intermediate inputs. (b) Second, the share of intermediates in unit costs can be lower in the more skill-intensive sector (i.e., $\theta_{I1} > \theta_{I2}$). (c) Third, the total labor share in unit costs can be lower in the skill-intensive sector (i.e., $\theta_{L1} > \theta_{L2}$). Together the last two conditions imply that the share of the remaining input (capital) is higher in the skill-intensive sector.

Technical Progress

Alternatively suppose there is (exogenous) *technical progress* in the two sectors, with no change in product prices. Such progress will also cause a shift in equilibrium relative factor returns. Technical progress can affect the input coefficients of both intermediate and primary inputs.[9] Changes in the former affect value-added prices. Let a'_{ij} denote the unit input requirements under the new technologies. Then, without loss of generality, we can decompose the change in input coefficients into

$$a'_{ij} = \delta_j a_{ij} + \Delta a_{ij}, \tag{3}$$

where δ_j and Δa_{ij} are defined such that[10]

$$w\Delta a_{Uj} + v\Delta a_{Sj} + r\Delta a_{Kj} + \sum_{k=1}^{n} p_k \Delta a_{kj} = 0. \tag{4}$$

Thus δ_j captures the change in total input productivity, and the Δa_{ij} measure the "input bias" (i.e., the change in the optimal input mix at the initial input prices) inherent in this change in technology. Then

$$wa'_{Uj} + va'_{Sj} + ra'_{Kj} + \sum_{k=1}^{n} p_k a'_{kj} = \delta_j \left[wa_{Uj} + va_{Sj} + ra_{Kj} + \sum_{k=1}^{n} p_k a_{kj} \right] + 0$$
$$= \delta_j p_j. \tag{5}$$

Note that technical progress implies that $0 < \delta_j < 1$, and the smaller is δ_j the larger the total input productivity improvement in sector j.

The changes in relative labor returns can then be solved from the competitive profit conditions at the new factor prices:

$$a'_{Uj}[w + \Delta w] + a'_{Sj}[v + \Delta v] + a'_{Kj}[r + \Delta r] + \sum_{k=1}^{n} a'_{kj} p_k = p_j, \tag{6}$$

which, using (5) and noting $\Delta r = 0$, implies

$$a'_{Uj}\Delta w + a'_{Sj}\Delta v = [1 - \delta_j] p_j. \tag{7}$$

In this case it is convenient to use the new equilibrium as a base from which to calculate the relative changes in labor returns. Equation (7) then translates into a system of equations:

$$\theta'_{U1}\hat{w} + \theta'_{S1}\hat{v} = 1 - \delta_1,$$
$$\theta'_{U2}\hat{w} + \theta'_{S2}\hat{v} = 1 - \delta_2, \tag{8}$$

where $\theta'_{Uj} = a'_{Uj}w'/p_j$ etc. denote the labor-cost shares in the new equilibrium, $\hat{w} = \Delta w/w'$ etc., and $|\theta'| = \theta'_{U1}\theta'_{S2} - \theta'_{U2}\theta'_{S1}$ (so sign $|\theta'|$ = sign $[s'_2 - s'_1] > 0$). These equations yield the solution

$$\hat{w} - \hat{v} = \frac{\theta'_{L2}[1-\delta_1] - \theta'_{L1}[1-\delta_2]}{|\theta'|}. \tag{9}$$

Note that $\Delta w/w' = \Delta w/(w + \Delta w)$, so that $\Delta w/w$ is greater or less than $\Delta v/v$ as $\Delta w/w'$ is greater or less than $\Delta v/v'$, implying that the sign of the term on the right side of (9) also determines the relative change in factor returns from the initial equilibrium. Since (9) has the same form as (2b), its interpretation follows accordingly.

The change in equilibrium relative factor returns depends on the relative rates of total input productivity change in the two sectors, and on the shares of labor in unit costs. There are two potential sources of change in relative labor returns. If labor shares are equal in the two sectors in the new equilibrium (i.e., $\theta'_{L1} = \theta'_{L2} = \theta'_L$), then

$$\hat{w} - \hat{v} = \frac{\theta'_L[\delta_2 - \delta_1]}{|\theta'|}, \tag{9a}$$

and the change in relative labor returns depends only on the relative total input productivity bias.[11] This outcome corresponds to that in the two-input case.[12] A higher rate of total input productivity improvement in the skill-intensive sector—*skill-biased technical change*—will (tend to) induce a decline in the relative return to unskilled labor. If rates of total input productivity change are the same in the two sectors (i.e., $\delta_1 = \delta_2 = \delta$), then

$$\hat{w} - \hat{v} = \frac{[\theta'_{L2} - \theta'_{L1}][1-\delta]}{|\theta'|}. \tag{9b}$$

In the absence of any sectoral bias in total input productivity changes, a fall in the relative return to unskilled labor will result if total labor has a larger cost share in the unskilled-labor-intensive sector in the new equilibrium.[13]

Summary

The conditions under which product price and technology changes will generate a decline in the relative return to unskilled labor in this extended model are consistent with those in the two-input case. A fall in the relative (value-added) price of the unskilled-labor-intensive output, or a higher rate of total input productivity improvement in the skilled-labor-intensive sector, will generate such a decline. When more than two inputs are considered, we note that decline in the relative return to unskilled labor is more likely, *ceteris paribus*, if the total labor and intermediate shares are lower in the more skill-intensive sector (i.e., the capital share is higher in this sector).

4. Technical Change Induced by Trade Liberalization

As noted in the introduction, the general consensus appears to be that skill-biased technical change has been the more important source of induced changes in relative labor returns. But it has also been argued here that the changes in relative product prices, and their accompanying changes in labor returns, may themselves have induced firms to change technologies. This possibility was illustrated for the case of two inputs in section 2. In this section we examine this process in the extended model and consider the implications of such trade-liberalization-induced technology change for relative labor returns.

To do this we suppose that there exist alternative ("new") technologies in each sector, whose unit input requirements are denoted by b_{ij}, and that these new technologies preserve the relative factor intensities of the two sectors. Since we are interested in the characteristics of technology choices *induced* by trade liberalization, we assume that these new technologies involve higher costs per unit of output at the initial factor prices—i.e., for each sector

$$a_{Uj}w + a_{Sj}v + a_{Kj}r + \sum_{k=1}^{n} a_{kj}p_k = p_j \leq b_{Uj}w + b_{Sj}v + b_{Kj}r + \sum_{k=1}^{n} b_{kj}p_k. \tag{10}$$

If we let $Da_{ij} = b_{ij} - a_{ij}$, then (10) implies that

$$wDa_{Uj} + vDa_{Sj} + rDa_{Kj} + \sum_{k=1}^{n} p_k Da_{kj} \geq 0. \tag{11}$$

Now suppose that product prices change (to p'_j and p'_k), as described in section 3. If firms continue to use the old technologies, the new production equilibrium will involve different labor returns that are the solution to

$$a_{Uj}w' + a_{Sj}v' + a_{Kj}r + \sum_{k=1}^{n} a_{kj}p'_k = p'_j. \tag{12}$$

In particular, suppose that the new equilibrium involves a relatively higher real return for skilled labor, in line with what we have observed in practice. Such a change in relative labor costs may make the adoption of more unskilled-labor-intensive technologies profitable in both sectors.[14] That is, trade liberalization can induce the adoption of new technologies, and they are likely to be skilled-labor saving in nature,[15] though we must also take into account interactions with changes in the cost of intermediates.

Suppose that the new technology would be preferred in sector j at the new factor and product prices; i.e.,

$$p'_j \geq b_{Uj}w' + b_{Sj}v' + b_{Kj}r + \sum_{k=1}^{n} b_{kj}p'_k. \tag{13}$$

Equations (12) and (13) can be combined to give

$$w'Da_{Uj} + v'Da_{Sj} + rDa_{Kj} + \sum_{k=1}^{n} p'_k Da_{kj} \leq 0. \tag{14}$$

Combining (11) and (14) we have

$$[w'-w]Da_{Uj} +[v'-v]Da_{Sj} + \sum_{k=1}^{n}[p'_k - p_k]Da_{kj} \leq 0. \tag{15}$$

Condition (15) implies a negative "correlation" between changes in input prices and changes in input usage. This is the (unsurprising) outcome that any shift in technology will be towards one which uses relatively more (less) of those inputs whose relative costs have fallen (risen) on average. One can infer no more than this in general.

Consider, however, the special case where the new technologies differ from the old only in their primary factor usage[16] (i.e., $Da_{kj} = 0$ for $k = 1, \ldots, n$.), and where $w' - w < 0$ and $v' - v > 0$.[17] Then (15) reduces to

$$[w'-w]Da_{Uj} +[v'-v]Da_{Sj} \leq 0, \tag{15a}$$

and this condition will *not* be satisfied if $Da_{Uj} < 0$ and $Da_{Sj} > 0$. That is, the alternative technology cannot use less unskilled labor *and* more skilled labor per unit of output. This leaves three possibilities: $Da_{Uj} < 0$ and $Da_{Sj} < 0$ (if $Da_{Kj} > 0$); $Da_{Uj} > 0$ and $Da_{Sj} > 0$ (if $Da_{Kj} < 0$); and $Da_{Uj} > 0$ and $Da_{Sj} < 0$. These possibilities can be narrowed further if one exploits the "complementarity" between capital and skilled labor inputs (i.e., that Da_{Kj} and Da_{Sj} have the same sign),[18] to $Da_{Uj} > 0$ and $Da_{Sj} < 0$. The fall in the relative value-added price of the unskilled-labor-intensive product is likely to induce a shift in both sectors to technologies that use more unskilled labor and less skilled labor and capital per unit of output.

This shift to new technologies will induce a further change in equilibrium factor returns. Let us denote these returns by $(\tilde{w}, \tilde{v})$. Then

$$p'_j = b_{Uj}\tilde{w} + b_{Sj}\tilde{v} + b_{Kj}r + \sum_{k=1}^{n} b_{kj}p'_k. \tag{16}$$

What are the implications of this shift in technologies for equilibrium relative labor returns? Let $\tilde{c}_j$ denote the reduction in unit cost in sector j from using the new technology (rather than the old) at the new equilibrium factor prices; i.e.,

$$\tilde{c}_j = a_{Uj}\tilde{w} + a_{Sj}\tilde{v} + a_{Kj}r + \sum_{k=1}^{n} a_{kj}p'_k - p'_j \geq 0. \tag{17}$$

Maintaining our assumption that there is no change in intermediate input usage, we can combine (17) with the equality in (12) to give

$$\tilde{c}_j = a_{Uj}[\tilde{w}-w']+a_{Sj}[\tilde{v}-v'] \geq 0,$$

which can be converted into proportional changes and cost shares as

$$\hat{c}_j = \tilde{\theta}_{Uj}\hat{w} + \tilde{\theta}_{Sj}\hat{v}, \tag{18}$$

where $\hat{c}_j = \tilde{c}_j/p'_j$, $\tilde{\theta}_{Uj} = a_{Uj}w'/p'_j$, and $\hat{w} = (\tilde{w} - w')/w'$, etc. Taking equation (18) for each of the two sectors gives a system that yields a solution for the proportional changes in labor returns of the same form as (2) above; i.e.,

$$\hat{w} - \hat{v} = \frac{\tilde{\theta}_{L2}\hat{c}_1 - \tilde{\theta}_{L1}\hat{c}_2}{|\tilde{\theta}|}, \tag{19}$$

where sign $|\tilde{\theta}|$ sign $[s_2 - s_1] > 0$. The effects of the trade-liberalization-induced changes in technology on relative labor returns depend on relative labor cost shares and relative cost reductions in the two sectors. Induced technology changes will further reduce the relative return to unskilled labor where the cost savings tend to be larger in the skill-intensive product, or where the total labor cost share is smaller in the skill-intensive product.

In summary, while a bias towards more unskilled-labor-intensive techniques might have been necessary for the alternative technologies to be adopted,[19] the effects of this choice on relative labor returns depends only on the relative cost savings so generated in the two sectors and their total labor cost shares. It is interesting that it is substantial cost savings in the skilled-labor-intensive sector, rather than the import-competing unskilled-labor-intensive sector, that are more likely to exacerbate the decline in the relative wage of the unskilled. To the extent that trade liberalization prompts the adoption of alternative technologies in the import-competing sector, this is likely to ameliorate the direct effects of the liberalization on relative wages.

5. Conclusions

We had two primary objectives in this paper. The first was to investigate the characteristics of any technology change in developed countries that might have been induced by the effects of trade liberalization in developing countries. The second was to determine whether these indirect effects of trade liberalization on relative wages, operating through switches to alternative technologies, are likely to ameliorate or exacerbate the direct effects of trade liberalization on relative wages, operating through value-added price changes.

To this end we set up a model that included skilled labor, unskilled labor, and capital as factor inputs and also allowed for intermediate inputs. Capital was assumed to be internationally mobile at a fixed return. We then examined the "biases" required for product price changes (as a result of liberalization by trading partners) and exogenous technology changes, respectively, to generate a fall in the relative wage of unskilled labor. For price changes, the biases required were that the unskilled-labor-intensive product had one or more of (a) a decline in its relative value-added price, (b) a larger share of intermediates in unit costs, or (c) a larger total share of labor (skilled and unskilled) in its unit costs. For technology changes the biases required were that this sector had (a) a lower rate of improvement in total input productivity, or (b) a larger total share of labor in unit costs.

Changes in the cost of inputs provided an incentive to switch to alternative technologies in both sectors, if such switches would be cost-reducing. Restricting attention to alternative technologies that differed only in their primary input usage and assuming complementarity between skilled labor and capital inputs, we concluded that such technologies would be adopted only if they were more unskilled-labor-intensive than current technologies. The effects of these induced technology changes on relative wages depended on the relative (potential) cost savings that they induced in the two sectors, and relative total labor cost shares. Substantial cost savings due to the adoption of alternative technology in the unskilled-labor-intensive sector would tend to ameliorate the original decline in the relative wage of unskilled labor. It is cost savings in the skilled-laborintensive sector that tend to exacerbate the original change. A decline in the relative return to unskilled labor will follow either exogenous or induced technology changes if the latter result in relatively larger cost reductions in the skilled-labor-intensive sector. Whether trade liberalization by developing countries has induced such changes in their developed trading partners is an empirical question worthy of further investigation.[20]

References

Arndt, S. W. and H. Kierzkowski (eds.), *Fragmentation: New Production Patterns in the World Economy* (forthcoming).
Autor, D. H., L. F. Katz, and A. B. Krueger, "Computing Inequality: Have Computers Changed the Labour Market?" *Quarterly Journal of Economics* 113 (1998):1169–213.
Bergstrom, V. and E. E. Panas, "How Robust is the Capital–Skill Complementarity Hypothesis?" *Review of Economics and Statistics* 74 (1992):540–52.
Berman, E., J. Bound, and Z. Griliches, "Changes in the Demand for Skilled Labour within US Manufacturing: Evidence from the Annual Survey of Manufactures," *Quarterly Journal of Economics* 109 (1994):367–97.
Berman, E., J. Bound, and S. Machin, "Implications of Skill-Biased Technological Change: International Evidence," *Quarterly Journal of Economics* 113 (1998):1215–44.
Bound, J. and G. Johnson, "Changes in the Structure of Wages in the 1980s: An Evaluation of Alternative Explanations," *American Economic Review* 82 (1992):371–92.
Falvey, R. E., "Trade Liberalization and Factor Price Convergence," *Journal of International Economics* 49 (1999):195–210.
Findlay, R. and H. Grubert, "Factor Intensities, Technological Progress, and the Terms of Trade," *Oxford Economic Papers* 11 (1959):111–21.
Francois, J. F. and D. Nelson, "Trade, Technology, and Wages: General Equilibrium Mechanics," *Economic Journal* 108 (1998):1483–99.
Haskel, J. and M. J. Slaughter, "Does the Sector Bias of Skill-Biased Technical Change Explain Changing Wage Inequality?" NBER working chapter 6565 (1998).
———, "Trade, Technology and UK Wage Inequality," Centre for Research on Globalisation and Labour Markets research chapter 99/2 (1999).
Jones, R. W. and S. L. Engerman, "Trade, Technology, and Wages: A Tale of Two Countries," *American Economic Review* 86(2) (1996):35–40.
Katz, L. F. and K. M. Murphy, "Changes in Relative Wages, 1963–1987: Supply and Demand Factors," *Quarterly Journal of Economics* 107 (1992):35–78.
Lucke, M., "Sectoral Value Added Prices, TFP Growth, and the Low-Skilled Wage in High-Income Countries," Presented at ETSG Conference, Rotterdam (1999).
Machin, S., "Changes in the Relative Demand for Skills in the UK Labour Market," in A. Booth and D. Snower (eds.), *Acquiring Skills*. Cambridge: Cambridge University Press (1996).
Machin, S. and J. van Reenen, "Technology and the Skill Structure: Evidence from Seven Countries," *Quarterly Journal of Economics* 113 (1998):1215–44.
Slaughter, M. J., "Globalisation and Wages: A Tale of Two Perspectives," *World Economy* 22 (1999):609–29.
Wood, A., "A New–Old Theoretical View of North–South Trade, Employment and Wages," IDS discussion chapter 292 (1991).
———, *North–South Trade, Employment and Inequality: Changing Fortunes in a Skill Driven World*. Oxford: Clarendon Press 1994.
———, "Globalisation and the Rise in Labour Market Inequalities," *Economic Journal* 108 (1998):1463–82.

Notes

1. See the symposia in the Summer 1995 and Spring 1997 issues of the *Journal of Economic Perspectives*, the September 1998 issue of the *Economic Journal*, and the discussion and references in Slaughter (1999).
2. These predictions carry over "on average" in more general models, depending on the source of comparative advantage; see Falvey (1999).
3. Discussion of the evidence on technology change can be found in Autor et al. (1998), Berman et al. (1994), Berman et al. (1998), Bound and Johnson (1992), Katz and Murphy (1992), Machin (1996), Machin and van Reenen (1998), and Lucke (1999). Some studies

find a major role for price changes, at least in the UK. See, for example, Haskel and Slaughter (1999).
4. This link has been emphasized by Wood (1994).
5. This avoids ambiguities concerning changes in factor proportions under a given technology (induced by a change in input costs for example) and changes in technology.
6. Haskel and Slaughter (1999) investigate the combined effects of product price changes and sectoral TFP changes on factor returns in a model with many goods and factors and including intermediate inputs. Francois and Nelson (1998) also consider the implications of generalizations of the two-sector model for relative factor returns.
7. Wood (1991) provides arguments and evidence justifying such an assumption.
8. That is, $s_2 > s_1$, where $s_j = a_{Sj}/a_{Uj}$. Empirically, relative factor usage across sectors does tend to be reasonably stable over time.
9. More generally, it has been argued that the globalization of markets has affected input usage in developed countries by inducing their industries to "narrow their product mix" or "outsource certain production operations"; see Wood (1998). For a general discussion of this "fragmentation" phenomenon, see Arndt and Kierzkowski (1999).
10. Equation (4), plus the system of $n + 3$ equations corresponding to (3), yields a system of $n + 4$ equations in $n + 4$ unknowns (δ_j, and Δa_{ij}, $i = L, S, K$ and $j = 1, \ldots, n$).
11. Haskel and Slaughter (1998) discuss the roles of sector-biased and factor-biased technical change in this context. They note that, for a large country, technical change will also have an indirect effect on relative factor returns through its effects on relative output supplies and, hence, relative product prices.
12. See Findlay and Grubert (1959) and Jones and Engerman (1996).
13. Note that the input-bias in the technology change will affect relative total labor cost shares in the new equilibrium relative to the old.
14. Were factor substitution possible under existing technologies, we would observe shifts towards more unskilled labor techniques.
15. Note that this is opposite to the assumption by Wood (1998) that import-competing firms will switch to unskilled-labor-saving techniques in response to import competition from the South. Such a switch could be related to the "fragmentation" of production (with unskilled-labor-intensive operations being moved offshore) or to a change in the output mix towards more skill-intensive products. The former could arise as a consequence of improvements in international communications—a change in a different technology from that considered in the text. The latter could arise as a result of relative product price changes.
16. Where alternative technologies differ only in their intermediate input usage, a change in intermediate product prices can induce a change in technology, but the impact of this change on relative wages will occur as result of the consequent change in value-added prices, as analyzed in section 3 above.
17. For example if $\hat{\pi}_1 < 0$ and $\hat{\pi}_2 = 0$.
18. For evidence on this complementarity, see Bergstrom and Panas (1992).
19. One should note that the empirical evidence does *not* find widespread shifts to more unskilled-labor-intensive techniques. See, for example, Berman et al. (1994), Berman et al. (1998), and Lucke (1999).
20. Though one should note that the empirical evidence to date does *not* indicate that there have been widespread shifts to more unskilled-labor-intensive techniques in developed countries. See, for example, Berman et al. (1994), Berman et al. (1997), and Lucke (1999).

4
Dynamics of Intraindustry Trade and Labor-Market Adjustment

Marius Brülhart

1. Introduction

There are two motivations for empirical research on intraindustry trade (IIT), the simultaneous import and export of very similar goods: (a) it is difficult to reconcile IIT with the predictions of neoclassical trade theory, and (b) IIT may herald comparatively smooth factor-market adjustment to trade liberalization. This paper examines aspects of the second issue, which is sometimes referred to as the "smooth adjustment hypothesis." Thanks to its intuitiveness this hypothesis has become widely accepted, but it has so far been subjected to little formal scrutiny.

A recent advance in this context was the development of dynamic IIT measures, labeled *marginal* IIT (MIIT), which conceptually relate more closely to adjustment processes than the traditional static indices. Progress was also made in linking trade data to sectorally disaggregated industrial statistics, which allows for direct tests of the correlation between (M)IIT and proxies for factor-market adjustment.[1]

Using data on manufacturing trade and job turnover in Ireland, this paper sheds light on three dynamic issues relating to the smooth-adjustment hypothesis. First, I review the case for using MIIT rather than IIT measures in analyses of adjustment. Second, I discuss the choice of the appropriate time horizon over which to calculate MIIT measures both conceptually and on the basis of empirical results. I find evidence that the MIIT-adjustment link works over relatively short time intervals. Third, I investigate the relative timing of trade and labor-market changes, and I find that the former tend to precede the latter.

An introductory review of the literature on the smooth-adjustment hypothesis is given in section 2. Section 3 sets out the empirical model and tests MIIT and static IIT measures. In section 4, I explore the issue of appropriate time intervals and lag structures. Section 5 concludes.

2. Conceptual Issues in Trade and Labor-Market Dynamics

Measuring Intraindustry Trade

IIT has traditionally been measured by the Grubel–Lloyd (GL) index:

$$GL_t = \left(1 - \frac{|X - M|}{(X + M)}\right)_t, \qquad (1)$$

where M stands for imports in a particular industry, X represents corresponding exports, and t is the reference year. This is a static measure, since it is based on trade data for one year only.[2] Hamilton and Kniest (1991) have argued that the observation of a high proportion of IIT in one particular time period does not justify *a priori* any prediction of the likely pattern of *change* in trade flows. Even an observed increase in static IIT levels between two periods (positive ΔGL) could "hide" a very uneven change in trade flows, akin to *inter-* rather than *intra-*industry adjustment. Motivated by this insight, a range of alternative measures have been developed to capture the MIIT concept empirically.[3]

In this paper, I retain the A index developed in Brülhart (1994) as the preferred measure of MIIT:

$$A_I = 1 - \frac{|\Delta_I X_t - \Delta_I M_t|}{|\Delta_I X_t| + |\Delta_I M_t|}, \qquad (2)$$

where Δ denotes changes in constant prices, t indicates the base year, and I denotes the length of the time interval between the base and end years. One feature of this index is its similarity with the GL coefficient. The A index also varies between 0 and 1, where 0 indicates that marginal trade in an industry is exclusively *inter-*industry and 1 indicates that it is entirely *intra-*industry, and the A index shares most of the statistical properties of the GL index. A share measure is preferred in the context of this chapter to measures that are based on levels, such as the C measure of Brülhart (1994) or *UMCIT* of Menon and Dixon (1997), because what we are interested in is the proportion of MIIT in total trade change, having controlled for the size of total trade in a sector.

The distinction between MIIT and IIT would appear superfluous if we found the two variables to be highly correlated in the data. However, Figures 1 and 2 clearly show that the A index is unrelated to levels and first-differences of the GL index in our Irish dataset (64 industries, 1977–91). The distinction between MIIT and IIT therefore seems relevant both conceptually and empirically.

Choice of Time Interval

The literature on MIIT has so far been concerned mainly with the identification of appropriate measures, and comparatively scant attention has been paid to questions of practical application. Given that (M)IIT measures are ultimately designed to guide

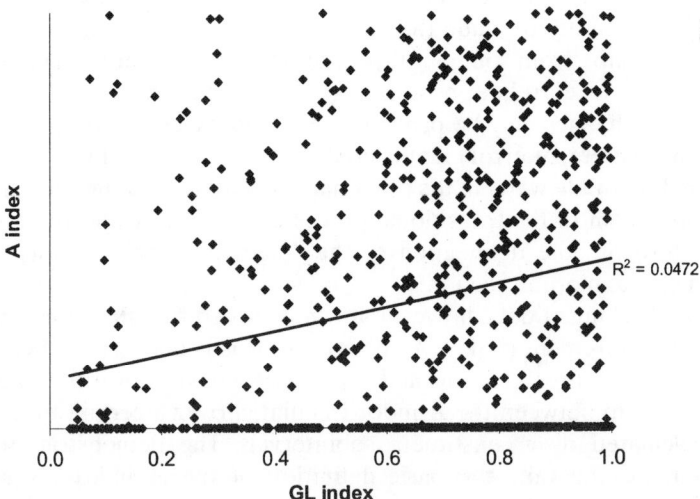

Figure 1. A and GL Indices: Scatter Plot and OLS Regression Line

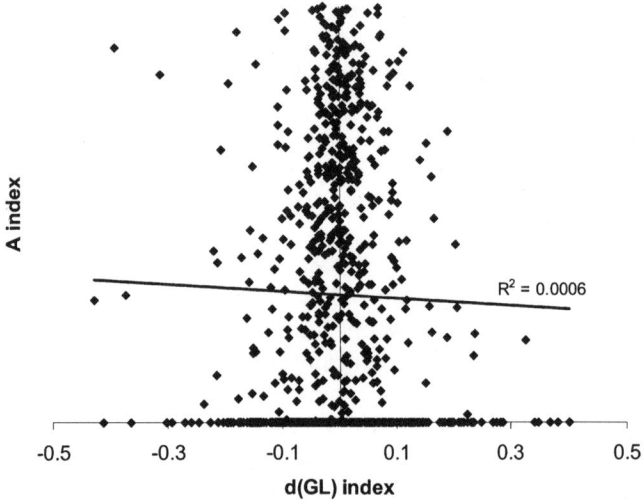

Figure 2. A and ΔGL Indices: Scatter Plot and OLS Regression Line

policy-relevant empirical work, it is important that the conceptual analysis be complemented by research on practical relevance and on questions of empirical implementation. There are a number of practical issues which matter for MIIT measures in a similar way as they affect the analysis of static IIT. These include topics such as the choice of the level of sectoral disaggregation, weighting methods in summing results over base sectors, and the appropriateness of correction for aggregate trade imbalance. Most of these issues have been analysed comprehensively and authoritatively by Greenaway and Milner (1986). There remain, however, some unexplored empirical questions relating to the appropriate measurement of MIIT. Two methodological issues are of specific relevance to MIIT: the choice of time interval for the calculation of MIIT measures, and the relative timing of trade and factor-market effects. It is on these aspects that I concentrate in this paper.

Measurement of MIIT indices necessitates a choice of the most appropriate time interval, Δ. There is little to guide the analysis *a priori* in selecting the relevant time period; apart, perhaps, from some intuitive notion that medium-term changes in trade patterns are likely to correlate most strongly with factor-market changes. Observed short-term trade changes may be prone to noise and excess volatility (some real and some due to measurement error) that is unlikely to affect firms' hiring and investment decisions in a discernible way. On the other hand, in looking at long-term trade changes one might loose sight of the transitional processes implied by the smooth adjustment hypothesis. However, the delineation of the "medium term" remains an empirical question, which I explore in section 4.

Even before looking at data, however, it can be noted that the choice of time interval for MIIT measurement is likely to be crucial. This is due to a particular statistical feature of MIIT measures. Oliveras and Terra (1997) have shown that there is no systematic relationship between the A index calculated over a certain time interval and A indices calculated over constituent subintervals. The demonstration is straightforward. First, we can take the basic definition of the A index for an interval I starting in base year t from equation (2), and apply the same formula to any subinterval i and base year s as follows:

$$A_{is} = 1 - \frac{|\Delta_i X_s - \Delta_i M_s|}{|\Delta_i X_s| + |\Delta_i M_s|}, \quad \text{where } \sum_i i = I, i > 0, \text{ and } t \leq s < t + I. \tag{3}$$

Next, define:

$$B_{is} = \frac{\Delta_i X_s - \Delta_i M_s}{|\Delta_i X_s| + |\Delta_i M_s|}, \quad \text{and} \quad w_{is} = \frac{|\Delta_i X_s| + |\Delta_i M_s|}{\sum_i (|\Delta_i X_s| + |\Delta_i M_s|)}, \tag{4}$$

where B_{is} is the "trade performance index" of Brülhart (1994), and w_{is} assigns trade-change weights to subintervals.

If the A index were a well-behaved weighted average of constituent subinterval A indices, the following relationship should hold:

$$A_{It} = \sum_i w_i A_{is}. \tag{5}$$

However, as demonstrated by Oliveras and Terra (1997), this regularity is only obtained if

$$\text{sg}(B) = \text{sg}(B_{is}) \forall is; \tag{6}$$

that is if the net balance of trade changes has the same sign in all subintervals. In other words, equation (5) holds, and a systematic link between the A index and its subinterval "components" exists, only if there is a continuous improvement/deterioration of the trade balance over subintervals in the sector at hand. Conversely, if net improvements and net deteriorations in the sectoral trade balance appear in different subintervals, no generalized relationship can be derived between the MIIT index for the full time interval, A_{It}, and the subinterval measures A_{is}. Inspection of most series of international trade data shows that net year-on-year changes in sectoral trade flows are rarely continuous, and the resulting dynamic "disjointedness" of the A index therefore needs to be taken into consideration in empirical application.

Timing of Trade and Labor-Market Effects

A second issue of empirical dynamics concerns the intertemporal sequencing of trade adjustments on the one hand, and factor-market adjustments on the other hand. Since the adjustment issue is mostly discussed with respect to reallocations in labor markets, this chapter abstracts from adjustments in markets for other production factors. It is well known that changes in firms' payrolls tend to follow changes in sales only with a certain time lag, as firms absorb sales variations in the short term through variations in stocks or temporary changes in hours worked ("hoarding").[4] Since there are no established theoretical or empirical priors on the size of this time lag, this is a fruitful object for more in-depth empirical scrutiny.

3. Testing the Smooth-Adjustment Hypothesis

An Empirical Model of Intraindustry Trade and Job Turnover

In this section I present an empirical test of the smooth-adjustment hypothesis, concentrating on adjustment in terms of plant-level employment changes. A fully specified empirical model must comprise three elements: (i) a dependent variable to represent labor-market adjustment; (ii) an independent variable representing (M)IIT;

and (iii) a set of independent variables to control for other exogenous influences on labor-market adjustment.

I use the index for intrasectoral job turnover of Davis and Haltiwanger (1992) as the dependent variable.[5] Derivation of this measure is as follows. Gross changes in plant-level job numbers within a particular industry are summed separately for plant births and expansions (*POS*) and for plant deaths and contractions (*NEG*) over the period starting in t and spanning the interval Δ_I:

$$POS_t = \sum_p \Delta_I E_{tp} \quad \text{for } \Delta_I E_{tp} > 0, \tag{7}$$

$$NEG_t = \sum_p |\Delta_I E_{tp}| \quad \text{for } \Delta_I E_{tp} < 0, \tag{8}$$

where E stands for the number of employees and p denotes plants. From this, one can derive the industry-level measure of excess job reallocation:

$$WITHIN_t = (POS_t + NEG_t - |POS_t - NEG_t|)/(POS_t + NEG_t), \tag{9}$$

where $WITHIN_t$ is the share of total plant-level job reallocation that is due to job reallocation in excess of net aggregate employment change of the particular industry. Like the IIT measures presented above, *WITHIN* takes values between zero and one. The left endpoint corresponds to instances where all plants within the sector experience either net job creation or job destruction; and the right endpoint corresponds to instances where the net change in job numbers of the sector is zero, and hence every job lost is offset by a job created simultaneously in the same sector.

The rationale for using *WITHIN* is its assumed relationship to labor-market adjustment costs. However, *WITHIN* is not a direct measure of labor adjustment *costs*, as it contains no information about flows into and out of unemployment, nor about relative wage changes and "adjustment services".[6] Nevertheless, the assumptions that need to hold for *WITHIN* to be a suitable inverse proxy for labor-market adjustment costs seem plausible. For *WITHIN* to be a valid proxy, labor should in general move more easily within than between industries. I cannot subject this crucial component of the smooth-adjustment hypothesis to an empirical test with the available data, but this assumption is strongly supported by empirical work in labor economics. Evidence that it is costlier for workers to move across industries instead of switching job within industries has been reported by Fallick (1993), Kletzer (1996), Neal (1995), and Shin (1997) for the United States, and by Greenaway et al. (1999) for the UK. In a comparative study for the US and the UK, Haynes et al. (1999) show that the likelihood of a displaced worker moving sectors relative to the likelihood of being re-employed in the original sector increases with the duration of the unemployment spell. This is compelling evidence that adjustment costs are higher for movers than for stayers. The link between intraindustry job turnover and low adjustment costs is therefore well documented.[7]

Moving on to the explanatory side of the model, there are three variables on which one can formulate well-founded priors.

1. One may expect highly concentrated industries to experience relatively low intrasectoral employment reallocation. Conversely, the larger the number of plants within an industry, the higher will be the share of intraindustry labor turnover, *ceteris*

paribus. The explanation is in two parts. First, simple arithmetic suggests that if an industry contains only a few plants, there may be less scope for intraindustry job moves between plants. Second, if plant and firm numbers are correlated, competitive pressures are likely to be weaker in sectors with small plant numbers, and plant-level payrolls are likely to be less volatile, because, for instance, larger profit margins allow for the absorption of negative demand shocks without labor shedding. Hence, it seems plausible to expect a negative relationship between *WITHIN* and a measure of plant concentration.

2. Second, based on similar reasoning, there is likely to be a positive relationship between *WITHIN* and trade exposure. If openness to trade means greater intensity of competition, then plant-level employment changes are likely to be required more frequently in order for firms to adapt to changing competitive positions *vis-à-vis* their competitors in low-margin activities. The expectation is therefore of a positive relationship between *WITHIN* and a measure of trade openness.

3. Most importantly, I have strong priors about the coefficients on the IIT variable. According to the smooth-adjustment hypothesis, the adjustment pressures induced by trade openness will be mitigated to the extent that trade flows are intraindustry. If the MIIT literature is correct and relevant, the *GL* index and *WITHIN* should be unrelated, but one would expect to find a significant positive relationship, *ceteris paribus*, between *WITHIN* and a measure of MIIT.

The first two of these expected relationships have been found to hold in a study of job turnover in Swedish industry by Andersson et al. (1998).

I consider four additional explanatory variables, which are known to be important in shaping industrial employment patterns in Ireland, but for which there are no clear-cut priors on expected coefficient signs. These variables are sectoral wages, technology intensity, exposure to foreign ownership, and changes in apparent demand. Hence, the baseline model is as follows:

$$WITHIN\_LOG_{xt} = \alpha + \beta_1 CONC_{xt} + \beta_2 TRADE_{xt} + \beta_3 WAGE_{xt} + \beta_4 TECH_{xt} + \beta_5 FOREIGN_{xt} + \beta_6 \Delta AD_{xt} + \beta_7 IIT_{xt} + \lambda_t + \varepsilon_{xt}, \quad (10)$$

where

$$WITHIN\_LOG = \ln(WITHIN/[1-WITHIN]), \quad (11)$$

and *CONC* is the four-plant concentration ratio, *TRADE* is imports plus exports as a share of production, *WAGE* is the average wage, *TECH* is the share of blue-collar workers in the total workforce, *FOREIGN* is the employment share of majority foreign-owned plants, ΔAD is the change in apparent consumption, *IIT* is either the *GL* or the *A* index, λ is a time dummy, and ε is an i.i.d. random error term. The subscripts x and t refer to industries and years, respectively. The logit transformation on *WITHIN* in equation (11) is performed in order to avoid problems due to the boundedness of the index. In the computation of *WITHIN_LOG*, values of 0 are set as 0.001 and values of 1 as 0.999. A fixed-effects panel data model is preferred to random effects, because the dataset consists of essentially the population of all Irish manufacturing industries.

The dataset is an industry-level panel of job turnover, trade, and other potentially relevant variables for the Irish manufacturing sector using three sources: a plant-level employment dataset provided by the Irish Agency for Enterprise and Technology

(Forfás), the Census of Industrial Production (CIP) published by the Irish Central Statistical Office, and a trade dataset provided by Eurostat. The panel is balanced, with observations on 64 industries for fourteen years, 1977 to 1990. A detailed description of the dataset can be found in Brülhart et al. (1998).

Year-on-Year Regression Results

Table 1 gives raw correlation coefficients among the variables of equation (10), with all the first-difference variables computed over one-year intervals. The first column, reporting correlations between *WITHIN_LOG* and the explanatory variables, supports all our priors: positive correlation with the *A* index (if lagged by one period), no correlation with the *GL* index or ΔGL, and the expected correlations with *CONC* and *TRADE* (lagged by one period).

Estimates of partial correlations in the full fixed-effects panel data model are reported in Table 2. The dependent variable *WITHIN_LOG* as well as the *A* index are again calculated over one-year intervals. Variables representing concentration ratios, trade exposure, and IIT are lagged by one year, since that structure gave consistently the most significant results in panel regressions as well as for bivariate correlations. I find strong confirmation of the priors on *CONC* and *TRADE* in all specifications. These results confirm the intuitive expectation that competitive pressures, induced by large plant numbers and openness to trade, lead to increased rates of job reallocation within industrial sectors.

Table 2 also confirms that it is not possible to find significant relationships between any definition of the *GL* index and intraindustry job turnover, whilst a modestly significant positive coefficient appears in the case of the one-year lagged *A* index. In regressions (1) to (3) of Table 2, I have estimated the full model with three different variables for IIT: the one-year-lagged *GL* index, first-differences in the *GL* index, and the one-year-lagged *A* index. Only in the last case is a significant partial correlation found. These results emerge with remarkable consistency across alternative specifications.[8]

Columns (4) and (5) of Table 2 report estimates of a parsimonious model consisting only of the variables on which we have theoretical priors. In addition to its congruence with *a priori* expectations, this specification is found to be very robust in a range of specification tests in Brülhart et al. (1998), and I therefore retain it here. Specification (4) shows that the one-year-lagged *A* index exhibits the predicted relationship with the dependent variable in the parsimonious version too. In column (5), a multiplicative interaction variable of lagged *A* indices and *TRADE* is added to the parsimonious model. One might expect MIIT to have a stronger impact in sectors that are relatively exposed to international trade, and hence the coefficient on the interaction term would be positive. However, the estimated regression coefficient on the interaction variable is only weakly positive, and dominated by the separate trade and MIIT variables. Other interactions of the IIT variables also failed to produce significant results. The empirical specifications used later in this chapter therefore omit interaction terms.

In conclusion, panel data regressions on a dataset for Irish industry suggest that year-on-year MIIT relates positively to the rate of intraindustry job turnover, while static IIT is unrelated to this proxy for labor-market adjustment. This evidence supports the MIIT version of the smooth-adjustment hypothesis. However, I find that two other variables, plant concentration ratios and trade exposure, exert even stronger influence on the rate of intraindustry job turnover than shares of MIIT.

Table 1. Raw Correlations Among Year-on-Year Variables

	WITHIN_LOG	CONC lagged	TRADE lagged	WAGE	TECH	FOREIGN	ΔAD	GL	GL lagged	ΔGL	A	A lagged	(A*TRADE) lagged
WITHIN_LOG	1												
CONC lagged	−0.39**	1											
TRADE lagged	0.16**	−0.20**	1										
WAGE	−0.15**	0.15**	−0.15**	1									
TECH	−0.01	−0.04	−0.16**	0.05	1								
FOREIGN	−0.15**	0.38**	0.21**	−0.05	−0.17**	1							
ΔAD	0.02	−0.13**	0.26**	−0.09**	−0.06*	0.06*	1						
GL	−0.02	0.03	−0.15**	−0.01	0.13**	0.13**	−0.11**	1					
GL lagged	−0.03	0.04	−0.14**	−0.01	0.14**	0.13**	−0.07	0.92**	1				
ΔGL	0.02	−0.02	−0.03	−0.01	−0.04	−0.01	−0.09**	0.18**	−0.22**	1			
A	−0.02	−0.01	0.04	−0.06*	−0.04	0.08*	0.07*	0.22**	0.23**	−0.03	1		
A lagged	0.07*	−0.01	0.05	−0.05	−0.07*	−0.09*	−0.01	0.21**	0.22**	−0.01	0.14**	1	
(A*TRADE) lagged	0.13**	−0.12**	0.71**	−0.09**	−0.18**	0.21**	0.20**	0.03	0.04	−0.01	0.08*	0.44**	1

Note: The number of observations ranges from 768 to 896.
**Indicates statistical significance at the 1% level of confidence, and *indicates statistical significance at the 10% level.

Table 2. Labor Turnover and Intraindustry Trade: Year-on-Year Fixed-Effects Panel Estimates

Explanatory variables	(1) GL index		(2) ΔGL index		(3) A index		(4) A index, parsimonious model		(5) A index interacted, parsimonious model	
	Beta	t-statistic	Beta	t-statistic	Beta	t-statistic	Beta	t-statistic	Beta	t-statistic
CONC lagged	−0.349	−7.44**	−0.349	−7.40**	−0.343	−7.16**	−0.370	−8.78**	−0.371	−8.80**
TRADE lagged	0.091	2.90**	0.091	2.99**	0.098	3.08**	0.087	2.94**	0.080	1.95*
WAGE	−0.087	−1.99*	−0.087	−1.98*	−0.090	−1.94*				
TECH	−0.010	−0.32	−0.011	−0.33	−0.005	−0.16				
FOREIGN	−0.031	−0.70	−0.031	−0.74	−0.044	−1.03				
ΔAD	−0.050	−2.40*	−0.050	−2.37*	−0.043	−1.99*				
GL lagged	−0.002	−0.04								
ΔGL			−0.001	−0.04						
A lagged					0.063	1.80*	0.064	1.84*	0.060	1.37
(A*TRADE) lagged									0.010	0.18
No. of explanatory variables	19		19		19		15		16	
No. of observations	832		832		768		768		768	
Adjusted R^2	0.162		0.162		0.168		0.166		0.161	

Notes: Dependent variable = logistically transformed *WITHIN* measure of intraindustry labor turnover. Year-dummies are included in all of the models although the coefficient estimates and associated *t*-statistics are not reported. Beta coefficients report how many standard deviations of the dependent variable can be explained by a one-standard-deviation movement in the explanatory variable. The *t*-statistics shown are based on heteroskedasticity-consistent (White-adjusted) standard errors.
** Indicates statistical significance at the 1% level of confidence, and * indicates statistical significance at the 10% level.

4. Dynamics

Time Intervals

In light of the purported sensitivity of MIIT measures to the size of the underlying time interval, I subject this issue to explicit scrutiny. The one-year periods used so far constitute the lower-bound possible interval size when applied to annual data, and they therefore correspond to the "short term" in the dataset used here. The question thus raised is: How are the results found in section 3 affected if we extend the length of the underlying time intervals?

The dataset covers 14 years (1977–91). Hence, the lower and upper bounds on feasible intervals are 2 and 14 respectively. In the empirical definition of these intervals, a choice must be made about the construction of the relevant base and end periods. It seems reasonable to postulate that those two subintervals should be nonoverlapping and of equal length. This still leaves room for alternatives. Taking the example of the 14-year interval, one could either define year 1 as the base period and year 14 as the end period; or, at the other extreme, the average over years 1–6 as the base period and the average over years 8–14 as the end period. I have opted for the latter version, since this is most congruent with the aim of eliminating short-term data volatility as the interval is extended.

The construction of medium-term A indices can be expressed formally as follows:

$$A_{\overline{BE}} = 1 - \frac{|(X_E - X_B) - (M_E - M_B)|}{|(X_E - X_B)| + |(M_E - M_B)|}, \tag{12}$$

where B and E stand for the base and end periods, respectively. Using the notation of section 3, which labels the first year of the interval as t and the number of years in the total interval as I, define:

$$X_B = \frac{\sum_{y=t}^{t+\text{int}(I/2)} X_y}{\text{int}(I/2)}, \quad \text{and} \quad X_E = \frac{\sum_{y=t+I-\text{int}(I/2)}^{t+I} X_y}{\text{int}(I/2)}, \tag{13}$$

assuming downward rounding in the integer function. Base- and end-period imports are defined equivalently.

In a similar vein, the other variables of my empirical model need to be recalculated for the relevant time interval. In the parsimonious model, the variables *WITHIN*, *CONC*, and *TRADE* require adaptation. For *CONC* and *TRADE*, this simply means averaging over the interval *I*. *WITHIN* is recalculated on the basis of year-on-year *POS* and *NEG* summed over the relevant time interval *I* (cf. equations (7)–(9)).

Some descriptive statistics confirm the sensitivity of the MIIT measure to the choice of interval. I have first calculated correlations across the 64 sample industries between, on the one hand, *WITHIN* calculated over the full 14-year interval, and, on the other hand, year-on-year values of *WITHIN* averaged over the 14 years.[9] The correlation coefficient is 0.48 and statistically significant at the 0.01% level. The same exercise was then conducted with *A* indices. The cross-industry correlation coefficient between, on the one hand, *A* indices calculated over the 14-year interval and, on the other hand, mean year-on-year *A* indices is 0.29 and statistically significant at the 5% level. Hence, there is a linear relationship in the data between MIIT measures over a certain interval and those of subintervals, but that relationship is rather weak. Another way of capturing this feature of MIIT indices is to look at their year-on-year serial correlations.

Table 1 reports correlations of current values with their lags for the *GL* and *A* indices. The one-year autocorrelation coefficient for the *GL* index is 0.92, but for the *A* index it is a mere 0.14. All these descriptive statistics support the conceptual analysis of Oliveras and Terra (1997), by confirming that the *A* index—and hence the results reported in section 3—are sensitive to the choice of time interval.

This sensitivity becomes even more apparent when the full regression model is re-estimated for variables calculated over different time intervals. Table 3 reports the result of the parsimonious model estimated for 2-, 5- and 10-year intervals. While the control variables *CONC* and *TRADE* are robust to those variations, the MIIT variable is not. Extending the time interval to two years (i.e., inserting a one-year gap in year-on-year computations of *A*) leaves a positive sign on the estimated coefficient for the *A* index, but statistical significance is lost. Indeed, the *A* index is never statistically significant when the size of the interval exceeds one year, and the estimated relationship with the intraindustry job turnover rate is (implausibly) negative in regressions (2) and (3) of Table 3.

This result also emerges from Figure 3, which reports beta coefficients on the three regressors of the parsimonious model for all interval sizes between 1 and 10 years (an asterisk denotes statistical significance at the 10% level). The chart visualizes the extent to which the effects of *CONC* and *TRADE* exceed those of MIIT, and it again becomes apparent that the significance of the *A* index hinges on the length of the chosen time interval. The coefficient on the *A* index is statistically insignificant for all interval sizes above one year. Moreover, seven of the eight interval sizes above two years produce negative (though statistically insignificant) coefficients on the *A* index—against our theoretical priors.

These results suggest that the relevant period over which to compute MIIT measures in analyses of trade-induced adjustment is shorter than one might have expected. In the dataset used here, one-year intervals are the only period over which the *A* index has a significant impact on the rate of intraindustry job turnover.

Lag Structure

For the reasons outlined in section 2, the sequencing issue also deserves explicit investigation. I have therefore re-estimated the model with four different lag structures on the two trade variables: contemporaneous changes with the regressand, one-year lag, two-year lag, and three-year lag.[10] Table 4 reports results for four corresponding regression runs, all based on one-year time intervals for *WITHIN* and *A*. *CONC* and *TRADE* again emerge statistically significant and with the expected signs throughout, while the *A* index is sensitive to the size of the lag. Contemporaneity is rejected, as the coefficient on the *A* index without lag is statistically insignificant and negative. Similarly, any lag that is larger than one year seems too long. Whilst the model with two-year lags still produces a positive but statistically insignificant coefficient estimate on the *A* index, the point estimate turns negative and insignificant in the version with three-year lags.

A picture is again given to visualize the effect of varying the dynamics of the model. Figure 4 tracks beta coefficients on the *A* index for the four lag structures across eight different sizes of the time interval. Only one specification stands out in yielding a statistically significant positive coefficient estimate on *A*, namely the original year-on-year model with one-year lags used in section 3. Contemporaneity as well as lags above one year are consistently rejected.[11]

Table 3. Fixed-Effects Panel Estimates of Parsimonious Model With Varying Time Intervals

Explanatory variables	(1) 2-year intervals		(2) 5-year intervals		(3) 10-year intervals	
	Beta	t-statistic	Beta	t-statistic	Beta	t-statistic
CONC lagged one year	−0.325	−8.09**	−0.308	−7.56**	−0.298	−5.84**
TRADE lagged one year	0.065	2.21*	0.100	2.74**	0.095	1.37
A lagged one year	0.037	1.01	−0.033	−0.87	−0.052	−0.90
No. of explanatory variables	15		12		7	
No. of observations	768		512		256	
Adjusted R^2	0.110		0.119		0.105	

Notes: Dependent variable = logistically transformed WITHIN measure of intraindustry labor turnover. See also the note to Table 2.

Table 4. Fixed-Effects Panel Estimates of Parsimonious Model With Varying Lags

Explanatory variables	(1) No lag		(2) 1-year lag		(3) 2-year lag		(4) 3-year lag	
	Beta	t-statistic	Beta	t-statistic	Beta	t-statistic	Beta	t-statistic
CONC lagged one year	−0.375	−9.04**	−0.370	−8.78**	−0.391	−8.65**	−0.387	−7.95**
TRADE (varying lags)	0.078	2.78**	0.087	2.94**	0.075	2.41*	0.079	2.50*
A (varying lags)	−0.023	−0.71	0.064	1.84*	0.014	0.40	−0.004	−0.10
No. of explanatory variables	16		15		14		13	
No. of observations	832		768		704		640	
Adjusted R^2	0.161		0.166		0.171		0.163	

Notes: Dependent variable = logistically transformed WITHIN measure of intraindustry labor turnover; one-year intervals. See also the note to Table 2.

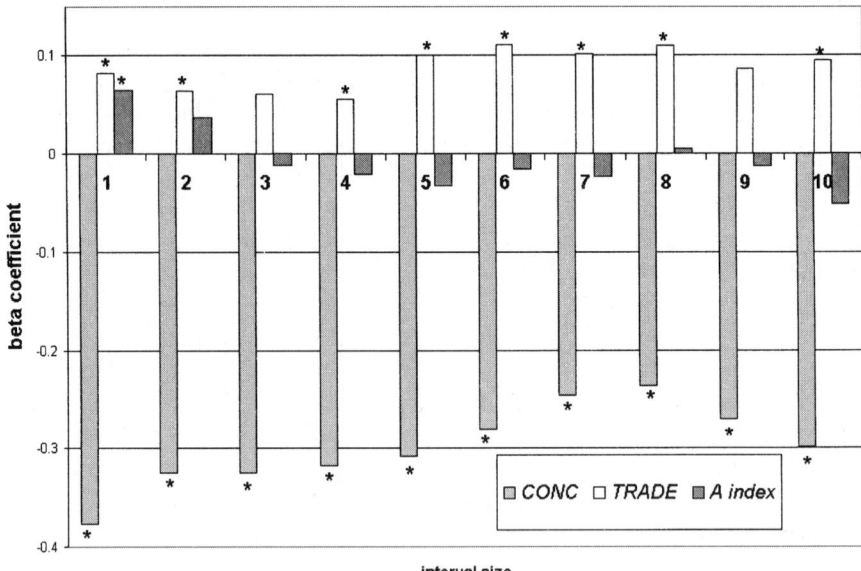

Figure 3. Beta Coefficients on CONC, TRADE, and A, with Varying Intervals

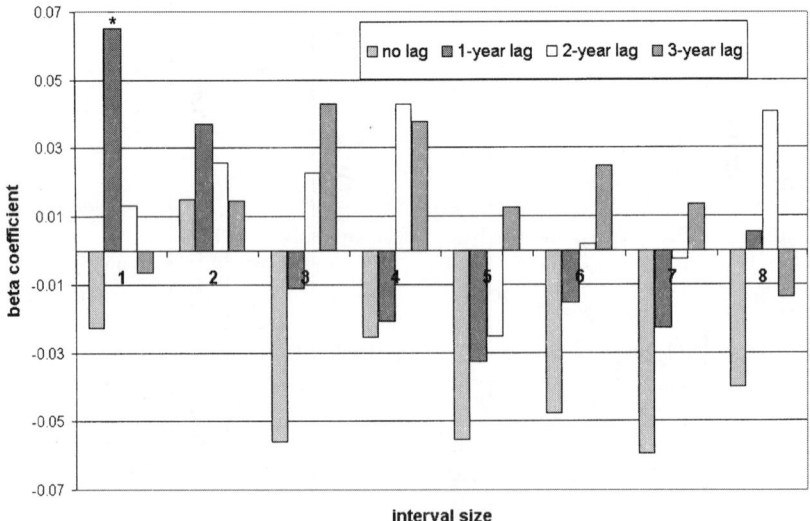

Figure 4. Beta Coefficients on the A Index, with Varying Lags and Time Intervals

In short, sensitivity analysis on various dynamic structures of the basic model suggests that MIIT measures computed over one-year intervals and lagged by one year relate most significantly to labor-market reallocation in the sense of the smooth-adjustment hypothesis.

5. Conclusions

I have explored some dynamic aspects of the "smooth-adjustment hypothesis" that is commonly associated with intraindustry trade. The analysis draws on a panel of Irish plant-level industrial employment data and of corresponding industry-level production and trade statistics for the 1980s. A concept borrowed from the empirical labor economics literature, the rate of intraindustry job turnover, is used as a proxy for labor-market adjustment.

Three questions were investigated. First, I explored the relevance of the traditional static IIT measure compared with that of an index measuring marginal IIT (MIIT). In some regression specifications, MIIT did appear with the expected sign and significance. However, no significant relationship was found between the proxy for labor adjustment and any variant of static IIT. Second, the appropriate size of the time intervals for MIIT and corresponding labor-market adjustment was investigated. The data clearly favor the shortest time period, namely year-on-year intervals. Third, I explored the relative timing of trade and labor-market changes by assuming different lag structures. The results suggest that labor-market effects follow changes in trade structure with a one-year lag.

It should be noted that by far the most significant determinants of the rate of intraindustry job turnover throughout was a sector-level measure of market concentration, followed by a measure of openness to trade. The share of MIIT in trade changes seems to have some bearing on the pattern of labor market adjustment in the short term, but over a long-term horizon these effects are swamped by changes in the intensity of competition among plants within a certain industry, be this trade-induced or not.

References

Andersson, Linda, Ola Gustafsson, and Lars Lundberg, "Structural Change, Competition and Job Turnover in the Swedish Manufacturing Industry 1964–96," FIEF working chapter 148, Trade Union Institute for Economic Research, Stockholm (1998).

Azhar, Abdul K., Robert J. R. Elliott, and Chris Milner, "Static and Dynamic Measurement of IIT and Adjustment: A Geometric Reappraisal," *Weltwirtschaftliches Archiv* 134 (1998): 404–22.

Baldwin, Robert E., John H. Mutti, and J. David Richardson, "Welfare Effects on the United States of a Significant Multilateral Tariff Reduction," *Journal of International Economics* 36 (1980):223–38.

Brülhart, Marius, "Marginal Intra-Industry Trade: Measurement and Relevance for the Pattern of Industrial Adjustment," *Weltwirtschaftliches Archiv* 130 (1994):600–13.

———, "Marginal Intra-Industry Trade and Trade-Induced Adjustment: A Survey," in M. Brülhart and R. C. Hine (eds), *Intra-Industry Trade and Adjustment: The European Experience*, London: Macmillan (1999).

Brülhart, Marius, Anthony Murphy, and Eric Strobl, "Intra-Industry Trade and Job Turnover," GLM research chapter 98/4, Centre for Research on Globalisation and Labour Markets, University of Nottingham (1998).

Davis, Steven J. and John Haltiwanger, "Gross Job Creation, Gross Job Destruction and Employment Reallocation," *Quarterly Journal of Economics* 107 (1992):819–64.

Fallick, Bruce C., "The Industrial Mobility of Displaced Workers," *Journal of Labor Economics* 11 (1993):302–23.

Feenstra, Robert C. and Tracy R. Lewis, "Trade Adjustment Assistance and Pareto Gains from Trade," *Journal of International Economics* 36 (1994):201–22.

Greenaway, David and Chris Milner, *The Economics of Intra-Industry Trade*, Oxford: Basil Blackwell (1986).
Greenaway, David, Robert C. Hine, Chris Milner, and Robert Elliott, "Adjustment and the Measurement of Marginal Intra-Industry Trade," *Weltwirtschaftliches Archiv* 130 (1994):418–27.
Greenaway, David, Richard Upward, and Peter Wright, "Sectoral Mobility in UK Labour Markets," GLM research chapter 99/1, Centre for Research on Globalisation and Labour Markets, University of Nottingham (1999).
Hamilton, Clive and Paul Kniest, "Trade Liberalisation, Structural Adjustment and Intra-Industry Trade: A Note," *Weltwirtschaftliches Archiv* 127 (1991):356–67.
Haynes, Michelle, Richard Upward, and Peter Wright, "Smooth and Sticky Adjustment: A Comparative Analysis of the US and UK," GLM research chapter 99/7, Centre for Research on Globalisation and Labour Markets, University of Nottingham (1999).
Kletzer, Lori G., "The Role of Sector-Specific Skills in Post-Displacement Earnings," *Industrial Relations* 35 (1996):473–90.
Levinsohn, James, "Employment Responses to International Liberalization in Chile," *Journal of International Economics*, 47 (1999):321–44.
Lovely, Mary and Doug Nelson, "Factor-Market Adjustment to Inter-Industry and Intra-Industry Trade in a Division of Labour Model," mimeo, Syracuse and Tulane Universities (1999).
Menon, Jayant and Peter B. Dixon, "Intra-Industry versus Inter-Industry Trade: Relevance for Adjustment Costs," *Weltwirtschaftliches Archiv* 133 (1997):164–9.
Neal, Derek, "Industry-Specific Human Capital: Evidence from Displaced Workers," *Journal of Labor Economics* 13 (1995):653–77.
Nickell, Stephen J., "Dynamic Models of Labour Demand," in: O. Ashenfelter and R. Layard (eds), *Handbook of Labour Economics*, Vol. 1, Amsterdam: North-Holland (1986).
Oliveras, Joaquín and Inés Terra, "Marginal Intra-Industry Trade Index: The Period and Aggregation Choice," *Weltwirtschaftliches Archiv* 133 (1997):170–9.
Shin, Kwanho, "Inter- and Intrasectoral Shocks: Effects on the Unemployment Rate," *Journal of Labor Economics* 15 (1997):376–401.
Thom, Rodney and Moore McDowell, "Measuring Marginal Intra-Industry Trade," *Weltwirtschaftliches Archiv* 135 (1999):48–61.

Notes

1. See Brülhart (1999) for an overview.
2. For the purpose of this analysis, it is useful to think of annual trade volumes as if they were stocks rather than flows.
3. Hamilton and Kniest (1991), Greenaway et al. (1994), Brülhart (1994), Menon and Dixon (1997), and Thom and McDowell (1999) have all proposed different measures of MIIT. For discussions, see Azhar et al. (1998), and Brülhart (1999). Lovely and Nelson (1999) have given the MIIT-adjustment link a theoretical underpinning.
4. For a survey of labor-demand responses to changes in product demand, see Nickell (1986).
5. For other recent applications of this job-turnover measure in the context of international trade, see Levinsohn (1999) and Andersson et al. (1998).
6. On different types of trade-induced adjustment costs, see Baldwin et al. (1980), and Feenstra and Lewis (1994).
7. An additional condition for accepting *WITHIN* as a useful proxy is that plant-level job turnover should correlate positively with total job turnover, since one of the main scenarios of smooth adjustment to IIT is where workers are redeployed within plants. Whilst it seems plausible to assume a positive correlation, we cannot verify it directly in our plant-level dataset.
8. Results are available from the author.
9. In the case of *CONC* and *TRADE*, the two definitions coincide, and the correlation is 1 by definition.

10. The one-year lag on *CONC* was maintained throughout.
11. Figure 4 shows that 2- and 3-year lags applied to *A* indices calculated over intervals of 2–4 years yield the expected positive coefficients, but they are never statistically significant even at the 10% level.

5
Marginal Intraindustry Trade and Labor Adjustment

Mary E. Lovely and Douglas R. Nelson

1. Introduction

In recent years there has been a boom in research measuring intraindustry trade (IIT) with the goal of studying the relationship between that trade and labor-market adjustment (Brülhart, 1998). This research proceeds from the widely held presumption that IIT is associated with lower adjustment cost in factor markets than interindustry, or "net", trade (NT). This revival of interest follows an important chapter in which Hamilton and Kneist (1991) argued that using the simple change in the Grubel–Lloyd index of IIT to identify low adjustment-cost trade can lead to potentially serious measurement error. In addition to a number of empirical applications, an interesting body of papers has developed examining the algebraic properties of various measures of *marginal* intraindustry trade (MIIT) to determine their relative suitability as measures of the low-adjustment-cost component of increased trade (Azhar et al., 1998). Because this work focuses on measures of IIT for a given sector, without incorporating adjustments of the overall equilibrium, the algebraic analysis of these measures is equivalent to a partial equilibrium analysis. The purpose of this chapter is to extend the analysis of MIIT to an explicitly general equilibrium environment.

The next section provides a very brief review of research on the relationship between IIT and adjustment to put the current chapter in context. Section 3 develops a general equilibrium framework based on Ethier's (1982) well-known division-of-labor model. Section 4 derives measures of change in IIT in the context of this model. Section 5 is the core of the paper, developing our analysis of MIIT and its economic consequences. The final section discusses the special properties of the model used and the extent to which our findings can be expected to carry over to alternative economic environments.

We find that the connection between MIIT and interindustry adjustment is not as direct in the general equilibrium context as presumed in partial equilibrium treatments. In particular, we show that a tariff reduction that influences only intraindustry trade causes interindustry adjustment. This result implies that increased IIT will generally be associated with some high-cost adjustment and with long-run changes in relative factor prices.

2. Related Literature

At least since the classic work of Verdoorn (1960), Drèze (1960), Kojima (1964), Balassa (1966), and Grubel (1967), it has been clear that IIT is in some fundamental way associated with trade liberalization, at least among industrial countries. Balassa in particular has argued that the empirically prominent role of IIT, along with a presumption that IIT is associated with lower adjustment cost than NT, helps to account for the unexpected sustainability of trade liberalization among industrial countries. In fact, Hufbauer and Chilas (1972), Lipson (1982), and Marvel and Ray (1987) invert

Balassa's logic as the basis of a political economic account of both intra-European and multilateral liberalization. Specifically, this line of research argues that, taking it as axiomatic that IIT is associated with lower adjustment cost than NT, not only will liberalization (either preferential or multilateral) be easier between countries whose trade can be expected to be characterized by a large share of IIT in total trade, but the intersectoral pattern of liberalization will be skewed toward sectors characterized by IIT. A survey of related research by Brülhart et al. (1998) strongly suggests widespread acceptance of the hypothesis that IIT induces lower adjustment cost than NT.[1]

If we accept that IIT really is intra-*industry* (i.e., not the result of problems with categorical aggregation) and, as we shall see, more importantly, that adjustment to changes in IIT is intraindustry, we can take advantage of substantial direct evidence from research by labor economists on the question of the relative costs of inter- versus intraindustry adjustment. Specifically, a substantial body of research uniformly finds that the cost of being displaced in terms of lower wages is substantially higher under interindustry adjustment (Jacobson, 1998). The modal explanation is quite clear: workers accumulate human capital which is portable between firms in the same sector, but is not portable between sectors; when a sector contracts (as the importable sector does under liberalization in the H–O–S model), labor is forced to move to the expanding (exportable-producing) sector (e.g., Topel, 1990; Neal, 1995; Kletzer, 1996). Because human capital is sector-specific, workers lose the value of their investment and, because accumulation is related to time in an industry, they may never fully recover from the move. Intraindustry adjustment is thought to be different: firms may go out of business, but liberalization does not generate (high-cost) interindustry adjustment. As with the other trade literature on this subject, we take these empirical findings as given. On the other hand, we do not assume an identity between intraindustry trade and intraindustry adjustment. Section 5 focuses on the relationship between these two magnitudes.

3. A Two-Country Model with Intraindustry Trade

Because we are interested in intersectoral adjustment, our analysis requires a model with at least two sectors; and because we are interested in the effects of intraindustry trade, the model requires that at least one of those sectors be characterized by IIT. While there are several models that meet these requirements, in this chapter we will be working with Ethier's (1982) model of trade in differentiated intermediate goods.[2] The model posits two factors of production, labor (l) and capital (k); and two final consumption goods, wheat (w) and manufactures (m). Wheat is taken to be produced with a standard neoclassical technology represented by a production function $f(k_w, l_w)$ which is twice-differentiable, linearly homogeneous, and concave. Both factors are costlessly mobile between sectors, and the markets for k, l, w, and m are perfectly competitive. Demand is taken to be generated by a representative agent with Mill–Graham preferences such that a share γ of income is spent on the manufactured final good. We will be considering a two-country world in which both countries are large, share the same technology sets, tastes, and endowments of capital and labor.[3] Importantly, we assume that countries share the same trade policies (i.e., we will assume that they levy the same *ad valorem* tariff on imports of intermediate goods, $t = T$).[4] Finally, we will focus only on international equilibria in which both countries produce both wheat and manufactures.

The Ethier model diverges from standard trade models in the technology of manufactures production: m is produced by costless assembly of components (x) which are, themselves, produced with internal increasing returns. Following the development in Ethier (1982), we suppose that in the relevant equilibrium there are n home firms and N foreign firms producing intermediates. Finished manufactures are costlessly assembled from intermediate components according to

$$m = \left[\sum_{j=1}^{n} x_j^{\beta} + \sum_{i=1}^{N} X_i^{\beta}\right]^{\frac{1}{\beta}}, \quad M = \left[\sum_{j=1}^{n} x_j^{\beta} + \sum_{i=1}^{N} X_i^{\beta}\right]^{\frac{1}{\beta}}, \tag{1}$$

where x_j is the input of intermediate component j, which is produced by the home country, and X_i is the input of intermediate component i, which is produced by the foreign country. Finished manufactures are produced in a similar way in the foreign country. Two features of this production technology are important. The first is the imperfect substitutability of differentiated components. The elasticity of substitution between any pair of component is $1/(1 - \beta)$ $(0 < \beta < 1)$. The second feature to note is that output is increasing in n and N, the number of distinct home and foreign varieties. The elasticity of output with respect to n or N is $1/\beta$, indicating increasing returns to variety.

To produce x_j units of intermediate variety j, a firm must purchase $b_j = ax_j + A$ bundles of k and l. The internal increasing returns to scale implies that a finite number of intermediates are produced, and each variety is produced by a different firm. These firms engage in large group monopolistic competition. Note that both the fixed (A) and marginal (a) costs are paid in bundles and are constant across firms in the component-producing sector. We assume all components have identical cost functions, which coupled with the symmetric form of (1) implies that all x_j and X_i are produced in the same quantity. If we let $b = \Sigma b_j$, and $x_j = x \; \forall \; j \in n$, and similarly for foreign producers of intermediates, then $b = n(ax + A)$ and $B = N(aX + A)$. With positive production of intermediates in both countries, producers of final manufactures will use all varieties of intermediates, so positive quantities of intermediates from both sources will be used by both home firms (x_h, X_h) and foreign firms (x_f, X_f). The total quantity of each input variety produced is the sum of sales to home and foreign firms: $x = x_h + x_f$ and $X = X_h + X_f$.

With a fixed endowment of factors of production, ($\bar{k}$, $\bar{l}$) and ($\bar{K}$, $\bar{L}$), we can summarize the resource constraint of the economy in terms of a transformation function between bundles and wheat: $w = s(b)$ and $W = S(B)$. We assume that bundles used in the production of components are produced using capital and labor according to a standard neoclassical production function, which is linearly homogeneous, twice-differentiable, and concave. Along with the equivalent assumptions on the production of wheat, and assuming no factor-intensity reversals, the function $w = s(b)$ is the concave transformation function of the H–O–S model. In particular, we know that $s'(b) < 0$ and $s''(b) \leq 0$.

Furthermore, given perfect competition in wheat and bundles, and taking wheat as the *numéraire*, the relative price of factor bundles for component production is $p_b = -s'(b)$. Since component producers purchase bundles under competitive conditions, total cost for a representative component-producing firm is $-s'(b)[ax_j + A]$. Total revenue is $q_j x_j$, so the condition that marginal revenue equals marginal cost can be rearranged to get an expression for q, the common price of intermediates:

$$q = \frac{-s'(b)a}{\beta}; \quad Q = \frac{-S'(B)a}{\beta}. \tag{2}$$

The profit of each component-producing firm is $\pi_j = q_j x_j + s'(b)[ax_j + A]$ which will be driven to zero by free entry and exit (abstracting from integer problems). Thus, setting $\pi_j = 0$ and substituting for q_j from equation (2), we get $x = X = A\beta/a(1 - \beta)$. Since this is made up entirely of parameters that are constant across component producing firms, scale is identical across firms.[5] Note also that these parameters are globally common, so all intermediate firms, regardless of location, produce the same quantity of the intermediate good.

It is important to note that while a representative home producer of intermediates produces exactly the same quantity as a representative foreign producer, it will not generally be the case that $x_h = X_h$ or $x_f = X_f$. In particular, the presence of tariffs creates a distortion in the choice of final manufacturers between home and foreign produced intermediates. Since this fact is essential to our analysis, we note that:

$$\frac{x_h}{X_h} = \left[\frac{Q(1+t)}{q}\right]^{1/(1-\beta)}; \quad \frac{X_f}{x_f} = \left[\frac{q(1+T)}{Q}\right]^{1/(1-\beta)}. \tag{3}$$

Ceteris paribus, a tariff shifts the input mix toward domestically produced intermediates. The elasticity of substitution between home and foreign inputs is $1/(1 - \beta)$.

Because the market for final manufactures is perfectly competitive, equilibrium is characterized by zero profits:

$$pm = qnx_h + Q(1+t)NX_h; \quad PM = QNX_f + q(1+T)nx_f, \tag{4}$$

which says that total revenue in manufactures is the sum of domestic and foreign input costs. Finally, our assumption of Mill–Graham demands ensures that a constant share, γ, of national income, inclusive of tariff revenue, will be spent on manufactured goods. Thus:

$$pm = \gamma(w + qnx + QtNX_h); \quad PM = \gamma(W + QNX + qTnx_f). \tag{5}$$

This system describes the two-country economy we use to examine the relationship between MIIT and resource allocation.

4. MIIT in a Two-Country Ethier Model

As we noted above, there is a widely held presumption that the larger the contribution of IIT to the change in total trade, the larger the contribution of intraindustry adjustment to total adjustment. This has led to a number of studies that use measures of the change in IIT more-or-less explicitly as a proxy for low-adjustment-cost trade. Most of this work measures IIT by the Grubel–Lloyd index, or one of its variants.[6] The Grubel–Lloyd index of IIT in sector j, G_j, gives IIT as a share of total trade in commodity j and, thus, takes values between 0 (no IIT, all trade is NT) and 1 (all IIT). The earlier research on liberalization–IIT–adjustment links, implicitly or explicitly, takes the change in the Grubel–Lloyd index to indicate the magnitude of that part of trade that does not generate high adjustment cost. That is, for the case of IIT in sector j, this research uses the measure

$$\Delta G_j := G_{j,t+1} - G_{j,t}. \tag{6}$$

To derive an expression for the Grubel–Lloyd index in terms of the framework developed in section 3, suppose the home country is (weakly) a net exporter of components. Because of the symmetry assumptions, there is no trade in wheat.[7] Thus, home exports are nx_f, and home imports are NX_h. In this context:

$$IIT = 2\min[nx_f, NX_h] = 2NX_h. \tag{7}$$

Using (7), the Grubel–Lloyd index, G, is

$$G = \frac{2NX_h}{nx_f + NX_h}. \tag{8}$$

Using circumflexes to denote proportional changes (i.e., $\hat{x} = dx/x$), we can express the change in the Grubel–Lloyd index as

$$\hat{G} = \frac{nx_f}{nx_f + NX_h}[\hat{N} + \hat{X}_h - \hat{n} - \hat{x}_f]. \tag{9}$$

By this measure, intraindustry trade increases when the number of foreign varieties or the quantity of each foreign variety used by home producers expands. In contrast, intraindustry trade is lower when the number of home varieties or the quantity of each home variety used by foreign producers expands. Note that the weight on the expansion of varieties in either country is the same—home exports as a share of total components trade.

As we noted in the introduction, Hamilton and Kniest (1991) argue, following Caves (1981, p. 213), that what is relevant to the analysis of factor market adjustment is not whether the amount of IIT has increased, but whether the share of IIT in trade has increased. That is, if one is interested in the effect of changed trading conditions on adjustment, it is necessary to identify the contributions of IIT and net trade (NT) to the change in total trade. In this chapter we will focus on a set of indexes due to Dixon and Menon (1997) which, like the Grubel–Lloyd index, have the attractive property that they can be derived from an identity with an intuitive relationship to both the theory and the data.[8] Specifically, Dixon and Menon's (1997) basic measure of the contribution of the change in IIT to the percentage change in total trade is

$$C_j := \frac{\Delta IIT_j}{TT_j} = \hat{IIT}_j G_j. \tag{10}$$

The second equality follows from the definition of the Grubel–Lloyd index, $G := IIT/TT$, and simple manipulation. Menon and Dixon prefer C_j to ΔG_j because the latter can lead to quite misleading inferences about the significance of MIIT in changing trade. Specifically, an increase in G_j is generally taken to imply an increase in the significance of IIT relative to NT. However, as Menon and Dixon (1996, pp. 7–8) show analytically, it is possible for $\Delta G_j > 0$ to be associated with a smaller increase in IIT than the increase in net trade.[9]

In terms of the model developed above, we can use (7) and (8) to write the C index as

$$C = \frac{2NX_h}{nx_f + NX_h}[\hat{N} + \hat{X}_h]. \tag{11}$$

This measure involves only expansion of foreign varieties and home usage of foreign varieties. Provided the home country remains the net exporter of components, changes in the number of home varieties and foreign usage of each home variety do not contribute to the measured change in intraindustry trade. Another distinction between this MIIT measure and the change in the Grubel–Lloyd index is that the weight used here is twice foreign intermediate exports as a share of total intermediates trade. If foreign production of components is small, changes in foreign exports of components lead to a small measured change in MIIT.

Thus, a first useful result from this analysis is that we confirm, in the context of a standard general equilibrium model, a result well known from the algebraic analysis of the Grubel–Lloyd index and the Menon–Dixon indices: these are measures of economically different things.

5. MIIT and Adjustment in a Two-Country Ethier Model

We now apply the analysis from sections 3 and 4 to our central question: What is the relationship between IIT and intraindustry adjustment? We proceed by totally differentiating the system given in section 3. Following Ethier (1979), we can express the international equilibrium in terms of national allocation curves. The home-country equilibrium requires that the market for finished manufactures clears. Because we assume the same import tariff that is levied on components is also levied on imports of finished manufactures, there is no trade in finished manufactures. Consequently, domestic equilibrium requires that the domestic demand price of finished manufactures equals the domestic supply price. This condition implies that the value of consumption of finished manufactures (given by equation (5)) equals the total cost of inputs to domestic manufactures (given by equation (4)).

As shown in an Appendix (available from the authors on request), the system reduces to two simultaneous equations that may be depicted as allocation curves. Letting $\tau = (1 + t)$ and $T = (1 + T)$, these equations take the form

$$\phi_n \hat{n} + \phi_N \hat{N} + \phi_t \hat{\tau} + \phi_T \hat{T} = 0,$$
$$\Gamma_n \hat{n} + \Gamma_N \hat{N} + \Gamma_t \hat{\tau} + \Gamma_T \hat{T} = 0. \tag{12}$$

The home allocation curve is depicted in Figure 1 as the curve HH' and the foreign allocation curve is depicted as FF'. We have assumed that the international equilibrium is stable and occurs at point A in the presence of identical tariffs on intermediates imports in each country. To understand the effect of liberalization, we note that a tariff reduction by the home country alone shifts both allocation curves. (The foreign curve is affected because the tariff reduction reduces home bias toward home intermediates, raising home demand for foreign intermediates.) The horizontal shift in HH' is given by

$$\left.\frac{\hat{n}}{\hat{\tau}}\right|_{HH'} = -\frac{\phi_t}{\phi_n}. \tag{13}$$

Domestic stability requires that ϕ_n be negative. ϕ_t may take either sign and we assume that $\phi_t > 0$. Thus, a decrease in the home tariff shifts HH' to the left. The foreign allocation curve also shifts, however, and its horizontal shift is given by

$$\left.\frac{\hat{n}}{\hat{\tau}}\right|_{FF'} = -\frac{\Gamma_t}{\Gamma_n}. \tag{14}$$

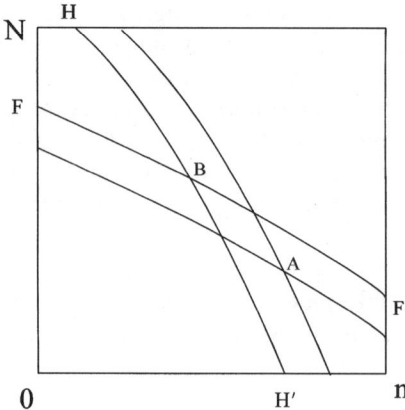

Figure 1. National Allocation Curves: Effect of a Decrease in the Home Tariff

As discussed in the Appendix, Γ_t is negative and Γ_n is negative. The sign of this derivative is therefore negative and FF' shifts right when the home tariff is reduced. Because HH' shifts left and FF' shifts right, the number of home input varieties falls while the number of foreign varieties rises when the home country reduces its tariff. The new equilibrium occurs at point B in Figure 1.

When both the home and foreign countries liberalize simultaneously, with the same percentage reduction in their tariffs, both countries influence the position of the two allocation curves. The net effect on the number of varieties depends on whether the effect of a tariff cut on one's own allocation curve induces a shift of the same, larger, or smaller magnitude (in absolute value) in the allocation curve of one's partner. Clearly, since the two countries cut tariffs by the same proportion, the net effect of the two policy changes will be the same for each country's total number of varieties. Whether the total number of varieties in each country rises or falls, these changes will be identical.

We can solve for the change in home varieties (the change in foreign varieties will be the same) as

$$\hat{n} = \frac{1}{D}[(\phi_N - \phi_n)(\phi_t + \phi_T)]\hat{\tau}, \tag{15}$$

where we have used the symmetry assumptions, as shown in the Appendix. Because the equilibrium is stable, the determinant, D, is positive. As in Ethier (1979), we also assume that an increase in either country's finished manufactures output reduces the demand price both absolutely and relative to that country's supply price and lowers the supply price of the other country. These assumptions imply that both ϕ_N and ϕ_n are negative but that $\phi_N > \phi_n$. Therefore, the sign of (15) depends on the sign of $\phi_t + \phi_T$. This sign will be positive if the rightward shift in the home allocation curve induced by an increase in the home tariff exceeds the leftward shift induced by an increase in the foreign tariff. If we assume this to be the case, the number of home varieties must fall when the home and foreign tariffs are reduced. Because the identical responses occur in the foreign country, liberalization reduces the total number of intermediates varieties.[10]

Now we turn to the measures of marginal intraindustry trade used in the empirical trade literature. These indices require measurement of changes in the amount of each variety that enters trade as well as their number. Using equations (3), we can derive expressions for changes in the amount of each imported intermediate. The change in home imports of each foreign variety is

$$\hat{X}_h = \frac{1}{1-\beta} \frac{X_f}{\Lambda} \left[x \varepsilon_h (\hat{n} - \hat{N}) + (x_f - x_h) \hat{\tau} \right], \tag{16}$$

where Λ is a measure of the home bias in input choices induced by the tariff and is positive, and ε_h is the elasticity of the supply price of factor bundles. We have also used symmetry of the two economies and of the policy changes. Similarly, the change in foreign imports of each home variety is

$$\hat{x}_f = -\frac{1}{1-\beta} \frac{x_h}{\Lambda} \left[X \varepsilon_h (\hat{n} - \hat{N}) + (X_f - X_h) \hat{\tau} \right]. \tag{17}$$

Because $\hat{n} = \hat{N}$, and $X_f > X_h$ while $x_f < x_h$ (home bias in input usage), it can be seen by inspection that the tariff reductions must increase both X_h and x_f.

Because symmetry ensures that $X_f = x_h$ and $X_h = x_f$, it can easily be confirmed that the change in the Grubel–Lloyd index, G, and in net trade, F, is zero. These results follow from the symmetry assumption: all trade is intraindustry. The liberalization by both countries does alter trade, however, in that fewer varieties are traded but each variety is now traded in larger quantities—the home bias in input use is reduced by the tariff reductions. Therefore, liberalization will induce changes in IIT.

The measure that captures the intraindustry trade induced by the mutual liberalization is the Menon–Dixon C index. For the present model, this expression is

$$C = \frac{2NX_h}{nx_f + NX_h} \left[\hat{N} + \hat{X}_h \right]. \tag{18}$$

The number of varieties falls while the amount of each variety traded rises, but the net effect on intraindustry trade in indeterminate. While we are unable to sign the MIIT measure, there is no presumption that it is zero.

Although the change in the volume of trade is indeterminate, the direction of adjustment is determinate. Because the number of varieties falls in each country, the total amount of domestic resources devoted to the manufacturing sector must fall. Trade generated or reduced is intraindustry, but the adjustment is interindustry. This observation leads us to the following propositions.

PROPOSITION 1. *For identical countries and interior equilibria before and after liberalization, mutual reductions in tariffs on imported intermediates can reduce the amount of resources employed in the manufacturing sector.*

PROOF. If $\hat{n} < 0$, then $\hat{b} < 0$. This follows from the positive (linear) relationship between n and b (see note 5). Resources are reallocated from the manufacturing sector to the wheat sector. All marginal trade is intraindustry but all adjustment is interindustry. □

This proposition suggests that MIIT measures may be poor guides to the share of adjustment that is low-cost adjustment. The link breaks down in that observations about changes in trade patterns do not map directly into changes in industry resource allocations. Moreover, as shown by the next proposition, observations about changes in trade patterns may be poor guides to the effect of trade on factor prices.

PROPOSITION 2. *For identical countries and interior equilibria before and after liberalization, mutual reductions in tariffs on imported intermediates alter the distribution of income. Assuming that the manufacturing sector is capital-intensive, liberalization reduces the return to capital and raises the wage.*

PROOF. Because n and N fall with liberalization, q and Q fall with liberalization. As shown by Ethier (1982, Proposition 4), a fall in the price of intermediates reduces the return to the factor used intensively in manufacturing and raises the return to the other factor. □

6. Conclusions

The two main results of this chapter have interesting implications for research on trade and labor-market adjustment. With respect to research on measuring MIIT with the goal of linking MIIT to factor-market adjustment costs, we conclude that the algebraic/partial equilibrium approach characterizing the earlier literature may be misleading. Our analysis shows that in a general equilibrium environment a change in net trade is not a necessary condition for high-cost (i.e., intersectoral) factor-market adjustment. The model we have used is a special case in that the extent of IIT is independent of scale parameters and is instead determined entirely by those parameters that determine the intersectoral allocation of resources. However, while the effect is shown in high relief here, as long as the change in IIT requires intersectoral reallocation, as it will if sectors shrink or expand in response to liberalization, changes in IIT will induce high-cost adjustment. This observation from our analysis holds true in alternative economic environments.[11]

In models in which liberalization induces scale effects as well as intersectoral reallocation, the relationship between MIIT and factor market adjustment will be more complex.[12] Liberalization may then alter the scale, as well as the number, of firms. Changes in trade patterns, then, may reflect both types of adjustment. It remains to be seen if, in the general equilibrium context, the contribution of MIIT to changes in total trade is a useful guide to the share of low-cost adjustment in total factor-market adjustment.

The second proposition takes us from the focus on short-run costs of adjustment to the long-run consequences of trade liberalization which has been the focus of so much recent empirical research (Gaston and Nelson, forthcoming). Specifically, the implication of Proposition 2 is that, not only may increases in IIT be associated with high-cost intersectoral adjustment, but as a result it may also be associated with long-run changes in relative factor returns. This suggests that worries about North–South trade, exemplified by rhetoric about a "giant sucking sound," as a culprit in the deterioration of the wages of unskilled workers may be missing the point in a way very different from the current stress on technological change. The culprit could conceivably be trade with other industrial nations.[13] It follows from the analysis leading to Ethier's (1982) fifth proposition that, even with pure intraindustry trade, the intersectoral adjustment will induce a change in the relative price of manufactures. This change in P_m/P_w can take, in general, either sign for a given change in P_b/P_w, though the change in the relative price of manufactures will be smaller than the change in the relative price of bundles.

Given the prominence of IIT among OECD economies, this suggests the possibility that both informal and econometric inference on the relationship between the relative prices of final goods and factors based on the H–O–S model may be faulty. At the very least, by using a model that incorporates IIT, which is such a prominent feature of trade data, we are alerted to aspects of the relationship between trade and wages that have been ignored in the focus on the Heckscher–Ohlin model.

References

Azhar, Abdul, Robert Elliott, and Chris Milner, "Static and Dynamic Measurement of Intra-Industry Trade and Adjustment: A Geometric Reappraisal," *Weltwirtschaftliches Archiv* 134 (1998):404–22.

Balassa, Bela, "Tariff Reductions and Trade in Manufactures Among the Industrial Countries," *American Economic Review* 56 (1966):466–73.

Brülhart, Marius, "Marginal Intra-Industry Trade and Trade-Induced Adjustment," in Marius Brülhart and Robert Hine (eds.), *Intra-Industry Trade and Adjustment: The European Experience*, London: Macmillan (1998).

Brülhart, Marius, Anthony Murphy, and Eric Strobl, "Intra-Industry Trade and Job Turnover," mimeo, University of Manchester (1998).

Caves, Richard, "Intra-Industry Trade and Market Structure in the Industrialised Countries," *Oxford Economic Papers* 33 (1981):203–23.

Dixit, Avinash and Victor Norman, *Theory of International Trade*, Cambridge: Cambridge University Press (1980).

Dixon, Peter and Jayant Menon, "Measures of Intra-industry Trade as Indicators of Factor Market Disruption," *Economic Record* 73 (1997):233–7.

Drèze, Jacques, "The Standard Goods Hypothesis," in A. Jacquemin and A. Sapir (eds.), *The European Internal Market: Trade and Competition*, Oxford: Oxford University Press (1989):13–32 (originally published in 1960, in French).

Ethier, Wilfred, "Internationally Decreasing Costs and World Trade," *Journal of International Economics* 9 (1979):1–24.

———, "National and International Returns to Scale in the Modern Theory of International Trade," *American Economic Review* 72 (1982):388–405.

Francois, Joseph, "Optimal Commercial Policy with International Returns to Scale,' *Canadian Journal of Economics* 25 (1992):184–95.

Francois, Joseph and Douglas Nelson, "A Geometry of Specialization," CEPR discussion chapter 1813 (1998).

Gaston, Noel and Douglas Nelson, "Trade and Wages in OECD Countries: Linking Theory and Evidence," in *Globalisation and Employment Patterns: Policy, Theory and Evidence*, Oxford University Press (forthcoming).

Greenaway, David and Chris Milner, *The Economics of Intra-Industry Trade*, Oxford: Blackwell (1986).

Grubel, Herbert, "Intra-Industry Specialization and the Pattern of Trade," *Canadian Journal of Economics and Political Science* 33 (1967):374–88.

Grubel, Herbert and Peter J. Lloyd, *Intra Industry Trade: The Theory and Measurement of International Trade with Differentiated Products*, London: Macmillan (1975).

Hamilton, Clive and Paul Kniest, "Trade Liberalisation, Structural Adjustment and Intra-industry Trade," *Weltwirtschaftliches Archiv* 127 (1991):356–67.

Hufbauer, Gary C. and John Chilas, "Specialization by Industrial Countries: Extent and Consequences," in H. Giersch (ed.), *The International Division of Labor: Problems and Perspectives*, Tubingen: J. C. B. Mohr (1972):3–38.

Jacobson, Louis, "Compensation Programs," in Susan Collins (ed.), *Imports, Exports, and the American Worker*, Washington, DC: Brookings, Institute (1998):473–537.

Kletzer, Lori, "The Role of Sector-Specific Skills in Post-Displacement Earnings," *Industrial Relations* 35 (1996):473–90.

Kojima, Kiyoshi, "The Pattern of International Trade Among Advanced Countries," *Hitot-subashi Journal of Economics* 5 (1964):17–36.

Lipson, Charles, "The Transformation of Trade: The Sources and Effects of Regime Change," *International Organization* 36 (1982):417–55.

Markusen, James, "Derationalizing Tariffs with Specialized Intermediate Inputs and Differentiated Final Goods," *Journal of International Economics* 28 (1990):375–83.

Marvel, Howard P. and Edward J. Ray, "Intra-Industry Trade: Sources and Effects of Protection," *Journal of Political Economy* 95 (1987):1278–91.

Menon, Jayant and Peter Dixon, "Regional Trading Agreements and Intra-Industry Trade," *Journal of Economic Integration* 11 (1996):1–20.

———, "Intra-Industry versus Inter-Industry Trade: Relevance for Adjustment Costs," *Weltwirtschaftliches Archiv* 133 (1997):164–9.

Neal, Derek, "Industry-Specific Human Capital: Evidence from Displaced Workers," *Journal of Labor Economics* 13 (1995):653–77.

Topel, Robert, "Specific Capital and Unemployment: Measuring the Costs and Consequences of Job Loss," *Carnegie–Rochester Conference Series on Public Policy* 33 (1990):145–76.

Verdoorn, P. J., "The Intra-Bloc Trade of BENELUX," in E. A. G. Robinson (ed.), *Economic Consequences of the Size of Nations*, London: Macmillan (1960):291–329.

Notes

1. Brülhart et al. (1998) refer to this as the "smooth adjustment hypothesis." This usage differs from the common use of the term "smooth adjustment," which refers to nondiscontinuous adjustment along a transformation function.

2. See Francois and Nelson (1998) for an expository development of the Ethier model and a variety of its applications.

3. Following Dixit and Norman (1980), we will denote home country magnitudes with lower-case letters and foreign country magnitudes with upper-case letters.

4. As in Markusen's (1990) analysis of derationalizing tariffs, we assume that each country levies the same tariff on imports of finished manufactures. Because final manufactures are costlessly assembled from intermediate goods, a tariff on finished manufactures eliminates the incentive to "jump" the tariff on intermediates through final goods imports.

5. Thus, from the fact that $b = n(ax + A)$, we can solve for the number of firms as a function of aggregate output of bundles: $n = (1 - \beta)b/A$. Note the implication that b and n are linearly related.

6. See Grubel and Lloyd (1975) for the original presentation of this index. The main variants attempt to correct for problems related to categorical aggregation or unbalanced trade, neither of which will concern us in our theoretical development, so we will focus on the Grubel–Lloyd index. For details on other measures, see ch. 5 of Greenaway and Milner (1986).

7. Note that wheat may be traded freely. However, because the two countries are identical, there is no neoclassical comparative advantage. Consequently, all trade is the exchange of component varieties.

8. The Grubel–Lloyd index follows straightforwardly from the fact that $IIT_j := 2\min[EX_j, IM_j] = EX_j + IM_j - |EX_j - IM_j|$, and normalization by total trade (TT). It is also quite natural to interpret G_j by noting that, since $NT_j := |EX_j - IM_j|$, we can rearrange the identity $TT \equiv IIT + NT$, and divide by TT to get an index that takes values in $[0, 1]$.

9. Perhaps more importantly, they develop extensive empirical evidence of precisely such an implication. For example, Dixon and Menon (1997) use Australian data at the 3-digit SITC level to illustrate the empirical significance of the measure one chooses to use in analyzing the effect of IIT in changing aggregate trade. They find that, of the 133 manufacturing industries that make up their dataset, about 14% in 1981–86 and 31% in 1986–91 were characterized by increases in G_j but larger contributions of marginal net trade than marginal *IIT*.

10. That protection raises the number of home varieties is the standard case, underlying arguments for optimal tariffs, as in Francois (1992). Markusen (1990) highlights the opposite

case when he derives conditions under which protection makes the number of domestic and foreign input varieties fall. He shows that a necessary condition for tariffs to be "derationalizing" is that the price elasticity of demand for finished manufactures exceeds the elasticity of substitution between home and foreign intermediate inputs. In the present model, this condition does not hold. Following Ethier (1982), we assume that the price elasticity of demand is unity, while the elasticity of substitution exceeds unity. Thus, in the present case, a liberalization may be derationalizing, in the precise sense that the liberalization reduces the total number of input varieties. See Markusen for references and further detail.

11. In any event, one implication of Proposition 1 would appear to be that, if we are interested in the link between trade and intersectoral adjustment, we will need measures of both intersectoral movement and trade. See Brülhart et al. (1998) for a first attempt in this direction.

12. Similarly, in the context of the current model, liberalization that reduces a firm's fixed costs will also produce a more complex relationship between MIIT and adjustment.

13. It is important to note, along with this theoretical possibility, that this is not a Stolper–Samuelson result. We have not shown that any factor experiences a *real* decline. As Ethier (1982, Proposition 6) makes clear, to make such a statement requires explicit attention to the interaction between intersectoral effects, of the usual Stolper–Samuelson sort, and scale effects.

6
Swedish Multinationals and Competition from High- and Low-Wage Locations

Henrik Braconier and Karolina Ekholm

1. Introduction

One major concern regarding the foreign operations of multinational enterprises (MNEs) is that they may reduce employment and wages in the MNEs' home countries. By these firms' ability to relocate activities to countries with lower wages, the home countries may become more exposed to factor price adjustment in terms of falling relative wages. Although a relocation of activities from the home country to affiliates abroad may enhance efficiency in production in the long run, there may be substantial adjustment costs associated with such relocations. Consequently, relocations may have a significant impact on the overall welfare and income distribution of the countries in which the MNEs operate.

However, the relationship between the MNEs' foreign employment and their domestic employment in the home country is not unambiguously a substitutionary one. With horizontal FDI, meaning foreign investments in the same type of activities as are conducted at home, we would expect mainly a substitutionary relationship between the firm's foreign and domestic activities as long as the produced good is a tradable.[1] Either the firm produces the good at home and exports it, or it produces the good in a foreign affiliate, in which case employment in the domestic part of the firm has to be lower than in the exporting case.[2] With vertical FDI, however, meaning foreign investment in activities that are either upstream or downstream in relation to the activities undertaken at home, there is an element of complementarity between the firm's domestic and foreign operations. Both upstream and downstream activities are undertaken to produce a good demanded by the firm's customers. When one of these activities expands, it tends to bring with it an expansion of the other activities as well.[3]

To examine the effect of the MNEs' foreign activities on the domestic economy is a difficult task. There are two strands in the literature dealing with such issues. First, there is a literature dating from the 1970s, where the relationship between affiliate production and exports from the home country is analyzed (e.g., Swedenborg, 1979; Lipsey and Weiss, 1981, 1984; Svensson, 1996). The earlier studies showed that there seemed to be a positive effect of outward FDI on exports, and this was taken to indicate that FDI tends to generate intrafirm trade because of the vertical nature of the firm's activities. However, it is not possible to infer from these studies whether an expansion of foreign activities tends to reduce or expand domestic employment. For instance, if a downstream activity were relocated from the home country to abroad, there could very well be a positive effect on home country exports even though home country employment was reduced. Similarly, if exports were to decrease as a consequence of increased overseas activities, home country employment could still increase if there were a more than offsetting expansion of production for the domestic market.[4]

There is also a more recent literature on the role played by outsourcing by MNEs in reducing demand for unskilled labor in the home country (e.g., Slaughter, 1995; Feenstra and Hanson, 1996a,b).[5] These studies are based on a Heckscher–Ohlin type of framework, where outsourcing is taken to lead to increased imports of unskilled labor-intensive goods. The upshot of this literature is that outsourcing seems to play a limited role in affecting the relative demand for skilled and unskilled labor. However, these studies are conducted on industry-distributed data, which means that important information at the firm level is lost in these studies.

In two recent working papers, Brainard and Riker (1997a,b) have used firm-level data for the US to analyze the effect of affiliate employment on the demand for labor in other parts of the firm. They estimate labor demand equations within MNEs, yielding estimates of cross-wage elasticities for labor demand in different parts of the firm. They find that for US MNEs, a substitutionary relationship seems to exist mainly between labor employed in affiliates located in the same type of locations with regards to their relative factor endowments. Between labor employed in affiliates located in different types of locations (i.e., one located in a high-wage country and the other located in a low-wage country), there seems to be mainly a relationship of complementarity.

This study employs a similar method to the one in Brainard and Riker (1997a,b) and applies it to firm-level data on Swedish MNEs. We thus estimate cross-wage elasticities, which enable us to assess the effect of wage changes in one type of location on the demand for labor in another location, and thus whether there is a relationship of complementarity or substitution between the employment in different parts of the firm.

In the analysis, we distinguish between affiliates located in high-income and lowincome countries on the assumption that cross-wage elasticities may vary depending on the type of location. In particular, we are interested in examining whether employment in the Swedish parts of the firms is affected differently by wage changes in low-wage countries compared with wage changes in other high-wage countries. Furthermore, we also want to study whether there are differences in the effect on affiliate employment of wage changes in locations that are either of the same or different type with regards to whether it is a high-wage or low-wage location.

Our study differs from the studies by Brainard and Riker in a number of respects. To begin with, the type of multinational activity conducted by firms from a small country such as Sweden is likely to differ markedly from the activities of firms from a large country such as the US (cf. Markusen et al., 1996). Therefore, the pattern of interaction between different parts of the firm may differ between Swedish and US MNEs. Furthermore, our empirical implementation differs somewhat from the one chosen by Brainard and Riker. In particular, we explicitly address, and try to control for, potential problems of endogeneity with respect to wages and productivity differences across locations.

What we find is some evidence of a substitutionary relationship between employment in the Swedish parts of the firms and employment in other high-wage locations. However, between employment in the different foreign affiliates, there seems to be mainly a relationship of complementarity.

The theoretical framework is presented in section 2. The data used in the analysis is presented in section 3, and the specification of the econometric model explained in section 4. Section 5 presents and discusses the results, and section 6 gives some concluding remarks.

2. Theoretical Framework

In order to analyze the different types of relationships that can prevail between the different parts of a multinational firm, we construct a simple model of a both horizontally and vertically integrated firm that has production plants in several locations.[6] More specifically, we assume that two distinct intermediate inputs have to be combined in order to supply the product in a market, and that high trade costs make one of these inputs nontraded. We assume that the firm has some monopoly power, while it is a price-taker in the labor market. Markets are assumed to be segmented so that the firm sets price independently in the different locations. The two different intermediate inputs are labeled X and Y, while the final product is labeled Q.

We assume the following production function for the firm:

$$Q = \min(X, Y), \quad X = \gamma L, \quad Y = \lambda L, \tag{1}$$

where L denotes labor. If either X or Y are shipped across borders, an iceberg trade cost has to be incurred. We assume that when one unit of a good is shipped across a border, only $\tau < 1$ arrives at the destination. These trade costs differ between goods and pairs of locations.

The firm maximizes total profits Π, which can be defined as net revenue over all its locations i:

$$\Pi = \sum_i \left(P_i^D(Q_i) Q_i - w_i \left(\frac{1}{\gamma} X_i + \frac{1}{\lambda} Y_i \right) \right), \tag{2}$$

where $P_i^D(Q_i)$ is the inverse demand function, $X_i = \Sigma_j X_{ij}$, $Y_i = \Sigma_j Y_{ij}$, the first subscript being the index for the location in which the intermediate input is produced and the second one being the index for the location in which the intermediate input is used to produce the final good, and w is the wage rate.

Because there are trade costs associated with trade between locations, cross-hauling of the inputs X and Y will never occur. For each location i, the following relationship must hold:

$$Q_i = X_i + T_{Xi} = Y_i + T_{Yi}, \tag{3}$$

where

$$T_{Gi} = -\sum_{j \neq i} G_{ij} \quad \text{if the affiliate exports good } G, \; G = X, Y, \tag{4}$$

$$T_{Gi} = \sum_{j \neq i} \tau_{Gji} G_{ji} \quad \text{if the affiliate imports good } G, \; G = X, Y. \tag{5}$$

If trade costs are high, production will be organized in a strictly horizontal fashion. This means that $T_{Gi} = 0$; i.e., there will be no intrafirm trade. In such a case, the different production units will operate completely independent of each other and wage changes in one location will not affect the demand for labor in another location.

To bring out the relevant results as clearly as possible, let us assume that trade costs associated with cross-border trade in X are prohibitively high. The motivation for this assumption is that, for some activities, especially the supply of services such as marketing and sales, there are very strong advantages with being in proximity to the consumers. We assume the following:

$$\tau_{Xij} w_i < w_j < \frac{w_i}{\tau_{Xij}} \quad \forall i, j, \tag{6}$$

which implies that $T_{Xi} = 0, \forall i$. X is thus now effectively nontraded and output of X will depend directly on the size of local demand:

$$Q_i = X_i. \tag{7}$$

The total demand for labor in location i then becomes:

$$L_i = \frac{1}{\gamma} Q_i(P_i^D, \mathbf{w}) + \frac{1}{\lambda} Y_i, \tag{8}$$

where $\mathbf{w}$ is the vector of wage rates in the different locations.

Expression (8) reveals that anything that affects the amount of final goods supplied in the domestic market will also affect the domestic labor demand. Q_i will depend on the domestic consumers' demand for the final product and cost factors affecting marginal costs of producing Q, which may not only include the domestic wage rates, but the wage rates in foreign locations as well. Labor demand will increase with an increase in domestic demand and decrease with increases in domestic wages. Labor demand will also depend of the amount of Y that is produced. Apart from the case where trade costs associated with Y are so high that Y becomes nontraded as well, there are two possible cases: the case where Y is produced and exported to other locations, and the case where Y is imported from other locations. Let us analyze each of these two cases in turn.

Case I: Y is Exported

If the production plant in location i exports Y to other parts of the firm, the amount exported will stand in direct proportion to the amount of the final good produced in each location and to the trade costs; i.e., $Y_{ij} = Q_j/\tau_{Yij}$, where τ_{Yij} is the trade cost associated with exporting from i to j.[7] Labor demand is then given by

$$L_i = \left(\frac{1}{\gamma} + \frac{1}{\lambda}\right) Q_i(P_i^D, w_i) + \frac{1}{\lambda} \sum_{j \in E} \frac{1}{\tau_{Yij}} Q_j\left(P_j^D, w_j, \frac{w_i}{\tau_{Yij}}\right), \tag{9}$$

where E is the set of locations that import Y from i (which will be the locations j for which the inequalities $w_i < \tau_{Yij} w_j$ and $\tau_{Ykj} w_i < \tau_{Yij} w_k, \forall k, k \neq i$ holds). Since Q_j will depend on local demand and wage rates in location j, it follows that an increase in product demand in location j will increase the demand for labor in location i, while an increase in wage rates in location j will decrease the demand for labor in location i. That is:

$$\frac{dL_i}{dw_j} < 0, \quad j \in E. \tag{10}$$

This is the case where the relationship between labor demand in different parts of the firm is one of complementarity. However, in the case where the wage change is sufficiently large to produce changes in the trade pattern within the firm, there may be a different outcome. Suppose that there is a decrease in the wage rate in location j that is sufficiently large for the following inequality to hold:

$$\tau_{Yij} < w_j w_i. \tag{11}$$

Production of Y may then shift from location i to location j, since it will be cheaper to produce Y in j than to import it from location i. An outcome with relocation of production will therefore lead to a substitutionary relationship of labor demand between different parts of the firm.

Case II: Y is Imported

Assume now that $w_j < \tau_{Yij} w_i$, $\exists j$, which implies that Y will be imported to location i. Domestic labor demand in location i is now given by

$$L_i = \frac{1}{\lambda} Q_i \left(P_i^D, w_i, \frac{w_m}{\tau_{Yim}} \right), \qquad (12)$$

where w_m is the wage in the location from which Y is imported, and τ_{Yim} is the trade cost associated with imports to i from m. For location m the following inequalities hold: $w_m < \tau_{Yim} w_i$ and $\tau_{Yij} w_m < \tau_{Yim} w_j$, $\forall j$. Because wage increases in the locations from which Y is imported will increase the marginal cost of producing Q in location i, Q_i is decreasing in the wage rates in those locations. Thus, a marginal increase in the wage rate in location m will have a negative effect on the domestic labor demand in location i:

$$\frac{dL_i}{dw_m} < 0. \qquad (13)$$

However, in the case where the wage change is sufficiently large to produce changes in the trade pattern within the firm, there may be a different outcome. Suppose the increase in the wages in location m is sufficiently large for the following inequality to hold:

$$w_m > \tau_{Yim} w_i. \qquad (14)$$

Production of Y may then shift from location m to location i, since it will be cheaper to produce Y than to import it from location m. However, this outcome would require that $w_j > \tau_{Yij} w_i$, $\forall j$; i.e., that it is cheaper to produce Y in location i than to import it from any other location in which the firm has production units. If this is not the case, the production of Y would instead shift to another foreign location, and the resulting increase in the cost of producing Y would feed into an increase in marginal costs in location i. Thus, even in this case, there would be a negative effect on the domestic labor demand in location i.

However, if the inequality $w_j > \tau_{Yij} w_i$, $\forall j$, holds after the wage increase in location m, production of Y will shift to location i and there will be a discrete increase in the domestic demand for labor. The size of this increase will depend on whether location i will only produce the amount of Y that is used domestically, or if it will also produce Y for exports to other locations. Thus, in the case where the change in foreign wages is sufficiently large to create a relocation of production activities, there may be a relationship of substitution between foreign and domestic labor. However, from the point of view of a particular location, this is not necessarily the case, because the relocation may shift production to a completely different part of the firm.

Under what circumstances is it likely that a change in foreign wages will result in a relocation of activities? Except for the trivial observation that this is likely to occur for very large wage changes, we may also not that a relocation is more likely between locations that have similar wages (i.e., similar relative factor endowments and technologies), and between locations for which trade costs are low.

To conclude, demand for labor in location i will depend on domestic and foreign product demand together with domestic and foreign wages. In reduced form, the equation for labor demand in location i can be written as

$$L_i = f(w_i, \mathbf{w}_E, \mathbf{w}_M, \tau_{YiE}, \tau_{YiM}, P_i^D, \mathbf{P}_E^D), \tag{15}$$

where $\mathbf{w}_E$ is the vector of wages in the locations to which location i is exporting, $\mathbf{w}_M$ is the vector of wages in the locations from which location i is importing, τ_{YiE} and τ_{YiM} denote vectors of trade costs for exports to and imports from other locations, while $\mathbf{P}_E^D$ is a vector of inverse demand for the final product in the locations to which location i is exporting. Whether changes in foreign wages have a positive or negative effect on domestic labor demand depends on whether they lead to a relocation of activities or simply to a change in marginal costs.

In the empirical analysis, we shall estimate a log–linear variant of (15) where we put restrictions on the way wages and measures of product demand in different locations enter into the equation. As we have no direct measures of trade costs, these will be captured by fixed-effect dummies.

3. Data

We use firm-level data on Swedish MNEs within the manufacturing sector. These data have been collected since the early 1970s about every fourth year. In our sample, we have data for six years: 1970, 1974, 1978, 1986, 1990, and 1994, and the full sample of Swedish MNEs cover some 700 observations at the firm level and some 3,000 observations at the affiliate level.[8] Only producing affiliates are included in the database.

In our analysis, we have eliminated affiliates that are operating in substantially different industries from the Swedish parent firm; i.e., conglomerates. This is done in order to ensure that the activities in the affiliates are sufficiently integrated with each other and the ones undertaken in the home part of the firm for there to be potential interactive effects on employment. We have not eliminated any affiliates belonging to the same two-digit ISIC group as the parent, as these can be considered to be either upstream or downstream in relation to the industry of the parent firm. Affiliates belonging to a different two-digit group from the parent have been eliminated on a case-by-case procedure.[9]

Moreover, we have eliminated all firms that appear only once or twice in the time series. Having done this, we are left with an unbalanced panel with about 200 observations at the firm level and 1,300 observations at the affiliate level. There are 44 firms included in the panel and 594 affiliates.[10]

We divide the host countries into a high-income group and a low-income group based on the level of per-capita income. The group of high-income countries consists of the western European countries (except Greece, Portugal, and Spain), the US, Canada, Japan, Australia, and New Zealand, while the group of low-income countries consists of all other countries. For our panel of MNEs, the relative importance of Sweden as a production location has decreased over time (Braconier and Ekholm, 1999). In this sense there is evidence of a substitution of foreign employment for domestic employment. However, it is mainly high-income countries that have gained employment in relative terms. The increase in the share of employment in low-income locations is very modest; only a few percentage points.

4. Estimation

In our econometric analysis we estimate two different types of labor demand equations; one that focuses on the relationship between employment in the parent firms in Sweden and the employment in the foreign affiliates, and one that focuses on the relationship between affiliate employment in different types of locations.

In the first type of equation, we estimate the effect of wage changes in high- and low-income foreign locations, respectively, on the employment in the Swedish parts of the firms. More specifically, we estimate the following equation:

$$\ln L_{it}^0 = \alpha + \delta_i + \gamma_t + \beta_0 \ln w_{it}^0 + \beta_1 \ln w_{it}^H + \beta_2 \ln w_{it}^L + \beta_3 \ln D_{it}^0 \\ + \beta_4 \ln D_{it}^E + \varepsilon_{it}, \qquad (16)$$

where L_{it}^0 is employment in the home part of firm i, w_{it}^0 is the wage rate in the home country, w_{it}^H is the wage rate in high-income countries, and w_{it}^L is the wage rate in low-wage countries. The wage variables w_{it}^H and w_{it}^L are averaged over all high- and low-income host-countries, respectively, in which firm i operates. The variable D_i^0 is a measure of domestic final demand and D_i^E a measure of demand in countries to which the firms export. The subscript t denotes time. The parameter δ_i captures a fixed firm-specific effect and γ_t a fixed time effect.

In order to reduce potential problems of endogeneity, our measures of w_{it}^0, D_i^0, and D_i^E are based on industry data for Sweden. The wage in Sweden, w_{it}^0, is measured by industry-distributed average labor costs in Swedish manufacturing.[11] The variable D_i^0 is proxied by industry-distributed domestic consumption and D_i^E by industry exports.[12] Ideally, we would like to have exogenous wage cost data for all the other countries too, but finding such data is difficult. The variables w_{it}^H and w_{it}^L are therefore instead calculated in the following way. First we construct a wage rate for each location in the sample by taking the average over all affiliates of all the firms in the sample that are located in that particular host country. Then we construct employment-based averages for each parent firm, distinguishing between high- and low-income locations.[13]

We expect β_0, the elasticity showing the effect of changes in the domestic wage on domestic employment, to be negative, while we expect β_3 and β_4 to be positive. The signs of β_1 and β_2, which can be interpreted as cross-elasticities showing the effect of changes in foreign wages on domestic employment, will depend on whether affiliate employment substitutes or complements employment in the home part of the firms.

In the second part of the analysis, we follow Brainard and Riker (1997b) in performing an analysis where we utilize the information on the affiliates in the dataset. More specifically, we estimate the following equation:

$$\ln L_{jt} = \alpha + \delta_j + \gamma_t + \beta_0 \ln w_{jt}^0 + \beta_1 \ln w_{jt}^H + \beta_2 \ln w_{jt}^L + \beta_3 \ln w_{jt}^S \\ + \beta_4 \ln D_{jt}^0 + \beta_5 \ln D_{jt}^S + \beta_6 \ln Y_{jt}^0 + \varepsilon_{jt}, \qquad (17)$$

where L_{jt} is the employment in affiliate j, w_{jt}^0 is the wage rate in the host country of affiliate j, w_{jt}^H and w_{jt}^L are the wage rates in the high- and low-income locations, respectively, that other affiliates of affiliate j's parent firm are located in, and w_{jt}^S is the wage rate in Sweden in the industry in which the parent firm operates. The wage variable w_{jt}^0 is an average over all the affiliates in the sample that produce in affiliate j's host country, subtracting affiliate j. The wage variables w_{jt}^H and w_{jt}^L are the employment-based averages of the wage rates in other host countries in which the parent firm of affiliate j operates.

The variable D_{jt}^0 is a measure of local demand, and here we follow Brainard and Riker (1997b) in proxying this with aggregate consumption of affiliate j's host country.[14] The variable D_{jt}^S is Swedish consumption in the industry in which affiliate j operates. It is included as a proxy for the demand for exports to the home country. Finally, the variable Y_{jt}^0 is a proxy for overall labor productivity in host country j (measured as real GDP per capita).[15] It is included in order to control for the fact that if labor productivity differs across locations, wage differences may partially reflect productivity differences instead of pure cost differences.

5. Results

Table 1 presents the results from the regressions based on (16). The first two columns contain the results from regressions on the subset of firms that have affiliates in both high- and low-income locations (in the second column, the wage rate in low-income locations has been dropped), whereas the third column contains results from regres-

Table 1. Results from Fixed-Effects Regression (Regressand: Parent-Firm Employment)

Regressors	(1)	(2)	(3)
w^0	0.17	0.16	−0.25
	(0.28)	(0.28)	(0.46)
w^H	0.77*	0.77*	−0.08
	(0.35)	(0.35)	(0.20)
w^L	0.06	—	—
	(0.11)		
D^0	0.08	0.07	0.41
	(0.13)	(0.13)	(0.48)
D^E	0.35*	0.35*	0.24*
	(0.09)	(0.09)	(0.11)
Constant	−7.84	−7.10	−1.44
	(6.34)	(6.17)	(12.1)
Number of observations	120	120	78
Obs. per group (min/avg/max)	2/4.0/6	2/4.0/6	2/4.0/6
R^2 (within)	0.35	0.35	0.16
F-test: Prob (firm dummies = 0)	0.00	0.00	0.00

Note: Regressions (1) and (2) were performed on a subsample consisting of firms with affiliates in both high- and low-income locations. Regression (3) was performed on the subsample of firms with affiliates in high-income locations only. Standard errors are reported in parentheses. The regressions also include time dummies, which are not reported. An asterisk indicates significance at the 5% level.

sions on the sample of firms that have affiliates in high-income locations only. As expected, the estimates of β_3 and β_4 are positive, but the regressions perform badly in other respects. The precision of the estimates is fairly low, and the point estimates of β_0 are positive.

In the regressions performed on the subsample of firms with affiliates in both high- and low-income locations, the only significant estimates are the ones for the cross-elasticity with respect to wages in high-income locations and for the export demand variable. Dropping the wage rate for low-income locations has very little effect on the point estimates, which means that they are at least robust to the elimination of this variable. The estimate of the cross-elasticity with respect to wages in high-income locations has a positive sign, indicating a relationship of substitution between parent firm employment and affiliate employment in high-income locations. The estimate indicates that a 1% increase in wages in other high-income locations in which Swedish MNEs operate would increase employment in the Swedish parts of the firms by 0.8%. However, we do not find any evidence of a substitutionary relationship between employment in the Swedish parts of the firms and affiliate employment in low-income locations.

In the third column we report the results for the sample with affiliates in only high-income locations. This estimation also yields positive estimates for the coefficients of the demand variables, whereas the estimate of the own-wage elasticity now has the expected negative sign (although it is still insignificant). The estimate of the cross-elasticity β_1, however, switches sign and becomes insignificant. Thus, while we do find some evidence of a substitutionary relationship between employment in Sweden and employment in affiliates in high-income locations for firms that have affiliates in both high- and low-income locations, we do not find any evidence of such a relationship for the sample of firms with affiliates in only high-income locations.[16]

We now turn to the regressions based on equation (17). In Table 2, results from regressions with affiliate employment in high-income and low-income countries, respectively, are reported. In the first two columns, results for affiliate employment in high-income locations are presented. The difference between the two regressions lies in the level on which the fixed effects enter into the equation. In regression (1) the fixed effects are based on the identity of the affiliate, as specified in (17). However, by specifying fixed effects on the firm level in regression (2), we are able to increase the number of observations relevant for the within-variation. Since location characteristics may be important, we control for locations in regression (2) by also including country dummies.

As can be seen from Table 2, the two different specifications yield similar results. As expected, the estimates of the elasticity for the local wage are negative and the estimates of the coefficient for local aggregate consumption are positive. The estimates of the cross-elasticities with respect to high- and low-income locations, respectively, are both negative, indicating a relationship of complementarity with both types of locations. The point estimates are somewhat higher in regression (2) than in regression (1). However, the precision of the estimates in (1) is higher. The estimated cross-elasticity with respect to the Swedish wage is insignificant.

The results suggest that there is a stronger complementarity between affiliates located in different high-income countries than between affiliates that are located in different types of locations. This result contrasts starkly with the findings of Brainard and Riker (1997b) for US firms, where there is a relationship of complementarity between affiliates in different types of locations and a substitutionary relationship between affiliates in the same type of locations. One interpretation of this result is that

Table 2. Results from Fixed-Effects Regressions (Regressand: Employment)

Regressors	High-income locations						ULC data	
	(1)	(2)	Low-income locations (3)	(4)	(5)	(6)	(7)	(8)
w^0	−0.41*	−0.56*	−0.36*	−1.27	−0.29*	−1.35	−0.57	−0.69
	(0.18)	(0.23)	(0.14)	(0.89)	(0.16)	(1.53)	(0.42)	(0.43)
w^H	−0.68*	−0.98	0.17	−0.22	0.02	0.77	−2.05*	−1.72
	(0.26)	(0.56)	(0.68)	(1.43)	(0.74)	(1.27)	(0.75)	(1.38)
w^L	−0.11	−0.21	−0.81*	−1.65*	−0.29	—	—	—
	(0.08)	(0.13)	(0.19)	(0.63)	(0.21)			
w^S	0.20	−0.07	−0.75	−0.64	−0.80	—	1.98	2.01
	(0.17)	(0.41)	(0.39)	(0.85)	(0.42)		(1.00)	(1.76)
D^0	0.22	0.23*	0.28*	1.91	−0.00	−0.13	0.34*	0.20*
	(0.14)	(0.03)	(0.06)	(1.01)	(0.10)	(0.16)	(0.08)	(0.03)
D^S	0.07	0.04	−0.10	0.28	−0.09	—	0.08	0.06
	(0.05)	(0.13)	(0.13)	(0.23)	(0.1)		(0.05)	(0.12)
D^E	—	—	—	—	—	0.21*	—	—
						(0.08)		
Y^0	−0.16	−0.39	0.44*	1.42	0.52*	—	—	—
	(0.50)	(0.38)	(0.17)	(1.71)	(0.20)			
Constant	9.51*	19.0*	16.6	−12.9	18.3	15.44*	2.90*	4.13
	(4.58)	(8.84)	(10.5)	(30.5)	(11.3)	(2.57)	(1.22)	(2.44)
Number of observations	880	919	380	71	309	197	1,048	1,083
Obs. per group (min/avg/max)	2/3.0/6	4/30.6/157	4/21.1/49	2/6.5/11	2/17.2/40	2/4.5/6	2/3.0/6	3/24.6/157
R^2 (within)	0.06	0.07	0.44	0.51	0.49	0.13	0.06	0.05
F-tests:								
Prob ($\beta_1 = \beta_2$)	0.03	0.18	0.17	0.31	0.69		0.00	
Prob (affiliate dummies = 0)	0.00							
Prob (firm dummies = 0)		0.00	0.00	0.00	0.00	0.00		0.00

Note: Standard errors are reported in parentheses. The regressions include time dummies, and regressions (2)–(5) include country dummies, which are not reported. The results reported in columns (1) and (7) refer to a regression with affiliate-specific fixed effects, whereas the other results refer to regressions with firm-specific fixed effects. An asterisk indicates significance at the 5% level.

trade costs really matter for the kind of vertical decomposition of production stages that we believe gives rise to a complementarity relationship between employment in different affiliates. While differences in production costs may be larger between affiliates located in high- and low-income countries, from the perspective of the affiliates in high-income countries, this difference may be offset by larger trade costs. Therefore, the vertical decomposition between different affiliates in high-income countries may be more extensive than between these affiliates and affiliates located in low-income countries.

In columns (3)–(5), we present results for affiliate employment in low-income countries. Here, the problem with our panel being unbalanced becomes crucial. To begin with, because the foreign activities of Swedish MNEs are heavily biased towards industrialized countries, the number of affiliates located in low-income countries is much lower than the number of affiliates located in high-income countries. Moreover, fairly few of the affiliates remain in the sample for more than three points of observation. This means that our estimation based on (17) performs very badly indeed. However, in regressions with firm-specific fixed effects instead of affiliate-specific fixed effects, we are able to increase the precision in our estimates considerably. Therefore, Table 2 presents results from the regressions with firm-specific fixed effects (see Braconier and Ekholm (1999) for results from regressions with affiliate-specific fixed effects).

Column (3) shows that the estimated own-wage elasticity is again negative, while the estimated coefficient of local aggregate demand is positive. The cross-elasticity showing the effect of wages in high-income countries is positive, but not significantly different from zero. However, the cross-elasticity for wages in other low-income locations is significantly negative, indicating a relationship of complementarity between employment in different low-income locations. This is a slightly odd finding, as it would suggest that affiliates located in different low-income locations are more strongly linked to each other through intrafirm trade in inputs than are affiliates located in different types of locations with respect to whether they are low- or high-income locations.

However, if we decompose the affiliates located in low-income locations along geographical lines, we find that the complementarity effect really stems from affiliates located in low-income countries in Europe. Columns (4) and (5) show the results from regressions for affiliates in low-income countries in Europe (to which we have included Turkey) and for affiliates in the rest of the low-income countries, respectively. As it turns out, the cross-wage elasticity with respect to wages in low-income countries is strongly negative for affiliates in the European low-income countries, while we cannot reject the hypothesis that the corresponding elasticity for the affiliates in other low-income countries is zero. Hence, there seems to be vertical linkages between affiliates in low-income locations and affiliates in low-income locations in Europe, while we do not find any evidence of linkages at all between affiliates in low-income locations in Asia and Latin America and other affiliates.

We may also note that, in these regressions, our control variable for differences in labor productivity is positive and significant, whereas it was insignificant in the regressions for affiliates in high-income locations. Again the estimated cross-elasticity with respect to the Swedish wage is insignificant.

In order to further explore whether the heterogeneity of labor may bias our results, we also use PPP-adjusted unit labor cost (ULC) data to check the robustness of our previous results.[17] The ULC data have the additional benefit of being exogenous to the

MNEs. However, a drawback is that we only have ULC data for high-income locations. Because ULC data are available only at the country level, we do not include country-specific dummies in the regression for affiliate employment in high-income locations.[18] ULC composites for individual firms are constructed in the same way as in the previous analysis and all the other data are the same.

Column (6) of Table 2 shows the results for employment in the parent firm in Sweden. The results are similar to those presented in column (2) of Table 1, with the exceptions that the estimated own wage elasticity is negative (but insignificant) while the substitutionary relationship with high-income locations is no longer significant (but the estimated coefficient is still positive). Exports is the only variable that turns out to be significant.

Columns (7)–(8) show the results for employment in high-income affiliates. The signs of all the estimated coefficients are the same as in columns (1)–(2), although the precision of the estimates is generally somewhat lower. The estimated cross-elasticity with respect to wages in other high-income locations is negative (indicating complementarity), while the estimated cross-elasticity with respect to Sweden is positive (indicating substitution), but insignificant.

6. Concluding Remarks

Based on data on Swedish MNEs, we find some evidence of a substitutionary relationship between parent-firm employment in Sweden and affiliate employment in other high-income locations. However, we do not find any evidence of a relationship in either direction between parent-firm employment and affiliate employment in low-income locations. We find mainly a relationship of complementarity between affiliate employment in different locations. Our results are in this respect different from what has previously been found for the US, where complementarity seems to prevail only between affiliates in locations with different relative factor endowments. One possible explanation for this difference in results is that Swedish MNEs are vertically integrated to a larger extent than US ones. This is consistent with the results found in recent models of FDI (e.g., Markusen et al., 1996), where vertically integrated MNEs tend to dominate in small and skilled-labor abundant countries.

References

Blomström, M., G. Fors, and R. E. Lipsey, "Foreign Direct Investment and Employment: Home Country Experience in the United States and Sweden," *Economic Journal* 107 (1997):1787–97.

Braconier, H. and K. Ekholm, "Swedish Multinationals and Competition from High- and Low-Wage Locations," CEPR working chapter 2323 (1999).

Brainard, S. L. and D. Riker, "Are US Multinationals Exporting US Jobs?" NBER working chapter 5958 (1997a).

Brainard, S. L. and D. Riker, "US Multinationals and Competition from Low Wage Countries," NBER working chapter 5959 (1997b).

Braunerhjelm, P. and K. Ekholm (eds.), *The Geography of Multinational Firms*, Boston: Kluwer Academic (1998).

Feenstra R. C. and G. H. Hanson, "Foreign Investment, Outsourcing, and Relative Wages," in R. C. Feenstra, G. M. Grossman, and D. A. Irwin (eds.), *The Political Economy of Trade Policy: Papers on Honor of Jagdish Bhagwati*, Cambridge, MA: MIT Press (1996a).

———, "Globalization, Outsourcing, and Wage Inequality," *American Economic Review* 86 (1996b):240–5.

Kravis, I. B. and R. E. Lipsey, "The Effect of Multinational Firms' Foreign Operations on their Domestic Employment," NBER working chapter 2760 (1988).

Lawrence, R. Z., "Trade, Multinationals, and Labor," NBER working chapter 4836 (1994).

Lipsey, R. E., "Outward Direct Investment and the US Economy," NBER working chapter 4691 (1994).

Lipsey, R. E. and M. Y. Weiss, "Foreign Production and Exports in Manufacturing Industries," *Review of Economics and Statistics* 63 (1981):488–94.

———, "Foreign Production and Exports of Individual Firms," *Review of Economics and Statistics* 66 (1984):304–8.

Markusen, J. R., "The Boundaries of Multinational Enterprises and the Theory of International Trade," *Journal of Economic Perspectives* 9 (1995):169–89.

Markusen, J. R., A. J. Venables, D. E. Konan, and K. H. Zhang, "A Unified Treatment of Horizontal Direct Investment, Vertical Direct Investment, and the Pattern of Trade in Goods and Services," NBER working chapter 5696 (1996).

OECD, *Economic Outlook No. 65*, Paris: OECD (1998).

Slaughter, M., "Multinational Corporations, Outsourcing, and American Wage Divergence," NBER working chapter 5253 (1995).

Svensson, R., "Effects of Overseas Production on Home Country Exports: Evidence based on Swedish Multinationals," *Weltwirtschaftliches Archiv* 132 (1996):304–29.

Swedenborg, B., *The Multinational Operations of Swedish Firms: An Analysis of Determinants and Effects*, Stockholm: Almqvist & Wicksell (1979).

Notes

1. See, for instance, the survey by Markusen (1995).
2. However, even in the case where a firm locates production abroad in order to supply a foreign market, complementary activities such as headquarter activities are likely to be undertaken at home.
3. However, if an upstream or downstream activity previously conducted in the home country becomes relocated to a foreign affiliate, there will be substitution associated with vertical FDI as well.
4. An early attempt to focus directly on the effect of outward FDI on home country employment was Kravis and Lipsey (1988) (see also Lipsey, 1994, and Blomström et al., 1997).
5. See also Lawrence (1994).
6. The model is inspired by the theoretical framework used in Brainard and Riker (1997b).
7. We assume that a unique location has the lowest cost (i.e., marginal costs plus trade costs) of supplying Y to another location.
8. A description of these data can be found in Braunerhjelm and Ekholm (1998).
9. In this process, we have eliminated less than 5% of the affiliates.
10. These MNEs employ between 74% and 86% of the total employment in Sweden that can be attributed to Swedish MNEs.
11. Wage data have been collected from Statistics Sweden, while information about payroll taxes have been supplied by the Swedish Employers' Confederation.
12. Data on industry-distributed consumption are from the 1998 STAN database (OECD) and on industry-distributed exports from Statistics Sweden.
13. The variables are defined as $w_{it}^g \equiv \sum_{k \in g} \frac{L_{ikt}}{\sum_{k \in g} L_{ikt}} w_{kt}$ $g = H, L$, where H and L are the sets of high- and low-income host countries, respectively, and w_{kt} is measured as an average over all affiliates in the sample that are located in country k.
14. Data have been collected from 1998 World Development Indicators on CD-ROM (World Bank).

15. The data have been collected from Penn World Tables 5.6.
16. Firms with affiliates in only high-income locations are located in natural-resource-intensive and capital-intensive low-tech sectors as pulp & paper, steel & iron, and rubber products. Changes in labor cost differences between locations may have a weaker effect on labor demand in such industries.
17. Our measure of ULC is defined as $ULC = \dfrac{wL}{GDP \times PPP}$, where w is the current wage cost, L is employment in the private business sector, GDP is volume GDP, and PPP the PPP exchange rate with respect to USD. All data are collected from *Economic Outlook* (OECD, 1998).
18. Both the own-labor cost and the local demand only vary across countries.

7
The Choice of Structural Model in Trade–Wages Decompositions

Lisandro Abrego and John Whalley

1. Introduction

This chapter seeks to contribute to the ongoing debate on the principal causes of increased wage dispersion seen in an elevated premium paid to skilled labor in OECD countries in recent years. Many papers have been written on the subject, and most focus on increased trade and skill-biased technological change as the two principal causes.[1] In this literature, Lawrence and Slaughter (1993), Krugman and Lawrence (1993), Leamer (1998), Baldwin and Cain (1997), and others have concluded that the role of trade is small; Wood (1994, 1995, 1998) points to a dominant role for trade.

The conclusions in this literature, however, rest largely on reduced-form regressions. Some, such as Murphy and Welch (1991), and Borjas et al. (1991), estimate the factor content of trade and use these estimates, via exogenous (literature-based) labor demand elasticities, to infer the wage change attributable to trade. They then compare this to observed wage changes. Others, such as Leamer (1998), Baldwin and Cain (1997), Haskel and Slaughter (1999), and Harrigan and Balaban (1999) use estimating equations derived from general equilibrium models. The numerical properties of alternative structural models seem not to be explicitly evaluated in any of this literature.

Our purpose here is to explore the use of structural models employing direct simulation methods and calibration procedures for decomposing observed wage changes resulting from trade and technology shocks into components attributable to each source, as an alternative to reduced-form methods. We first use a Heckscher–Ohlin-type trade model with two factor inputs (skilled and unskilled labor) and two outputs (skilled-labor-intensive and unskilled-labor-intensive outputs), where the economy in question is modeled as a taker of goods prices on world markets.[2] Skilled and unskilled labor are mobile between sectors, while internationally immobile. Trade shocks are modeled as world price changes, and technology shocks as sector-specific shocks to Hicks-neutral production function parameters. We calibrate the model both to UK data for 1990, and to the relative wage and price changes observed over the period 1976–90.[3] We then explore the use of the model in decomposition by first removing technology only, and subsequently removing trade, and computing equilibria for each case. These allow for an assessment directly from the structural model of the separate role of trade and technology in contributing to observed changes in wage inequality over the period.

Results using a simple Heckscher–Ohlin-type model suggest that with conventional functional forms this structure is unlikely to be suitable for decomposition analysis of actual country experiences. First, the model can only be solved for relatively small international price shocks with the CES functional forms we use (or indeed any convenient functional form), since the production frontier is close to linear and so specialization accompanies even small changes.[4] Thus, international price changes of the type which show up in data on country experiences cannot be easily accommodated by such a model in decomposition experiments. Second, there are multiple model parameterizations consistent with the same reduced-form data across the periods, and those can each yield considerably divergent decompositions of the same trade-and-technology-driven wage change. We conclude that there are potentially significant and somewhat disturbing degrees of ambiguity associated with decompositions even for the small changes that this model can be solved for. Reduced forms estimated in the literature typically do not allow for discrimination between these alternative parameterizations for use in decomposition. Third, as Leamer (1994, 1998) has argued, such a Heckscher–Ohlin-type structure can only meaningfully accommodate sector-biased technical change as a source of wage inequality in the small open economy case, since factor-augmenting technical change is neutral with respect to relative wage rates.

We consider an alternative differentiated-goods model for which the first Heckscher–Ohlin structure is a special case. In this, goods imported from world suppliers and import-substituting domestic products are treated as imperfect substitutes in demand, and as the substitution elasticity between them approaches infinity the model reverts to the more classical Heckscher–Ohlin form. This second structure is able to accommodate large price changes, and while some ambiguity of decomposition remains, this is lessened here. For finite substitution elasticities, this model weakens and typically removes the specialization properties of the Heckscher–Ohlin-type model, allowing actual technology and wage changes to be decomposed into constituent parts. It also incorporates endogenous domestic price determination in response to world price changes with imperfect passthrough onto prices of domestically produced import-substituting goods (in simple Heckscher–Ohlin models all external shocks fully impact domestic goods prices). In addition, this structure allows for direct model calibration to import demand elasticity estimates, something that in simple Heckscher–Ohlin is considerably more difficult.

Decompositions of the same UK data performed with this model reveal strikingly different results relative to the simple Heckscher–Ohlin case. Trade shocks can now be absorbed on the import demand side of the model, without full transmission to domestic producer prices, and technology now plays a larger role. The portion of the increase in wage inequality attributed to trade changes can even change sign depending upon whether the demand-side substitution elasticity between domestic and foreign goods is greater or less than one. In addition, the model structure implies implausibly large parametric changes to accommodate sector-biased technical change.

Our conclusion is that models widely used in the literature would seem to have numerical properties (given our choice of functional forms) seemingly unsatisfactory for decomposition analysis. Further exploration of the numerical properties of alternative structural models rather than reduced forms seems the way forward to more satisfactorily sort out trade and technology effects on wage dispersion, in contrast to the direction taken in recent literature.

2. The Trade and Wage Inequality Debate

Recent literature on trade and wages focuses on understanding the quantitative significance of trade in explaining the sharp increase in OECD wage inequality which has occurred during the 1980s. This issue is important because of the associated pressures for protection which arise if trade is deemed to be the main source. This increase in inequality has been documented for a number of OECD countries, most notably the US and the United Kingdom (e.g., Davis, 1992; Kosters, 1994; OECD, 1997; Gottschalk and Smeeding, 1997). The pattern has been observed across different types of workers according to their skills (low vs. high skill), education levels (college vs. non-college graduates), and experience. Even among "observably similar workers" wage inequality has increased (e.g., Davis, 1992). There has also been documentation of a rise in unemployment in some European countries without major increases in wage inequality (Kosters, 1994; OECD, 1997; Dewatripont et al., 1998)—as well as of a decline in wage inequality in some key developing countries (Korea, Venezuela, Colombia, and Brazil) (Davis, 1992; UNCTAD, 1997; Wood, 1997).

A large volume of literature has emerged on the explanation of increased wage inequality, especially for the US case.[5] Two major factors have been discussed as primarily responsible for this phenomenon: increased trade (particularly with low-wage developing countries) and technological change biased against unskilled labor. The great majority of research has concluded that skilled-biased technological change,[6] rather than trade, is the main source of this increase in wage inequality.[7]

This literature uses a variety of econometric methods. Early papers focused on how trade changes labor demand via the factor content of trade (e.g., Borjas et al., 1991; Murphy and Welch, 1991; Katz and Murphy, 1992). They typically ran regressions which linked labor demand (by type of labor) and trade flows, and then used actual trade flows to infer the changes in labor demand they imply. They then combined these labor demand changes with wage elasticity of labor demand estimates culled from the literature, to infer what portion of actual wage changes are due to trade changes. This work generally came to the conclusion that the portion of actual wage change attributable to trade is small.

Conclusions based on factor content of trade calculations, were, however, criticized by Wood (1994), who argued that trade is a considerably more important factor than these analyses show. He argued that for many products, and especially those from developing countries, there is no comparable domestic product, and so factor substitution effects attributed to trade using conventional elasticities are understated. He also argued that technological response to trade will occur in expectation of future trade surges, and so some of what is attributed to technology in factor content analyses should in reality be attributed to trade.

Later papers in the area use a different approach, and relate relative product price changes to relative wage changes (e.g., Lawrence and Slaughter, 1993; Baldwin and Cain, 1997; Leamer, 1998; Harrigan and Balaban, 1999; Haskel and Slaughter, 1999). Many of these work with estimating equations derived from general equilibrium models of a Heckscher–Ohlin type. The majority of these studies conclude that skilled-biased technical change was the main source of increased wage inequality during the 1980s, with the role of trade being insignificant.

Other recent work regresses measures of factor shares on measures of outsourcing and other factors (Feenstra and Hanson, 1996; Anderton and Brenton, 1998; Autor et al., 1998), concluding that trade may be more important than in earlier analyses. Anderton and Brenton (1998), in particular, find that trade is more important when only trade with developing countries rather than with all countries is used as an explanatory variable.

However, virtually all of these analyses use reduced-form data in their estimations, with little work explicitly employing structural models.[8] As explained in more detail below, structural models are needed to make a meaningful decomposition of an observed relative wage change into a portion due to trade and a portion due to technological change. Because the model parameters consistent with given reduced-form data are not unique, different parameterizations can generate different decomposition results between trade and technological change as sources of an observed change in inequality. Some attention to the numerical behavior of structural models seems to be required.

3. A Heckscher–Ohlin Model for Inequality Decomposition in the UK

We first explore decompositions of combined wage and technology shocks using numerical simulations from a simple and theory-consistent Heckscher–Ohlin-type general equilibrium model calibrated to UK data. We use 1990 data on production, consumption, factor use, and trade, aggregated into a two-factor, two-commodity classification, and calibrate the model to estimates on trade shocks and wage changes over the period 1976–90.[9] Technology shocks are implied for the model by the wage outcome over the period and the data on trade shocks. Because, following Leamer (1994, 1998), factor-augmenting technical change is neutral for relative wage rates in the small open economy case, we are forced to consider only sector-biased technical change.

We use a two-good (importable/exportable), two-factor (skilled/unskilled labour) Heckscher–Ohlin CES[10] model to incorporate both trade shocks and skilled-biased technological change. We perform decomposition analysis by first generating a parameterization for the model which is consistent with the combined trade and technology shock (as reflected in data on wage change). We then remove individual components of the joint change from the model to assess the contribution of each to the observed total change generated by the joint shock.

Production

For our simple Heckscher–Ohlin-type model, we consider a small, open, price-taking economy that produces two goods, M and E (importable and intensive in unskilled labor, and exportable and intensive in skilled labor, respectively), both of which are traded at fixed world prices. The production of each good requires the use of two factors: skilled labor, S, and unskilled labor, U. Each good is produced using a constant-returns-to-scale CES technology, with constant elasticity of substitution between S and U.

$$Y_i = \gamma_i \left[\beta_i U_i^{-\rho_i} + (1-\beta_i) S_i^{-\rho_i} \right]^{-\frac{1}{\rho_i}}, \quad i = M, E \qquad (1)$$

where Y_i represents output, γ_i denotes sector-specific measures of technical achievement, β_i is a share parameter, and ρ_i determines the elasticity of substitution, η_i, between U_i and S_i, with $\eta_i = 1/(1 + \rho_i)$. Changes over time in γ_i represent sector specific technical change. Factor augmenting technical change (increases in the effective units of U and S economy-wide) are not considered since, following Leamer's (1994) argument, such changes have no effect on relative wages since the zero-profit conditions remain unaffected.

Labor Market

We take the endowment of unskilled and skilled labor to be fixed (there is no labor–leisure choice), and to equal $\bar{U}$ and $\bar{S}$, respectively. Full employment of each type of labor is assumed. We also assume competitive labor markets so that each type of labor is paid its marginal value product; i.e.

$$W_U = \beta_i P_i (Y_i/U_i)^{1+\rho_i} / \gamma_i^{\rho_i}, \quad i = M, E \tag{2}$$

$$W_s = (1-\beta_i) P_i (Y_i/S_i)^{1+\rho_i} / \gamma_i^{\rho_i}, \quad i = M, E, \tag{3}$$

where W_U and W_S denote unskilled and skilled wage rates respectively, and P_i is the (fixed) world price of good i.

Trade

Imports and domestically produced goods are homogeneous, as is also the case with exports (i.e., trade is of Heckscher–Ohlin form). This homogeneity assumption implies that trade flows involving any good are only one-way; i.e., one of the goods is exported and the other imported.

In equilibrium trade balance will hold; i.e.

$$\sum_{i=M,E} P_i T_i = 0, \tag{4}$$

where the T_i denotes the net trade of the country in the two goods, M and E. If good i is exported, domestic production less consumption is positive; if good i is imported, this difference is negative.

Equilibrium and Market-Clearing Conditions

Given the small open-economy assumption, equilibrium in this model is given by unskilled and skilled wage rates, such that the two domestic labor markets clear:

$$\sum_i U_i = \bar{U}, \quad i = M, E \tag{5}$$

$$\sum_i S_i = \bar{S}, \quad i = M, E \tag{6}$$

as well as by the zero-profit conditions in each sector:

$$P_i = g_i(W_U, W_S), \quad i = M, E$$

where g_i are the unit cost functions derived from the CES production function (1).

Consumption of each good i is given by the difference between production and trade:

$$C_i = Y_i - T_i, \quad i = M, E \tag{7}$$

where C_i denotes consumption of good i.

Production of each good, in turn, is given by using equations (2), (3), (5), and (6) and solving for Y_i along with W_U and W_S as part of the equilibrium.

Decomposing the Effects of Trade and Technology on Wage Inequality

We can use the Heckscher–Ohlin-type model presented above to investigate the decomposition of a total wage rate effect from joint trade and technology shocks into separate portions attributed to each source. To do this, we consider trade shocks to be represented by world price changes which generate more trade—in this case, falls in the relative price of the unskilled-intensive products. Our data for the UK indicate a relative price decline of 7.9% for unskilled-intensive goods over the period 1976–90.[11] Given the fall of roughly 15% in the relative wage of unskilled workers over the period, we determine the sector-biased technology shock by residual as that needed to yield the observed wage change as a model solution in the presence of the combined trade and technology shock.

Specialization and Simple Heckscher–Ohlin-type Models

This simple Heckscher–Ohlin-type model immediately proves unsatisfactory for the task of decomposing UK data on wage inequality into separate trade and technology components. This is because of the near linearity of the production frontier alluded to above, and the associated problems of specialization. The model simply cannot accommodate a 7.9% change in traded goods prices and seemingly for any combination of calibrated parameters. Table 1 presents the maximum size of relative price changes—for different production-side elasticities—allowed by the model before reaching full specialization. Given the close-to-linear production frontier, the model is unable to accommodate the observed relative price change even for fairly small elasticities of substitution between the two types of labor.

Near linearity is a well-known numerical property of production frontiers generated from conventional functional-form production functions and fixed economy-wide endowments (Johnson, 1966). If, alternatively, a production frontier with sufficient curvature to prevent specialization were directly specified, the problem would remain that there is no known way to recover sector production functions consistent with such a frontier, and they anyway would be inconsistent with the observed base-case equilibrium data.

Ambiguity in Decompositions

We can, however, solve the model for smaller trade and technology changes than those observed, but such solutions raise further problems since they also indicate ambiguity

Table 1. Maximum Relative Price Changes Consistent with Incomplete Specialization for Different Production-Side Elasticities

	P_M/P_E increase	P_M/P_E decrease
$\eta_M = \eta_E = 0.5$	8.2	6.2
$\eta_M = \eta_E = 1.1$	3.4	3.1
$\eta_M = \eta_E = 1.5$	2.4	2.3

Note: Since our model contains no intermediate goods, the elasticities (η_i) presented here are elasticities of substitution between skilled and unskilled labor.

in the decomposition results. To illustrate this, we have simulated the effects of a 1% fall in the world relative price of the unskilled-intensive good, P_U/P_S, and obtained residually the size of the sector-biased technological change required to produce a −15% change in the relative wage of unskilled workers, W_U/W_S. We represent technical change by an increase in the Hicks-neutral technical change term in the production of the skilled-intensive importable good, γ_S. This is in contrast to the pervasive unskilled-biased technological change, which, as we indicated earlier, the bulk of the literature finds to be responsible for the surge in wage inequality during the 1980s (e.g., Berman et al., 1994; Berman et al., 1997; Baldwin and Cain, 1997; Machin and van Reenen, 1998), but which this model, as Leamer (1994) argues, cannot accommodate.

In Table 2 we report two alternative model parameterizations chosen such that, given the combined trade and technology shocks, both generate the same change in W_U/W_S (−15%), but with different decomposition results as to portion due to each factor. As we note above, there are, in fact, many such parameterizations that can be calculated, and Table 2 presents merely two that we have been able to find using a GAMS (Generalized Algebraic Modelling System) code.

These two model parameterizations differ substantially in the share parameters and production-side elasticities, chosen, in part, to illustrate the ranges of ambiguity that can be involved in decomposition experiments more than representing firm literature estimates. In both parameterizations the importable good utilizes unskilled labor intensively—which we, for now, take as a stylized fact for the UK and other OECD economies. We have only varied production parameters (elasticities of substitution and labor shares), leaving demand parameters unaltered since this is a small open-economy model.

Table 2 also presents decomposition results for each of the two model parameterizations. These are obtained by first allowing only technology to change, and then

Table 2. *Two Parameterizations of the Heckscher–Ohlin-type Model Giving the Same Relative Wage Change, and Decompositions of the Wage Change*

	Parameterization A		Parameterization B	
	Good M	Good E	Good M	Good E
Share parameters				
Production				
Unskilled labor	0.33	0.31	0.44	0.26
Skilled labor	0.67	0.69	0.56	0.73
Consumption	0.60	0.40	0.60	0.40
Elasticities of substitution				
Production	1.05	1.75	3.1	1.30
Consumption	1.25		1.25	
Decompositions			A	B
Change in W_U/W_S from trade and technology shocks (%)			−15.0	−15.0
Fraction of change in W_U/W_S due to technology			0.58	0.42
Fraction of change in W_U/W_S due to trade			0.42	0.58

only the world price change to occur, and computing a new equilibrium in each case. The resulting wage change is compared with that observed under the joint shock (shown in Table 2). Although the overall change in wage inequality is the same for both parameterizations, the relative importance of trade and technology in each case is different. For parameterization A, the technology shock is dominant, where as for parameterization B the opposite occurs. Were we to regress, say, factor price changes from the joint shock on goods price changes (the trade shock) and some measure of the technology change, such a regression would not allow differentiation to be made between competing parameterizations of the structural model, all of which are consistent with reduced-form data, but each of which gives a different decomposition.

This ambiguity in the decomposition results can be reduced either by restricting key elasticity parameters—such as production substitution elasticities between skilled and unskilled labor—to a narrower range of values, appealing to literature estimates.[12] Alternatively, we could also move to increasingly constrained calibration where calibration to other observed changes, such as changes in factor shares, for instance, is required simultaneously.[13]

In passing we also comment on a further feature of this Heckscher–Ohlin-type model illustrated by Table 1—that large wage changes occur from only relatively small product price changes. This reflects the same feature alluded to earlier, that with a production frontier close to linear, a small change in output prices from a trade shock (1% here) moves the economy a substantial distance along the frontier with a large change in output composition and hence a large relative wage change. In our simulations, the result of this is that changes in goods prices which constitute only a small fraction of the actual change over the period we consider here can generate wage effects much larger than those observed.

4. Trade and Technology Decompositions Using a Differentiated-Goods Model

Results in the preceding section suggest that the small-economy Heckscher–Ohlin-type trade model may be inappropriate for trade–technology decomposition analyses of wage changes. In this section we examine an alternative structural trade model with differentiated goods, similar to the one set out in de Melo and Robinson (1989), and recently discussed in Bhattarai et al. (1999). In this model, imports and domestically produced goods are imperfect rather than perfect substitutes. Imports are not produced domestically, and one of the domestically produced goods is not traded. The model remains a two-produced-goods, two-factor model with two traded goods, but embodies three goods in aggregate when the consumption side is included.[14] Imports and exports are traded at fixed world prices. The domestic good—which is an imperfect substitute for imports—and the exportable are the two produced goods. Each uses skilled and unskilled labor. Imports and the (nonexportable) domestic good enter consumption.

This model weakens the problems of specialization associated with the simple Heckscher–Ohlin model when performing trade–technology decompositions, since imports are not produced domestically. The new structure becomes the Heckscher–Ohlin model as the elasticity of substitution in demand between domestically produced goods and imports approaches infinity.

The Model

Denoting imports by M, exports by E, and domestic goods by D, preferences are defined over M, D, and E, with D and E being the produced goods. Using the same two factor inputs U and S (high- and low-skilled labor), production occurs for only two of the three goods, D and E. Effectively the same two-by-two structure is preserved, but imported and domestically produced goods are differentiated. Unlike in the Heckscher–Ohlin-type model above, preferences now enter the picture and a product price is determined endogenously, even in the small-country case. Thus, preferences are denoted by

$$U(M^D, E^D), \tag{8}$$

where E^D denotes demand for the exportable good, M^D is the composite of imports, M, and the domestic import substitute, D^D; i.e.

$$M^D = H(M, D^D).$$

Technology is represented by

$$D^S = D(U^D, S^D), \tag{9}$$
$$E = E(U^E, S^E), \tag{10}$$

where U^D, S^D, U^E, and S^E denote inputs of high- and low-skilled labor used in domestic good and export production; D^S is production of the imperfect import substitute domestic good.

The economy is a taker of prices for exports and imports, $\bar{P}_E$, $\bar{P}_M$, but now the price for the domestic good, P_D, is determined endogenously. The per-unit cost functions for the production of E and D, consistent with zero profits, are

$$P_D = g_D(W^U, W^S), \tag{11}$$
$$\bar{P}_E = g_E(W^U, W^S), \tag{12}$$

where W^U and W^S are the wage rates of high- and low-skilled labor, and g_D and g_E are per-unit cost functions.

Full employment conditions for factors yield

$$f_D^U D^D + f_E^U E = \bar{U}, \tag{13}$$
$$f_D^S D^D + f_E^S E = \bar{S}, \tag{14}$$

where $f_D^U, f_E^U, f_D^S, f_E^S$ are per-unit cost-minimizing factor demands for U and S in the production of D and E.

The representative household in this economy maximize the utility function (8) subject to the budget constraint

$$P_D D^D + \bar{P}_M M + \bar{P}_E E^D = W^U \bar{U} + W^S \bar{S}. \tag{15}$$

In equilibrium, the price of the domestically produced good, P_D^*, will be determined such that market clearing occurs in D; i.e.

$$D^D = D^S. \tag{16}$$

No market clearing is required in either E or M. Walras' law, which holds for demand functions generated from utility maximization subject to a budget constraint, also implies that trade balance will hold; i.e., in equilibrium:

$$\bar{P}_M M = \bar{P}_E E. \tag{17}$$

In this structure, relative to the simple Heckscher–Ohlin case discussed earlier, one additional endogenous variable, P_D, enters the model. Additional parameters enter the model in terms of preferences over D^D and M. Thus, in the case where the elasticity of substitution in preferences between D^D and M is unity, changes in world prices of imports can be fully accommodated by changes in import volumes. In this case, trade shocks have no impact on domestic production patterns, and hence no impact on the relative wages of skilled and unskilled labor. The role of trade in affecting the relative wages of the skilled and unskilled in trade and technology decompositions will be zero. In addition, we note that empirical studies of import demand elasticities (Reinert and Roland-Holst, 1992; Shiells and Reinert, 1993) consistently produce estimates in the neighborhood of one; and in a CES function the own-price demand elasticity approaches the negative of the substitution elasticity as the relevant share parameter approaches zero.

Decomposition Results

With specialization problems weakened in this model, we are able to consider the full change in relative wages and goods prices in a decomposition exercise for the UK economy. As in the previous section, we use the figure of –7.9% for the change in the relative price of the unskilled-intensive good, and 15% for the fall in W_U/W_S. The size of technological change is again calculated residually in our decomposition experiments; i.e., such that given the observed product price change, the joint shocks produce a decline of 15% in W_U/W_S.

As in the previous section, we assume that technological change is of Hicks-neutral type, and sector-specific. The model, however, has difficulties accommodating this type of technical change to the extent that, unrealistically, large changes in γ_i are needed to generate even modest relative wage rate changes. This is because with an endogenously determined price for the domestic import substitute, P_D, changes in γ_S can be largely offset by changes in, P_D, so that little impact on relative wage rates occurs. For example, the size of technical change required—in combination with the 7.9% relative price change—to generate a 15% decline in W_U/W_S, for consumption and production-side elasticity values of 2 and 1.5, implies that (for an unchanged γ_U) γ_S must increase by a factor of around 19.

Also, when the value of the elasticity of substitution between domestic goods and imports is unity, the fraction of the change in W_U/W_S due to trade is zero, independently of the parameterization used for the model.[15] This is because, in this case, trade shocks are fully accommodated on the demand side of the model. We therefore carry out decomposition experiments where we vary a particular type of elasticity (consumption or production-side) within a range consistent with literature estimates, while holding the other elasticity type constant. We first consider values between 0.5 and 2 for the elasticity of substitution in preferences between the domestic good and imports,[16] and set the value for the elasticity of substitution between skilled and unskilled labor equal to 1.5. In a second set of decomposition experiments, we vary the production-side elasticity between 1.05 and 3, and set the consumption-side elasticity

Table 3. *Range of Technology–Trade Decompositions over Alternative Values for the Elasticity of Substitution in Preferences (σ) and Production (η_i)*

	$\sigma = 0.5$–2.0^a	$\eta_i = 1.05$–3.0^b
Range for fraction of change in W_U/W_S due to technology	1.018–0.974	0.991–0.997
Range for fraction of change in W_U/W_S due to trade	−0.018–0.026	0.009–0.003

[a] Production-side elasticity held constant, and equal to 1.5.
[b] Consumption-side elasticity held constant, and equal to 1.25.

equal to 1.25. In all these experiments, the degree of technological change is obtained residually.

In Table 3 we report decomposition results for parameterizations where the elasticity of substitution in preferences departs from unity, but in all cases the contribution of trade to wage inequality is small. Again, with imports and their domestic counterparts now being imperfect substitutes, the change in relative prices is accommodated largely by changes in consumption rather than production—exactly the opposite to the outcome under the simple Heckscher–Ohlin-type model.

We also note that the trade contribution to wage inequality changes sign as the elasticity of substitution in consumption moves below one, so that it is only when this elasticity is greater than one that the trade shock causes W_U/W_S to fall. With an elasticity of substitution in preferences of less than one, when the world price of imports decreases, the resulting increase in the volume of imports is not enough to offset the price fall, so that if trade is to remain balanced, exports—and the production of E—must go down. The latter implies that the production of the import-competing good, D, will then go up, and since D is intensive in U, W_U/W_S will increase. Similarly, with a consumption elasticity above one, the trade shock causes the production of D to decrease, and W_U/W_S falls.

The problem of ambiguity of decomposition depending upon parameter specification discussed for the Heckscher–Ohlin structure is also present in the differentiated-goods model, but the degree of ambiguity is now considerably smaller since, owing to the demand side of the model now absorbing world price changes, technical change is always the dominant factor behind increased wage inequality. This is shown in Table 4, which presents alternative model parameterizations consistent with the same 15% decline in W_U/W_S, and the corresponding decompositions into trade and technology portions. Unlike in Table 3, the size of technical change in Table 4 is held constant across parameterizations, and only production and consumption-side elasticities are varied to calibrate to the same jointly-determined wage change.

These decomposition experiments show clear differences between the differentiated goods model and the earlier Heckscher–Ohlin-type structure. First, decompositions with larger relative price changes can now be made, and the difficulty of simultaneously accommodating large price and wage changes is no longer present. Second, demand-side parameters are now critical for the results of such decompositions, with the trade contribution to wage inequality changing sign as the consumption-side elasticity goes above or below one—becoming zero when it equals unity. In addition, unlike the Heckscher–Ohlin model, there are now numerical difficulties in accommodating sector-biased technical change. These are radically

Table 4. Two Parameterizations of the Differentiated-Goods Model Giving the Same Relative Wage Change, and Decompositions of the Wage Change

	Parameterization A		Parameterization B	
	Good D	Good E	Good D	Good E
Share parameters				
Production				
Unskilled labor	0.37	0.28	0.19	0.07
Skilled labor	0.63	0.72	0.81	0.93
Elasticities				
Production	1.5	1.5	0.52	0.52
Domestic and imports	2.5		1.5	
Composite and exportable	1.0		1.0	
Decompositions			A	B
Change in W_U/W_S from trade and technology shocks (%)			−15.0	−15.0
Fraction of change in W_U/W_S due to technology			0.961	0.998
Fraction of change in W_U/W_S due to trade			0.039	0.002

different properties from those found for the Heckscher–Ohlin-type model, indicating the importance of the choice of structural model for trade–wage–technology decompositions.

5. Summary and Conclusions

This chapter uses general equilibrium numerical simulation techniques to explore the significance of the choice of structural model when assessing the contribution of trade and technological change to the increase in wage inequality documented for a number of OECD countries for the 1980s (most notably the US and the UK). Our purpose has been to explore the numerical properties of alternative structural models, and assess their suitability for performing decompositions.

Using a simple Heckscher–Ohlin-type model for a small open economy, we first show how problems of specialization can occur for even modest trade shocks, and how different model parameterizations are consistent with a given change in wage inequality from trade and technology shocks but yield substantially different decompositions results. To remove the problem of specialization, we also use a differentiated-goods model with imports and domestically produced goods as imperfect rather than perfect substitutes in preferences. Our results with the second model indicate an ability to examine larger trade shocks in decomposition experiments, and produce a significantly reduced variation in results across parameterizations owing to trade becoming less important in most cases. This is because now the demand side of the model can absorb a large portion of any trade shock (indeed all of such shock when the elasticity of substitution in preferences is one).

From these results we suggest that it is important to explore explicitly the numerical properties of particular structural models when contemplating decompositions, rather than only appealing to them as theoretically consistent models for reduced-form analyses. The choice of structural model, perhaps not surprisingly, seems to matter in this case for trade–wages decompositions.

References

Anderton, B. and P. Brenton, "The Dollar, Trade, Technology and Wage Inequality in the USA," mimeo, CEPS, Brussels (1998).

Autor, D., L. Katz, and A. Krueger, "Computing Inequality: Have Computers Changed the Labor Market," *Quarterly Journal of Economics* 113 (1998):1169–213.

Baldwin, R. E. and G. G. Cain, "Shifts in US Relative Wages: The Role of Trade, Technology and Factor Endowments," NBER working chapter 5934 (1997).

Berman, E., J. Bound, and Z. Griliches, "Changes in the Demand for Skilled Labor within US Manufacturing: Evidence from Annual Survey of Manufactures," *Quarterly Journal of Economics* 109 (1994):367–98.

Berman, E., J. Bound, and S. Machin, "Implications of Skill-Biased Technological Change: International Evidence." *Quarterly Journal of Economics* 113 (1998):1245–79.

Bhattarai, K., M. Ghosh, and J. Whalley, "On Some Properties of a Trade Closure Widely Used in Numerical Modelling. *Economics Letters* 62 (1999):13–21.

Blonigen, B. and M. Slaughter, "Foreign-Affiliate Activity and US Skill Upgrading," NBER Working chapter 7040 (1999).

Borjas, G., R. Freeman, and L. Katz, "On the Labor Market Effects of Immigration and Trade," in G. Borjas and R. Freeman (eds.), *Immigration and the Work Force*, Chicago: University of Chicago Press (1991).

———, "How Much Do Immigration and Trade Affect Labor Market Outcomes?" *Brookings Papers of Economic Activity* 0 (1997):1–85.

Brenton, P. A., "Rising Trade and Falling Wages: A Review of the Theory and the Empirics," in P. A. Brenton and J. Pelkmans (eds.), *Globalization and European Workers*, London: Macmillan (1998).

Burtless, G., "International Trade and the Rise in Earnings Inequality," *Journal of Economic Literature* 33 (1995):800–16.

Card, D., "Falling Union Membership and Rising Wage Inequality: What's the Connection?" NBER working chapter 6520 (1998).

Davis, S., "Cross-Country Patterns of Changes in Relative Wages," in *NBER Macroeconomics Annual* (1992):239–91.

Deardorff, A. and D. S. Hakura, "Trade and Wages: What are the Questions," in J. Bhagwati and M. Kosters (eds.), *Trade and Wages: Levelling Wages Down?*, Washington: AEI Press.

de Melo, J. and S. Robinson, "Product Differentiation and the Treatment of Foreign Trade in Computable General Equilibrium Models of Small Economies," *Journal of International Economics* 27 (1989):47–67.

Devarajan, S., J. Lewis, and S. Robinson, "Policy Lessons from Trade-Focused, Two-Sector Models," *Journal of Policy Modeling* 12 (1990):625–57.

———, "External Shocks, Purchasing Power Parity, and the Equilibrium Real Exchange Rate," *World Bank Economic Review* 7 (1993):45–63.

Dewatripont, M., A. Sapir, and K. Sekkat, "Labour Market Effects of Trade with LDCs in Europe," in M. Dewatripont, A. Sapir, and K. Sekkat (eds.), *Trade and Jobs in Europe: Much Ado about Nothing*, Oxford: Clarendon Press (1998).

Feenstra, R. and C. Hanson, "Globalization, Outsourcing and Wage Inequality," *American Economic Review*, May (1996):240–45.

Fortin, M. and L. Thomas, "Institutional Changes and Rising Wage Inequality," *Journal of Economic Perspectives* 11 (1997):75–96.

Francois, F. and D. Nelson, "Trade, Technology and Wages: General Equilibrium Mechanics," *Economic Journal* 108 (1998):1483–99.

Gottschalk, P. and T. Smeeding, "Cross National Comparisons of Earnings and Income Inequality," *Journal of Economic Literature* 35 (1997):633–87.

Hamermesh, D. S., *Labour Demand*, Princeton: Princeton University Press (1993).
Harrigan, J. and R. Balaban, "US Wages in General Equilibrium: The Effects of Prices, Technology, and Factor Supplies, 1963–1991," NBER working chapter 6981 (1999).
Haskel, J. and M. Slaughter, "Trade, Technology and UK Wage Inequality," NBER working chapter 6978 (1999).
Johnson, H. G., "Factor Market Distortions and the Shape of the Transformation Frontier," *Econometrica* 34 (1966):686–98.
Katz, L. and K. Murphy, "Changes in Relative Wages, 1963–1987: Supply and Demand Factors," *Quarterly Journal of Economics* 107 (1992):35–78.
Kosters, M., "An Overview of Changing Wage Patterns in the Labor Market," in J. Bhagwati and M. Kosters (eds.), *Trade and Wages: Levelling Wages Down?*, Washington: AEI Press (1994).
Krugman, P. and R. Lawrence, "Trade, Jobs and Wages," in P. Krugman (ed.), *Pop Internationalism*, Cambridge, MA: MIT Press (1996).
Lawrence, R. and M. Slaughter, "International Trade and American Wages: Giant Sucking Sound or Small Hiccup," *Brookings Papers of Economic Activity* 161 (1993):226.
Leamer, E., "Trade, Wages and Revolving Door Ideas," NBER working chapter 4716 (1994).
———, "In Search of Stolper–Samuelson Linkages between International Trade and Lower Wages," in S. M. Collins (ed.), *Imports, Exports, and the American Worker*, Washington, DC: Brookings Institution (1998).
Machin, S. and J. van Reenen, "Technology and Changes in Skill Structure: Evidence from Seven OECD Countries," *Quarterly Journal of Economics* 113 (1998):1215–44.
Murphy, K. and F. Welch, "The Role of International Trade in Wage Differentials," in M. Koster (ed.), *Workers and their Wages: Changing Patterns in the United States*, Washington: AEI Press (1991).
Neven, D. and C. Wyplosz, "Relative Prices, Trade and Restructuring in European Industry," in M. Dewatripont, A. Sapir, and K. Sekkat (eds.), *Trade and Jobs in Europe: Much Ado about Nothing?*, Oxford: Oxford University Press (1999):60–78.
OECD, "Trade, Earning and Employment: Assessing the Impact of Trade with Emerging Economies on OECD Labor Markets," *Employment Outlook*, OECD (1997).
Perroni, C. and T. Rutherford, "Regular Flexibility of Nested CES Functions," *European Economic Review* 39 (1995):335–43.
Reinert, K. and D. Roland-Holst, "Armington Elasticities for United States Manufacturing Sectors," *Journal of Policy Modelling* 14 (1992):631–9.
Shiells, C. and K. Reinert, "Armington Models and Terms of Trade Effects: Some Econometric Evidence for North America," *Canadian Journal of Economics* 26 (1993):299–316.
Slaughter, M., "What Are the Results of the Product-Price Studies and What Can We Learn from Their Differences," NBER working chapter W6591 (1998).
UNCTAD, *Trade and Development Report*, Geneva: UNCTAD (1997).
Wood, A., *North–South Trade, Employment and Inequality*, Oxford: Clarendon Press (1994).
———, "How Trade Hurt Unskilled Workers," *Journal of Economic Perspectives* 9 (1995): 57–80.
———, "Openness and Wage Inequality in Developing Countries: the Latin American Challenge to East Asian Conventional Wisdom," *World Bank Economic Review* 11 (1997): 33–57.
———, "Globalisation and the Rise in Labor Market Inequalities," *Economic Journal* 108 (1998):1463–82.

Notes

1. Immigration, reduced labor market imperfections, and foreign direct investment also enter as possible additional factors in some literature (Borjas et al., 1997; Fortin and Thomas, 1997; Card, 1998; Blonigen and Slaughter, 1999).
2. The structure differs from the conventional two-country, two-good, two-factor Heckscher–Ohlin model in which relative factor abundance across countries determines the pattern of trade.

Our model contains two goods, two factors and homogeneous products, but there is only one (small price-taking) country and our base-case pattern of trade is determined by the own-country comparative advantage, not relative factor abundance. We label it a Heckscher–Ohlin-type model owning to its use of homogeneous goods and industry mobile factors, but it is not a strict Heckscher–Ohlin global model.

3. Our choice of this period is based both on data availability for international product prices and the fact that a considerable change in wage inequality took place in the UK over it.

4. This is a similar finding to that in Johnson (1966), who simulates production frontiers for cases where the underlying sectoral technology is either Cobb–Douglas or CES, and shows them to be close to linear. Fixed-factor variants of the same model can be used to remove specialization, but these have the property that price shocks can be largely borne by the fixed factors, rather than by the mobile skilled and unskilled labor types.

5. See, for instance, the surveys by Burtless (1995), Gottschalk and Smeeding (1997), and Brenton (1998). For a critical assessment of some of the literature, see Deardorff and Hakura (1994) and Slaughter (1998).

6. Although, as indicated earlier, Leamer (1998) has argued that from the zero-profit conditions in a two-sector, two-factor small open economy model skill (or factor) biased technical change should have no impact on relative wages. This logic suggests that only sector-biased technical change should be considered in such a case.

7. Exceptions to this conclusion include Borjas et al. (1991), Wood (1994, 1995, 1998), and Feenstra and Hanson (1996). The latter identify outsourcing as a significant cause.

8. In the literature using econometric-modeling techniques, exceptions are Leamer (1998), and Harrigan and Balaban (1999), where structural forms are estimated. Francois and Nelson (1998) are seemingly the other authors who use an applied general equilibrium model to look at the effects of trade and technology on wage inequality. They also compare the pure Heckscher–Ohlin structure with differentiated goods models as well as with a Heckscher–Ohlin version including intermediate goods. However, the focus of their numerical simulation discussion is on the relative intensity of trade effects on wages (presence or absence of a magnification effect, and/or absolute losers) under different model structures, and they do not analyse decomposition results.

9. A more detailed description of the data used is available upon request.

10. An important issue for our analysis is whether the results we report are specific to our choice of functional form, or whether they have more generality. We use the family of convenient forms widely used in the modeling literature, but do not use flexible functional forms (generalized Leontief, translog). The latter do not satisfy global concavity property, and can as a result pose problems in computing equilibria; although Perroni and Rutherford (1995) have developed globally concave flexible forms. The more general and well-known problem is that generally there are no known analytical structures which allow us to move easily between production functions (needed here for wage effects) and production frontiers which give the link between wage and price change. CES are widely used functions, and we acknowledge that our results may be function-specific.

11. This estimate is based on information from Neven and Wyplosz (1999), combined with information on UK imports by country of origin (developed/developing countries).

12. Hamermesh (1993) provides ranges for empirical estimates of production-side elasticities which could be used, although these are for three-factor production functions (skilled and unskilled labor, and capital).

13. A more stringent restriction would be explicit two-period calibration, a feature apparently little used in the applied general equilibrium literature. This, however, has the problem that non-technology parameters must also be allowed to change across periods, which would substantially complicate trade and technology decompositions.

14. In de Melo and Robinson's model, three goods are also considered two of which are domestically produced, but only two of them (the imported and the domestic good) enter preferences.

15. Devarajan et al. (1990, 1993) also discuss the role of the elasticity of substitution in consumption in this model.

16. A referee has correctly pointed out to us that a consumption-side elasticity below one implies gross complementarity between domestic goods and imports, and is therefore implausible. We still consider values less than one for this elasticity in our experiments because the range of empirical estimates available for industrialized countries (the US) includes them (e.g., Reinert and Roland-Holst, 1992).

8
Policy Implications of the Trade and Wages Debate

Alan V. Deardorff

1. Introduction

For the last ten years or so there has been a lively debate among trade and labor economists in America regarding "trade and wages." The issue is the extent to which "trade" has been the cause of the increasing skill differential in the US economy. A parallel issue has occupied European economists, where, on the continent at least, the symptom to be explained has been changes not so much in relative wages but in unemployment. In both cases, "trade" is shorthand for increasing competition with low-skilled labor in global markets, owing to a combination of global trade liberalization and growth of the labor-abundant countries, especially in Asia.

Among several alternatives to trade as causes for these changes in labor markets, the most prominent is "technology," that is, technological progress that has been biased in favor of skilled labor, either within industries or across industries. The outcome of that debate, it seems, is a near consensus that trade has indeed been a significant cause of these labor market changes, but also that it has been less important quantitatively than other causes, and most likely less important than technology. In spite of that consensus, the debate continues over the appropriate methodology to use for drawing these conclusions.[1] In this paper, however, I want to ask a different question: Does it really matter for policy whether trade or technology (or something else) is the cause?

This is a question that I have already touched on elsewhere, in Deardorff (1997). There I primarily merely stated the usual trade economist's argument against restricting trade as a first-best policy, and then noted that this argument holds regardless of whether labor markets have been impacted by changes in trade or by changes in technology. My argument here will be the same, but somewhat more formal. I will lay out a simple explicit model of trade and income distribution in which it is possible to examine the effects on income distribution of both trade and technology, as well as of certain policies to redistribute income. The point will be to show that, while the socially optimal level of policy for redistributing income certainly changes when trade or technology worsens the income distribution, neither the choice of which policy is best to use, nor the decision of whether to use it at all, really depends upon the cause. Thus if it is true that trade has caused a certain worsening of the income distribution, the optimal policy response will be the same as if technology had caused the same worsening.

In particular, like most trade economists I will argue against the use of trade policies to solve the problem, on the grounds that better policies exist. Thus in normal circumstances, even if trade were the cause of a need for greater efforts at redistribution, these efforts should not take the form of restricting trade, even though this might be a workable second-best policy. And if for some reason trade restrictions are the best available policy for redistribution, the case for using them would be just as strong if technology were the source of the increased inequality. In short, the cause does not matter for the cure.

In what follows I will first, in section 2, lay out the model that I will use to address these issues. This is just a minor extension of the usual two-sector, two-factor Heckscher–Ohlin (H–O) trade model, extended to allow heterogeneous workers to choose whether or not to become skilled. As I have shown in Deardorff (1997), this model incorporates an interaction between trade and income distribution that causes some redistribution policies to affect trade. Here I will use the model in section 3 to identify optimal redistribution policies, and then to see how changes in trade and technology alter these in section 4. To this point, I retain the standard H–O assumption of FPE. In section 5, however, I consider the possibility of moving out of the cone of diversification, so that factor prices paid by firms can change, and also the possibility of multiple cones of diversification. Since this raises the possibility of using changes in factor supplies themselves to change factor prices, I consider these in section 6. Section 7 concludes.

2. The Model[2]

The model builds upon the standard two-factor, two-good H–O structure with perfect competition. The two factors are skilled and unskilled labor, which are assumed to be imperfect substitutes in the production of both goods. One of the goods, X, uses skilled labor relatively intensively compared with good Y. Given the endowments of the two factors (to be determined endogenously below), the model can be analyzed with the familiar Lerner–Pearce diagram as in almost any modern textbook on international trade.

The number of workers in a country is fixed at a number, L, that is large enough so that I can treat it as continuous. Each of these workers can be thought of as innately unskilled, but they are capable of acquiring skill by giving up some fixed amount of their own time. Workers are heterogeneous, some able to acquire a great deal of skill through this process, others not, with the amount of skill that they can acquire distributed continuously over the population, representing their diverse abilities. The model is static, but one can think of each worker as living a fixed lifetime, then being replaced with another worker with the same ability but who must make anew the choice of whether to acquire skill or not. The distribution of births/deaths is constant over time, so that at any moment there is a constant flow of new workers coming on the scene. The distribution of ability across new workers also remains constant over time.

If a new worker chooses to remain unskilled, then she[3] will supply one unit of unskilled labor over her lifetime and earn the unskilled wage w_u. For worker i to become skilled, the only resource she requires is her own time, and the result is that she acquires an amount of skill S_i that is available to her over the remainder of her life.[4] It is this number, S_i, that is taken as given by worker i, and that is distributed unequally across the population. The market will determine a wage per unit of skill, w_s, which I will call the skilled wage, even though it is not paid per person and therefore should not be compared to w_u. It follows that worker i will earn an income of $w_s S_i$ over her lifetime if she chooses to become skilled.

The decision to acquire skill depends, then, simply on the comparison of $w_s S_i$ with w_u. It may seem that a unit of skilled labor should be paid more than unskilled labor, and this is true (that is, presumably $w_s > w_u$); but because of the time spent in skill acquisition the fraction of their lives that skilled workers are paid this higher wage is smaller than one. Since S_i is that fraction multiplied by the level of skill acquired, it too will be less than one for some workers who are not able to acquire very much skill. Such workers will opt to remain unskilled.

Given a pair of market-determined wages, w_s and w_u, then, workers with low ability will remain unskilled, while workers of high ability will become skilled, the dividing line being at

$$S_{\hat{i}} = \frac{w_u}{w_s}. \tag{1}$$

That is, the marginal worker, $\hat{i}$, will earn a lifetime income just equal to what they could have earned remaining unskilled. Clearly I am ignoring discounting here, which would complicate matters only slightly.

The distribution of income that emerges from this simple model has all workers of low ability earning the same low lifetime wage, w_u, while workers of high ability, because their skill levels differ, earn different lifetime incomes all of which are higher than w_u. In the model, ability matters only for the return on skill acquisition, not for the unskilled worker's productivity on the job, and that is why they all earn the same. This is not enough diversity for realism, but it suffices to incorporate the incentive effects that will distinguish at least some policies for redistribution. That is, policies that change the relative wages of skilled and unskilled workers in (1) will change some workers' choices of whether or not to become skilled, and will therefore alter the economy's "endowment" of factors, its production and trade, and its total income.

Once trained, all workers work the same amount of time, and there is no alternative for leisure. This means that another margin for choice that might respond to income redistribution policies is omitted, so that the range of redistribution policies that will be considered below is correspondingly limited. In particular, a simple proportional income tax, because it does not change relative wages, will not here introduce any distortion into worker choice, as it would if they could substitute leisure for work.

Figure 1 shows the tradeoff that these assumptions imply between skilled and unskilled labor for the economy as a whole, and the corresponding wages. In the top panel, curve *MEL* shows the "endowment possibilities" for skilled and unskilled labor. Since each unit of labor can supply a unit of unskilled labor if it does not acquire skill, the maximum amount of unskilled labor is L. If some workers do choose to acquire skill, it will be those with the greatest ability, and (minus) the slope of the curve as it rises to the left from L is therefore the skill per worker acquired by the most able individual. As we move to the left along the curve, less and less able individuals opt for skill, and the curve therefore flattens out. At the vertical intercept, all workers acquire skill and the slope there reflects the ability of the least able. Various points along the horizontal axis from O to L therefore represent the individuals in the economy, ordered least able to most able from left to right.

Now introduce wages of skilled and unskilled labor determined by the market. In the lower panel, the horizontal line *CED* at $y_u = w_u$ represents the lifetime income that a worker can acquire by remaining unskilled, and this is the same for all individuals. Curve *AEB*, in contrast, shows the income that these same individuals can earn if they become skilled, starting low for the least able and rising to the right. This income is just $w_s S_i$, and it is therefore equal to the given wage w_s multiplied by (minus) the slope of the curve *MEL* above it. All workers choose the highest of these two incomes, and therefore all workers above $\hat{U}$ become skilled. This corresponds to point E in the

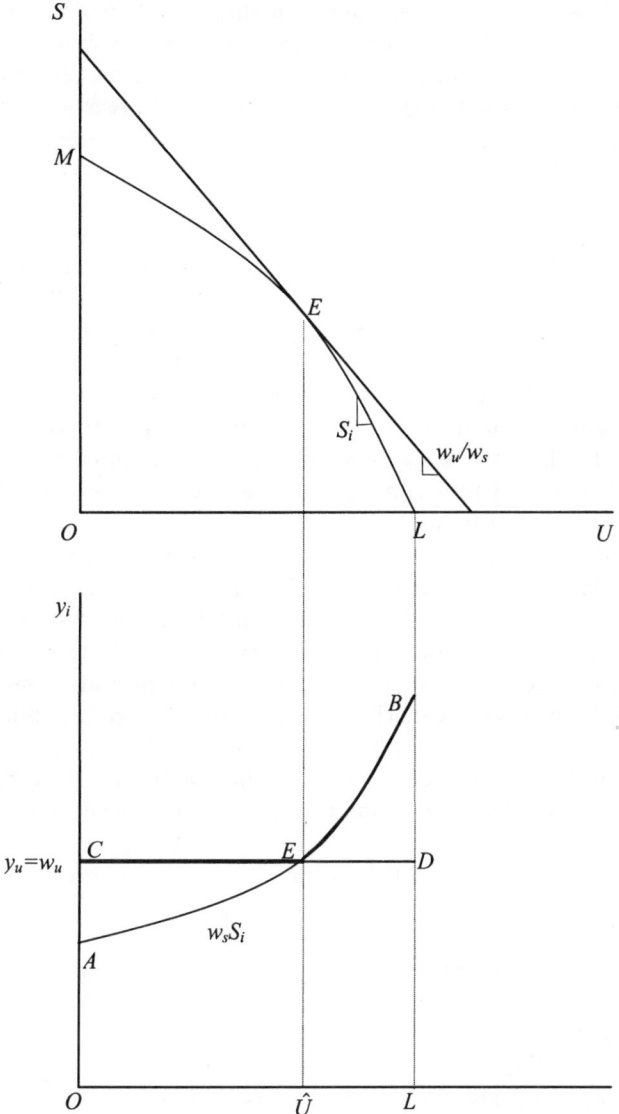

Figure 1

upper panel, which is the tangency between the endowment possibility curve and a downward-sloping factor price line with slope w_u/w_s, as shown. Note that the choice by individuals maximizes the value, at these factor prices, of the endowment point selected for the country.

The bottom panel shows the complete income distribution in the economy. Unskilled workers, on the left, all earn the same income, y_u. Skilled workers earn more, as shown by the rising curve. Thus the income distribution is unequal. Furthermore, those with the highest incomes are not working harder, as they would for example in Leamer's (1996) model of effort. They are simply lucky, having arrived in the world with higher levels of ability. The market rewards them for this, in part as a mechanism to induce them to use that ability to acquire high levels of productive skill. But a side-effect of that mechanism is that incomes are unequal, solely as an accident of birth.

The extent of this inequality depends directly on the two wages. Assuming that all individuals share the same tastes in their roles as consumers and that they face the same prices,[5] a rise in the skilled wage relative to the unskilled wage, w_s/w_u, will increase inequality by raising the incomes of all those who would already have opted to become skilled. Further, it will induce those unskilled workers nearest the margin $\hat{i}$ to become skilled after all, and to raise their incomes too above y_u. Meanwhile the less able unskilled workers fall relatively further behind their skilled (and now more numerous) colleagues. By any measure, the income distribution has become more unequal.

Figure 1 does not determine these wages, but the rest of the model (the H–O part) does. Let the country be small and open, so that prices of goods are determined exogenously in world markets. Then as long as factor endowments, now endogenous, are within the H–O diversification cone, goods prices will determine factor prices à la factor price equalization (FPE).

Figure 2 incorporates the familiar Lerner–Pearce diagram of H–O trade theory into the top panel of Figure 1. Solid curves $X = 1/p_x$ and $Y = 1/p_y$ are unit-value isoquants for the two goods, incorporating both their technologies and the prices of the goods taken from world markets. Absent factor-intensity reversals, their common tangent, CD, defines the unique factor prices and factor ratios that are consistent with producing both goods at these prices. These factor ratios, s_x and s_y, define the diversification cone.

In the same figure, the solid curve MEL is the endowment possibility curve from Figure 1, and a line parallel to the common tangent, CD, now determines which factor

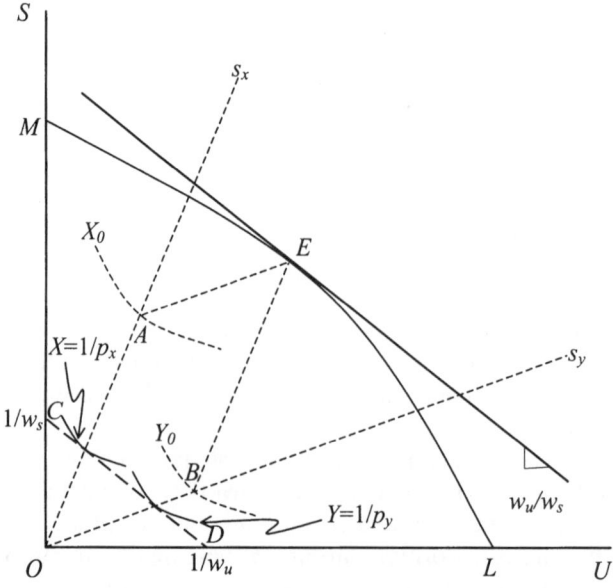

Figure 2

endowment will be chosen in a diversified equilibrium by individuals deciding on skill acquisition. Point E is that endowment, and it can now be used together with the factor ratios to determine allocations of the factors to the two industries, at points A and B. Point E determines, together with the origin of the diagram, the corners of a standard Edgeworth production box leading to these allocations, although I omit the sides of the box to avoid additional clutter.

Figure 2, expanded to include also the lower panel of Figure 1, can and will be used below to work out the effects of various exogenous changes in the model on income distribution, as well as on the more familiar variables of the H–O model. As a simple example, I note in passing that mere enlargement of a country will not change the proportions of anything, unless the economy is or becomes large enough to matter for world prices. That is, suppose that a country's population become larger, the distribution of abilities across that population remaining the same. This will expand the endowment possibility curve outward also in proportion and leave the tangency with the factor price line on the same (undrawn) ray from the origin as point E. The result will be exactly the same distribution of income as before, but with proportionally more people at each income.

However, if such a country is large enough to affect world prices, then this expansion will matter after all. At unchanged prices the country's supplies, demands, and quantities traded all increase in the same proportion. This increases the supply of its export good on world markets, as well as the demand for its import good, and prices will move against it. We cannot tell from Figure 2 which good is exported, but the resulting price change will change factor prices against the factor used intensively in its production. Suppose, for example, that this was a country with an abundance of ability and therefore an (endogenous) abundance of skilled labor. Then it will have exported the skill-intensive good X prior to the expansion. The price of good X will therefore fall on world markets, as will the relative (and real) wage of skilled labor. Working through the rest of the model, income distribution will become more equal.

More relevant to the current discussion is the opposite case, however, of expansion by a low-ability, low-skill country. This will cause the price of the unskilled-labor-intensive good to fall, lower the corresponding relative wage of unskilled labor, and make the income distribution more unequal both at home and abroad.

3. Redistribution

I will consider four policies for income redistribution in the context of this model. The first is nondistorting lump-sum redistribution that simply taxes some individuals and subsidizes others in ways that do not change their behavior. In the real world this would be almost impossible to do, but within the model it is feasible since a proportional income tax does not distort behavior in the absence of a labor/leisure choice. Nonetheless, while I will examine this policy, I will normally assume that it is not available, and I discuss it only as a benchmark.

The second policy is a tax on skilled labor together with a subsidy to unskilled labor. This is feasible, both in the model and in the real world via a progressive income tax, but it does distort behavior: the choices by some workers of whether or not to become skilled.

The third policy is a tax/subsidy on outputs. By taxing the output of the sector that uses skilled labor intensively and simultaneously subsidizing output in the other sector, policymakers can again tilt the ratio of the two factors' wages, although here it is the wages paid, not just the wages received, that are changed. This too distorts workers' choices regarding skill acquisition, and in addition it distorts producer choices of what to produce.

Finally, the fourth policy is a tax on imports of unskilled-labor-intensive goods. This too alters wages paid, not just wages received, and indeed it has all of the effects of a tax/subsidy on production. Thus it too will have redistributive effects. But it also causes the extra distortion of quantity demanded that is familiar from trade theory.

In each case, while the model can display, as in the bottom panel of Figure 1, the complete distribution of income, this does not summarize it in a way that facilitates discussion of social preferences. And this is difficult, since the model includes a continuum of individuals with different incomes. Therefore, I will focus—and suppose that society also focuses—on only two of them: those individuals at percentiles l and h from the bottom of the income distribution. For example, we might compare the real incomes of individuals whose incomes are above $l = 25\%$ of the population (the lth percentile) with those whose incomes are above $h = 75\%$ of the population (the hth percentile), in order to capture the essential inequality. Since, in the model, all unskilled workers earn the same wage, I will require only that l be small enough to lie within that group, and that h be large enough to lie outside it, at least prior to any policies to redistribute income.

With this assumption, we can think of social preferences as being represented by a social welfare function defined over the real incomes, or utilities, of only these two percentiles, and we can represent these preferences with social indifference curves defined on these two utilities. Obviously, if policies could be constructed without constraint, maximization of social preferences defined in this peculiar way would yield crazy results, concentrating subsidies on just the chosen percentiles. But with only the above-mentioned policies to choose from, I don't think that this simplification will particularly distort the results.

The first step in using this approach is to determine what real income or utility combinations are possible for the chosen percentiles, using each of the eligible mechanisms for redistribution. I will consider them in turn, looking in each case only at the simplest case of a diversified small open economy with free trade. The country therefore takes as given both the prices of the two goods on world markets and the associated (by FPE) wages of the two kinds of labor. In the absence of any redistribution policy, the latter determine the real incomes both of the unskilled lth percentile and of the skilled hth percentile. These are graphed in Figure 3 at the point E, where utilities of the two percentiles are u_l^0 and h_h^0 respectively.[6]

Nondistorting Redistribution

Nondistorting lump-sum redistribution simply transfers real income from one group to another, and it therefore might seem to reallocate simply along the downward-sloping 45° line that is drawn in Figure 3 through point E. That would be the case if the redistribution took only from percentile h or l and gave only to the other, but that is not very interesting. For comparability with the policies to be addressed below, we should think instead of a policy that redistributes among the entire population, even though we focus only on these two percentiles.

Suppose, then, that the nondistorting policy is a simple proportional income tax, the proceeds of which are given back equally to all individuals. The tax does not distort

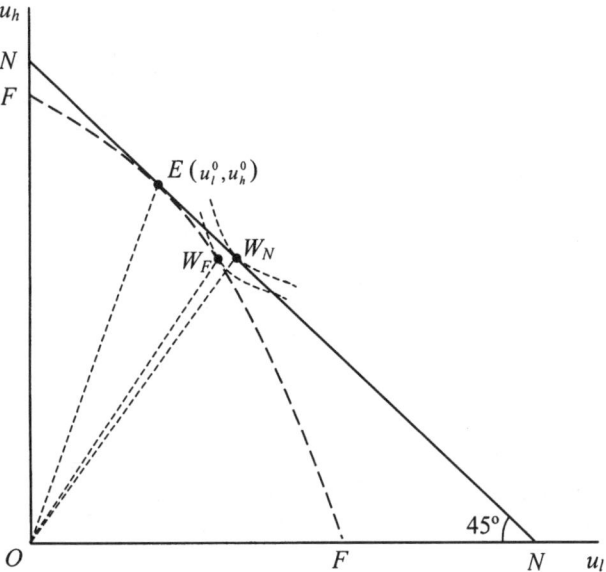

Figure 3

because there is no leisure option and because the skill choice is dependent only on the ratio of wages, which are taxed equally. This will raise incomes of those whose incomes before the policy were below average, and vice versa. However, for arbitrary percentiles l and h, these changes will not usually be equal. In general, therefore, the frontier representing real income combinations that are attainable with nondistorting redistribution will not be a 45° line, or even necessarily straight. But it is harmless, and most easily recognized, if I draw it that way.

Factor Taxes

In this small open economy with the factor prices that are paid by industries determined via FPE on world markets, a tax on a factor (supply or demand) will be borne entirely by the factor. Therefore an easy way to redistribute income from skilled to unskilled workers is to tax the former and subsidize the latter. Wages received by skilled workers will fall by the amount of the tax, and wages received by unskilled workers will rise by the amount of the subsidy. Of course, those skilled workers closest to the margin will now opt not to become skilled in the first place, and the economy's endowment of skilled labor will decline. Figure 4 illustrates the policy, which leaves the Lerner–Pearce part of the picture unchanged. But it raises the relative take-home wage of unskilled labor, to the steeper tangent to the endowment possibility curve at E'. In the lower panel, the income distribution changes from CEB to $C'E'B'$. Just how far the unskilled take-home wage rises and the skilled one falls depends on the numbers and incomes of both groups, since the payments to the unskilled should just exhaust the proceeds from the tax.

Looking at the incomes of our focus groups, the l and h percentiles, it would seem that we only know that one gains and the other loses, without knowing how much

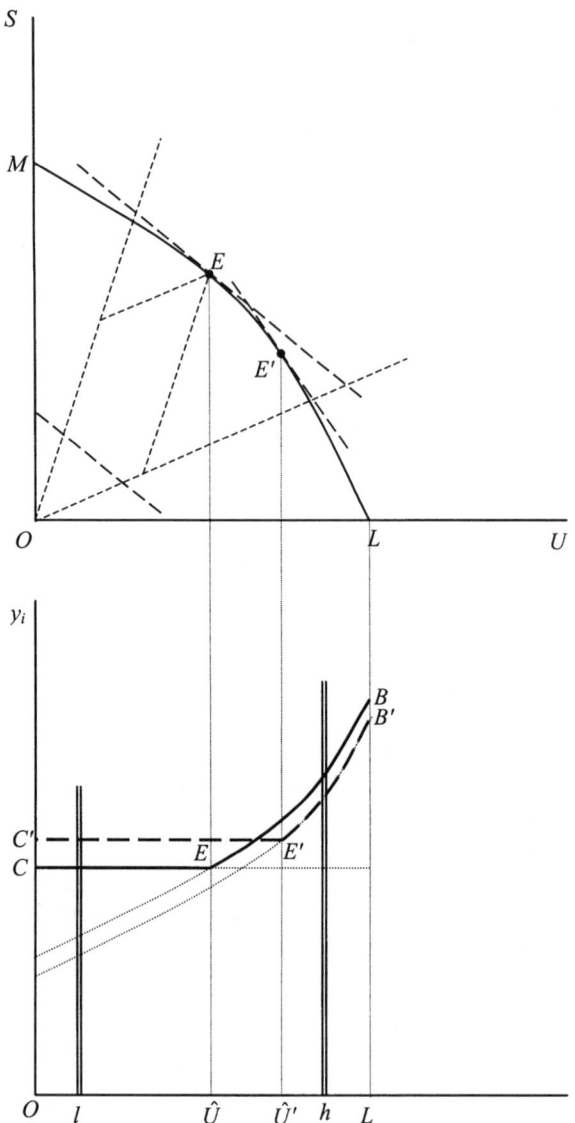

Figure 4

they gain and lose. But in fact, we can say more. For the distortion of the choice to acquire skill has led to an endowment of the two factors that is worth less, at world prices, than the previous endowment choice was worth. This is seen in the top panel of Figure 4 from the fact that E' lies below the tangent to E. Therefore real national income must be lower with this policy than without, suggesting that the utility possibilities for this distorting factor tax must lie below those of the nondistorting tax above. Such a curve is labeled FEF in Figure 3, lying inside NEN except at E. Curve FEF is the utility possibility curve, or UPF, attainable using a factor tax/subsidy for redistribution.

If we now introduce a social welfare function defined on the utilities of our two focus percentiles, we can use the indifference curves from that function to identify optimal policy. Of course, such a social welfare function could have many forms, but I will draw the social indifference curves as looking much like we see in other contexts. In Figure 3, these identify social optima at W_N with the nondistorting policy and at W_F with the factor tax. This proves nothing, but it does suggest the plausibility of the result that it is the poor who are likely to bear the costs of distortions that arise in attempts to redistribute income. That is, as drawn, the curvature of *FEF* has caused the high-income percentile to be left with almost as much income as it would have enjoyed if nondistorting redistribution had been possible.

There is one more point worth noting before moving on. In the present model, utility is real income. This depends on net nominal income, which varies across groups, and on prices, which do not. Thus the ratio of utilities captures the ratio of net nominal incomes—gross wages, when there are no taxes, and net wages otherwise. In Figure 3, therefore, we can use rays from the origin to index relative net wages, as well as the changes worked upon them by policy. The fact that W_F is drawn on a higher ray than W_N therefore says that the nondistorting policy would be used to lower the relative net wage of skilled workers by more than would be optimal if only factor taxes were available. This too is not inevitable, of course, but it seems to follow if the social welfare function is homothetic.

Production Taxes

A production tax drives a wedge between world prices and those faced by domestic producers, with the latter being those that determine domestic factor prices. A tax on the skill-intensive sector (combined with a subsidy on the other sector to keep the budget balanced) will be borne entirely by domestic producers, whose price will fall by the amount of the tax. As is familiar from the Stolper–Samuelson theorem, this will cause a magnified drop in the relative wage of skilled labor compared with unskilled labor, and once again, it will redistribute real income, or utility, from the high to the low percentiles.

Compared with a factor tax that would have the same effect on relative net wages, this policy will cause exactly the same distortion of factor endowments and therefore the same drop in the value of the country's endowments at world prices. However, in this case there is an additional distortion, as the country also fails to produce the most valuable bundle of goods along its production possibility frontier. I will skip drawing that, since the story is so familiar. But the lesson is that the UPF for nonzero production taxes will lie even further inside that of the nondistorting policy, being itself everywhere inferior to the factor tax.

Trade Taxes

Finally, consider a tax on trade. If the country in question is an importer of the unskilled-labor-intensive good, as I will assume,[7] then a tax on trade will raise the domestic relative price of the imported good, having the same effect on producer prices and factor prices as the production tax. In addition, however, it will also distort consumption and again produce an inferior combination of utility possibilities, even compared with the already inferior production tax. Again the story here is too well known to require much explication.

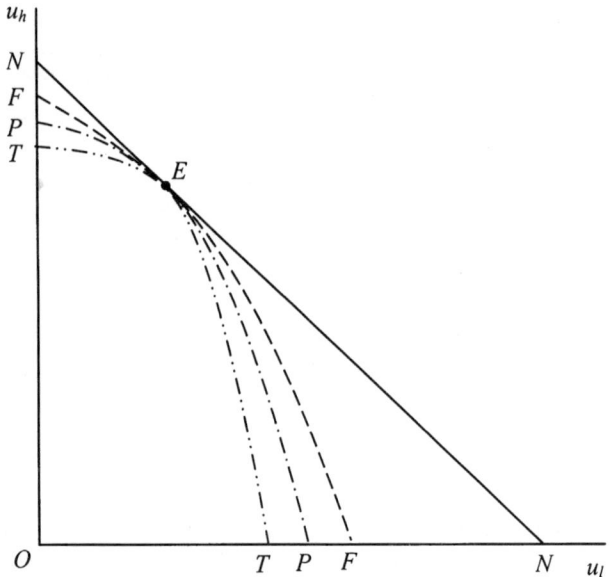

Figure 5

To sum up, then, Figure 5 shows the UPFs together for the four different redistribution policies: *NEN* (nondistorting policy); *FEF* (factor tax); *PEP* (production tax); and *TET* (trade tax). The four curves coincide at point *E* where the policies are all zero. Everywhere else, they possess a clear rank ordering, with utility possibilities falling as we move down the list.

4. Response to Change

I now consider how redistribution policy should respond to a worsening of the income distribution, first if it arises from trade, and second if it arises from technology.

A Trade Shock

Suppose simply that the world relative price of the unskilled-labor-intensive good now falls. Figure 6 shows in three panels what happens to the economy and its choices. In the top panel with good *Y* as *numéraire*, the fall in the price of good *Y* means an increase in the price of good *X*, which shifts its unit-value isoquant inward from *X* to *X'*. This flattens the common tangent and lowers the relative wage of unskilled labor. That in turn moves the tangency with the endowment possibility curve up and to the left, from *E* to *E'*, leaving a smaller fraction of the population unskilled.

The middle panel shows the resulting income distribution, with the unskilled workers worse off than before, including even some of the new skilled workers who are worse off than when they were unskilled before the shock. The more skilled are doing quite well, thank you. Secure within these two groups lie our focus percentiles, *l* worse off and *h* better off, as expected.

In the bottom panel, then, the new equilibrium without any policy, *E'*, is therefore above and to the left of the old one, *E*. Moreover, continuing the assumption made

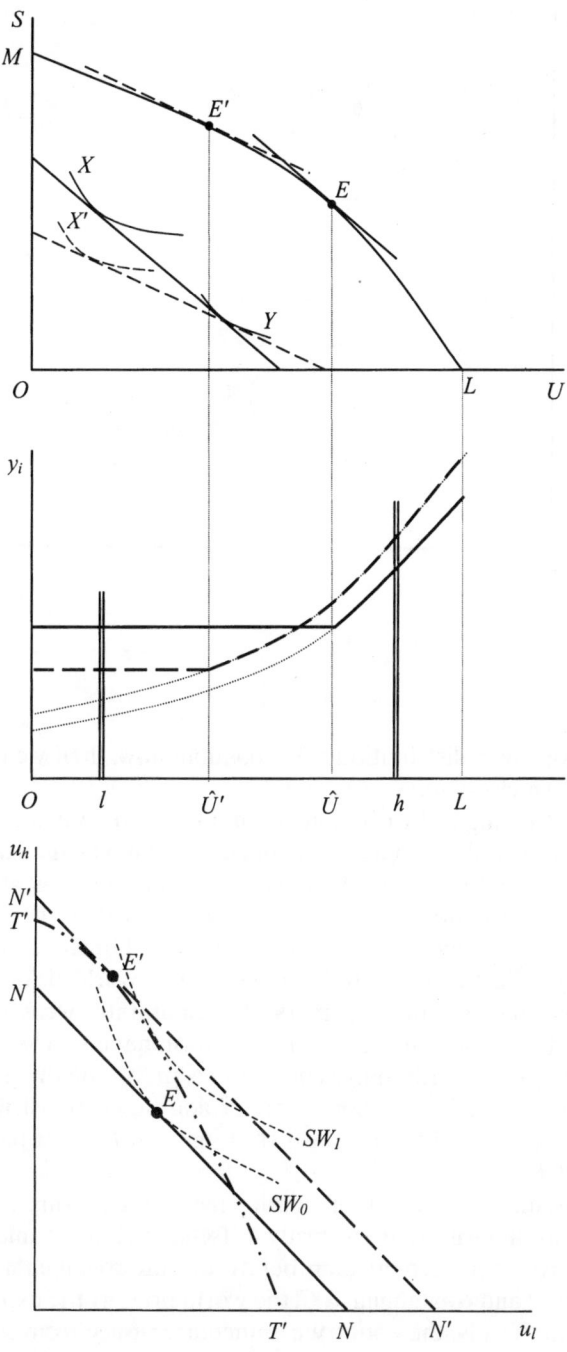

Figure 6

before that this country is an exporter of skilled-labor-intensive goods—that is, a developed country—I assume that real national income of the country has been increased by this price change. Thus the new equilibrium lies outside the utility possibilities that could have been attained before even with nondistorting redistribution. Likewise, of

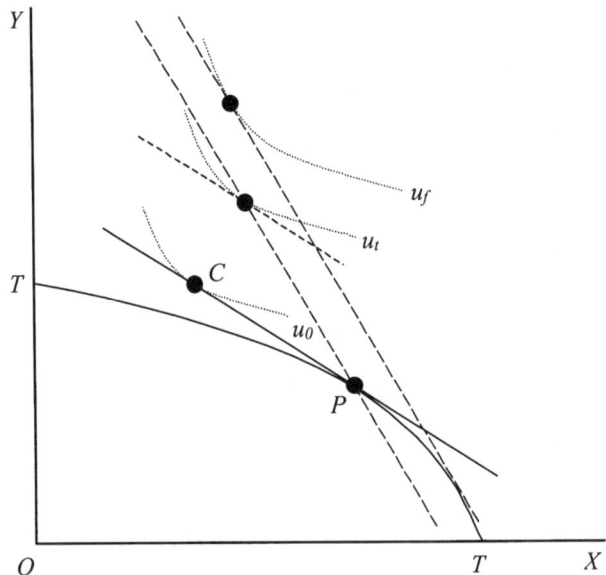

Figure 7

course, if nondistorting redistribution were possible now, then we could make everybody better off if we chose to.

However, nondistorting redistribution is not an option, only a benchmark, and the question is what we can do with available policies, whatever they are. We know from Figure 5 that the new UPFs for our various policies are all tangent to one another at E', but what we want to know now is where any one of them lies relative to E. That turns out to be easy to know. Consider the worst of the bunch: the tariff. Suppose that a tariff were used to just exactly offset the change in world prices, leaving domestic prices for both producers and consumers exactly as they were before. This would restore the upper two panels in Figure 6 to their original configurations, thus yielding exactly the same income distribution as before, except for one thing: the tariff revenue. This would become available for some sort of additional redistribution, perhaps to everybody. Therefore, the UPF for a tariff starting from E' must pass above the original equilibrium at E.

In case this seems like sleight of hand, Figure 7 confirms in a more conventional context that a tariff that perfectly offsets an improvement in a country's terms of trade leaves it better off than before the improvement. Starting from free trade producing at P and consuming at C, the world price of the exported good X rises. Continuing to trade freely, the country can increase utility from u_0 to u_f. But even a tariff that restores the original domestic prices to both producers and consumers leaves the country free to trade along the new world price line, and the country still achieves a higher utility, u_t, than it had before. This is in fact exactly what is going on in our model in this case, since by leaving domestic producer prices unchanged, this tariff has also prevented any change in domestic factor prices and endogenous factor endowments.

Returning to the bottom panel of Figure 6, then, what can we say about optimal policy? Not much, without some assumptions about social preferences. But suppose we assume that the initial equilibrium was considered optimal. Then there is a social indifference curve tangent to UPF_N at E, regardless of which of the several redistribution policies were available. And without too much more restriction on these social preferences, the new social optimum after the change in world prices will require some redistribution toward the low-skilled population, now that the equilibrium has shifted to E'. This is shown in Figure 6 by the tangencies with the two social welfare contours SW_0 and SW_1.

Thus, if a tariff is the only available means of redistributing income, and if the optimal tariff was zero before the trade shock, then after the trade shock one should indeed restrict trade. The figure also suggests (and homothetic social preferences would assure) that, even here, one should not restrict trade enough to restore the original income distribution, even though that can be done without eliminating all gains from the improved terms of trade. On the contrary, the optimal policy is likely to dampen only slightly the distributional effects of the shock, leaving the beneficiaries (skilled workers) far better off and the unskilled workers still suffering, relatively if not absolutely.

Of course, all of this will be true of the other policies as well, if they are available, and they always dominate the tariff. Thus if a factor tax can be used, its UPF will lie between $T'E'T'$ and $N'E'N'$. This means not only that the factor tax will dominate the trade tax, as we already knew. It also means that the beneficiary of having it available, instead of a trade tax, will be mostly the unskilled. The skilled may actually suffer from having this more efficient redistribution policy tool in the arsenal.

A Technology Shock

The simplest technology shock that can yield a comparable change in income distribution is not, in fact, the most plausible. If the technology for producing the skilled-labor-intensive good were to improve, but only within our small open economy, then while prices would be unchanged, the unit-value isoquant of the skill-intensive sector would shift inward, more or less as it did in the top panel of Figure 6.[8] Yet it makes little sense that technology would change only locally. If technology improves for producing the skilled-labor-intensive good everywhere, then of course world prices will change too, and things are a bit messier. But as long as the price falls by less than the technology has improved, the net effect of the two together will still be a picture much like Figure 6. That is the case I will consider.

That is, assume a worldwide Hicks-neutral technological improvement of some percentage, say α, in the skill-intensive industry, X.[9] Assume also that this causes the world price of good X to fall, but by a smaller percentage, $\beta < \alpha$. The net effect in our small country will be to shift the unit-value isoquant for X inward toward the origin by the percentage $\alpha - \beta$, exactly as in Figure 6, with all of the same implications that this change had there. The relative unskilled wage falls, the income distribution worsens, and fewer workers choose to remain unskilled even as some of those who now choose to become skilled are made worse off by the entire event. And once again, since the country enjoys higher real income as a result of the shock, the new equilibrium in the bottom panel is, like E', above and to the left of E. But it is nonetheless above and to the right of the old UPF for nondistorting policy.

This time, constructing a policy to reproduce the original income distribution, as we did in showing that $T'E'T'$ lay outside of E, is not quite as simple as just setting a tariff equal to a price change. But it is not that much harder. A tariff on imports of Y, set at the percentage $\alpha - \beta$, will reduce the domestic relative price of X still further, pushing the unit-value isoquant back to where it started and restoring factor prices, factor endowments, and income distribution to their original levels. And once again, there will be some tariff revenue left over to make incomes higher than before the shock. So once again, the use of a tariff for redistribution is capable, in spite of its many distortionary effects, of completely redressing the income distribution without fully undoing the benefits of the shock.

Indeed, one basis for the major conclusion of this paper—that the source of the shock does not really matter for policy—is simply the fact that the same Figure 6, without even relabeling, represents both.

5. Specialization and Multiple Cones

Until now I have assumed that the country remains inside the single cone of diversification that exists in the two-good model. With factor supplies changing in response to both shocks and policies, it is possible that the country may move into or out of this cone. Recognizing this, we should also consider the possibility, with more than two goods, of more than one diversification cone. Both possibilities are addressed in Figure 8, where four goods and three cones serve to illustrate the relevant possibilities.

The country now faces given world prices for four goods, $p_1 \ldots p_4$, and therefore the four unit-value isoquants shown. These permit production of at most two of the goods at a time, within the three cones $s_1 O s_2$, $s_2' O s_3$, and $s_3' O s_4$. Together, since the linear homogeneity of the production functions implies that production techniques can be used in linear combinations, these unit-value isoquants imply that the isoquant for producing, in effect, a unit of value is the convex hull of the separate isoquants. That is, the heavy dashed curve labeled NEK and composed of alternating straight and curved

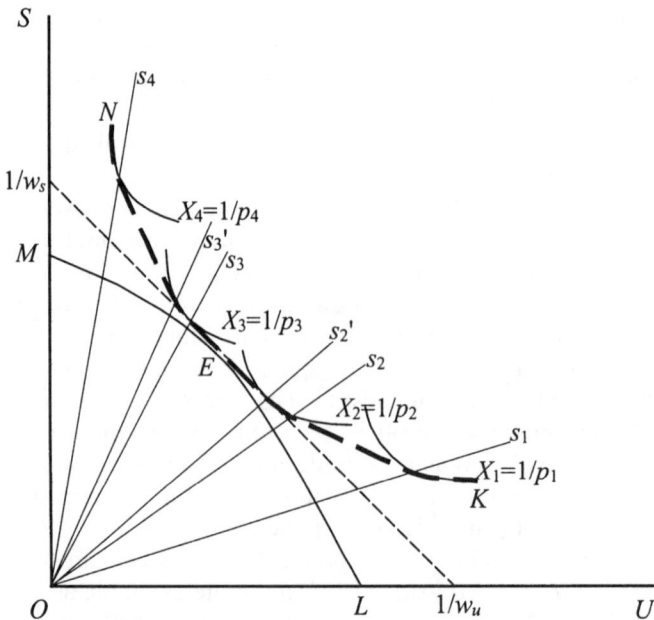

Figure 8

segments is the isoquant for producing a dollar, if that is the *numéraire*, by producing whatever combination of one or more goods can do this most efficiently.

For convenience, I take this *numéraire* to be the value of the small country's output under free trade without distortions, so that the endowment possibility curve, *MEL*, just touches this convex hull. Thus, as before, in the absence of policy the country's endowment is at *E*, which in this case means that it produces goods 2 and 3, importing goods 1 and 4. Wages are given by the straight segment of the hull within the middle diversification cone.

The big difference that this makes for an H–O economy is by now well known. Factor prices now vary with factor endowments as we pass into and out of the several cones. In addition, a change in the price of an import leaves relative factor prices unchanged if that import is not produced domestically, and it matters for real wages only through the price index of goods consumed. This and other behavior of a multi-cone model has been the subject of several recent papers, such as Davis (1996) and Deardorff (1998b).

The first implication of this for the analysis here is that any of the policies that redistribute income by changing factor prices and therefore endowments may, if they are strong enough, move the country outside its initial diversification cone and perhaps into another. This means that patterns of specialization will change and, more importantly, that factor prices paid by producers will also change, rather than being fixed by FPE. Thus a subsidy to unskilled labor will not, after all, accrue entirely to workers, but will instead also cause the unskilled wage paid by firms to fall somewhat after the country exits from its initial cone. For example, if the subsidy reduces the ratio of skilled to unskilled labor to, say, s_2 in Figure 8, then the relative wage received by unskilled workers rises to the slope of *MEL* where it crosses the Os_2 ray, while the relative wage paid by firms falls to the slope of *NEK* along the same ray. Thus a larger subsidy is needed to reach this point than if we were still in the same cone.

It remains true that any distorting policy for redistribution—one that does alter the relative wages received by workers and thus changes the choices of some of them to become skilled—will lower national income below what it could have been. This can be seen in Figure 8 from the fact that the endowment possibility curve, *MEL*, is below the aggregate unit-value isoquant *NEK* at every point but *E*, just as *E'* was below the straight line through *E* in Figure 4. The possibility of specialization and additional cones only increases this effect by increasing the amount of factors needed to attain the same level of income at different factor ratios compared with the case with FPE.

A second implication of specialization and multiple cones is that shocks involving goods that are not produced do not change factor prices. In particular, a fall in the world price of an unskilled-labor-intensive good that is not produced in the country will not change relative wages at all. It will matter only for real wages, by increasing both, as all workers can afford more of the good. By the same token, a tariff on imports of such a good will not help to improve the income distribution unless it is large enough to cause it to be produced. Up to that point, it only lowers real wages and real incomes through its consumption effects. That is, in Figure 8 a change in the price of good 1 changes the shape of the aggregate unit-value isoquant, but not within the middle cone where the country is operating. In general, then, it does no good for the domestic income distribution to have a tariff on the imports of a good that is not produced at home, and it only does harm overall. This too is true regardless of whether any worsening of the income distribution has been due to trade or technology.

Others have noted, in the context of this discussion, that shocks to world prices cannot change domestic relative wages if they occur outside the country's diversification cone. Some have suggested that therefore a cure for the adverse effects of falling world prices of unskilled-labor-intensive goods would be to move the country out of the cone where they are produced. The model here confirms the importance of which cone you are in, but it also draws attention to the further implications of attempts to move across cones. Suppose for example that the relative unskilled wage has previously fallen for the country in Figure 8, for any of the reasons I have discussed that could have shifted the unit-value isoquant of good 2 outward. And suppose that the country now wants to do something about this. To what extent is moving to the higher cone, $s'_3 Os_4$, an option? Presumably, it could do this by somehow acquiring more skilled labor, perhaps by subsidizing its wage to induce workers to become skilled. But doing this would make the income distribution worse, not better.

A subsidy to the skilled wage will accrue entirely to skilled workers as long as the economy remains inside the same diversification cone, and it will be shared between workers and firms if the supplies of factors move the economy outside the cone. Thus, in Figure 8, a large enough subsidy to skilled labor could move the factor supplies to, say, ratio s'_3. At that point, while the relative wage received by unskilled labor would fall to the slope of MEL where it crosses s'_3, the skilled wage paid by firms would fall, so that the relative unskilled wage paid by firms rises to the slope of NEK where it crosses s'_3. The income distribution, which depends on the first of these, not the second, worsens.

6. Changing the Supply of Skilled Labor

Until this last result, I did not mention changing the supplies of skilled and unskilled labor as a means to altering the income distribution. The reason was that, in the standard one-cone, small-open-economy model with FPE, factor supplies do not matter for factor prices.[10]

Thus, for example in Figure 4, suppose that we were somehow to override the choices of workers to become skilled and force more of them to do so, moving the endowment point northwest of E instead of southeast. With FPE, factor prices will remain unchanged, and we will simply get a larger group of skilled workers and a smaller group of unskilled workers. This may sound good, but in fact the additional skilled workers are worse off than before, since their higher skilled wage is not high enough to compensate them for the time spent acquiring skill. Thus this group of workers is worse off, while all others are unchanged. The loss to these workers is reflected also in the fall of national income that is observed when the endowment point, northwest of E on MEL, lies inside the factor price line tangent to MEL at E. Thus there was no point in talking about changing factor supplies as long as we were constrained by FPE.

With allowance for specialization and more cones, however, factor prices can change. I have already shown that, in spite of this, changing factor supplies by taxing and subsidizing their employment will not help. But suppose instead that we interfere with the process of skill acquisition itself, leaving the workers free to earn whatever wage the market generates. Then we may be able truly to make a difference for good.

Suppose, then, that we subsidize workers during the time that they acquire skill, replacing a part of their lost wages. The subsidy must be financed somehow, and I will assume this can be done by taxing either the time or the income of all workers. With their lost wages from skill acquisition reduced, all workers will have their potential skilled wage increased by the amount of the subsidy (recall that it was previously defined net of the time cost of skill acquisition). Therefore, for initially given wages, the curve *AEB* in the lower panel of Figure 1 is shifted up, and it is no longer simply equal to the absolute slope of *MEL* in the upper panel. In addition, both curves in the lower panel must be shifted down by the amount of any tax used to finance the subsidy.

The effect of the subsidy, of course, is to encourage more workers to become skilled, and the endowment point moves northwest of *E* as discussed above. If we remain inside the cone, then FPE insulates the curves from any further change, and the effect is, again, a worsening of the income distribution. Those workers who remain unskilled more than pay for the gain to those who become skilled.

However, if we move outside the cone or to a different cone, then factor prices paid by firms do change and the workers get them. The relative wage paid to unskilled labor rises with the slope of the hull *NEK* in Figure 8 in response to the greater scarcity of unskilled workers. This causes the wage curves in the lower panels of earlier figures to shift endogenously, making finding the new equilibrium somewhat awkward. The unskilled wage curve shifts up, while the skilled wage curve shifts down, moving their intersection yet again. In the end, we cannot know for sure whether the income distribution has improved or worsened. But the possibility of a real improvement seems to be clear, if we can move far enough outside the initial cone and if diminishing returns to both skill acquisition and skilled labor employment are not too severe.

This then seems to be the best hope for improving the distribution of income in this model: subsidy to skill acquisition (if one can believe such a result coming from a likely beneficiary of such subsidies in the real world). Note once again that this policy is appropriate regardless of whether the initially worsened income distribution was due to trade or to technology. The source of the worsening does not matter.

7. Conclusion

What really matters, of course, is not what matters, but only what should be done. The fact is that we have seen increasing inequality in the United States and elsewhere over the last two decades, and we must decide what, if anything, to do about that. That increasing inequality has in turn been due, in part, to the growing wage differential, and we must also decide what if anything to do about that. The literature on trade and wages has seemed to imply that the answers to these questions would be at least a little easier if we could only sort out the causes of these events. I disagree. If we have a problem with the income distribution, it is the same problem, whether or not its cause was trade or its cause was technology. And the solution will also be the same, if we can only figure out what it is.

It is time we turn to the harder questions of whether in fact a policy remedy is needed; if so, which of many available policies will handle the problem best; and then how far to go with it. These are important and difficult questions to which I do not have the answers. But I am convinced that the answers, when we find them, will not depend on the relative contributions of trade and technology as causes of these problems. And incidentally, for these problems like most others, trade restrictions are almost certainly *not* the best answers.

References

Davis, Donald R., "Trade Liberalization and Income Distribution," NBER working chapter 5693 (1996).

Deardorff, Alan V., "International Externalities in the Use of Domestic Policies to Redistribute Income," Research Seminar in International Economics, University of Michigan, discussion chapter 405 (1997).
———, "Technology, Trade, and Increasing Inequality: Does the Cause Matter for the Cure?" *Journal of International Economic Law* 1 (1998a):353–76.
———, "Fragmentation across Cones," Research Seminar in International Economics, University of Michigan, discussion chapter 427 (1998b).
———, "Factor Prices and the Factor Content of Trade Revisited: What's the Use?" *Journal of International Economics* 50 (2000):73–90.
Krugman, Paul R., "Technology, Trade, and Factor Prices," *Journal of International Economics* 50 (2000):51–71.
Leamer, Edward E., "Effort, Wages and the International Division of Labor," NBER working chapter 5803 (1996).
———, "What's the Use of Factor Contents?" *Journal of International Economics* 50 (2000):17–49.
Leamer, Edward E. and James Levinsohn, "International Trade Theory: The Evidence," in Grossman and Rogoff (eds.), *Handbook of International Economics*, Vol. III, Amsterdam: North-Holland (1995).

Notes

1. See Leamer (2000) and the responses by Deardorff (2000) and Krugman (2000).
2. This section draws heavily on Deardorff (1997).
3. It seems customary these days to let the economic actors in our models be female. I am not entirely comfortable with that custom, especially, as here, in models where the workers are actually sexless and far less interesting than the female pronoun would connote in real life. But I made these workers male in Deardorff (1997), so in fairness, I hope, I make them female here.
4. It does not matter how long this process of skill acquisition takes, since a longer time would merely mean that S_i is concentrated over a shorter period.
5. Not a realistic assumption, of course, but probably of second-order importance compared with the wages themselves.
6. I am really thinking here simply of real incomes—nominal wages net of any taxes or subsidies, deflated by a price index that is common to all individuals owing to the assumption of identical tastes. I call them utilities only because a utility possibility frontier, UPF, is more familiar and comfortable terminology than real-income possibility frontier.
7. If not, then a subsidy to trade will be needed here.
8. If the change is Hicks-neutral the shift will be exactly as shown in Figure 6. If it is factor-biased in the Hicks sense, then the shift will be further northwest or southeast, but this will not matter.
9. Again, the story is not much different if the change is, say, "skill-biased," as some empirical evidence seems to suggest. The isoquant will shift inward but also drift to the northwest due to the technical change, then shift back outward radially with the subsequent price change. Aside from the (unlikely?) possibility that the latter shift could be larger than the former, the analysis is unchanged.
10. This *is* the FPE theorem, or as Leamer and Levinsohn (1995) call it more relevantly, the factor-price insensitivity theorem.

9
Technical Progress, Price Adjustments, and Wages

Ronald W. Jones

A standard result in the theory of international trade is that in a Heckscher–Ohlin 2×2 model, if a country faces fixed commodity prices and experiences technical progress, the impact on factor prices depends only upon which sector experiences the greater (Hicksian) degree of cost reduction. If this should be the labor-intensive sector, the real wage will unambiguously rise. This is a corollary of the Stolper–Samuelson result on the effect of price changes on factor prices—the connection arising from the analogy of technical progress to a commodity subsidy or price rise for producers. Two principal caveats are required, however. The first is that such a result holds primarily for *small* changes in technology—for larger changes the *pattern* of production might change (or the country could become completely specialized), and this would alter the results (Jones, 1998; Findlay and Jones, 2000). The second caveat is that, if commodity prices adjust to the changed market conditions represented by technical progress, these price adjustments have a further effect on factor prices, leaving the net result on income distribution in doubt and opening up room for the *bias* in technical change to affect factor returns because such bias obviously affects relative outputs. Recent work in this area (Krugman, 2000; Davis, 1998; Xu, 2000) has done much to resolve this second issue, albeit often with restrictions on technology or tastes, or with technical progress captured in the use of augmenting coefficients to the inputs of the production function. In the present note, I explicate the role of induced commodity price changes by using the analysis of technical progress on factor prices presented in Jones (1965), which relies on the Hicksian decomposition of technical change and factor bias in technology.

If the kind of technical progress being examined were spread equally to all countries, it would be necessary to solve for changes in the relative commodity prices that clear global markets. But if tastes and technical conditions in the rest of the world are sufficiently well-behaved (i.e., homothetic and constant returns) and identical to those of the home country, the connection between progress and price changes might as well be analyzed in the context of a closed economy. This is the procedure I shall follow.

First consider the relationship between factor prices, commodity prices, and the sectoral distribution of technical progress that follows directly from the competitive profit conditions in a Heckscher–Ohlin 2×2 setting. Let X and Y denote the two outputs, with X being the labor-intensive sector. To align the discussion with the current concerns with income distribution in the literature, think of "labor" (L) as unskilled labor, and the other factor, which I shall call capital (K), as "skilled labor," possessing human capital. Technology is expressed in the set of input/output coefficients, a_{ij}. Letting w and r indicate the returns to unskilled and skilled labor (or capital) respectively, the competitive profit conditions are given by

$$a_{LX}w + a_{KX}r = p_X,$$
$$a_{LY}w + a_{KY}r = p_Y. \tag{1}$$

Letting a circumflex over a variable indicate a relative change (e.g., $\hat{x} \equiv dx/x$), differentiation of these competitive profit conditions yields the standard result that the distributive share (θ_{ij}) weighted average of factor price changes equals the relative change in the commodity price less the distributive share weighted average of the input/output coefficients. The latter would vanish if there were no technical progress, because techniques are selected by firms in order to minimize unit costs.

The Hicksian measure of the degree of cost saving in an industry at given factor prices would be captured by the distributed-share weighted average of the reduction in input/output coefficients because of technical progress. In general, decompose the change in any input/output coefficient as in (2):

$$\hat{a}_{ij} = \hat{c}_{ij} - \hat{b}_{ij}. \tag{2}$$

The first term on the right-hand side represents movements along a given unit isoquant, triggered by changes in factor prices. Indeed, in the X-industry such changes would be shown by[1]

$$\hat{c}_{LX} = -\theta_{KX}\sigma_X(\hat{w} - \hat{r}),$$
$$\hat{c}_{KX} = \theta_{LX}\sigma_X(\hat{w} - \hat{r}). \tag{3}$$

The σ represent the elasticities of substitution in each of the two industries. The second term in (2) is positive if technical progress brings about a reduction in the input/output coefficient at the initial set of factor prices.

The terms reflecting technical progress can be aggregated for the two changes within an industry as well as for the two changes for a given factor between industries. For the sectoral changes, let

$$\pi_j \equiv \theta_{Lj}\hat{b}_{Lj} + \theta_{Kj}\hat{b}_{Kj}, \quad j = X, Y. \tag{4}$$

Each of these is the Hicksian measure of the relative reduction in that industry's costs that would be obtained at the initial factor prices. Using this measure seems appropriate if firms select techniques without considering the effect of their actions in changing wages and rents. An alternative aggregate measure sweeps together, say, the reductions in labor coefficients over the two industries, weighting them by the fraction of the total factor supply used in each sector; e.g., λ_{LX} for the fraction of the labor force used in the X-sector. Thus for labor:

$$\pi_L \equiv \lambda_{LX}\hat{b}_{LX} + \lambda_{LY}\hat{b}_{LY} \tag{5}$$

Such an aggregate denotes the relative saving in the economy in the use of labor at initial factor prices. The λ-weighted average of changes in input/output coefficients *along* a unit isoquant is also of relevance. Call these δ_L and δ_K. For example, for labor, after substituting from (3):

$$\lambda_{LX}\hat{c}_{LX} + \lambda_{LY}\hat{c}_{LY} \equiv -\delta_L(\hat{w} - \hat{r}), \quad \delta_L = \lambda_{LX}\theta_{KX}\sigma_X + \lambda_{LY}\theta_{KY}\sigma_Y. \tag{6}$$

Now differentiate the competitive profit conditions to obtain the sought-for relationships among factor prices changes, commodity price changes, and Hicksian measures of technical progress:

$$\theta_{LX}\hat{w} + \theta_{KX}\hat{r} = \hat{p}_X + \pi_X,$$
$$\theta_{LY}\hat{w} + \theta_{KY}\hat{r} = \hat{p}_Y + \pi_Y. \tag{7}$$

It is easier to focus on changes in the factor price ratio instead of individual changes in factor returns. Subtract the second equation in (7) from the first, and let $|\theta|$ denote the expression $(\theta_{LX} - \theta_{LY})$, which is also the determinant of the distributive-share coefficients in (7). This expression must be a positive fraction because I have assumed the X-sector to be labor-intensive. Thus:

$$(\hat{w} - \hat{r}) = \frac{1}{|\theta|} \{(\hat{p}_X - \hat{p}_Y) + (\pi_X - \pi_Y)\}. \tag{8}$$

I termed the expression $(\pi_X - \pi_Y)$ the *differential industry effect* in Jones (1965). Expression (8) confirms that *if* commodity prices are held constant, as would represent the situation for a small open economy in which technical progress was limited to that country, the differential industry effect *alone* would determine factor price changes.

The principal task remaining is to solve for the effect of such progress on commodity prices so that (8) can be used to net out the direct and indirect effects of such progress on factor prices. This requires solving for the changes in outputs and the required change in commodity prices. On the supply side, the full-employment conditions, in (9), show outputs being constrained by technology and endowments:

$$a_{LX}X + a_{LY}Y = L,$$
$$a_{KX}X + a_{KY}Y = K. \tag{9}$$

Differentiation, letting endowments change as well, yields

$$\lambda_{LX}\hat{X} + \lambda_{LY}\hat{Y} = \hat{L} + \pi_L + \delta_L(\hat{w} - \hat{r}),$$
$$\lambda_{KX}\hat{X} + \lambda_{KY}\hat{Y} = \hat{K} + \pi_K - \delta_K(\hat{w} - \hat{r}). \tag{10}$$

Subtracting the second equation from the first and letting $|\lambda|$ represent the determinant of factor-allocation fractions, which also equals $(\lambda_{LX} - \lambda_{KX})$, a positive fraction because X has been assumed to be produced by labor-intensive techniques, the solution for relative output changes is

$$(\hat{X} - \hat{Y}) = \frac{1}{|\lambda|}\{(\hat{L} - \hat{K}) + (\pi_L - \pi_K) + (\delta_L + \delta_K)(\hat{w} - \hat{r})\}. \tag{11}$$

This expression reveals that technical progress, in the form of the *differential factor effect*, $(\pi_L - \pi_K)$, works to change outputs precisely as would a change in factor endowments. Having made this point, I now assume that endowments do not change. Furthermore, use equation (8) to substitute for the factor price change in (11) to obtain equation (12), where the symbol σ_s has been introduced to represent the *elasticity of relative supply* of X along the transformation schedule. Thus:

$$(\hat{X} - \hat{Y}) = \frac{1}{|\lambda|}(\pi_L - \pi_K) + \sigma_S\{(\hat{p}_X - \hat{p}_Y) + (\pi_X - \pi_Y)\},$$
$$\sigma_S \equiv \frac{(\delta_L + \delta_K)}{|\lambda||\theta|}. \tag{12}$$

On the demand side, I assume tastes are homothetic so that the ratio of commodities demanded, D_X/D_Y, depends only upon the commodity price ratio. Taking relative changes:

$$(\hat{D}_X - \hat{D}_Y) = -\sigma_D(\hat{p}_X - \hat{p}_Y), \tag{13}$$

where σ_D is defined as the *elasticity of substitution in relative demand*. Bringing these changes together requires prices to adjust so that:

$$(\hat{p}_X - \hat{p}_Y) = -\frac{|\theta|}{\sigma}\{(\pi_L - \pi_K) + |\lambda|\sigma_S(\pi_X - \pi_Y)\},$$

$$\sigma \equiv |\lambda||\theta|(\sigma_S + \sigma_D). \tag{14}$$

The term, σ, as defined in Jones (1965), represents the economy's aggregate elasticity of substitution. Its inverse tells how much a 1% increase in the relative supply of labor in this closed economy would reduce the wage/rental ratio, taking into account not only the changes in techniques in each industry, but also the substitution by consumers towards labor-intensive commodity X as it becomes cheaper. Indeed, this aggregate elasticity is a positive weighted average of the three sources of substitution in this model:

$$\sigma = A_X\sigma_X + A_Y\sigma_Y + |\lambda||\theta|\sigma_D,$$

$$A_X \equiv \theta_{LX}\lambda_{KX} + \theta_{KX}\lambda_{LX},$$

$$A_Y \equiv \theta_{LY}\lambda_{KY} + \theta_{KY}\lambda_{LY},$$

$$A_X + A_Y + |\lambda||\theta| \equiv 1. \tag{15}$$

Finally, substitute expression (14) into equation (8) for the factor price change:

$$(\hat{w} - \hat{r}) = -\frac{1}{\sigma}\{(\pi_L - \pi_K) - |\lambda|\sigma_D(\pi_X - \pi_Y)\}. \tag{16}$$

The effects of technical progress on the commodity price ratio and on the factor price ratio are captured in equations (14) and (16). I assume that technical progress favors the X-sector, in the sense that $(\pi_X - \pi_Y)$ is positive. Clearly this differential industry effect *by itself* serves to lower the relative commodity price of labor-intensive X, but not by as much as $(\pi_X - \pi_Y)$, so that the relative (and real) wage rate rises. What is left out of account is the simultaneous influence of the differential factor effect. If this is also positive, so that the aggregate measure of labor input reductions exceeds that of capital input reductions, the relative drop in the price of labor-intensive X is enhanced, which serves to dampen, and perhaps reverse, the favorable effect on wages.

The rationale behind this result can be conveyed by means of Figure 1. The original relative demand and supply curves are drawn to illustrate an equilibrium at point A, with the relative price of X (compared with Y) shown by p_0. The supply curve marked $(X/Y)'$ shows the changes in quantities produced if the differential industry effect were the only factor affecting supplies. The supply curve shifts down by the relative amount, $(\pi_X - \pi_Y)$, since by (8) at that price (denoted p') relative factor prices would be unaltered and (ignoring the differential factor effect) the relative quantity of X/Y supplied would be the same (at B) as originally (at A). It is clear from Figure 1 that if the differential factor effect could be ignored, the relative wage rate must rise because the commodity price adjustment (from A to E) would be outweighed by the differential industry effect of technical progress. Alternatively phrased, at p', the price ratio at which there is *no* change in factor prices, there is excess demand for commodity X

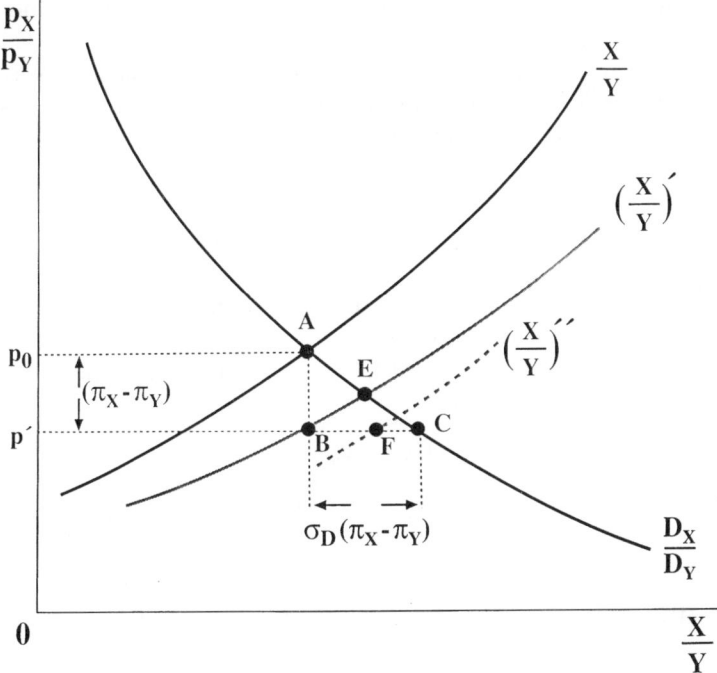

Figure 1

(relative to Y), measured by BC. Therefore in equilibrium X's relative price would be higher than p'.

The differential factor effect cannot be ignored, however. If technical progress is, in the aggregate, labor-saving (as I will now assume), from point B the relative supply curve shifts to the right, by the amount $\{1/|\lambda|\}(\pi_L - \pi_K)$, as confirmed in equation (11). The crucial question is whether this rightward shift at the price p' results in a *net* excess relative demand or supply for labor-intensive X. If the increase in demand at the lower price, shown by BC, exceeds the relative increase in the ratio of quantities supplied, X's relative price cannot fall as much as p', which would mean that relative wages will rise. Crucial distance BC shows how much the relative demand for X increases as a consequence of a price fall from p_0 to p', and this amount is related to the substitution elasticity of demand, σ_D. Indeed, at p' excess demand for labor-intensive commodity X appears if and only if:

$$\sigma_D(\pi_X - \pi_Y) > \frac{1}{|\lambda|}(\pi_L - \pi_K). \tag{17}$$

This condition is satisfied for the supply curve, $(X/Y)''$ in Figure 1. This criterion is what is displayed in the explicit solution for factor price changes in equation (16).

Note the role *not* played by the elasticity of relative supply, σ_S. High underlying values for the separate elasticities of substitution in production would serve to enhance the aggregate elasticity of substitution, σ, and thus to dampen price changes, but σ_S does not affect the criterion for a rise or fall in relative wages.

Both the differential industry effect and differential factor effect depend on the constellation of the $\hat{b}_{ij}$, and are therefore related. The expression $(\pi_L - \pi_K)$ will tend to be positive if, in each industry, the labor input coefficient is reduced relatively more than the capital input coefficient. To be more precise, define the degree of Hicksian labor-saving bias in each sector by the β in (18):

$$\beta_j \equiv \hat{b}_{Lj} - \hat{b}_{Kj}, \quad j = X, Y. \tag{18}$$

The case of Hicksian neutrality is one in which the appropriate β_j is zero. Note that even if each industry's technical progress were to be characterized by Hicksian neutrality, the differential factor effect would not vanish if the extent of technical progress in the labor-intensive X-sector should exceed that in the Y-sector. With X receiving a heavier weight, so would the extent of labor-saving be greater than that of capital-saving. Indeed it can be shown that[2]

$$(\pi_L - \pi_K) = A_X \beta_X + A_Y \beta_Y + |\lambda|(\pi_X - \pi_Y). \tag{19}$$

Now substitute this expression for the differential factor effect into the criterion for the increase in relative wages shown by (17):

$$\text{Relative wages rise iff } (\sigma_D - 1)(\pi_X - \pi_Y) > \frac{A_X \beta_X + A_Y \beta_Y}{|\lambda|}. \tag{20}$$

Krugman (2000) has pointed out that in the Cobb–Douglas case for demand, with σ_D equal to unity, sectoral bias (as in the term $[\pi_X - \pi_Y]$) matters not at all in the question of the effect of technical progress on factor prices when commodity prices are endogenous. In this special case, only the factor bias in each industry matters. More generally, what criterion (20) reveals is that the more heavily biased towards saving labor in each industry is technical progress, the greater must the elasticity of demand be in order to ensure that relative wages nonetheless increase.

The consequences of technical progress on commodity and factor prices become easier to analyze once it is recognized that such progress has a two-pronged effect on markets. It acts like a relative subsidy to production for the industry experiencing a greater Hicksian measure of progress. But it also acts like a relative endowment increase for the factor which, in the aggregate, has experienced the greater reduction in need. This latter measure encompasses not only the extent of factor bias in each sector, but also the difference in factor intensities of the two industries.

References

Davis, Donald R., "Technology, Unemployment, and Relative Wages in a Global Economy," *European Economic Review* 42 (1998):1613–33.

Findlay, Ronald and Ronald W. Jones, "Factor Bias and Technical Progress," forthcoming, *Economics Letters* (2000).

Jones, Ronald W., "The Structure of Simple General Equilibrium Models," *Journal of Political Economy* 73, December (1965):557–72.

———, "Trade and Wages: Comment," in S. Collins (ed.), *Imports, Exports and the American Worker*, Washington, DC: Brookings Institute (1998):83–94.

Krugman, Paul, "Technology, Trade and Factor Prices," (forthcoming), *Journal of International Economics* (2000).

Xu, Bin, "Factor Bias, Sector Bias, and the Effects of Technical Progress on Relative Factor Prices," forthcoming, *Journal of International Economics* (2000).

Notes

1. Following the treatment in Jones (1965), the solutions are obtained from the pair of equations stating that the θ-weighted average of changes in input/output coefficients vanishes, on the one hand, and the definition of the elasticity of substitution in production, on the other.

2. If the coefficient of the last term in (19) is written as $\lambda\theta$, with the differential industry effect divided by θ, the sum of the weights would add to unity. See equation (15).

10
The Effect of International Trade on Labor-Demand Elasticities: Intersectoral Matters

Sébastien Jean

1. Introduction

The impact of international trade on the labor market is not only a problem of absolute levels: it is also worth evaluating the modifications induced in the functioning of the labor market. In particular, as argued by Rodrik (1997), the strengthening of competition in goods markets may increase the sensitivity of factor demands.

A first illustration is provided by the factor proportions theory, which concludes that the price-elasticity of labor demand turns out to be infinite for a non-specialized, small economy in a situation of free trade. Through the weakening of mark-ups, new trade theories also show that this elasticity might rise. However, the result of the traditional approach appears somewhat caricatured, while the main available assessment of the impact linked to the lowering of mark-ups (Slaughter, 1997) provides "mixed support, at best," as the effects highlighted are not robust.

The analysis developed here is intermediate, and focuses on the intersectoral factor reallocations induced by an exogenous change in the cost of a production factor. The intuition is that an increase in the cost of a production factor has an effect on the sectoral trade specialization of an economy, at the expense of production using this factor most intensively, and that this effect is more important, the more open the economy is.

This mechanism is illustrated with a model of perfect competition, using the Armington hypothesis. Starting from an initial competitive equilibrium, I study analytically how the employment cost of imposing an exogenous rise in the real wage of unskilled labor (above its competitive level) depends on trade openness. An empirical assessment is then presented for France.

2. International Trade and Labor-Demand Elasticity in the Main Theories

Lessons from the Neoclassical Theory of International Trade

In the H–O–S neoclassical framework, the price-elasticity of labor demand is infinite for a nonspecialized small economy in a context of free trade: the FPE theorem stipulates that real and relative factor rewards are determined by international goods prices. This extreme result does not apply to a large country, because its influence on international terms of trade reduces the price sensitivity of its labor demand. However, this sensitivity remains higher than under autarky. Davis (1996) illustrates this by studying the case of free trade between two economies identical in their consumer preferences, their production functions, and their endowments in skilled and unskilled labor. One (assimilated to the US) is supposed to have a perfectly competitive labor market, while the other (Europe) sets a minimum wage for unskilled labor, superior the full-employment equilibrium level. Davis shows that under these conditions,[1] the unemployment caused by the minimum-wage constraint doubles under free trade, with respect to autarky. If, in addition, the opening to trade with low-wage countries reduces the demand for unskilled labor, Davis shows that the minimum-wage economy has to bear the whole of the adjustment, at least as long as it is not completely specialized in the production of skill-intensive goods. More generally, the same conclusion would apply to any exogenous shock involving a lowering of unskilled labor demand. For the minimum-wage economy, openness then magnifies the consequences of the shock, with respect to autarky.

Through the constraint introduced over relative good prices, trade openness is thus likely, in the traditional trade theory, to modify the price elasticity of labor demand. However, this analysis remains somewhat schematic. In particular, the notion of an infinite elasticity of labor demand under free trade seems unrealistic. As a matter of fact, recent studies have focused more on the analysis through new trade theories.

Lessons from the New Trade Theories

So far, I have been reasoning in terms of the price elasticity of aggregate labor demand, for the whole economy. Instead, the analysis through new trade theories focuses on the price elasticity of an individual firm's labor demand. Such an elasticity can be decomposed into two components.[2] The first, always negative, corresponds to the pure *substitution effect*. The second is the *scale effect*. It reflects the fact that a wage increase raises the firm's production cost, hence a negative effect on its output, which implies a lowering in labor demand, except under exceptional configurations of labor demand.[3] Generally speaking, the scale effect reinforces the substitution effect.

From this decomposition, Slaughter (1997) highlights two influences of international trade on labor-demand elasticities. The first one concerns the substitution effect: if the production process of a firm is decomposed vertically into various stages with different factor intensities, then this firm has the possibility, consecutively to increased wages, to relocate production or to use foreign outsourcing for the most labor-intensive production stages. This widening of substitution possibilities is likely to increase the elasticity of substitution between labor and other production factors.

The second influence of international trade put forward by Slaughter concerns the scale effect. This effect is higher when the firm's output level is more price-sensitive, and this sensitivity depends negatively on firms' mark-ups. Now, different international trade models predict that trade openness lowers mark-ups. By increasing the elasticity of goods demand addressed to each firm, trade thus increases the price elasticity of their labor demand.

Empirical estimates of these effects would require working on firms' individual data. Given the lack of satisfactory individual data for this type of estimate, Slaughter works on the basis of industries defined at a detailed level of classification (4-digit SIC), which he assimilates to firms, before grouping them into "aggregated industries." His estimates provide only little support to the hypotheses formulated: for production workers as well as for nonproduction workers, several trade variables have a significant explanatory power, with the expected sign, when only industry dummies are considered, but their significance disappears when time dummies are introduced. The variations in labor-demand elasticities are therefore mainly explained by a temporal trend. Interestingly, this trend is upward, in absolute terms, for production workers, whereas it is downward for nonproduction workers.

A similar methodology has been applied by Faini et al. (1998) for Italy, with elasticities estimated on the period 1985–95, distinguishing 14 manufacturing industries. It is difficult to conclude from these 14 points, but a weak correlation appears between the degree of openness to trade and the labor demand elasticity.[4] Greenaway et al. (1999) introduce, in their dynamic equation of labor demand, a term corresponding to interactions between the wage rate and import or export intensities. They also find a weak, positive impact of import and export volumes on the labor-demand elasticity in manufacturing industries, but this impact is not significant.[5]

In sum, this second approach is more realistic than the neoclassical one, but it has so far received weak empirical support. Moreover, it deals with *firms'* individual labor-demand elasticities. It is therefore concerned with firms' reactions to firm-specific shocks. From an economic policy standpoint,[6] however, the central problem is not to understand firms' individual reactions but rather to understand the behavior of the aggregate labor demand.

An Intermediate Approach: Aggregate Scale Effect and Sectoral Specialization, in a Context of Finite Elasticities

In spite of the fact that the aggregate labor demand is the sum of individual labor demands, the price-elasticities of these demands are not necessarily linked in a simple way, as emphasized by Slaughter (1997, p. 8). In the neoclassical model, for example, trade openness radically modifies the aggregate labor-demand elasticity, without modifying firms' individual labor-demand elasticity which, in the context of perfect competition, was already infinite in autarky.

The aggregate labor-demand elasticity is therefore a subject on its own, which cannot be studied merely through the study of the individual labor demand function. Just as with individual labor-demand elasticities, this elasticity can be decomposed into two effects. The substitution effect corresponds to the consequences of within-firm factor substitutions, as a consequence of a shift in relative factor costs: it is a weighted sum of firms' individual substitution effects.

In contrast, the scale effect (i.e., the effect resulting from the variation in outputs) corresponds to mechanisms different from those described at the individual level. On the one hand, the problem is no longer to describe the reactions of firms with respect to each other, but rather to analyse the global evolution of national output. On the other hand, the output level is no more a unidimensional variable when considered at the aggregate level. Intersectoral differences in output variations can modify relative factor demand, especially when these differences are linked to initial factor intensities. And there are good reasons for this to be the case: a shift in production factors' relative costs modifies trade specialization determinants.

Assume, for example, that the cost of unskilled labor is increased exogenously. The *ex-ante* effect is to increase goods prices, in a higher proportion for the most unskilled-intensive good (as a consequence of the Shepard lemma). This will depress the domestic demand, but it will also reduce the competitiveness of domestic producers, and this loss of competitiveness will thus be higher for the most unskilled-intensive industries. As a consequence, domestic producers will suffer losses in market shares, which will be higher, the more unskilled-intensive the industry is (except if the elasticity of substitution between domestic and foreign goods is systematically higher for skilled-intensive goods, which does not seem to be the case in practice). Moreover, these losses in market shares will be higher, the more exposed domestic production is to foreign competition.

Such a shock also induces general equilibrium effects, through the constraint on the total employment of the other factor (say, skilled labor), through the evolution of national income, or through the trade balance constraint. However, these effects do not present, *a priori*, the same kind of systematic bias with regards to factor intensity. Thus, the global effect of an exogenous increase in the cost of unskilled labor is likely to be a change in the trade specialization of the economy, at the expense of the most unskilled-intensive industries.

This would mean that trade openness increases the elasticity of unskilled-labor demand, by reinforcing the scale effect following an increase in the cost of unskilled labor. However, different complex mechanisms are at stake, and the economy undergoes various constraints. A more detailed analysis is thus necessary, and the next section aims at illustrating the argument put forward above, through a simple model. In order to avoid the crude aspect of the results obtained with the pure neoclassical theory, however, we will work with finite elasticities of substitution between domestic goods and foreign goods.

3. Trade Openness and the Aggregate Scale Effect: A Simple Model

This section uses a simple model describing a small economy, producing N goods with two factors, say skilled labor (S) and unskilled labor (U). There is perfect competition between domestic producers, and trade flows are represented using the Armington hypothesis. As I want to focus on the scale effect, it is assumed, for the sake of simplicity, that the production factors are perfectly complementary, thus implying that the substitution effect is equal to zero.

I first present the model and describe rapidly the static equilibrium obtained when wages are perfectly flexible. I then determine analytically what the consequences are, for unskilled labor, of imposing on it a real wage superior to the competitive level.

The Setup

The demand side is modeled through a representative consumer, which maximizes a two-tier utility function:

$$U = \prod_{k=1,\ldots,N} \left[\left(\delta_k X_{D,k,D}^{(\sigma-1)/\sigma} + (1-\delta_k) X_{F,k,D}^{(\sigma-1)/\sigma} \right)^{\sigma/(\sigma-1)} \right]^{\gamma_k}, \qquad (1)$$

where index k refers to industry, $X_{D,k,D}$ (resp. $X_{F,k,D}$) is the quantity of good k produced domestically (resp. abroad) and sold in the domestic market,[7] δ_k and γ_k are share coefficients (with $\Sigma \gamma_k = 1$), and σ is the elasticity of substitution between domestic and foreign goods.

This utility function is a nesting of a Cobb–Douglas function, describing the choice of consumption between indusries (γ_k is the share of industry k in the consumption in value), and of a CES function for the tradeoff between domestic and foreign products. The latter function corresponds to the Armington hypothesis (1969): goods produced in the home country are homogenous, but they are differentiated from foreign goods, with a constant elasticity of substitution $\sigma > 1$. This is a rough hypothesis, but it is a convenient way to account for the finite elasticities observed in trade flows, without the complexity inherent to the models with imperfect competition. For the sake of simplicity, we assume in addition that the elasticity of substitution is the same for all industries.

If R is the total income spent on consumption, then the resolution of the consumer's problem is summarized through the two following equations, for each industry:

$$p_{D,k}X_{D,k,D} + p_{F,k}X_{F,k,D} = \gamma_k R, \tag{2}$$

$$\ln\left(\frac{p_{D,k}X_{D,k,D}}{p_{F,k}X_{F,k,D}}\right) = \sigma \ln\frac{\delta_k}{1-\delta_k} + (1-\sigma)\ln\left(\frac{p_{D,k}}{p_{F,k}}\right). \tag{3}$$

The foreign demand for domestic goods is assumed to be

$$X_{D,k,F} = \mu_k\left(\frac{p_{D,k}}{p_{F,k}}\right)^{-\sigma}, \quad \forall k = 1, \ldots, N \tag{4}$$

where $X_{D,k,F}$ is the foreign demand for domestic goods in industry k, μ_k is a constant, and $p_{D,k}$ (resp. $p_{F,k}$) is the price of domestic (resp. foreign) goods in industry k, in domestic currency. The demand for exports has thus a constant price elasticity equal to σ. This is the case, in particular, if the elasticity of substitution between foreign goods and domestic goods is the same abroad as it is domestically, and if in addition the market share of domestic producers is assumed to be negligible in the foreign market.

On the supply side, production is represented through a Leontief function:

$$Q_k = \min\left(\frac{U_k}{a_{U,k}}, \frac{S_k}{a_{S,k}}\right), \quad \forall k = 1, \ldots, N \tag{5}$$

where Q_k is the domestic output in industry k, U_k (resp. S_k) is the input of unskilled labor (resp. skilled labor) used in industry k, $a_{U,k}$ and $a_{S,k}$ are technical coefficients. Production factors are thus perfectly complementary, and there are constant returns to scale. The average (and marginal) cost is equal to

$$C_k = a_{U,k}w_u + a_{S,k}w_s, \quad \forall k = 1, \ldots, N \tag{6}$$

where w_u (resp. w_s) is the wage rate for unskilled (resp. skilled) labor. As there is perfect competition between domestic producers, the price of domestic goods is equal to their cost ($p_{D,k} = C_k$).

The closing rules are the following. The economy is assumed to be small, so the price of foreign goods expressed in foreign currency ($p_{F,k}^*$) is exogenous. Trade is supposed to be balanced, so that consumption expenditure R is exactly equal to income:

$$\sum_{k=1}^{N} p_{D,k}X_{D,k,D} + p_{F,k}X_{F,k,D} = R = w_u U + w_s S, \tag{7}$$

where $U = \Sigma U_k$ and $S = \Sigma S_k$ are the total inputs of unskilled labor and skilled labor in the economy. The nominal exchange rate $e = p_{F,k}/p_{F,k}^*$ is therefore endogenous. Factor supplies ($\bar{U}$ and $\bar{S}$) are assumed to be exogenous. Finally, one of the prices in domestic currency has to be chosen as the *numéraire*.

Assuming in addition that both skilled and unskilled labor markets are perfectly competitive (and therefore that these factors are fully employed[8]), the setup described above enables the static equilibrium of the economy to be determined without difficulty: for given prices, the maximization of utility under income constraint sets the

The Employment Cost of a Wage Constraint for Unskilled Labor: Comparative Statics for Small Changes

Now that the model and its static equilibrium have been presented, I will address the following question: What is the employment cost of imposing a real wage for unskilled labor (which is assumed to be the scarce factor here, in the sense specified below) above its competitive level? Such a constraint could, for example, be the result of a minimum wage constraint, or of an increase in the cost of unskilled labor (because of labor standards, for example), in a context of the real rigidity of this wage. Whatever the reason, I will thus assume the real wage for unskilled labor to be set exogenously above its competitive level, while the wage for skilled labor remains perfectly flexible. A new equilibrium is then obtained, where skilled labor is still fully employed, but where unskilled employment has decreased.

While studying analytically the consequences of this constraint, I will assume the differences between the constrained wage and the competitive wage to be small, so that the changes studied are sufficiently small to make first-order approximations. More specifically, I will use log–linearized equations to analyze the changes between the previous competitive equilibrium and the new equilibrium obtained imposing exogenously the increase in the unskilled wage.

To begin with, for this comparative statics exercise, let us choose as the *numéraire* the GDP price index, based on an arithmetic average with the weights from the initial equilibrium:

$$\sum_{k=1}^{N} Q_k^0 p_{D,k} \equiv 1, \tag{8}$$

where Q_k^0 is industry k's output in the initial equilibrium. Instead of being one single price, the *numéraire* is thus a linear combination of various prices (with constant weights, of course); this has no influence on the evolution of variables in real terms. Now, for a small change from the initial equilibrium, this implies that (see the Appendix for details on calculations)

$$\sum_{k=1}^{N} \lambda_k \hat{p}_{D,k} = 0, \tag{9}$$

where the parameter $\lambda_k = Q_k^0 p_{D,k}^0 / (\Sigma Q_j^0 p_{D,j}^0)$ is the share of industry k in GDP, in the initial equilibrium. A hat above a variable refers to logarithmic changes. This also implies that the nominal change, $\hat{w}_u$, in the wage for unskilled labor is equal to the real change exogenously imposed (assuming that the deflator used is a Laspeyres index for GDP price).

Given (6), the price change for industry k is

$$\hat{p}_{D,k} = \alpha_k \hat{w}_u + (1 - \alpha_k) \hat{w}_s, \quad \forall k = 1, \ldots, N \tag{10}$$

where $\alpha_k = a_{U,k}w_u^0/p_{D,k}^0$ (the subscript 0 refers to the initial equilibrium) is the share of unskilled labor in the price of good k, in the initial equilibrium. If we note by $\alpha = \Sigma \lambda_k \, \alpha_k$ the weighted mean of α_k, which is equal to the share of unskilled labor in the initial GDP, then equation (9) implies that

$$\hat{w}_s = -\frac{\alpha}{1-\alpha}\hat{w}_u, \tag{11}$$

and (10) can be rewritten as

$$\hat{p}_{D,k} = \frac{\alpha_k - \alpha}{1-\alpha}\hat{w}_u, \quad \forall k = 1, \ldots, N. \tag{12}$$

On the other hand, the changes in import prices are only the consequence of the variations in the nominal exchange rate (given the hypothesis of small economy):

$$\hat{p}_{F,k} = \hat{e}, \quad \forall k = 1, \ldots, N. \tag{13}$$

The output of industry k is

$$Q_k = X_{D,k,D} + X_{D,k,F}. \tag{14}$$

Thus, if $x_k = X_{D,k,F}^0/Q_k^0$ is the export intensity of industry k in the initial equilibrium, the logarithmic variation of the industry's output can be written, as a first-order approximation:

$$\hat{Q}_k = (1 - x_k)\hat{X}_{D,k,D} + x_k\hat{X}_{D,k,F}. \tag{15}$$

The changes in exports are obtained directly from equation (4):

$$\hat{X}_{D,k,F} = -\sigma(\hat{p}_{D,k} - \hat{p}_{F,k}). \tag{16}$$

For the variation of the domestic output sold on the domestic market, note first that differentiating relations (1) and (2) yields

$$(1-m)(\hat{X}_{D,k,D} + \hat{p}_{D,k}) + m(\hat{X}_{F,k,D} + \hat{p}_{F,k}) = \hat{R}, \tag{17}$$

$$(\hat{X}_{D,k,D} + \hat{p}_{D,k}) - (\hat{X}_{F,k,D} + \hat{p}_{F,k}) = (1-\sigma)(\hat{p}_{D,k} - \hat{p}_{F,k}), \tag{18}$$

where $m_k = (p_{F,k}^0 X_{F,k,D}^0)/(p_{D,k}^0 X_{D,k,D}^0 + p_{F,k}^0 X_{F,k,D}^0)$ is the penetration rate of imports in industry k, in the initial equilibrium. Rearranging, these two equations give

$$\hat{X}_{D,k,D} = \hat{R} - \hat{p}_{D,k} + (1-\sigma)m(\hat{p}_{D,k} - \hat{p}_{F,k}). \tag{19}$$

Note, in particular, that this relation shows that the higher the penetration rate of imports in an industry, the more sensitive domestics sales on the domestic market are to the relative price of imports. In this sense, it reflects the market power that domestic producers taken as a whole have in the domestic market, owing to the imperfect substitutability between domestic and foreign goods. Now, relations (15), (16), and (19) enable the variation in the domestic output to be written as

$$\hat{Q}_k = (1 - x_k)\hat{R} + [(\sigma - 1)(m_k + x_k - m_k x_k) + x_k]\hat{p}_{F,k} \\ - [(\sigma - 1)(m_k + x_k - m_k x_k) + 1]\hat{p}_{D,k}. \tag{20}$$

Given the above expressions of price changes ((11) and (12)), this implies

$$\hat{Q}_k = (1-x_k)\hat{R} + [(\sigma-1)t_k + x_k]\hat{e} - [(\sigma-1)t_k + 1]\frac{\alpha_k - \alpha}{1-\alpha}\hat{w}_u, \qquad (21)$$

where I have noted, for the sake of simplicity, $t_k = m_k + x_k - m_k x_k = (1 - x_k)m_k + x_k$. The second expression of t_k shows that it refers to the average market share of foreign producers in the markets where domestic firms sell their products (assuming that the market share of domestic producers in foreign markets is negligible): this market share is 1 in the foreign market, where domestic producers sell x_k% of their output, and it is equal to m_k in the domestic market, where domestic producers sell $(1 - x_k)$% of their output. t_k can thus be interpreted as the degree of exposure of domestic production to foreign competition or, in the words of Orléan (1986), as the internationalization rate of the industry.

In order to express the endogenous variation of the exchange rate as a function of other variables, we have to take into account the fact that trade remains balanced. This implies that the logarithmic variation in the consumption expenditure ($\hat{R}$) is equal to the variation in the national income, that is the value of the national production:

$$\sum_{k=1}^{N} \lambda_k (\hat{p}_{D,k} + \hat{Q}_k) = \hat{R}. \qquad (22)$$

Using equations (9) and (21) and rearranging, we then obtain:

$$\hat{e} = \frac{x}{(\sigma-1)t + x}\hat{R} + \frac{\sigma-1}{(\sigma-1)t + x}\left(\sum_{k=1}^{N} \lambda_k t_k \frac{\alpha_k - \alpha}{1-\alpha}\right)\hat{w}_u. \qquad (23)$$

In this expression, $t = \Sigma_k[\lambda_k t_k]$ and $x = \Sigma_k[\lambda_k x_k]$ refer, respectively, to the average degree of exposure to foreign competition and to the average export intensity of the economy.[9]

On the other hand, the national income is also the sum of the wage bill of unskilled labor and skilled labor, as expressed in the right-hand side of equation (7). As a consequence (knowing that total skilled employment is constant):

$$\hat{R} = \alpha(\hat{U} + \hat{w}_u) + (1-\alpha)\hat{w}_s; \qquad (24)$$

or, given equation (11):

$$\hat{R} = \alpha\hat{U}. \qquad (25)$$

Sectoral output variation can now be expressed as a function of $\hat{U}$, $\hat{w}_u$, and of the characteristics of the initial equilibrium:

$$\hat{Q}_k = \left[1 - x_k + x\frac{(\sigma-1)t_k + x_k}{(\sigma-1)t + x}\right]\alpha\hat{U}$$

$$+ \left[(\sigma-1)\frac{(\sigma-1)t_k + x_k}{(\sigma-1)t + x}\left(\sum_{j=1}^{N}\lambda_j t_j \frac{\alpha_j - \alpha}{1-\alpha}\right) - [(\sigma-1)t_k + 1]\frac{\alpha_k - \alpha}{1-\alpha}\right]\hat{w}_u. \qquad (26)$$

Now, as the initial share of industry k in unskilled total employment is $\lambda_k \alpha_k$, the variation in unskilled employment is, as a first-order approximation (see the Appendix):

$$\hat{U} = \sum_{k=1}^{N} \frac{\lambda_k \alpha_k}{\alpha} \hat{Q}_k. \tag{27}$$

Replacing sectoral output variations $\hat{Q}_k$ by their expression obtained in (26) and rearranging, we are finally able to characterize the elasticity of unskilled employment with respect to an exogenous increase in the real wage for unskilled labor:

$$\frac{\hat{U}}{\hat{w}_u} = -\frac{1}{\alpha} \frac{\sum_{k=1}^{N} \lambda_k \alpha_k \frac{\alpha_k - \alpha}{1-\alpha} + t\psi}{1 - \alpha - t(\sigma-1)\varphi}, \tag{28}$$

where we have noted

$$\psi = (\sigma-1) \sum_{k=1}^{N} \lambda_k \frac{t_k}{t} \frac{(\alpha_k - \alpha)(\alpha_k - \tilde{\alpha})}{1-\alpha}$$

with $\tilde{\alpha} = \sum_{j=1}^{N} \lambda_j \alpha_j \frac{(\sigma-1)t_j + x_j}{(\sigma-1)t + x}$, and $\varphi = \sum_{k=1}^{N} \lambda_k \alpha_k \frac{x \frac{t_k}{t} - x_k}{(\sigma-1)t + x}$.

As α and $\tilde{\alpha}$ are two weighted averages of the α_k (a mixed measure of openness enters the weight in the second one, in addition to the share of the industry in GDP), ψ will be positive, except under very particular circumstances. As far as the sign of φ is concerned, it should be remembered that I assumed the country in question to be scarcely endowed with unskilled labor. It can then be assumed that the country has a comparative advantage in skill-intensive industries. This means that, on average, the more unskilled-intensive an industry, the less export-oriented it is. As soon as this is the case on average, φ is positive.

Note in addition that ψ and φ are both homogenous of degree zero in the variables of openness (t or x): they depend on the sectoral structure of the degrees of openness but, for a given intersectoral structure (i.e., for t_k/t and x_k/t fixed), they do not depend on t, the degree of exposure of domestic production to foreign competition.

Thus, equation (28) shows that $-\hat{U}/\hat{w}_u$ is an increasing function of t. This means that, for a developed country, the higher the degree of exposure of domestic production to foreign competition, the bigger the employment cost of a given constraint on the real wage for unskilled labor.

This conclusion illustrates the mechanisms mentioned before. An increase in the cost of unskilled labor increases the cost of unskilled-intensive goods compared with skill-intensive goods. For an open economy this implies losses of market shares in the unskilled-intensive industries, compared with skill-intensive industries. The sectoral specialization of the economy is thus modified, in a sense that is unfavorable to unskilled-intensive industries, and therefore unfavorable to unskilled-labor demand. Moreover, the more open the economy, the more important this mechanism is.

It is no surprise to observe that this effect is stronger, the higher the elasticity of substitution between domestic and foreign goods. What is perhaps more surprising is that the more pronounced the comparative advantage the economy has in skill-intensive industry, the stronger the effect of openness on unskilled labour demand elasticity (because in (28), φ will be higher). This is due to the fact that the more export-oriented an industry is, the less it will suffer from the negative impact on the national consumption observed here.

Empirical Assessment

What is the practical importance of this effect of international trade on the price elasticity of unskilled-labor demand? Equation (28) enables the described effects to be assessed, on the basis of real data. As the mechanisms described concern mainly the industrial sector, we will limit the analysis to this part of the economy. A reservation has first to be made: such an assessment depends on the sectoral classification chosen. The data used here come from the classification NAP 100 of French national accounts. The field of industry, excluding energy and quarrying, is disaggregated into 39 sectors. The definition for unskilled labor includes manual workers and employees, as opposed to intermediate and superior professions, which are supposed to be skilled.

For simplicity, intermediate consumption is not considered in the analysis. Implicitly, the production has so far been assumed to be totally integrated vertically. In order to fit this hypothesis more closely, it would be necessary to include direct *and* indirect national, unskilled-labor input, and to base the calculation on the share of its wage bill in production costs. A plainer calculation is made here, as a proxy; it takes into account only direct employment and is therefore based on its share in value-added.

Table 1 displays the results obtained for $\hat{U}/\hat{w}_u$, on the basis of equation (28), for the French industry in 1977, 1985, and 1993. As a basis of comparison, I also show the results obtained with this equation, without taking into account the terms related to trade. The result strongly depends on the choice made for the Armington elasticity, which in each case is assumed to be identical for all industries. With a fairly low

Table 1. Assessment of the Price Elasticity of Unskilled-Labor Demand Associated with the Scale Effect for French Industry in 1977, 1985, and 1993[a]

	1977	1985	1993
Scale effect without taking into account effects linked to foreign trade (elasticity)	−0.043	−0.062	−0.043
Total scale effect (elasticity) with an elasticity of substitution between domestic goods and foreign goods equal to:			
1.2:	−0.047	−0.071	−0.051
1.5:	−0.053	−0.081	−0.059
2:	−0.062	−0.098	−0.071
3:	−0.081	−0.132	−0.096
4:	−0.100	−0.165	−0.121
5:	−0.118	−0.199	−0.145
For information:			
Share of unskilled labor wage bill in value-added (%)	33.1	28.2	22.3
Average export intensity (%)	23.3	29.2	32.0
Average import penetration rate (%)	20.5	26.7	30.6
Average degree of exposure to foreign competition:			
weighted average of sectoral degrees (%)	38.0	46.3	50.1
direct calculation for the whole industry (%)	39.0	48.1	52.8

[a] The data presented concern all industries, excluding energy and quarrying.
Sources: French national accounts, INSEE; *Enquêtes sur la structure de l'emploi*, INSEE; *Déclarations Annuelles de Données Sociales* (DADS), INSEE-DARES. All data are based on the classification NAP 100 of the French national accounts.

elasticity of 1.2, the scale effect linked to trade is rather small. With an elasticity of 1.5, however, it already corresponds to 25–30% of the "autarkic" effect, and international trade accounts for more than half the total scale effect when the elasticity is assume to equal 4 or more.

These calculations can only give orders of magnitude. They are sufficient, however, to show that trade openness explains an important share of the scale effect linked to a variation in unskilled labor cost, for a country like France. In other words, the price elasticity of unskilled-labor demand is significantly higher than it would be under autarky.

4. Conclusion

The influence of international trade on labor-demand elasticities has so far been analyzed essentially through two approaches. According to the neoclassical theory of trade, this elasticity is infinite at the aggregate level, for a small economy under free trade. Recent studies, on the other hand, have focused on the effect induced by trade openness on the elasticity of individual firms' labor demand, through the lowering of their mark-ups.

The analysis proposed here is intermediate, and focuses on the intersectoral dimension of the scale effect linked to a variation in the cost of a production factor. The intuition is that an increase in the cost of a production factor has an effect on the sectoral trade specialization of an economy, at the expense of the production using this factor intensively. This effect is more important the more open the economy is, because the market share of domestic producers taken together is then more sensitive to their relative price, compared with imports. This is not linked to imperfect competition; it is rather the consequence of the imperfect substitutability between domestic and foreign goods, which enables domestic producers taken together to enjoy some kind of market power, with respect to foreign producers.

This mechanism is illustrated through a model of perfect competition, using the Armington hypothesis. Starting from an initial competitive equilibrium, I have shown that the employment cost of imposing an exogenous rise in the real wage of unskilled labor (above its competitive level) is increasing with trade openness. This result is proved to hold, except in very particular configurations, as soon as the economy has a comparative advantage in skill-intensive industries. The interest of the latter condition is linked to the fact that the more export-oriented an industry is, the less it will suffer from the negative impact on the national consumption observed here. The empirical assessment for France shows that trade openness can indeed have a significant effect on labor-demand elasticities through this mechanism. And this effect would be far higher for small rich countries, like Belgium or The Netherlands for example, that are far more open to international trade.

Appendix: Some Details of the Calculations

From Equation (8) to (9)

A simple differentiation of equation (8) gives

$$\sum_{k=1}^{N} Q_k^0 \Delta p_{D,k} = 0; \quad \text{i.e.} \quad \sum_{k=1}^{N} P_{D,k} Q_k^0 \frac{\Delta p_{D,k}}{p_{D,k}} = 0.$$

As we have assumed the changes to be small, we can make the following first-order approximations: $p_{D,k} \approx p_{D,k}^0$, and $\Delta p_{D,k}/p_{D,k} \approx \Delta \ln(p_{D,k}) = \hat{p}_{D,k}$. Thus:

$$\sum_{k=1}^{N}(p_{D,k}^0 Q_k^0)\hat{p}_{D,k} = 0.$$

Noting, $\lambda_k = p_{D,k}^0 Q_k^0/R^0$, this gives equation (9).

The approximation made corresponds to the hypothesis that the logarithmic change (i.e., approximatively the growth rate) of the sum is the weighted average of the logarithmic changes of the terms, with the weights equal to the ratio of the term to the sum, in the initial equilibrium. A similar approximation is made in other cases in the text: to obtain equation (10) from the differentiation of equation (6); to obtain equation (15) from the differentiation of equation (14); to obtain equation (17) from the differentiation of equation (2).

Equation (27)

The expression of $\hat{U}$ in (27) is obtained in a similar way. Note first that

$$U = \sum_{k=1}^{N} U_k = \sum_{k=1}^{N} a_{U,k} Q_k,$$

which gives by simple difference:

$$\Delta U = \sum_{k=1}^{N} a_{U,k} \Delta Q_k = \sum_{k=1}^{N} a_{U,k} Q_k \frac{\Delta Q_k}{Q_k}.$$

As we have assumed the changes to be small, we can make the following first-order approximations: $Q_k \approx Q_k^0$, and $\Delta Q_k/Q_k \approx \Delta \ln(Q_k) = \hat{Q}_k$. In addition, note that $a_{U,k} Q_k^0/U = \lambda_k \alpha_k/\alpha$. Using these three equations in the previous expression gives equation (27).

References

Cahuc, P. and Zylberberg, A., *Economie du Travail*, Bruxelles: De Boeck (1996).
Davis, D. R., "Does European Unemployment Prop Up American Wages?" NBER working chapter 5620 (1996).
Faini, R., Falzoni, A. M., Galeotti, M., Helg, R., and Turrini, A., "Importing Jobs and Exporting Firms? A Close Look at the Labour Market Implications of Italy's Trade and Foreign Direct Investment Flows", mimeo (1998).
Greenaway, D., Hine, R., and Wright, P., "An Empirical Assessment of the Impact of Trade on Employment in the United Kingdom," *European Journal of Political Economy* 15 (1999):485–500.
Hamermesh, D. S., *Labor Demand*, Princeton, NJ: Princeton University Press (1993).
Orléan, A., "L'insertion dans les Échanges Internationaux: Comparaison de Cinq Grands Pays Développés," *Economie et statistique* 184 (1986):25–40.
Rodrik, D., *Has Globalization Gone Too Far?* Washington, DC: Institute for International Economics (1997).
Slaughter, M. J., "International Trade and Labor-Demand Elasticities," NBER working chapter 6262 (1997).

Notes

1. However, this result is valid only if the free-trade equilibrium leads to an incomplete specialization of both economies.

2. For a more detailed description, see for example Hamermesh (1993) or Cahuc and Zylberberg (1996).
3. If the relative use of labor decreases strongly with the output level, this effect can be inverted. This, however, corresponds to exceptional configurations and it is incompatible with the hypothesis of homogeneity of the production function.
4. The correlation is stronger when internationalization is measured by the share of foreign affiliates in the employment of national enterprises, but this measure is rather linked to the question of FDIs.
5. Note, however, that only a short-term effect is in question in this case, as the estimates are based on annual variations, with two lags.
6. For a description of the potential consequences of an increased labor-demand elasticity, see Rodrik (1997, pp. 16–27).
7. Index D refers to the "domestic" country, and F to the "foreign" country. In the three subscripts of quantity variables, the first one indicates the country of production, the second one the industry, and the third one the country of consumption.
8. I assume that there exist at least two industries k_0 and k_1 such that $a_{U,k_0}/a_{S,k_0} < \overline{U}/\overline{S} < a_{U,k_1}/a_{S,k_1}$.
9. Note, however, that the degree of exposure to foreign competition is not additive. As a consequence, the calculation of this indicator at the level of the whole economy would not give the same result as the weighted average used here.

11
Smooth and Sticky Adjustment: A Comparative Analysis of the US and UK

Michelle Haynes, Richard Upward, and Peter Wright

1. Introduction

A purported characteristic of intraindustry trade is its allegedly low adjustment costs in the face of trade liberalization. It has become an chapter of faith that the European Community's early liberalization succeeded because of intraindustry trade. Grant et al. (1993)

The proposition that labor market adjustments to intraindustry trade are less costly than adjustments to interindustry trade is a widely held belief amongst trade economists.[1] If it is the case that there are significant sector-specific skills, then this "smooth adjustment hypothesis" seems intuitive. Such reasoning has been used to argue that both the 1992 Single Market and further expansion to encompass Eastern Europe can be achieved relatively costlessly. However, direct evidence relating to this issue remains largely anecdotal.

The movement of labor between sectors is also of interest to labor economists. The importance of the sectoral reallocation of labor as a source of aggregate unemployment is the subject of ongoing debate. Frictional unemployment which occurs as workers move between jobs has long been a focus of research, but with the general increase of unemployment over the last two decades it has reassumed importance. Is it the case that unemployment has increased as a result of individuals becoming less mobile? If so, how mobile is labor and how long does this imply it will take an economy to adjust? These are important questions, since it has been argued (e.g., Haskel and Slaughter, 1999; Slaughter, 1999) that a defining contrast between "trade" and "labor" economists is how they view the mobility of labor. Trade theorists generally deal with multisector general equilibrium models, which assume that labor is mobile. Labor economists typically model labor as immobile in the short, and even medium run.

In this chapter we adopt the methodology of the microeconometric labor literature to analyse the assertion by some trade economists that reallocation within sectors is less costly than between sectors. In the context of this paper, "costs" are defined as the duration of unemployment spells; these costs could also be thought of in terms of lost wages resulting from a period of unemployment. An alternative interpretation, more closely related to the trade literature, is that costs consist of lost production incurred during the adjustment from one equilibrium to another.

We construct data on unemployment spells for heads of households in both the US and the UK, and use these data to compare unemployment durations for those who find work in the same sector in which they were originally employed, and those who find work in a new sector. We analyze how the personal and economic circumstances of individuals affect the probability of moving between sectors, and we also examine what factors affect the duration of individual unemployment spells. By comparing the United Kingdom and the United States, we compare economies with very different unemployment experiences, and ask whether the "flexibility" of the US labor market manifests itself in terms of unemployment incidence, unemployment duration, or the probability of moving sectors.

Section 2 provides a summary of previous work in this area. Section 3 describes the data used and provides some basic descriptive statistics. Section 4 explains the techniques we use to model unemployment durations with multiple outcomes. Section 5 describes the results, and section 6 concludes.

2. Some Earlier Work

The intraindustry trade literature contains only limited direct evidence on the relative ease of intra- as opposed to intersectoral adjustment. Lundberg and Hansson (1986) and Tharakan and Calfat (1994) approach this issue by comparing factor intensities between and within industries. They find that factor intensities are more homogenous within rather than between sectors, though differences are still considerable. By contrast, Finger (1975) and Rayment (1976) found evidence of greater variation within than between sectors. All of these studies do, of course, offer only indirect evidence, rather than focusing directly on the costs of adjustment. The fact that intraindustry adjustment costs may vary considerably depending on the sector being considered is borne out by Adler (1970). He finds that the reorganization of the steel sector following the formation of the European Coal and Steel Community was relatively painless. In contrast, Reker (1994) found that adjustment processes in the machine tool industry were considerably more traumatic, with the industry being highly heterogeneous.

Adopting a political economy approach, Lundberg and Hansson (1986) found that the demand for defensive measures to protect jobs was low in industries subject to intraindustry trade, suggesting the adjustment costs were also relatively small. A similar finding was obtained by Marvel and Ray (1987) for the USA, though these results were contradicted by Ratanayake and Jayasuriya (1991) for Australia. Greenaway and Torstensson (1997) refer to several other industry-specific studies.

The labor economics literature, on the other hand, contains far more direct evidence on the cost to individual workers of moving jobs. First, there is aggregate evidence on the relationship between sectoral reallocation of labor and the aggregate unemployment rate. The proposition that sectoral shocks and the subsequent movement of workers between sectors are the main source of fluctuation in the aggregate unemployment rate has been widely investigated in the US, following Lilien (1982), who proxied intersectoral shocks by the variance of industry employment growth rates and found that they were positively correlated with US unemployment. This methodology has been questioned: Abraham and Katz (1986) point out that, if manufacturing employment is more cyclical than that of services, then the dispersion of employment growth rates may increase anyway during slumps, even without any permanent reallocation of labor. Hence, a positive correlation between the variance of employment growth and unemployment is not necessarily evidence for the impact of restructuring. A number of more recent studies—Loungani et al. (1990), Brainard and Cutler (1993), Mills et al. (1995)—have sought to remedy this shortcoming and have generally been supportive of the "sectoral shift hypothesis" that intersectoral shocks are the main source of fluctuations in the unemployment rate.

Second, there is evidence at the individual level on the wage effects of changing or staying within the same sector. It is often assumed that the wage changes are less negative (or more positive) for "stayers" since, if skills are job-specific, then an individual is more likely to remain in the same occupation if they stay in the same industry (Kletzer, 1996). Evidence to this effect is found by Neal (1995), who finds that workers can transfer skills acquired in one firm to another in the same sector. Workers who change industry, on the other hand, suffer wage losses, as they are not rewarded for their (now) redundant skills.

Third, there is evidence at the micro level that individuals who change industry ("movers") tend to have longer unemployment durations than do those who return to the same industry ("stayers"). The fact that changing industry may entail greater wage losses has led authors such as Murphy and Topel (1987) and Fallick (1993) to argue that individuals may be prepared to stay unemployed for longer periods in order to return to their original sector and avoid losing sector-specific skills. Unemployment may then increase because higher skilled workers become increasingly unwilling to move. This hypothesis has been tested on Canadian data by Thomas (1996a), who finds that the link between increased aggregate unemployment and increased immobility of labor is rather weak.

3. The Data and Some Basic Statistics

Despite the interest of labor economists in the effects on workers of changing jobs, occupations, and industries, the analysis has not been directed towards assessing directly the relative costs of inter- and intrasectoral adjustment, nor has it attempted to compare different countries using comparable datasets. This is the approach taken here.

This study makes use of two datasets. US data are from waves 21 to 26 of the Panel Study of Income Dynamics (PSID), covering the period 1988–93, described in detail in Hill (1992). The UK data come from waves 1 to 6 of the British Household Panel Survey (BHPS), covering the period October 1990 to January 1997, described in Taylor et al. (1998). From each we construct a complete sequence of labor market spells, recorded to the nearest calendar month. For heads of household who appear in every wave, we select all spells of unemployment and "out of the labor force." For each spell of unemployment we record the length of the spell, the previous industry of employment, and the industry of employment following the spell. Industries are defined using the 1980 UK 2-digit SIC classification.

The use of panel data in the construction of labor market spells allows us to largely avoid the problem of recall bias associated with retrospective data collection (e.g., Elias, 1997). The data used are never more than 12 months old, and the overlapping of recall and contemporaneous information has been used to make a variety of consistency checks. The construction of the data is described in detail in a technical appendix (Upward, 1999).[2]

Table 1 describes the spells of unemployment. Note that for some individuals employment status is not available either before or after the beginning of the sample period, owing to left- or right-censoring. Left-censoring occurs when a spell of unemployment starts before the beginning of the sample period; right-censoring occurs when a spell of unemployment is still in progress at the end of the sample period. We select only those spells of unemployment preceded by a spell of employment; i.e., we exclude left-censored spells (the third row), and those spells of unemployment preceded by another spell of unemployment (the second row).[3]

Table 1. Sample Sizes and Mean Unemployment Durations[a]

Status at t − 1	Status at t + 1			
	Employed same industry	Employed new industry	Unemployed/ out of labor force	Censored[b]
BHPS				
Employed	152 (7.01)	270 (8.34)	125 (11.30)	197 (28.21)
Unemployed/out of labor force		78 (9.46)	112 (13.43)	116 (28.70)
Censored[c]		109 (19.06)	92 (24.14)	109 (73.35)
PSID				
Employed	855 (4.04)	438 (4.07)	270 (7.43)	276 (14.92)
Unemployed/out of labor force		216 (5.16)	555 (6.71)	210 (17.21)
Censored		212 (7.38)	162 (13.99)	120 (60.00)

[a] Numbers in parentheses indicate mean duration in months.
[b] Following status not known because of right-censoring (occurs after end of sample period).
[c] Previous status not known because of left-censoring (occurs before start of sample period).

The final sample for the UK consists of a balanced panel of 563 individuals, who experienced 785 spells of unemployment between 1991 and 1996. For the US there are 1,345 individuals who experienced 2,340 spells of unemployment between 1988 and 1993. Looking at the first row of Table 1, the average duration of unemployment was shortest for those spells ending in a return to the same industry, and longest for those which did not end before the end of the sample period. In both countries the spells which ended in a move were slightly longer. However, as we show in section 4, this is somewhat misleading because each outcome censors the other. For example, an individual who is unemployed for a long time, but who finds a job in a new sector, would have taken even longer to find a job in the same sector.

Table 2 describes sample characteristics for those spells in the first row of Table 1. Each individual in the US data experiences 1.74 spells over the 5-year period (1,839/1,055); in the UK this ratio is 1.32 (744/563). This conforms to our expectations: unemployment incidence is higher in the US, but average durations are shorter. Less obviously, a much smaller proportion of spells in the UK end in a return to the same sector than in the US: 20.4% compared with 46.5%. A correspondingly higher proportion of UK spells therefore end in a movement to a new sector. Note also that the proportion of spells that are censored is higher in the UK. This occurs because the average duration of spells in the UK is longer.

Table 2 also describes the sample means for the explanatory variables used in the analysis. Where possible we have constructed comparable measures for the two countries. These include the usual covariates in an analysis of unemployment duration (see, e.g., Narendranathan and Stewart (1993) for the UK, and Meyer (1990) for the US).

Table 2. Sample Characteristics

	BHPS	PSID
Number of individuals	563	1,055
Number of spells of unemployment	744	1,839
Exit into job, of which:	0.567	0.703
(a) Exit into same industry	0.204	0.465
(b) Exit into new industry	0.363	0.238
Censored	0.433	0.297
Temporarily laid off	—	0.136
Out of the labor force	0.355	0.298
Female	0.233	0.249
Age	42.585	38.674
Has children	0.406	0.484
Married	0.715	0.516
No qualifications[a]	0.230	0.267
Years of labor market experience since 18[b]	23.408	14.671
Previous job skilled[c]	0.535	0.423
Previous job manual	0.573	0.487
Tenure of previous job (months)	60.108	52.784
Previous job in manufacturing[d]	0.355	0.288
Industry of previous job:		
Agriculture, forestry and fishing	0.018	0.043
Energy and water supplies	0.030	0.019
Extraction of minerals and ores; manufacture of minerals, mineral products and chemicals	0.036	0.037
Metal goods, engineering & vehicles industries	0.144	0.097
Other manufacturing industries	0.128	0.092
Construction	0.077	0.158
Distribution, hotels & catering (repairs)	0.172	0.210
Transport & communication	0.077	0.057
Banking, finance, insurance, business services & leasing	0.106	0.087
Other services	0.214	0.201
Self-employed in previous job	0.148	0.137
In receipt of unemployment benefit	0.306	0.243
Mean monthly unemployment benefit income	£234.37	$704.94
Local unemployment (%)[e]	8.708	5.699
Owns own home	0.156	0.160
Buying house (mortgage)	0.535	0.280
Private renter[f]	0.081	

[a] Proxied by failure to graduate from high school in PSID data.
[b] Proxied by (age–age left school) in UK data; this is one reason for the disparity between the two means.
[c] Skilled job defined as (BHPS) managers & administrators; professional; associate professional; craft and related and (PSID) professional and technical; managers and administrators; craftsmen.
[d] Manufacturing industries defined according to UK 1980 SIC divisions 0–4.
[e] Local unemployment (%) at UK Standard Region and US County level.
[f] Missing category for UK is public renters; for US missing category is any renter.

One notable difference in the US data is that 13.6% of spells are coded as "temporarily laid off." This phenomenon is rare in the UK, and is not recognized as an explicit category in the data. We would expect that individuals who report being temporarily laid off are more likely to return to their previous employer, and therefore remain in the same sector.

We have included spells of "out of the labor force" in the sample. This is because, despite reporting themselves as out of the labor force, these respondents often return to employment. As can be seen, they constitute a significant proportion of the sample.

4. Modeling Unemployment Durations with Multiple Outcomes

The modeling framework that will be adopted in this chapter is a competing risk model, which is commonly used in the estimation of unemployment durations with multiple outcomes (e.g., Katz and Meyer, 1990; Narendranathan and Stewart, 1993; Thomas, 1996a). This allows a comparison of the length of unemployment of those who change sector with those that do not, as well as an assessment of those factors that affect choice of sector. In such models, the duration of unemployment spells of those individuals returning to the same industry (t_A) is assumed to be distributed with density $f_A(t_A)$, whilst the duration of unemployment spells of those returning to a different industry (t_B) is given by $f_B(t_B)$. For a given individual, the industry into which he or she exits will depend on drawings of t_A and t_B. If $t_A < t_B$ then the individual will exit into the same industry, whilst if $t_A > t_B$ the person will exit into a different industry. The observed duration (t^*) will therefore be the minimum of these two underlying factors:

$$t^* = \min(t_A, t_B).$$

For a given individual in the sample, the drawings of t_A, t_B will be unknown. The probability of observing a spell with duration t^* which ends with a return to the same industry is given by the joint probability:

$$\Pr(T_A = t^*) \cdot \Pr(T_B \geq t^*) = f_A(t^*)(1 - F_B(t^*)).$$

The probability of a duration t^* which ends in an exit into a new industry will similarly be given by

$$\Pr(T_B = t^*) \cdot \Pr(T_A \geq t^*) = f_B(t^*)(1 - F_A(t^*)).$$

These probabilities may be estimated using maximum likelihood techniques, and the dependence of the transition probabilities on the characteristics of the individuals may be assessed.

In order to simplify the log-likelihood function, note that the *hazard rate* is the probability of exiting unemployment in the period of time between t and $t + dt$ as $dt \to 0$, conditional on having reached t:

$$h(t) = \frac{f(t)}{1 - F(t)} = \frac{f(t)}{S(t)}.$$

We can now partition the log-likelihood into two separate terms, according to the exit industry of the individual if it is assumed that $f_A(t_A)$ and $f_B(t_B)$ are independent.

Right-censoring (failing to find a job before the end of the sample period) is treated as another outcome.

The assumption that the draws from $f_A(t_A)$ and $f_B(t_B)$ are independent (conditional on observed characteristics) is problematic if it is thought that there are unobserved factors which jointly influence the hazard to exiting into either state. However, an alternative approach, which is to allow for a joint distribution of the two outcomes (e.g., Card and Olson, 1995) relies on a restrictive functional form. As noted by Thomas (1996a), conditioning on the distribution of unobserved heterogeneity can be very sensitive to the choice of distribution. We choose therefore to maintain the independent-risks assumption, and rely on the measured covariates in our regression to control for differences in search intensity between individuals. Hence the likelihood can be written in terms of the hazard as

$$\log L = \sum_{i=1}^{N} d_i \log h_A(t_i^*) + \sum_{i=1}^{N} \log S_A(t_i^*) + \sum_{i=1}^{N} (1 - d_i) \log h_B(t_i^*) + \sum_{i=1}^{N} \log S_B(t_i^*),$$

where $d = 1$ if the individual returns to the same industry and $d = 0$ if the return is to a different industry. To allow for the fact that durations are recorded to the nearest month, we use the sequential binary response form of the likelihood (Jenkins, 1995). The discrete-time hazard rates for person i in each duration interval $j = 1, \ldots, t_i$ are given by

$$h_r(\mathbf{x}, j) = 1 - \exp(-\exp(\mathbf{x}_{ij}'\beta_r) + D_r(j)), \quad r = A, B$$

where $\mathbf{x}_{ij}'$ is a vector of covariates, which may vary across individuals and across time, β_r is a vector of parameters to be estimated which vary across outcome r, and $D_r(j)$ is a function describing the duration dependence in the hazard. The parameters of $D_r(j)$ are also to be estimated, and also vary across r; i.e. the hazard is allowed to vary by outcome. We allow for three different functional forms for $D(j)$. First, we specify $D(j) = \ln(j)$ in which case the hazard has a Weibull distribution. Second, we specify $D(j)$ as a (quartic) polynomial, which allows for nonmonotonicity in the hazard. This may be important if, for example, the hazard is initially increasing but then decreasing. Finally, we replace $D(j)$ with a set of dummy variables, d_j, for each time period, $j = 1, \ldots, t_i$. This allows the baseline hazard to take any value for any interval, and is therefore the least restrictive form.

Although the Weibull distribution is more restrictive, it does allow for an intuitive interpretation of the baseline hazards across outcomes. The Weibull distribution is $\alpha_r t^{\alpha_r - 1}$, where α_r is a parameter determining whether the hazard increases or decreases over the duration of a spell. If $\alpha_A < 1$, for example, then the conditional probability of exiting unemployment into the same industry is declining as the spell continues. Further, if $\alpha_A < \alpha_B$, then the probability of exiting a spell into a new industry is increasing relative to the probability of exiting into the same industry over the course of a spell. If the hazard to returning to the same industry is initially higher than the hazard to moving industry, this provides some support for the idea that individuals find employment more easily in the sector from which they came, and hence supports the smooth adjustment hypothesis.

Table 3 gives guidance on interpreting competing risk models (Thomas, 1996b). In a proportional hazard model of the type estimated, covariates serve to shift up or down the baseline hazard. Thus, in the table, a negative sign indicates that the variable shifts the hazard down and hence decreases the likelihood of a transition.

Table 3. Interpreting Competing Risk Estimates

Coefficient (stayers) β_A	Coefficient (movers) β_B	Predicted probability of moving sector	Predicted unemployment duration
<0 Takes longer to find a job in the same sector	>0 Takes less time to find a job in a new sector	<0 Probability of moving sector is increased	? Ambiguous effect on predicted unemployment duration
>0 Takes less time to find a job in the same sector	<0 Takes longer to find a job in a new sector	>0 Probability of moving sector is decreased	? Ambiguous effect on predicted unemployment duration
<0 Takes longer to find a job in the same sector	<0 Takes longer to find a job in a new sector	? Ambiguous effect on probability of moving sector	>0 Unemployment durations increased
>0 Takes less time to find a job in the same sector	>0 Takes less time to find a job in a new sector	? Ambiguous effect on probability of moving sector	<0 Unemployment durations decreased

Table 3 shows that if both β_A and β_B are negative, then the influence of that covariate is to unambiguously increase the unemployment durations, since the hazard to both outcomes is reduced. However, the effect on the probability of changing sector depends on the relative size of the coefficients. For example, if $\beta_A < \beta_B$ then the effect of that covariate is to increase the probability of moving sector. Conversely, if β_A and β_B have opposite signs, the effect of moving sector is unambiguous, whereas the impact on unemployment duration depends on relative magnitudes. This is because the hazard to one outcome is reduced (increasing durations), but the hazard to the other outcome is increased (reducing durations).

5. Results

Figure 1 plots the estimated baseline hazards that result from the three specifications of $D(j)$. In both the UK and the US, and for both outcomes, the Weibull parameter is less than one, which indicates that the baseline hazard is declining and hence individuals are less likely to exit unemployment as the spell proceeds. The polynomial estimates are very similar, also suggesting a (near) monotonic declining hazard for both outcomes. The piecewise constant baseline hazards are more variable. In the UK, in particular, a spike in the hazard is observed at 12 months. However, the suggested pattern is similar to the parametric estimates: hazards for both outcomes decline. Crucially, all three specifications suggest that the hazard for stayers declines *faster* than the hazard for movers. This implies that the likelihood of an individual moving sector increases the longer they remain unemployed. Using the Weibull specification (not reported) one can test the hypothesis that $\alpha_A < \alpha_B$, and this effect is significant at conventional levels.

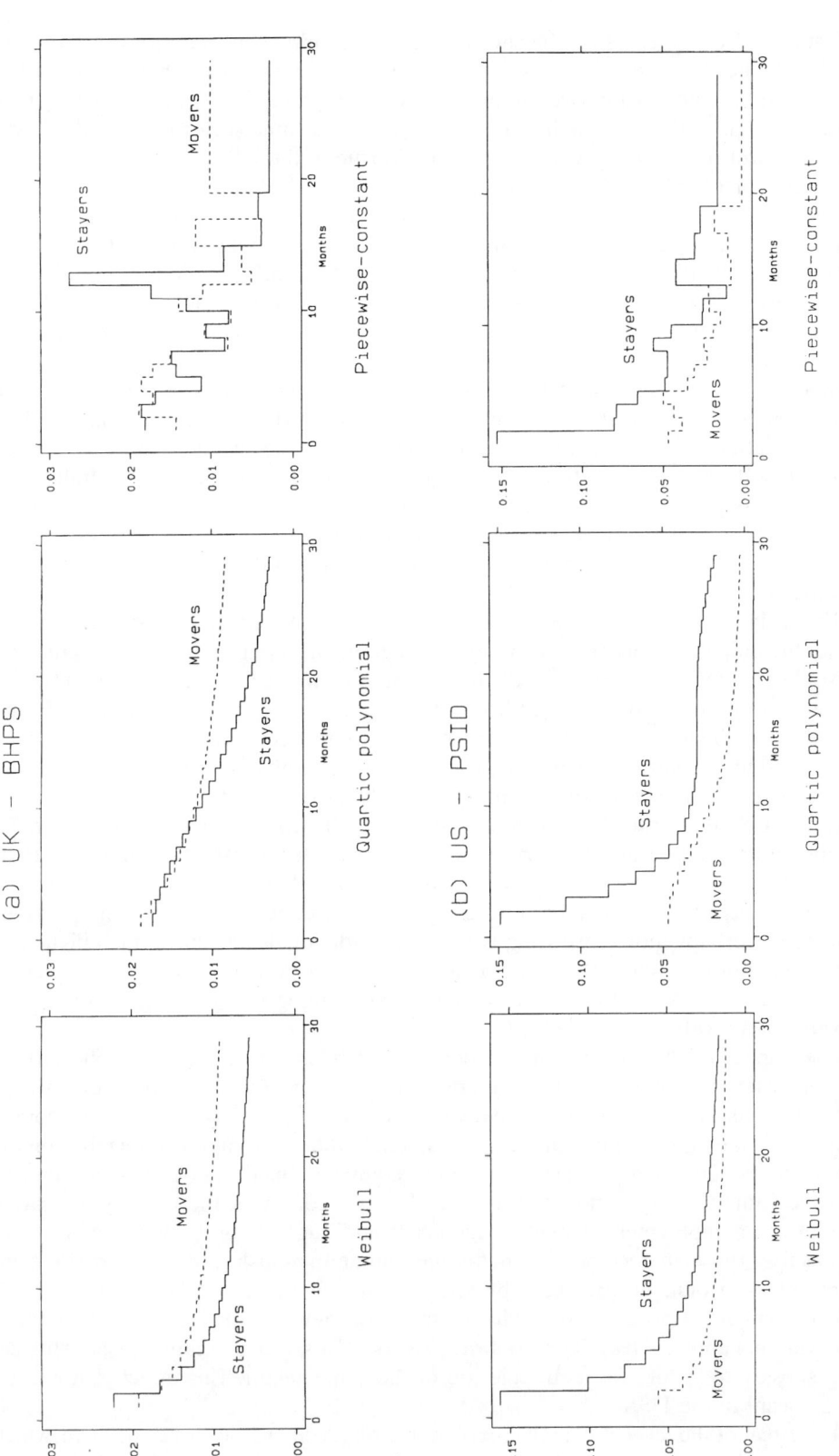

Figure 1. Predicted Baseline Hazards

Figure 1 also suggests that the shorter mean unemployment durations observed in the US are not the result of a less sharply declining unemployment hazard but rather the effect of a much higher overall hazard in the US, picked up by the constant terms. Note also that in the UK the hazard to staying in the same sector is generally lower than the hazard to moving, while the reverse is true in the US.

The fact that the hazard to staying in the same sector declines faster than the hazard to finding a job in a new sector in both countries is supportive of the hypothesis that individuals initially concentrate their search for re-employment in the sector in which they were originally employed. This in turn suggests that adjustment for individuals is less "costly" within than between sectors. It is also interesting to note that the UK has a much higher proportion of sectoral movers amongst the unemployed and also has lower re-employment hazards.

In Table 4 we report estimates of β_A and β_B from the piecewise-constant model, since it imposes least restrictions on the baseline hazard, and yields the largest log-likelihood. In fact, estimates of β_A and β_B from all three specifications are very similar, so our results are robust with respect to specification. The results are generally consistent across the two countries. Of the 42 estimated parameters which are shared by both countries, 31 have the same sign across countries. Of those 11 covariates where the estimates differ in sign, only three are significantly different from zero in either country.

The variable that relates most directly to the "sectoral shifts hypothesis" is whether or not the individual was previously employed in the declining sector (manufacturing). It would be expected that such individuals would be more likely to move sector, and this is exactly what is observed, although the results are not always significant. In the UK, those in the manufacturing sector have lower hazards to finding a job in the same sector, and higher hazards to moving. The net effect in both countries is that those who were employed in manufacturing are significantly more likely to move sector.

In the US, temporary layoffs may help to explain why a large proportion of the sample return to the same industry. As would be expected, those who report that their spell of unemployment is a temporary layoff are more likely to stay in the same sector than otherwise, presumably because a significant number return to their previous employer. Perhaps more surprising is that such individuals also have unambiguously longer unemployment durations, as the estimate of β_A as well as β_B is negative. It seems that individuals who are temporarily laid off are willing to wait longer to reap the rewards of a recall.

The impact of the unemployment benefit system is rather more complicated. In both datasets the measure of unemployment benefit is available for every month in the sample, and is therefore included as a covariate, which may vary over the course of a spell of unemployment. Our measure of benefit therefore captures the most important features of the benefit systems in the two countries: the duration of benefit receipt and the (time-varying) amount of benefit. In both countries, the dummy indicating receipt of unemployment benefit is significant and negative on both outcomes, indicating that those in receipt of benefits have unambiguously longer unemployment durations, as would be predicted by standard search theory. In both countries the effect is smaller (more negative) for exits into a new sector, indicating that those receiving benefits are less likely to switch sectors. This, too, is intuitive if benefits act as a subsidy to "wait" for a suitable job in the same sector. This effect is, however, insignificant in the US.

The effect of the *level* of benefits (conditional on receipt), is however, positive, which is less intuitive. In fact, only 47.4% of the UK sample and 34.6% of the US sample

Table 4. Piecewise-Constant Proportional Hazard Competing Risk Estimates[a,b]

	BHPS			PSID		
	Stayers	Movers	Difference	Stayers	Movers	Difference
Temporarily laid off				−0.411**	−0.985**	0.574**
Out of the labor force	−0.915**	−2.278**	1.363**	−0.547**	−0.518**	−0.029
Female	0.719**	0.391*	0.328	0.044	−0.183	0.227
Age 26–35	0.581	−0.036	0.617	0.036	−0.402**	0.439**
Age 36–45	0.655	−0.257	0.912*	−0.091	−0.446**	0.355
Age 46–55	0.443	−0.545*	0.988*	−0.165	−0.938**	0.773***
Age 56+	0.299	−1.234**	1.533**	−0.138	−1.014**	0.877**
Has children	0.282	−0.492**	0.774**	−0.113	−0.027	−0.086
Married	0.036	0.654**	−0.618**	0.130	−0.064	0.194
No qualifications	−0.188	−0.289	0.101	−0.069	−0.337**	0.269*
>10 years in labor market	−0.267	−0.011	−0.257	0.172	0.128	0.044
Previous job skilled	0.231	0.026	0.205	0.052	0.101	−0.049
Previous job manual	−0.074	0.071	−0.145	0.166**	−0.102	0.268*
Tenure of previous job 1–5 years	−0.447**	−0.034	−0.414*	−0.031	−0.010	−0.021
Tenure of previous job >5 years	−0.521**	−0.318*	−0.203	−0.301**	−0.266*	−0.035
Previous job in manufacturing	−0.296	0.114	−0.410*	−0.241**	0.197*	−0.438**
Self-employed in previous job	0.399*	−0.081	0.481	0.347**	−0.150	0.498**
In receipt of unemp. benefit	−0.933**	−1.806**	0.873**	−1.304**	−1.890**	0.586
Monthly UB income	0.052	0.093**	−0.040	0.202**	0.278**	−0.076
Local unemployment (%)	0.215	−0.562	0.778	−0.136	−0.020	−0.115
Owns own home	0.730**	0.493*	0.237	0.135	0.139	−0.004
Buying house (mortgage)	0.826**	0.367*	0.459	0.100	0.127	−0.027
Private renter	0.828**	−0.103	0.931**			
1989				−0.100	0.399**	−0.499**
1990				−0.155	0.507**	−0.662**
1991				−0.115	0.420**	−0.535**
1992	−0.429	0.489	−0.919	−0.166	−0.360*	0.193
1993	−0.302	0.437	−0.739			
1994	−0.116	0.339	−0.455			
1995	−0.661**	0.379	−1.040**			
1996	−0.578*	0.170	−0.749*			
Number of spells		744			1,839	
Total time at risk		10,287			11,358	
Log-likelihood	−697.39	−1,006.65		−2,739.49	−1,680.99	

[a] Estimates are maximum likelihood using the sequential binary response form to take account of the discrete measurement of duration, which is measured to the nearest month (Jenkins, 1995). Estimates include 16 time dummies to capture piecewise variations in the baseline hazard (not shown).
[b] Estimates were also made using a Weibull and a quartic polynomial specification. The piecewise constant results are reported as they impose the least restriction on the baseline hazard. Coefficient estimates were very similar for all three specifications. All other estimates available on request from the authors.
[c] Two asterisks denote 95% significance level; one denotes 90% significance level.

report themselves as receiving unemployment benefit (see Table 2). This seems low, and suggests that individuals are reporting a particularly narrow definition of benefit. It may be that those in our sample who report high levels of unemployment benefit receive low levels of other out-of-work benefits, and vice versa. This seems plausible if other out-of-work benefits are means-tested. It should be noted that the predicted mean effect of benefit is still negative for the great majority, since the absolute value of the coefficient on receipt of benefits is much smaller than that on the level of benefits.

Because the estimates cover several years, during which time macroeconomic and institutional features changed, we also include a set of year dummies. The base year for the UK is 1991, for the US it is 1988. In both countries, relative to the base year, hazards to staying in the same sector are lower, while hazards to moving are usually higher. In most years the net effect is that the probability of moving sector is higher than in the base year, although this is not always significant. Thus an unemployment spell which began later in the sample period was more likely to end with a switch to another sector. It is not clear whether this is the result of macroeconomic conditions: unemployment peaked in the UK in 1993, in the middle of the sample period, while it peaked in the US in 1992, at the end of the period. It is the case, however, that the inclusion of year dummies reduces the significance of the coefficient on local unemployment rates.

One of the largest and most consistent effects on unemployment durations occurs if the individual reports being "out of the labor force" rather than unemployed. As noted earlier, these spells are included because they are preceded and often followed by a spell of employment. These individuals presumably regard themselves as being less attached to the labor force, and this is reflected in the significantly lower re-employment hazards. Spells out of the labor force are on average longer than spells of unemployment. Less obviously, spells out of the labor force in the UK are *less* likely to result in a move to a new sector. This effect is insignificant in the US.

Turning to the impact of the other covariates, there is a consistent monotonic age effect on hazards to changing sector: older workers have lower hazards, which is consistent with the idea that older workers have a greater value of industry-specific human capital accumulated with experience. As a result, older workers are also less likely to switch sector, as shown by the increasingly positive coefficients in the third column.

The effect of tenure with previous employer is also consistent across the two countries. Tenure also ought to relate to skill specificity. Presumably, a high tenure signals that the quality of the pre-unemployment match was high and that job specific skills will have been accumulated. This may serve to hinder mobility. In fact, in the UK there appears to be a strong negative effect of tenure on unemployment hazards to both moving and staying: those with longer tenure take significantly longer to find a job in the same sector, as well as in a new sector. A similar result is found in the US: those with the longest tenures have longer unemployment durations. This result is consistent with the hypothesis that high tenure workers spend longer searching for re-employment in the same sector, because the relative value of the sector-specific skills is higher. After controlling for age and tenure, general labor market experience is insignificant.

Turning to qualifications, the estimates have the expected signs but are generally insignificant. Individuals with no qualifications have lower hazards to moving and staying in both the US and the UK and thus have longer unemployment durations. They also appear to be less flexible in that they are increasingly likely to stay in the same sector the longer they are out of work. This gives weak support to the view that high levels of general education aid mobility.

In order to assess the impact of specific skills on mobility, we also considered whether the previous job was skilled and whether it was manual. We would expect that skilled workers would be in relatively high demand, and hence have shorter spells of unemployment. However, because of the specific nature of many skills, their mobility between sectors might be reduced. The effect of skill was, however, insignificant, whilst for the US it was found that manual workers have a significantly higher hazard to staying in the same industry, with the net result that manual workers are less likely to switch sectors.

Finally, we also investigated the role of the housing market on sectoral mobility and unemployment durations. It has been suggested that owner-occupiers (Oswald, 1997) and public-sector renters (Hughes and McCormick, 1981) may be unable to move between geographical regions, and are therefore less mobile between sectors. In the context of a comparison between the UK and the US, this hypothesis is particularly interesting because the structure of the housing market is so different: Table 2 shows that over 69% of the UK sample are buying or own their home, compared with 42% in the US.

In the UK, the housing variables do have a significant impact on unemployment durations. However, we find no evidence to support the hypothesis that owner-occupiers are less mobile in terms of sectors.[4] Public-sector renters (the base group) have significantly longer unemployment durations. Those who own their own home and those with mortgages appear to be more mobile both within and between sectors, though they are not more likely to change sector. Private renters have an increased probability of staying in the same sector, presumably to retain the rewards that accrue to specific skills. Interestingly, we find no significant housing effects in the US data: although owner-occupiers have higher hazards, the effect is insignificantly different from zero.

6. Summary and Conclusions

This chapter has examined the intra- and intersectoral mobility of labor. It provides evidence on what factors determine how long an individual remains unemployed, and what factors affect whether an individual moves sector following a period of unemployment. In doing so we examine the hypothesis that adjustment within industries is less costly, in terms of unemployment duration, than adjustment between industries.

The raw data confirm the stylized facts that, although US workers experience a higher incidence of unemployment, the spells have shorter duration. A further key difference between the two countries is that unemployment spells in the US are less likely to end in a move to another sector than they are in the UK. This may suggest one reason for the superior labor market performance of the US economy in the last two decades.

We also find that individuals are more likely to switch sector the longer they are unemployed in both countries. A plausible explanation for this is that individuals initially attempt to find jobs that complement their general and specific skills in order to accrue the associated rewards, but move sector as this prospect diminishes. This finding is consistent with the hypothesis that finding a job in the original sector is less costly than finding a job in a new sector, at least for shorter unemployment durations. Indeed, even if it were the case that rewards in the new sector were in fact higher, our results suggest that other costs of moving are sufficiently large to encourage search in the original sector. Our interpretation of these results does not, therefore, necessarily imply that potential wages in the original sector are greater than in any other sector.

The use of individual-level data enables us to say more about which types of worker are more or less likely to change sector. It is clear that, although the average effect (as measured by the difference between the baseline hazards) suggests that workers initially search in the sector in which they were previously employed, there is great variation in the probability of moving sector. As suggested in some of the previous work in section 2, the smooth adjustment hypothesis is perhaps too simple a view, since some industries contain heterogeneous workers, some of whom find it more difficult to change sectors than others. For example, we find that workers who would be expected to have higher levels of sector-specific skills (older workers, for example) are less mobile between sectors.

A further interesting result is that workers in both countries who enter unemployment from the manufacturing sector are more likely to change sectors. If, as is thought to be the case, the manufacturing sector has experienced adverse interindustry trade pressures, this provides some evidence of a relationship between trading patterns and factor mobility, as would be predicted. An obvious direction for future research would be to directly relate sectoral-specific trade pressures to the sectoral outcomes of individual unemployment spells.

Finally, our results are also suggestive of the appropriate framework for thinking about labor market adjustment. There do indeed appear to be significant costs associated with moving between sectors, as witnessed by the longer unemployment spells of movers. Nevertheless, it would also seem to be the case that a significant proportion of unemployment spells end in a switch to a new sector within what might be regarded as the "short-term," lending support to the notion that a multisector model is more appropriate.

References

Abraham, K. and L. Katz, "Cyclical Unemployment: Sectoral Shifts or Aggregate Disturbances?" *Journal of Political Economy* 94 (1986):507–22.

Adler, M., "Specialisation in the European Coal and Steel Community," *Journal of Common Market Studies* 8 (1970):175–91.

Brainard, S. L. and D. M. Cutler, "Sectoral Shifts and Cyclical Unemployment Reconsidered," *Quarterly Journal of Economics* 108 (1993):219–43.

Brülhart, M., "Marginal Intraindustry Trade and Trade-Induced Adjustment," in M. Brülhart and R. C. Hine (eds.), *Intra-Industry Trade and Adjustment: The European Experience*, London: Macmillan (1998).

Card, D. and C. Olson, "Bargaining Power, Strike Durations and Wage Outcomes: An Analysis of Strikes in the 1880s," *Journal of Labor Economics* 13 (1995):32–61.

Elias, P., "Who Forgot They were Unemployed?" ESRC Research Centre on Micro-Social Change, working chapter 97-19 (1997).

Fallick, B. C., "The Industrial Mobility of Displaced Workers," *Journal of Labor Economics* 11 (1993):302–23.

Finger, J. M., "Trade Overlap and Intra-Industry Trade," *Economic Inquiry* 13 (1975):581–9.

Grant, R. J., M. C. Papadakis, and J. D. Richardson, "Global Trade Flows: Old Structures, New Issues, Empirical Evidence," in C. F. Bergsten and M. Noland (eds.), *Pacific Dynamism and the International Economic System*, Washington DC: Institute for International Economics (1993).

Greenaway, D. and R. C. Hine, "Intra-Industry Specialisation, Trade Expansion and Adjustment in the European Economic Space," *Journal of Common Market Studies* 29 (1991):603–21

Greenaway D. and J. Torstensson, "Back to the Future: Taking Stock of Intra-Industry Trade," *Weltwirtschaftliches Archiv* 133 (1997):249–69.

Haskel, J. and M. Slaughter, "Trade, Technology and UK Wage Inequality," Centre for Research on Globalisation and Labor Markets research chapter 99/2 (1999).

Hill, M., *The Panel Study of Income Dynamics: A User's Guide*, Newbury Park, CA: Sage Publications (1992).

Hughes, G. and B. McCormick, "Do Council House Policies Reduce Migration Between Regions?" *Economic Journal* 91 (1981):919–37.

Jenkins, S. P., "Easy Estimation Methods for Discrete-Time Duration Models" *Oxford Bulletin of Economics and Statistics* 57 (1995):129–38.

Katz, L. and B. Meyer, "The Impact of Potential Duration of Unemployment Benefits on the Duration Of Unemployment," *Journal of Public Economics* 41 (1990):45–72.

Kletzer, L. G., "The Role of Sector Specific Skills in Post-Displacement Earnings," *Industrial Relations* 35 (1996):473–90.

Lancaster, T., *The Econometric Analysis of Transition Data*, Cambridge: Cambridge University Press (1990).

Lilien, D., "Sectoral Shifts and Cyclical Unemployment," *Journal of Political Economy* 90 (1982):777–93.

Loungani P., M. Rush, and W. Tave, "Stock Market Dispersion and Unemployment," *Journal of Monetary Economics* 25 (1990):367–88.

Lundberg, L. and P. Hansson, "Intraindustry Trade and its Consequences for Adjustment," in D. Greenaway and P. K. M. Tharakan (eds.), *Imperfect Competition and International Trade*, Brighton: Wheatsheaf (1986).

Marvel, H. P. and E. J. Ray, "Interindustry Trade: Sources and Effects on Protection," *Journal of Political Economy* 95 (1987):1278–91.

Meyer, B., "Unemployment Insurance and Unemployment Spells," *Econometrica* 58 (1990):757–82.

Mills, T. C., G. Pelloni, and A. Zervoyianni, "Unemployment Fluctuations in the United States: Further Tests of the Structural Shifts Hypothesis," *Review of Economics and Statistics* 77 (1995):294–304.

Murphy, K. and R. Topel, "The Evolution of Unemployment in the United States 1968–1985," in S. Fischer (ed.), *NBER Macroeconomics Annual*, Cambridge, MA: MIT Press (1987).

Narendranathan, W. and M. Stewart, "Modelling the Probability of Leaving Unemployment: Competing Risks Models with Flexible Baseline Hazards," *Journal of the Royal Statistical Society (Series C) Applied Statistics* 42 (1993):63–83.

Neal, D., "Industry-Specific Human Capital: Evidence from Displaced Workers," *Journal of Labor Economics* 13 (1995):653–77.

Oswald, A., "The Missing Piece of the Unemployment Puzzle," Inaugural Lecture, Department of Economics, University of Warwick (1997).

Ratanayake, R. and S. Jayasuriya, "Intraindustry Trade and Protection: Which Way Does Causation Go?" *Economics Letters* 35 (1991):71–6.

Rayment, P., "The Homogeneity of Manufacturing Industries with Respect to Factor Intensity: the Case of the UK," *Oxford Bulletin of Economics and Statistics* 38 (1976):203–9

Reker, C., "Adjustment Pressures and Adjustment Processes in the Machine Tool Industry: The Role of Intraindustry Trade," mimeo, University of Dusseldorf (1994).

Slaughter, M., "Globalisation and Wages: A Tale of Two Perspectives," Centre for Research on Globalisation and Labor Markets, University of Nottingham research chapter 99/5 (1999).

Taylor, M. F. (ed.) with J. Brice, N. Buck, and E. Prentice-Lane, *British Household Panel Survey User Manual Volume A: Introduction, Technical Report, and Appendices*, Colchester: University of Essex (1998).

Tharakan, P. K. M. and G. Calfat, "Adjustment and Interindustry Trade: A Factor Heterogeneity Test Using Firm Level Data," mimeo, University of Antwerp (1994).

Thomas, J. M., "An Empirical Model of Sectoral Movements by Unemployed Workers," *Journal of Labor Economics* 14 (1996a):126–53.

———, "On the Interpretation of Covariate Estimates on Independent Competing Risks Models," *Bulletin of Economic Research* 48 (1996b):27–39.

Upward, R., "Constructing Data on Unemployment Spells from the PSID and the BHPS," University of Nattingham: Centre for Research on Globalisation and Labor Markets, mimeo (1999).

Notes

1. For reviews of the relevant literature, see Greenaway and Hine (1991) and Brülhart (1998).
2. Available from http://www.nottingham.ac.uk/economics/leverhulme/publications.
3. The sample is therefore a *flow* rather than a *stock* sample. If we were to include left-censored spells we would be oversampling long spells of unemployment because the probability of a spell being sampled is proportional to its length (Lancaster, 1990).
4. Of course, sectoral mobility is not synonymous with geographical mobility, since workers may move regions in order to stay in the same sector.

12
Relative Demand for Skills in Swedish Manufacturing: Technology or Trade?

Pär Hansson

1. Introduction

A striking feature in most OECD countries is a sharply growing share of skilled labor in the labor force. A clear result from several decompositions of the changes in skill shares (shift-share analyses) in various countries[1] is that the bulk of the increase is driven by rapid within-industry changes in skill utilization rather than between-industry employment shifts. This precludes explanations involving shifts in production from less-skilled-intensive industries to more-skilled-intensive industries as the main causes of the significant skill upgrading.

Two factors put forward, consistent with within-industry increases in skill shares, are skilled-biased technological change and increased globalization pressure. Skilled-biased technological change means technical progress that reduces the need for unskilled labor. The prime suspect for widespread recent technological changes that could have led to drastic changes in the relative demand for skills is the diffusion of computers and related technologies. Another factor that may have accelerated technological changes is the larger R&D expenditure in many OECD countries.

Increased globalization pressure may affect the relative demand for skills within industries through increased competition from the South. I will show that industries, even if they are defined on the lowest level of industry aggregation, are by no means composed of activities with similar skill shares. Increased exposure to competition from the South may then lead to switches from domestic low-skill producers to foreign suppliers in countries abundantly endowed with unskilled labor. Outsourcing is another possibility, which means that firms in developed countries find it profitable to offload the most unskilled-labor-intensive activities to overseas production in countries where unskilled labor is relatively cheap. The relative demand for skilled workers increases in the developed countries since the remaining activities then, on average, become more skill-intensive.[2]

The purpose of this chapter is an attempt to quantify the relative importance of these factors in Swedish manufacturing over the past 25 years. The chapter is in a vein emanating from Berman et al. (1994). I estimate a reduced-form model at industry level originating from a labor demand function derived from a translog cost function. I assume that technological changes can be related to investment in physical capital and knowledge. New technologies are often embodied in new machinery and the latest production methods are usually put into practice in newly set-up plant. As in several other similar studies, a positive relationship can be established between accumulation of physical capital and demand for skills.[3]

Investments in R&D are expected to result in technological improvements. By cumulating R&D expenditure we can construct knowledge capital stocks. The knowledge stocks can be smoothly integrated into the analytical framework and make it possible to examine whether knowledge capital and skilled labor are relative complements. The findings show that they are, and that the rapid growth in knowledge capital in Sweden is a major explanation of the increased relative demand for skills in Swedish manufacturing over the last decade. Moreover, the degree of complementarity between knowledge capital and skill has strengthened over time. I also try to evaluate the impact of international technology spillovers, and the results indicate some influence on the relative demand for skills.

Many studies have examined the hypothesis that trade has led to deterioration in the position of less-skilled workers. Generally, growth rates in the shares of imports and exports in consumption (production) are included as explanatory variables of shifts in skill structures.[4] I argue that growth in the share of imports in consumption is an indicator of increased import competition. In order to investigate the influences of increased competition from the South more rigorously, the imports have to be disaggregated by country of origin; in the present analysis I let the import share be based solely on imports from non-OECD countries.[5] A small, positive impact of increased Southern import competition is observed on the relative demand for skills in Swedish manufacturing. A closer examination of individual sectors shows that this result is essentially driven by the textile industry.

Finally, I broaden the horizon outside manufacturing and discuss what has happened to Swedish manufacturing as a whole in relation to other sectors. Has the manufacturing share of total employment been shrinking in Sweden as in other OECD countries? A reasonable consequence of a falling manufacturing share due to increased competition from the South would be a decrease in employment of less-skilled labor in manufacturing. Such a development may in turn have effects on the skill intensity in the less trade-exposed nonmanufacturing sector. In this context I compare the employment pattern of the skilled and less-skilled in Swedish manufacturing and nonmanufacturing sectors in the late 1980s up to the mid-1990s. An indicator of the position of skilled and less-skilled workers on the labor market, in particular in the European countries, is the relative unemployment rate. I investigate its development in Sweden since the beginning of the 1970s and make a comparison with the situation in other OECD countries.

Section 2 outlines the analytical framework and suggests various technology indicators. Section 3 first analyzes the technology impact on skill upgrading in Swedish manufacturing over the last decade. It then deals with whether we can observe acceleration in the relative demand for skills, and examines the effects of competition from the South on skill upgrading. Section 3 also widens the analysis to the whole Swedish economy, discussing employment patterns in the manufacturing and nonmanufacturing sectors and the relative unemployment rate of skilled and less-skilled workers. Section 4 concludes.

2. Analytical Framework

I follow the standard setup in this literature and derive an econometric specification from a nonhomothetic translog cost function.[6] Skilled and less-skilled labor are variable factors, and physical capital K and knowledge capital S are treated as fixed. Cost minimization implies that we obtain the share of skilled labor cost in total wage cost by employing Shephard's lemma. The cost share of skilled labor P^W is

$$P^W = b_0 + b_1 \ln(w_s/w_u) + b_2 \ln Y + b_3 \ln K + b_4 \ln S + b_5 T, \tag{1}$$

where w_s and w_u are wage rates of skilled and less-skilled workers, Y is real output, and T is an index of the state of technology.

Differentiating (1) with respect to time, assuming the parameters to be invariant across industries i and appending an error term ε_i, gives our basic regression model:

$$\Delta P_i^W = \beta_0 + \beta_1 \Delta \ln(w_s/w_u)_i + \beta_2 \Delta \ln Y_i + \beta_3 \Delta \ln K_i + \beta_4 \Delta \ln S_i + \beta_5 \Delta T_i + \varepsilon_i. \quad (2)$$

The sign of β_1 depends on whether the elasticity of substitution between skilled and less-skilled labor σ is greater or less than one; β_1 is negative when σ is larger than one.[7] Despite an opportunity to calculate relative wages—by using the sum of labor income and the number of employed divided into skilled and less-skilled categories at industry level—β_1 is not estimated. The reason is that it is questionable whether such relative wages can be considered exogenous. According to Berman et al. (1994), some of the relative wage changes depend on cross-sectional differences in skill upgrading, which means that we confound price changes with quality changes. On the whole, compositional changes (due to age and education) of the skilled and less-skilled groups may largely affect the calculated relative wages. Moreover, there is a definitional relationship between the dependent variable and the measure of relative wage.

If we instead assume labor to be perfectly mobile across industries, the wage of the skilled is equalized across industries, as well as the wage of the less skilled, and $\Delta \ln(w_s/w_u)_i$ is a constant. The exclusion of the relative wage variable will then affect the intercept β_0 or the coefficients of the time dummies only in a panel study. The estimate of β_2 shows whether the growth in output is related to changes in the wage bill share of skilled labor. If $\beta_2 = 0$, we cannot reject the hypothesis that the production function is homothetic.

The coefficient of $\Delta \ln K$ indicates whether skilled labor is complementary ($\beta_3 > 0$) or substitute ($\beta_3 < 0$) to physical capital in the production process. I assume that new machinery and equipment make use of the latest technologies and that modern methods of production are practiced in newly built plants. Technology innovations alter the demand in favor of better-educated workers because they have a comparative advantage in implementing new technology.[8] Computerization and other information technology upgrade the workforce by automating manual tasks and giving workers more time to concentrate on conceptual and decision-making tasks. Others may argue that new technology de-skills the workforce. Mass production and other radical technological advances in the nineteenth century led to the substitution of highly skilled artisans with physical capital, raw materials, and unskilled labor.[9]

Similar arguments also apply to knowledge capital, and the estimate of β_4 shows whether skilled labor is complementary ($\beta_4 > 0$) or substitute ($\beta_4 < 0$) to knowledge capital. To calculate knowledge capital stocks, I use time series of R&D expenditure. Following Hall and Mairesse (1995):

$$S_{it} = (1-\delta_s)S_{it-1} + RD_{it-1}, \quad (3)$$

where S_{it} is the knowledge (R&D) capital stock in industry i at the beginning of period t, RD_{it-1} is expenditure on R&D in industry i at time $t-1$, in constant prices, and δ_s is the rate of depreciation of knowledge (i.e., the rate at which knowledge becomes obsolete). A benchmark S_{i1} is obtained as

$$S_{i1} = \frac{RD_{i1}}{g+\delta_s}, \quad (4)$$

where g is the rate of growth of R&D (assumed constant over time). I assume a depreciation rate of knowledge δ_s of 15% (cf. Hall and Mairesse, 1995) and a presample growth in R&D expenditure of 6%. I also assume that investments in research add to the stock of productive knowledge with a lag of three years.[10]

As alternative measures of $\Delta \ln S$, I employ R&D expenditure as a share of value-added, $(RD/Y)^{Sweden}$, which has been used frequently in other similar studies; or the proportion of technicians among the employees, $TECH$. New technologies are continuously introduced at a high rate in R&D-intensive industries, and a high proportion of technicians enhances the ability to develop, adopt, and implement new technologies. ΔT includes technological changes not captured by changes in the industry's own physical or knowledge capital stock. One would expect a higher rate of technological change in industries where the potential for international technology spillovers is large. Following Machin and Van Reenen (1998), I construct a spillover pool simply by calculating the worldwide (13 OECD countries excluding Sweden) R&D intensity, $(RD/Y)^{OECD}$, for each industry.[11]

Models use various types of technology indicator to measure different aspects of technological change.[12] It could be of interest to show the correlation among these indicators. I therefore calculate a correlation matrix for the technology indicators in a panel of 19 industries for the period 1986–95. A complete description of the data is given in the Appendix.

Most of the variables in the correlation matrix in Table 1 are positively correlated, and the R&D intensity in Sweden and the proportion of technicians are very strongly correlated (0.80). In the analysis I will use these two variables interchangeably; $TECH$ has the advantage of being available in industries at low levels of aggregation. Other variables that are strongly correlated are $(RD/Y)^{Sweden}$ and the R&D intensity in other OECD countries, $(RD/Y)^{OECD}$. Yet the correlation is far from one (0.69), which indicates that it is not exactly the same industries that are R&D-intensive in Sweden and in other OECD countries. Finally, the R&D intensity in Sweden and the relative growth in the knowledge stock, $\Delta \ln S$, are not strongly correlated (0.50); the R&D intensity

Table 1. Correlation Matrix: Technology Indicators

	$\Delta \ln K$	$\Delta \ln S$	$(RD/Y)^{Sweden}$	$TECH$	$(RD/Y)^{OECD}$
$\Delta \ln K$	1.000				
$\Delta \ln S$	0.215	1.000			
$(RD/Y)^{Sweden}$	0.318	0.495	1.000		
$TECH$	0.355	0.359	0.805	1.000	
$(RD/Y)^{OECD}$	0.564	0.325	0.687	0.715	1.000

Note: The correlations are calculated on variables in the panel of 19 manufacturing industries 1986–95. OECD is 12 countries: Australia, Canada, Denmark, Finland, France, Germany (West), Italy, Japan, The Netherlands, Norway, the United Kingdom and the United States.
Variable definition:
$\Delta \ln K$ 100 × the change in the log of the physical capital stock
$\Delta \ln S$ 100 × the change in the log of the knowledge capital stock
$(RD/Y)^{Sweden}$ 100 × R&D expenditure as a share of value added in Sweden
$TECH$ 100 × the share of employees with technical post-secondary education
$(RD/Y)^{OECD}$ 100 × R&D expenditure as a share of value added in OECD excluding Sweden

may underestimate (overestimate) knowledge capital accumulation in "low-tech" ("high-tech") industries.[13]

3. Empirical Results

Technology and Skill Upgrading

The econometric analysis estimates various specifications based on the model in equation (2). Owing to the availability of data, I use two datasets.[14] The first is a panel of 19 manufacturing industries for the period 1986–95. In the second the time period is extended, 1970–93, and data are pooled for two time periods, 1970–85 and 1986–93, for which average annual changes have been calculated. Here, we use two levels of aggregation: the same 19 industries as in the 1986–95 panel and a more disaggregated one, consisting of 34 manufacturing industries. The definition of skilled labor is based on educational attainment.[15] Thus skilled labor is employed workers with a post-secondary education; i.e., with more than 12 years of education. The dependent variable in the 1986–95 panel study is change in skilled labor wage bill share, ΔP^W; and in the pooled 1970–93 dataset the dependent variable is change in skilled labor employment share, ΔP^E.[16] The results from the 1986–95 panel are given in Table 2, and from the 1970–93 pooled model in Table 6.

As a comparison with similar studies, in particular Machin and Van Reneen (1998),[17] I start in Table 2 specification (1) by using the R&D intensity in Sweden in period $t-1$, $(RD/Y)^{Sweden}$, as a technology indicator. I use lagged R&D intensity[18] to take into account that new knowledge will not be implemented immediately (cf. the construction of knowledge stocks). Another reason is that I want to avoid picking up an identity between R&D expenditure and changes in the share of skilled labor; most R&D spending is made up of the employment cost of scientists and other skilled workers. On the other hand, the number of R&D workers in manufacturing is relatively small.[19]

The results agree with other studies. The coefficient on the change in physical capital is positive and significant in specification (1) and in all other specifications in Table 2. This implies complementarity between physical capital and skilled labor. The coefficient is also positive, and strongly significant, on Swedish R&D intensity; this means that over the decade R&D intensive industries were more likely to increase their skill shares.[20] In columns (2) and (3) in Table 2, Swedish R&D intensity are replaced with changes in knowledge capital. The yearly variation in skill shares and technology measures tend to be small, and therefore in (3) we use longer fre-quency differences, three-year differences instead of one-year differences. Moreover, such a specification is more useful for comparisons with some of the later results. From the results in columns (2) and (3) we can evaluate and compare the impact of investment in new plant and machinery and investment in knowledge on the relative demand for skills in Swedish manufacturing during the late 1980s and the beginning of the 1990s.[21] The coefficient on the growth in knowledge capital is less than the coefficient on the growth in physical capital, but from column (5) we can see that the knowledge capital has grown faster than the physical capital. Using this in a back-of-the-envelope calculation in column (5) (the regression coefficients are from specification (3)), the growth in knowledge capital "explains" almost 17% of the overall change in the skill structure in manufacturing, while the contribution of physical capital is 14%.[22]

Table 2. *Wage-Bill Share Equations Based on a 19 Manufacturing Industry Panel in Sweden, 1986–95*

Variables	(1) Regression one-year changes	(2) Regression one-year changes	(3) Regression annualized three-year changes	(4) Mean value	(5) Contribution
Dependent:					
ΔP^W				0.798 (0.96)	
Independent:					
$\Delta \ln Y$	−0.005 [−0.71]	0.001 [0.10]	0.020 [1.48]	2.213 (9.57)	5.3%
$\Delta \ln K$	0.035 [2.35]	0.052 [2.27]	0.063 [2.00]	1.783 (3.89)	14.0%
$\Delta \ln S$		0.025 [2.06]	0.035 [2.28]	3.800 (5.14)	16.6%
$(RD/Y)^{Sweden}$	0.015 [2.84]				
$(RD/Y)^{OECD}$		0.026 [1.71]	0.010 [0.56]	5.552 (5.53)	7.0%
Time dummies	8.70 /0.00/	8.89 /0.00/	14.70 /0.00/		57.1%
$\bar{R}^2$	0.483	0.533	0.695		
Observations	169	160	53		

Notes: All regressions and mean values are computed over 19 industries for the period 1986–1993 and over 18 industries for the period 1993–95 (see the Appendix in Hansson, 1999). I exclude the observations on $(RD/Y)^{OECD}$ in ISIC 3845 Aircraft. Owing to the large amount of military/government expenditure in ISIC 3845 there appear to be problems in constructing reasonable R&D figures, in particular in the US and the UK, two large OECD countries that heavily influence $(RD/Y)^{OECD}$ (Machin and Van Reenen, 1998). I weigh regressions and means values by the average industry share of the manufacturing wage bill. The impact in total manufacturing is larger from large manufacturing industries. Furthermore, the weighing procedure reduces the influence of noise in the data owing to measurement errors particularly evident in small industries (Berman et al., 1994). Square brackets [ ] give White's heteroskedasticity-consistent *t* statistics, and slashes // the significance level of the *F*-test. The fourth column contains mean values, and in parentheses ( ) are standard deviations of the dependent and independent variables. The fifth column shows the contribution of each of the independent variables in specification (3).
Variable definition:
ΔP^W 100 × the change in the skilled labors' share in the wage bill
$\Delta \ln Y$ 100 × the change in the log of real output
Other variables are defined in Table 1, and the Appendix gives more details.

Since the change in knowledge capital, $\Delta \ln S$, is a key variable, I also check whether outliers drive the estimates on the coefficient of $\Delta \ln S$. Figure 1, which shows the partial association between change in skilled labor wage share and change in knowledge capital, indicates that this is not the case.[23] The effect of potential international technology spillovers is positive and significant at the 10% level in (2), while we get a lower, and statistically insignificant, coefficient when we base our estimates on longer frequency differences (column (3)). According to the evaluation in column (5),

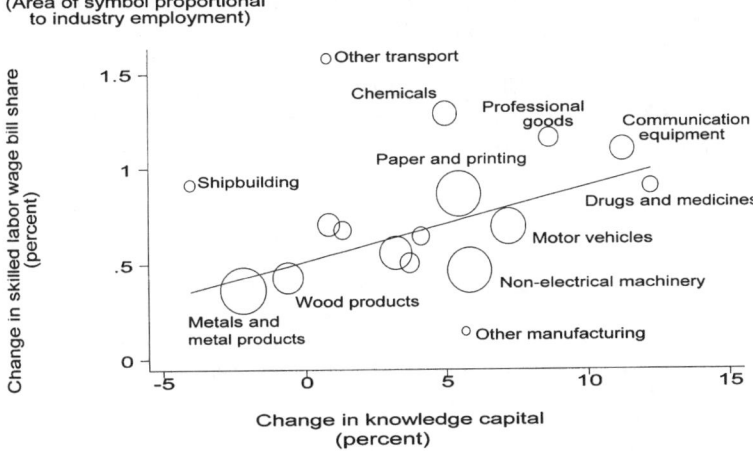

Figure 1. Partial Association Between Change in Skilled-Labor Wage Bill and Change in Knowledge Capital

international technology spillovers seem to have some economic impact. Another interesting observation is that an exclusion of $(RD/Y)^{OECD}$ will bias the coefficients on $\Delta \ln S$ and $\Delta \ln K$ upwards;[24] they pick up some of the effects of international technology spillovers.

The results in Table 2 indicate that, in particular, investment in knowledge capital (i.e., growth in R&D stocks) seems to have played an important role in explaining the increased relative demand for skills in Swedish manufacturing over the decade. This impression is strengthened by the fact that, until the beginning of the 1980s, the R&D intensity in Sweden and the R&D intensity in other OECD countries developed in similar pattern. By the mid-1980s the Swedish R&D intensity was slightly larger, but then the gap between them has widened. The investment ratios, on the other hand, have fluctuated around the same level (15%) over the period 1973–94.[25] Calculations of the annual growth in the physical and the knowledge capital stocks in manufacturing, presented in Table 3, indicate that the growth rate in knowledge capital has been about one percentage point higher in Sweden than in other OECD countries, and the growth rate in physical capital has been more than two percentage points lower. The lower rate of physical capital accumulation, despite an average OECD investment ratio in Sweden over the period studied, can be explained by the fact that Sweden had a fairly high physical capital–output ratio in the middle of the 1980s.[26] Consequently, a great deal of the investment in buildings and machinery was replacement of depreciated capital.

Acceleration in Skill Upgrading

One intriguing question is whether we can observe acceleration in the relative demand for skills during the last few decades.[27] To analyze this we have to extend the period under study. The educational attainment of employees in manufacturing increased continuously over the period. The proportion with post-secondary education increased from 2.6% in 1970 to 16.3% in 1995, and the proportion with post-secondary

Table 3. Physical and Knowledge Capital Investments in Sweden and OECD Countries, 1986–95

Country	I/Y	RD/Y	$\Delta \ln K$	$\Delta \ln S$
Sweden	15.65	8.78	1.91	5.80
OECD	14.81	6.72	4.09	4.77

Notes: I/Y is the average gross fixed capital formation as a share of value-added for the period 1985–94, and RD/Y is the average R&D expenditure as a share of value-added for the period 1983–92 $\Delta \ln K$ and $\Delta \ln S$ are the average annual changes in physical and knowledge capital, 1986–95. To calculate the physical and knowledge capital stocks, I use the methods described in the Appendix. I get the benchmark physical capital stock K in 1986 from OECD (1993) and investments I in constant prices from OECD (1996). OECD is 12 countries (see Table 1).

education of more than three years increased from just over 1% in 1960 to a little under 6.4% in 1993.[28] If we calculate the average annual changes in the manufacturing skill share over different periods, we find that the rate of change has increased over time.[29]

Partly, the shift over the period 1970–85 may be explained by growing relative demand for skills; but, as put forward by Edin and Holmlund (1995), an increase in the supply of labor with higher education seems to have played the more important role. According to Table 4, the relative wages of skilled labor fell over the period 1970–85. This implies that firms had an incentive to substitute less-skilled labor with skilled. Moreover, the changes in the international specialization pattern of Swedish manufacturing are consistent with a Rybczynski effect: the large increase in the supply of skilled labor led to shifts in specialization towards more production in skilled-labor-intensive industries.[30]

Table 4 also documents a moderate rise in the relative wages of skilled labor from 1984 until at least 1991. Edin and Holmlund (1995) argue that even over this period the explanations for the relative wage changes are found on the supply side; i.e., a slowdown in the supply of educated workers in the mid-1980s. One argument against this is the increased rate of change in the manufacturing skill share, despite slightly rising relative wages of skilled labor. In their analysis the demand side is modeled in a rudimentary fashion. A time trend, which is positive and significant, is used to pick up influences of technological changes in a regression on relative wages.[31] Furthermore, they examine the extent to which employment has shifted towards skill-intensive industries (cf. the between-industry component below) and find that the allocation between industries was less favorable to skilled labor in the late 1980s.

However, recent studies have decomposed the change in the share of skilled labor into two components, where one captures reallocations between industries and the other the effect of changing skill ratios within industries. Table 5 makes this type of analysis on the changes in the employment structure in Swedish manufacturing in 1970–96. We can see the same pattern as in other studies, namely that the bulk of the increase in the manufacturing skill share has occurred within industries. The result is not dependent on the aggregation level of industries; the within-industry component is large even on a fairly low level of industry aggregation. This emphasizes the impor-

Table 4. Skilled-Based Relative Wages in Sweden, 1968–91

	1968	1974	1981	1984	1986	1988	1991
University/upper secondary	1.80	1.33	1.23	1.22	1.27	1.24	1.31

Notes: The relative wages are based on standardized wage equations. "University" means 16 years of education, and upper secondary 12 years of education. The table is from Holmlund (1997).

Table 5. Between- and Within-Industry Decomposition of Changes in Employment Structure in Swedish Manufacturing, 1970–96 (annualized changes in percentage points)

Period	Number of industries	Total change	Between-industry component	Within-industry component	Contribution of within-industry component
1970–85	34	0.442	0.040	0.402	91.0%
1986–93	34	0.916	0.111	0.805	88.0%
1986–93	146	0.916	0.112	0.804	87.8%
1990–96	275	0.765	0.132	0.633	82.7%

Note: The first part (the between-industry component) captures the effect of employment shifts between industries. The second part (the within-industry component) measures the impact of changes in skill-intensities within industries.
Decomposition of changes in skill shares:

$$\Delta P^E = \sum_{i=1}^{n} \Delta S_i \overline{P_i} + \sum_{i=1}^{n} \Delta P_i^E \overline{S_i}$$

P_i^E: share of the employees in industry i with post-secondary education
S_i: industry i's share of total employment in manufacturing
$\overline{P_i^E}$ and $\overline{S_i}$ are period averages.

tance of trying to explain the within-industry shifts in skill shares in order to understand skill share trends in Swedish manufacturing.

The rate of the within-industry shift towards higher skill shares has been increasing over time, and it was particularly strong during the late 1980s and at the beginning of the 1990s.[32] To explain this pattern, I estimate the preferred model in Table 2 (specification (3)) for the two time periods 1970–85 and 1986–93 on the same 19 (18) manufacturing industries as in the 1986–95 panel study, and I allow the coefficients to vary between the periods. It is found that the only variable of importance for which the coefficient differs significantly between the two periods is the knowledge capital accumulation, $\Delta \ln S$. Therefore, in Table 6 specification (1), all other coefficients are restricted to being equal across the two time periods. The result is quite interesting since knowledge capital accumulation has a significantly larger effect on the relative demand for skills in the more recent period.[33] One interpretation is that the degree of complementarity between knowledge capital and skills has increased over time.

In some contrast to the results in the panel study in Table 2, potential international technology spillovers have a positive and clearly significant impact on the relative demand for skills. This is a reasonable outcome given the fact that Sweden is

Table 6. Employment Share Equations in Swedish Manufacturing, 1970–93

Variables	(1) Regression annualized changes 1970–93	(2) Regression annualized changes 1970–93	(3) Mean value	(4) Contribution
Dependent:				
ΔP^E			0.595	
			(0.38)	
Independent:				
$\Delta \ln Y$	0.033	0.028	0.431	2.4%
	[2.30]	[2.64]	(3.21)	
$\Delta \ln K$	0.019	0.047	2.969	9.4%
	[0.63]	[2.83]	(1.48)	
$\Delta \ln S$ 1970–85	−0.0003		6.497	−0.1%
	[−0.02]		(2.74)	
$\Delta \ln S \times$ dummy	0.047		3.983	15.6%*
1986–93	[2.62]		(3.99)	
TECH		0.031		
		[4.80]		
$(RD/Y)^{OECD}$	0.023		4.491	17.7%
	[2.34]		(5.03)	
Intercept	2.03×10^{-3}	-5.02×10^{-4}		17.0%
1970–85	[2.42]	[−0.61]		
Dummy	2.50×10^{-3}	5.44×10^{-3}		38.0%*
1986–93	[2.84]	[7.12]		
$\bar{R}^2$	0.839	0.699		
Observations	36	68		
Industries	18	34		

Notes: I weigh the regressions and mean values by the average industry share of the manufacturing employment. As in Table 2 I exclude the observations on $(RD/Y)^{OECD}$ in ISIC 3845. Square brackets [ ] give White's heteroskedasticity-consistent *t*-statistics. The third column contains mean values, and in parentheses ( ) are standard deviations of the dependent and independent variables. The fourth column shows the contribution of each of the independent variables in specification (1). *The contribution is calculated for the period coefficient, i.e., 0.047 for $\Delta \ln S$ 1986–93 and 4.53×10^{-3} for the intercept 1986–93.
Variable definition:
ΔP^E 100 × the change in the skilled labors' share in the employment
Other variables are defined in Tables 1 and 2, and the Appendix gives more details.

a small open economy, and is in line with other studies on international technology spillovers; e.g., Coe and Helpman (1995).[34] The influence of physical capital accumulation is insignificant, however, yet still positive. The back-of-the envelope calculations in Table 6 column (4) indicate that there is a considerable contribution to the relative demand for skills from international technology spillovers and knowledge capital accumulation in the more recent period, and also to some extent from physical capital accumulation.

Specification (2) in Table 6 uses the more disaggregated dataset (34 manufacturing industries). On this level of aggregation I have no access to data on R&D expenditures. The correlation matrix in Table 1 demonstrates, however, strong correlation at the industry level between the R&D intensity in Sweden, $(RD/Y)^{Sweden}$, the R&D intensity in other OECD countries, $(RD/Y)^{OECD}$, and the share of technicians, $TECH$. Specification (2) replaces $\Delta \ln S$ and $(RD/Y)^{OECD}$ with $TECH$ and the coefficient on $TECH$ is positive and strongly significant.[35] A notable difference in comparison with specification (1) is the coefficient on physical capital accumulation, which is larger and clearly significant in specification (2).

Skill Upgrading and Competition from the South

One argument advanced against international trade as an explanation of increased relative demand for skills is the outcome from decomposition studies such as those presented in Table 5. It has been argued that, in a developed country, increased competition from less-developed and newly industrialized countries (LDCs and NICs) shift employment from low-skill to high-skill industries, while changes in the within-industry shares are a result of technological changes. Since the bulk of the increased skill share has occurred within industries, the conclusion has been that international trade played a minor role in explaining the increased relative demand for skills. From Table 5 it appears that Sweden is no exception in this respect; even on the lowest level of industry aggregation the contribution of the between-industry component is less than 20%.

However, trade may just as well affect the within-industry share. Theoretically, industries are often assumed to be homogeneous with respect to factor intensities. In practice, they are composed of a wide range of activities, in which final and intermediate products are produced with varying factor intensities. Table 7 shows the variation in skill shares among plants within industries defined on the lowest level of industry aggregation in Swedish manufacturing. In the analysis of variance, the F-values indicate that there are significant differences in skill shares between industries. Yet the variations among plants within industries are substantial. Between 60% and 70% of the total variance in skill shares are within industries, even though we observe a tendency towards decreasing variances within industries. This means that there has been, and still is, a great potential for specialization with respect to skill shares within industries.

Table 7. Analysis of Variance in Skill Shares Among Swedish Manufacturing Plants Within Industries, Defined on the Lowest Level of Industry Aggregation

Variable	F-value	$\bar{R}^2$	Number of plants	Number of industries
Skill share 1986 (SNI69)	135.44	0.323	40,898	146
Skill share 1990 (SNI69)	140.09	0.336	39,876	146
Skill share 1990 (SNI92)	79.52	0.337	41,727	271
Skill share 1996 (SNI92)	90.02	0.409	35,330	274

Notes: The total variance, SS_{total}, in skill shares on plant level is separated into two components: the variance between averages for industries defined on the lowest level of aggregation in SNI (Swedish Standard of Industrial Classification), $SS_{between}$, and the variance within these industries, SS_{within}; i.e., $SS_{total} = SS_{between} + SS_{within}$. To establish whether skill shares differ between industries I assume that the variable F is F-distributed: $F = (SS_{between}/k - 1)/(SS_{within}/N - k)$, where k is the number of industries and N is the number of plants. A measure of the between-industry variance of the total variance in skill shares is $\bar{R}^2$. A more complete description of analysis of variance is given in standard textbooks in statistics, for example Mendenhall et al. (1990).

One example of such specialization is outsourcing. In many firms different stages of production are heterogeneous with respect to skill intensity. Firms in developed countries may then, in response to competition from low-wage countries, move their low-skill-intensive production abroad. Modern production techniques and improvements in communication technology have made it easier to split up the manufacturing process of production into separate activities performed in different countries. By moving the low-skill-intensive part of the production (for example assembly of components) overseas, but continuing to carry out the high-skill-intensive activities themselves, a firm can take advantage of lower wages for the less skilled. Once the low-skilled activities have been accomplished the goods are imported back, either to be used as intermediate inputs or sold as finished goods. Hence, a reasonable variable to proxy the impact of outsourcing on the relative demand for skills within an industry is the change in imports from non-OECD countries as a share of consumption. Such a variable captures more than just the effect of outsourcing. Narrowly defined outsourcing takes place within multinationals. Nevertheless, increased competition from low-wage countries also entails that domestic consumers and producers may switch from buying low-skill-intensive final or intermediate goods from domestic producers to foreign suppliers in countries like the LDCs and the NICs.

In my econometric analysis I use a similar approach as in Feenstra and Hanson (1996, 1997) to analyze the effect of outsourcing on the relative demand for skills within industries. I append the variable $\Delta(M/C)^{Non-OECD}$, the average annual change in import competition from non-OECD countries, to the regression models previously estimated. Feenstra and Hanson (1996) proxy outsourcing by the share of imports from all countries (including imports from advanced industrialized countries) in US shipments plus imports. There is no reason, however, to expect that Swedish multinationals would outsource low-skilled activities to other countries where less-skilled labor is expensive, or that increased competition from nations with abundant supply of high-skill labor would severely affect the situation of the low-skilled in Sweden. Table 8 presents the results from this analysis. Both specifications use the most disaggregated dataset (34 manufacturing industries), which means that the variables based on R&D expenditures ($\Delta \ln S$ and $(RD/Y)^{OECD}$) are replaced with the share of technicians, $TECH$.[36] In column (1), the coefficient on $\Delta(M/C)^{Non-OECD}$ is positive and significant.[37]

An interesting hypothesis set out by Wood (1998) is that most of the recent acceleration in the growth rate of the relative demand for skilled labor has been caused by increased globalization. The reasons are reduced policy barriers to international transactions (fewer restrictions on trade and foreign direct investment), and technical changes resulting in lower transport and communication costs. Moreover, many less-developed countries have shifted development strategies from import substitution to export promotion, and large countries, such as China and India, and the former Soviet bloc countries have become more outward-oriented. A simple test of the hypothesis is to allow the coefficient on $\Delta(M/C)^{Non-OECD}$ to vary between the two periods. Contrary to Wood's hypothesis, the estimate on $\Delta(M/C)^{Non-OECD}$ in Table 8 column (2) is significant only for the earlier period 1970–85. However, it is not significantly different from the coefficient in the later period, 1986–93.[38]

The partial association plot in Figure 2, using the coefficients from Table 8 column (2), shows that many of the results in Table 8 are driven by development in the textile industry.[39] The non-OECD import competition increased sharply in textiles over the whole period, while employment fell precipitously.[40] From the plot we can see that the average relative size of the textile industry was larger in the 1970–85 period (circle)

Table 8. *Effects of Increased Competition from the South on Skill Upgrading in Swedish Manufacturing, 1970–93*

Variables	(1) Regression annualized changes	(2) Regression annualized changes	(3) Mean value	(4) Contribution
Dependent:				
ΔP^E			0.601	
			(0.39)	
Independent:				
$\Delta \ln Y$	0.032	0.032	0.218	1.2%
	[3.11]	[3.07]	(3.53)	
$\Delta \ln K$	0.057	0.057	3.181	30.2%
	[3.43]	[3.41]	(1.80)	
TECH	0.029	0.030	7.298	35.2%
	[4.95]	[5.01]	(5.57)	
$\Delta(M/C)^{Non\text{-}OECD}$	0.116		0.280	5.4%
	[1.97]		(0.51)	
$\Delta(M/C)^{Non\text{-}OECD}$ 1970–85		0.178 [3.13]		
$\Delta(M/C)^{Non\text{-}OECD}$ 1986–93		0.093 [1.41]		
Intercept 1970–85	-9.13×10^{-4} [−1.12]	-1.04×10^{-3} [−1.25]		−7.6%
Intercept 1986–93	4.25×10^{-3} [4.72]	4.32×10^{-3} [4.60]		35.4%
$\bar{R}^2$	0.718	0.720		
Observations	68	68		
Industries	34	34		

Notes: I weigh the regressions and the mean values by the average industry share of the manufacturing employment. Square brackets [ ] give White's heteroskedasticity-consistent *t*-statistics. The third column contains mean values, and in the parentheses ( ) are standard deviations of the dependent and independent variables. The fourth column shows the contribution of each of the independent variables in specification (1).

than in the 1986–93 period (square). Since the regressions are weighted, the impact of the textile industry is larger on the estimate on $\Delta(M/C)^{Non\text{-}OECD}$ in the 1970–85 period. Furthermore, the changes in non-OECD import competition on industry level are more scattered over the latter period, which may give rise to the less precise estimate we get on $\Delta(M/C)^{Non\text{-}OECD}$ in the 1986–93 period.

Evidently the results in Table 8 give some support for a statistically significant impact of increased import competition from the South on the relative demand for skills in Swedish manufacturing industries. How important is this effect economically? Feenstra and Hanson (1996) detect considerable influences on skill upgrading of the increased import competition in US manufacturing, using the same method as used in Tables 2 and 3 to evaluate the contribution of different independent variables. They estimate that the growth of imports explains 15–33% of the increase in the nonproduction (skilled) labor share over the period 1979–87. Since the magnitude of

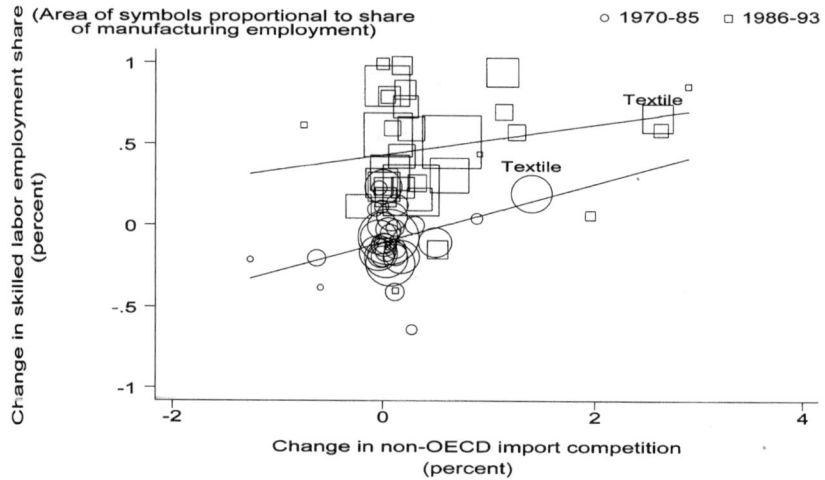

Figure 2. Partial Association Between Change in Skill Share and Change in Non-OECD Import Competition Over Periods 1970–85 and 1986–93

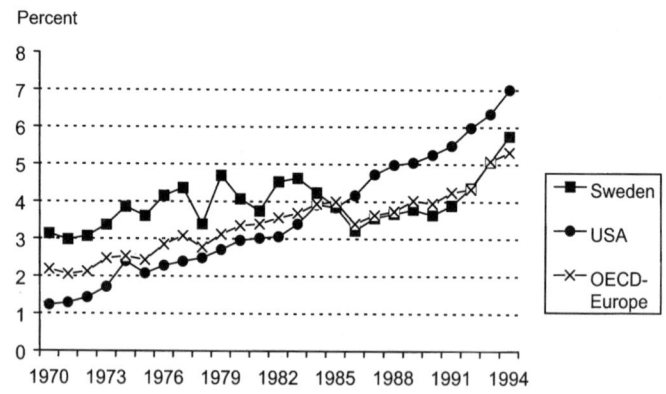

Figure 3. Non-OECD Manufacturing Import Share in Sweden, the US, and OECD–Europe, 1970–94 (OECD, 1998)

the contribution is determined by the development of the non-OECD imports (together with the coefficient on $\Delta(M/C)^{Non\text{-}OECD}$), I begin the evaluation by demonstrating, in Figure 3, how the non-OECD import competition progressed in Swedish manufacturing between 1970 and 1994. As a benchmark, I show the development of non-OECD manufacturing imports in the US and in OECD–Europe (excluding Sweden)[41] over the same period. Figure 3 shows that, at the beginning of the 1970s, Sweden had a larger non-OECD import share than the US and OECD–Europe. One explanation may be that Sweden was more free-trade oriented; the tariffs were lower than in most other developed countries.[42] However, the non-OECD imports in Sweden have grown less than in the US, while the development in Sweden is more in accordance with the development in OECD–Europe.

Not surprisingly, we find, in Table 8 column (4), that the contribution of increased import competition from the South on the relative demand for skilled labor has been of minor importance in comparison with physical capital accumulation and technological change. Just over 5% of the increase in skill shares is "explained" by intensified competition from the South. The corresponding figures for physical capital accumulation and my technology indicator are 30% and 35%.

Nonmanufacturing Employment and Relative Unemployment Rate of Skilled and Less-Skilled Labor

So far, I have, as in most other similar studies, focused on variations across industries within the manufacturing sector. However, increased competition from the South may involve contracting employment of less skill in the manufacturing sector, resulting in excess supply of less-skilled labor. We would then expect to find increased employment of less-skilled people in the nonmanufacturing sector or, since the relative wage between skilled and less skilled has been fairly constant (Table 4), a higher unemployment rate among the less skilled.

The development of manufacturing employment as a share of total employment shows almost the same pattern in Sweden as in the OECD; in Sweden, the share fell from around 29% in 1970 to less than 19% in 1994.[43] Since there seems to be a robust relationship among the OECD countries between increased non-OECD imports and falling employment in manufacturing,[44] one would hypothesize that increased competition from the South has increased the skilled labor employment shares more in the more trade-exposed manufacturing sector than in the nonmanufacturing sector.[45] Yet Table 9 indicates that this does not appear to be the case in Sweden. Certainly, over the period 1986–96, the relative increase in skilled labor employment and the relative decrease in less-skilled labor employment are larger in manufacturing, and the share of skilled labor employment almost doubled in manufacturing. However, the absolute increase in the share of skilled labor employment is less in manufacturing than in non-manufacturing.[46]

Finally, if we look at the unemployment rates by skills, in Figure 4, we can see that the unemployment rate of the less skilled is higher and seems to be more responsive to business cycles. Between 1975 and 1990, the unemployment rate of the skilled was more or less tied to 1%, whereas the unemployment rate of the less skilled varied between 2% and 4%. Over the period 1971–91, the Swedish unemployment rate was low in comparison with other OECD countries, but the macroeconomic shock that hit Sweden in the early 1990s pushed the unemployment rates up to an average OECD level.[47] If we use the data in Figure 4 to calculate the ratio of and the difference between the unemployment rates,[48] we find that, whereas the ratio fluctuates around

Table 9. Employment of Skilled and Less-Skilled Labor in Swedish Manufacturing and Nonmanufacturing, 1986 and 1996 (thousands)

Sector	Skilled labor			Less-skilled labor			Skill share		
	1986	1996	Δ96–86	1986	1996	Δ96–86	1986	1996	Δ96–86
Manufacturing	86	128	48.8%	844	623	−26.2%	9.2	17.0	7.8%
Nonmanufacturing	679	933	37.4%	2,613	2,090	−20.0%	20.6	30.9	10.3%

Source: SCB Regional Labor Statistics.

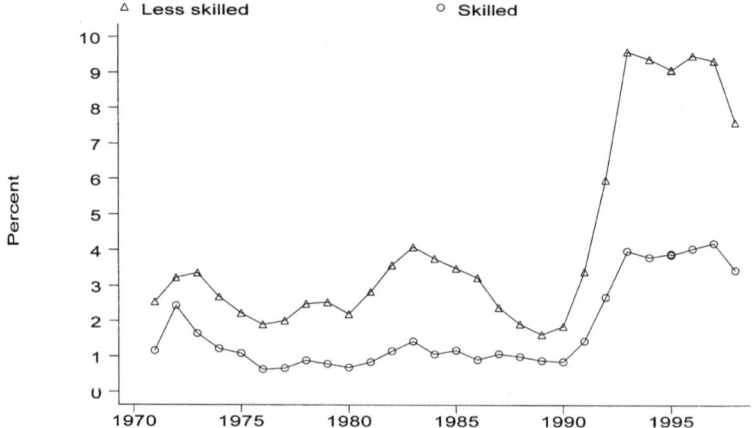

Figure 4. Unemployment Rates by Skill in Sweden, 1971–98 (SCB Labor Force Survey)

2.6, the difference has an upward-sloping trend.[49] The latter means that the gap between the unemployment rates of the skilled and less skilled has widened over the 25 years. The pattern is comparable with many other OECD countries[50] and indicates that the position of the less skilled has deteriorated in the Swedish labor market.

4. Concluding Remarks

A steady increase has been observed in the rate of change towards higher skill shares in Swedish manufacturing over the 35-year period from 1960 to 1995. Contrasting the development over the periods 1970–85 and 1986–93, the falling relative wages of skilled labor during the period 1970–85 suggests that the relative supply of skilled labor grew faster than the relative demand for skills. On the other hand, slightly rising relative wages over the more recent period of 1986–93, together with an increased rate of skill upgrading, indicate acceleration in the relative demand for skills in Swedish manufacturing. In accordance with this are the findings that the degree of complementarity between knowledge capital and skills appears to have strengthened over time, and that Sweden was a heavy investor in R&D in the late 1980s and at the beginning of the 1990s. Another factor behind acceleration in the relative demand for skills may be the rapid diffusion of computer technology. Autor et al. (1998) establish a strong positive relation between computer usage and skill upgrading, and according to SCB (1995) computer usage among the employed in Sweden doubled between 1984 and 1995.

Given the fact that Sweden is a small, open economy, it is not surprising that international technology spillovers affect the relative demand for skills positively. This study also gives some support for the belief that intensified competition from the South has increased the relative demand for skilled labor. However, the economic impact appears to be small; increased import competition from non-OECD countries "explains" relatively little of the skill upgrading. Furthermore, the textile industry played a crucial role in the outcome. Lastly, in most respects the Swedish experience has been similar to that in many other OECD countries. In particular, that applies to the main result, i.e., that both technology and trade matter for the deterioration of the less skilled, but the former is more important.

Appendix: Definitions and Data Sources

The Panel of 19 Manufacturing Industries 1986–95

Until 1993, data were classified according to SNI69. After 1993, a new system of classification (SNI92) was introduced. It is possible to achieve concordance at a fairly high level of aggregation. Hansson (1999) gives more details of the concordance between SNI69 and SNI92. The variables are listed below (*see also Hansson, 1999):

- *Wage incomes W*: Total wage incomes for employees with post-secondary education. Source: SCB Regional Labor Statistics.
- *Wage incomes skilled labor W^S*: Wage incomes for employees with post-secondary education. Source: SCB Regional Labor Statistics.
- *Skilled labors' share of the wage bill P^W*: $P^W = W^S/W$.
- *Employment E*: Number of employees. Source: SCB Regional Labor Statistics.
- *Technicians T*: Employees with technical post-secondary education. Source: SCB Regional Labor Statistics.
- *Share of technicians TECH*: $TECH = T/E$.
- *Physical capital K:** Stocks of fixed assets at replacement costs, 1991 prices. Source: SCB (1996a).
- *Real output Y:** Value-added, 1991 prices. Source: SCB (1997) and SCB (1995).
- *R&D intensity in Sweden and in OECD:* $(RD/Y)^{Sweden}$ and $(RD/Y)^{OECD}$
    RD: Expenditure on R&D, current prices. Source: OECD (1997).
    Y: Value added, current prices. Source: OECD (1996).
- *Knowledge capital S*: $S_{it} = (1 - \delta_s)S_{it-1} + R_{it-1}$.
    S_{it}: Knowledge capital (R&D) stock, industry i at time t, 1991 prices.
    R_{it}: Expenditure on R&D, industry i at time t, 1991 prices. R&D expenditure are simply deflated by the manufacturing sector level value added deflator. Source: OECD (1996) and OECD (1994).
    δ_S: Depreciation rate of knowledge (0.15).
    Benchmark year 1976.
- *Import competition* $(M/C)^{All}$ *and* $(M/C)^{Non\text{-}OECD}$:
    Import M^{All} and $M^{Non\text{-}OECD}$: Total import and import from non-OECD countries. Source: 1986–93 OECD (1998) and OECD (1996) and 1993–95 SCB Foreign Trade Statistics.
    Export X^{All}: Total export. Source: 1986–93 OECD (1998) and OECD (1996) and 1993–95 SCB Foreign Trade Statistics.
    Production Q: Sales value. Source: 1986–93 SOS Manufacturing various issues and 1993–95 SCB Manufacturing.
    Consumption C: $C = Q + M^{All} - X^{All}$.

The 34 (19) Manufacturing Industries 1970–93

- *Employment E*: Number of employees. Source: 1970–85 SCB (1991) and 1986–93 SCB Regional Labor Statistics.
- *Skilled labor E^S*: Employees with post-secondary education. Source: 1970–85 SCB (1991) and 1986–93 SCB Regional Labor Statistics.
- *Technicians T*:
    1970–85: Employees with technical secondary education of more than two years or technical post-secondary education. Source: SCB (1991).
    1986–93: Employees with technical post-secondary education. SCB Regional Labor Statistics.

- *Physical capital K:*** Capital stock, 1980 prices. Capital stock estimates are derived by the Perpetual Inventory Method (PIM). This implies that capital formations are added to and capital assets withdrawn are subtracted from an initial estimate of the capital stock. We assume linear depreciation, which means that the gross capital stock at time t is

$$K_t = K_{t-i}[1-(i/2a)] + \sum_{m=0}^{i-1} I_{t-m-1}[1-(m/2a)]$$

  K_{t-i}: Capital stock in the beginning of year $t - i$, 1980 prices.
  I_{t-m-1}: Gross fixed capital formation year $t - m - 1$, 1980 prices.
  a: Average service life in manufactures.
  Buildings 45 years and machinery 20 years (Meyer-zu-Schlochtern 1994).
  Benchmark year 1970. Source: SCB (1985).
  Investment, constant prices. Sources: SCB (1987) and SCB (1996b).
- *Real output Y:*** Value-added, 1980 prices. Source: SCB (1986) and SCB (1995).
- *R&D intensity in OECD* $(RD/Y)^{OECD}$: *(19 industries)*
  1970–85: Average 1973–84
  1986–93: Average 1985–92
  RD: Expenditure on R&D, current prices, US dollar: Source: OECD (1997)
  Y: Value-added, current prices, US dollar: Source: OECD (1996)
- *Knowledge capital S: (19 industries)*: $S_{it} = (1 - \delta_s)S_{it-1} + R_{it-1}$.
  S_{it}: Knowledge capital (R&D) stock, industry i at time t, 1980 prices
  R_{it}: Expenditure on R&D, industry i at time t, 1980 prices. R&D expenditure are simply deflated by the manufacturing sector level value added deflator. Sources: OECD (1996), SCB (1995), SCB (1986), OECD (1983), and SCB (1975).
  δ_s: Depreciation rate of knowledge (0.15).
  Benchmark year 1967.
- *Import* M^{All} *and* $M^{Non-OECD}$: Total import and import from non-OECD countries. Source: SCB Foreign Trade Statistics.
- *Export* X^{All}: Total export. Source: SCB Foreign Trade Statistics.
- *Production Q*: Sales value. Source: SOS Manufacturing, various issues.
- *Consumption C*: $C = Q + M^{All} - X^{All}$.

Data Sources

- Meyer-zu-Schlochtern, F. J. M. (1994), *An International Sectoral Database for Fourteen OECD Countries*, 2nd edn, Economics Department no. 145, OECD, Paris.
- OECD (1983), Science and Technology Indicators, Basic Statistical Series, Vol. D: Research and Development in the Business Sector 1963–1979.
- OECD (1993), *International Sectoral Database (ISDB)*. OECD (1994), *DSTI (STAN/ABERD Database), 1994*. OECD (1996), *DSTI (STAN Industrial Database), 1996*. OECD (1997), *DSTI(STAN/ANBERD Database), 1997*. OECD (1998), *DSTI(STAN/BTD) 1998*.
- SCB (1975), *Production and Factor Income 1950–1974*, SM N 1975: 98. SCB (1985), *Capital Formation and Stocks of Fixed Capital*, SM N 1984: 5.5. SCB (1986), *Production and Factor Income*, N 10 SM 8601. SCB (1987), *Capital formation*, N 10 SM 8601. SCB (1991), Utbildning och Produktivitet: En Studie av Svensk Industri under de Senaste Decennierna (Education and Productivity: A Study of the Swedish Industry over the Last Decades), *Information om Arbetsmarknaden 1991: 2*, Statistics Sweden Örebro. SCB (1995), *Production and Employment 1980–1994*, detailed tables, N 10 SM 9501, Statistics Sweden, Örebro. SCB (1996a), *Stocks of Fixed Assets and National Wealth*, N 10 SM 9501, Statistics Sweden, Örebro. SCB (1996b), *Expenditure of GDP*, N 10 SM 9501. Statistics Sweden, Örebro. SCB (1997), *National Accounts 1980–1995*. N10 SM 9601. Statistics Sweden, Örebro.

References

Anderton, B. and P. Brenton, "Did 'Outsourcing' to Low-Wage Countries Hurt Less-Skilled Workers in the UK?" in P. Brenton and J. Pelkmans (eds.), *Global Trade and European Workers*, London: Macmillan (1998).

Autor, D., L. Katz, and A. Krueger, "Computing Inequality: Have Computers Changed the Labor Market?" *Quarterly Journal of Economics* 113 (1998):1169–213.

Berman, E., J. Bound, and Z. Griliches, "Changes in the Demand for Skilled Labor within US Manufacturing: Evidence from the Annual Survey of Manufactures," *Quarterly Journal of Economics* 109 (1994):367–98.

Bernard, A. and B. Jensen, "Exporters, Skill Upgrading, and the Wage Gap," *Journal of International Economics* 42 (1997):3–31.

Berndt, E., *The Practice of Econometrics: Classic and Contemporary*, New York: Addison-Wesley (1991).

Braverman, H., *Labor and Monopoly Capital*, New York: Monthly Review Press (1974).

Coe, D. and E. Helpman, "International R&D Spillovers," *European Economic Review* 39 (1995):859–87.

Desjonqueres, T., S. Machin, and J. Van Reenen, "Another Nail in the Coffin? Or Can the Trade Based Explanation of Changing Skill Structures Be Resurrected?" *Scandinavian Journal of Economics* 101 (1999):533–54.

Edin, P.-A. and B. Holmlund, "The Swedish Wage Structure: The Rise and Fall of Solidarity Wage Policy," in R. Freeman and L. Katz (eds.), *Differences and Changes in Wage Structures*, Chicago: University of Chicago Press and NBER (1995).

Feenstra, R. and G. Hanson, "Foreign Investment, Outsourcing and Relative Wages," in R. Feenstra, G. Grossman, and D. Irwin (eds.), *The Political Economy of Trade Policy: Papers in Honour of Jagdish Bhagwati*, Cambridge, MA: MIT Press (1996).

———, "Productivity Measurement and the Impact of Trade and Technology on Wages: Estimates for the US, 1972–1990," NBER working chapter 6052 (1997).

Freeman, R., "The Demand for Education," in O. Ashenfelter and R. Layard (eds.), *Handbook of Labor Economics, Vol. 1*, Amsterdam: North-Holland (1986).

Hall, B. H. and J. Mairesse, "Exploring the Relationship Between R&D and Productivity in French Manufacturing Firms," *Journal of Econometrics* 65 (1995):263–93.

Hansson, P., "Trade, Technology and Changes in Employment of Skilled Labor in Swedish Manufacturing," in J. Fagerberg et al. (eds.), *Technology and Trade*, Cheltenham: Edward Elgar (1997).

———, "Relative Demand for Skills in Swedish Manufacturing: Technology or Trade?" FIEF working chapter 152 (1999).

Hansson, P. and L. Lundberg, *Från Basindustri till Högteknologi? Svensknäringsstruktur och Strukturpolitik* (From Natural Resource Processing to Hi-Tech? Industrial Structure and Industrial Policy in Sweden), Stockholm: SNS-förlag (1995).

Holmlund, B., "Löneskillnader och Arbetslöshet (Wage Differences and Unemployment)," in V. Bergström (ed.), *Arbetsmarknad och Tillväxt* (Labor Market and Growth), Stockholm: Ekerlids-förlag (1997).

Horn, H., H. Lang, and S. Lundgren, "Managerial Effort, Incentives, X-inefficiency and International Trade," *European Economic Review* 39 (1995):117–38.

Katz, L. and K. Murphy, "Changes in Relative Wages, 1963–1987: Supply and Demand Factors," *Quarterly Journal of Economics* 107 (1992):35–78.

Keller, W., "Trade and the Transmission of Technology," NBER working chapter 6113 (1997).

Leamer, E., "Trade, Wages and the Revolving Door Ideas," NBER working chapter 4716 (1994).

Leibenstein, H., "Allocative Efficiency versus 'X-efficiency'," *American Economic Review* 56 (1966):392–415.

Lundberg, L., *Handelshinder och Handelspolitik* (Trade Barriers and Trade Policy), Stockholm: Almqvist & Wiksell (1976).

Machin, S., "Changes in the Relative Demand for Skill in the UK," in A. Booth and D. Snower (eds.), *Acquiring Skills*, Cambridge: Cambridge University Press (1996).

Machin, S. and J. Van Reenen, "Technology and Changes in Skill Structures: Evidence from Seven OECD Countries," *Quarterly Journal of Economics* 113 (1998):1215–44.

Marx, K., *Capital: Vol. 1*, London: Lawrence & Wishart (1867).

Mendenhall, W., D. Wackerly, and R. Scheaffer, *Mathematical Statistics with Applications*, 4th edn, Belmont: Duxbury Press (1990).

Mishel, L. and J. Bernstein, *Inside the Black Box: Estimating Technology's Impact on Wage Inequality Trends, 1973–94*, Washington, DC: Economic Policy Institute (1996).

Nickell, S. and B. Bell, "Changes in the Distribution of Wages and Unemployment in OECD Countries," *American Economic Review* 86 (1996):302–8.

OECD, "Trade, Earnings and Employment: Assessing the Impact of Trade with Emerging Economies on OECD Labor Markets," in *Employment Outlook*, Paris: OECD (1997).

Saeger, S., "Globalization and Deindustrialization: Myth and Reality in the OECD," *Weltwirtschaftliches Archiv* 133 (1997):579–608.

SCB, *Datorvanor 1995* (Computer Usage 1995), Stockholm: Nordstedts (1995).

US Bureau of Labor Statistics, "The Impact of Research and Development and Productivity Growth," Bulletin 2331 (1989).

Wood, A., *North–South Trade, Employment and Inequality: Changing Fortunes in a Skill-Driven World*, Oxford: Clarendon Press (1994).

———, "Globalisation and the Rise in Labor Market Inequalities," *Economic Journal* 108 (1998):1463–82.

Notes

1. See, for example, Berman et al. (1994) for the US and Machin (1996) for the UK; Sweden is no exception, which is shown in Hansson (1997) and in section 3.
2. The outsourcing argument has been elaborated and examined for the US in Feenstra and Hanson (1996, 1997).
3. For example, Autor et al. (1998) and Machin and Van Reenen (1998).
4. Among others, Autor et al. (1998), Bernard and Jensen (1997), Hansson (1997), and Machin and Van Reenen (1998).
5. Surprisingly few studies have hitherto disaggregated imports by country of origin. Examples are Anderton and Brenton (1998), Desjonqueres et al. (1999), and Machin and Van Reneen (1998).
6. A complete derivation is given in, e.g., Berndt (1991).
7. Katz and Murphy (1992) get a point estimate of σ on aggregate level around 1.4 using US annual time-series information on relative wages and quantities of college and high-school equivalents. At the same time they make the reservation that there is substantial uncertainty concerning the magnitude of σ. Edin and Holmlund (1995) obtain, in a similar study on Swedish data, an estimate on σ of 2.9 between labor with upper secondary and university education. According to Freeman (1986), earlier estimates of σ tend to be between 0.5 and 2.5. Thus an assumption of $\sigma = 1$, which implies that $\beta_1 = 0$, is possible, but probably too low.
8. The way our stocks of physical capital are constructed (see the Appendix) means that we will not capture this effect in full; rather a vintage approach would have been more appropriate.
9. The de-skilling hypothesis originates from Marx (1867) and was revived by Braverman (1974). Braverman's argument is essentially that capitalism has not changed. He asserts that work is getting more fragmented and monitored; there is a separation of conception from execution and the conceptual activities are concentrated on as few workers as possible.
10. According to a study by the US Bureau of Labor Statistics (1989), the mean lag for basic research appears to be five years, and two years for applied research.
11. An alternative, more elaborate, measure, suggested by Coe and Helpman (1995), would be to construct import-weighted R&D intensities. The idea is that trade is a mechanism through

which technological knowledge is transmitted internationally. On the other hand, as Keller (1997) has noted, technology diffusion need not be related to goods trade; for example, in reverse engineering or attending conferences where the state-of-the art technology is demonstrated.

12. Another factor that may boost technological changes is increased import competition. Some loose theoretical underpinning can be found in the literature on X-efficiency; e.g., Leibenstein (1966) and Horn et al. (1995). The basic idea is that managers, in particular in oligopolistic industries, do not maximize profits. One reason may be that they prefer leisure before profit; another is that they appreciate the power and satisfaction an excess number of employees can afford. A rent-threatening disturbance, such as increased import competition, implies, however, that managers take action, for example, by eliminating excess labor or by introducing labor-saving techniques. Changes in the import share of consumption would capture this effect. However, the results in Hansson (1999) suggest that imports from all partners do not affect the relative demand for skilled workers.

13. The R&D intensity, RD/Y, and the relative growth in knowledge stock, $\Delta \ln S$, need not be highly correlated at industry level. After some manipulation of equation (3) we can show that $\Delta \ln S = (RD/Y)(Y/S) - \delta$. Since we assume the depreciation rate of knowledge δ to be equal across industries, the relative change in the knowledge stock is equal to the R&D intensity times the inverse of the knowledge–output ratio. Large knowledge–output ratios characterize R&D intensive industries. This means that $\Delta \ln S$ is not necessarily high in R&D intensive industries.

14. The Appendix in Hansson (1999) contains details of the industries in the two datasets.

15. Most likely such a division of labor into skilled and less-skilled is more appropriate than the often used, but criticized (e.g., Leamer, 1994), nonproduction/production worker classification. Obviously, educational attainment has its imperfections too: it does not capture experience, it partially understates participation in further education and training, and there are variations in the quality of schooling over time and between regions/countries. However, educational attainment seems to be strongly correlated with occupation and earnings, and initial attainment is a good predictor of whether a person will participate in further education and training. Yet, with such a division into skilled and less-skilled labor we miss a distinction which is very important within manufacturing, namely between skilled and less-skilled manual workers; in Sweden, almost all manual workers have less than 12 years of education.

16. Over the period 1970 to 1985, the Censuses of Population 1970 and 1985 are the only sources of data on educational attainment of the Swedish population. From 1986 onwards, there is annual data on educational attainment and wage incomes of the employees in ÅRSYS, SCB Regional Labor Statistics.

17. Machin and Van Reneen (1998) examine a panel of 15 manufacturing industries in seven OECD countries, including Sweden, over the period 1970–90. The model setup is the same as mine, but their dependent variable is different since they apply the nonproduction/production worker definition of skill. They also exclude the transport industry (ISIC 384); in Sweden 1990, the transport industry had 14.3% of the employment in manufacturing.

18. I have also experimented with the R&D intensity dated $t-2$ and $t-3$. The precise dating is not important but produces very similar results. This is not surprising noting that most of the variation in the R&D intensity is between industries rather than over time. If we regress the R&D intensity over the studied industries and time period on industry and time dummies, we find that the F-value of the industry dummies is 59.27 (0.000), whereas the F-value of the time dummies is 1.27 (0.263); significance level in parentheses.

19. The number of full-time employees in R&D in Sweden 1991 was 28,961; i.e., 3.5% of those employed in manufacturing.

20. As an alternative to $(RD/Y)^{Sweden}$, I use the share of technicians of the employed in the beginning of each period, $TECH$, and the coefficient is positive and strongly significant (Hansson, 1999). This implies that the labor demand is more skilled-biased in technology-intensive industries.

21. A word of caution. In this econometric analysis we assume that investments in plants and machinery and R&D expenditure are exogenous variables. Most economists would argue that

these variables respond to profit opportunities; i.e., they are endogenous variables. Technological changes or increased globalization may affect expected profits so that investments in physical and knowledge capital increase and at the same time give rise to skill upgrading. Then we will observe a correlation between growth in physical and knowledge capital and higher skill shares, but the correlation is not causal. We should therefore be careful when we make causal interpretations of the results.

22. These computations simply involve taking the mean of the independent variable in column (4), multiplying it by its regression coefficient in column (3), and taking that as a percentage of the mean of the dependent variable.

23. In Figure 1, the dependent variable equals the residuals from a regression on all independent variables in the model in Table 2, columns (2) and (3), except for $\Delta \ln S$. The regression line is $0.513 + 0.039 \times \Delta \ln S$, and the t-value of the slope coefficient is 1.76. Unlike in columns (2) and (3), we estimate the model on annualized nine-year changes over the period 1986–95.

24. If we exclude $(RD/Y)^{OECD}$ in specification (3), the coefficient on $\Delta \ln K$ is 0.067 and on $\Delta \ln S$ 0.040.

25. See Figures 1 and 2 in Hansson (1999).

26. $\Delta \ln K = (K/Y)(I/Y) - \delta$, which means that even though the investment ratio is rather high, $\Delta \ln K$ may be low due to a high physical capital–output ratio in the beginning of the period (cf. note 13).

27. See, for example, Mishel and Bernstein (1996) and Autor et al. (1998).

28. I use the share with post-secondary education of more than three years to obtain a comparable measure of skills that includes the 1960s.

29. The annual average change in skill share was 0.44 percentage points between 1970 and 1985, 0.66 between 1985 and 1990, and 0.78 between 1990 and 1995. For more details see Hansson (1999).

30. Hansson and Lundberg (1995, ch. 3).

31. They estimate the following model: $\ln(W_u/W_g) = \beta_0 + \beta_1 T + \beta_2 \ln(L_u/L_g)$. Their dependent variable is the university/upper-secondary log-wage differential among male white-collar workers in mining, manufacturing, and construction. $L_u(L_g)$ is the number of labor force participants with university (upper-secondary) education, and T is a time trend.

32. This is indicated in Table 6, and is even more evident if we examine statistically whether the annual average rate of growth in skill shares within industries differs between time periods. Hansson (1999) presents results showing that, in comparison with a reference period 1970–86, the growth rate was significantly higher in the later period 1986–93 and significantly lower in the earlier period 1960–70.

33. Also worthy of remark is the fact that, whereas the coefficient on $\Delta \ln S$ in the 1970–85 period is insignificant, it is positive and strongly significant in the 1986–93 period (0.047 [3.57] t-value in square brackets).

34. Machin and Van Reenen (1998) also obtain a positive and significant coefficient on $(RD/Y)^{OECD}$, while the inclusion of the spillover variable drives the coefficient on own R&D, in their study measured by the R&D intensity in Sweden $(RD/Y)^{Sweden}$, to insignificance.

35. The coefficient on $TECH$ is larger in the period 1986–93, but yet not significantly different from the estimate in the earlier period. A test for structural differences over time shows that we cannot reject the hypothesis of equal coefficients over the two time periods on the variables in specification (2).

36. Hansson (1999) gives a detailed presentation of the effects of increased Southern competition on skill upgrading using all the different datasets.

37. There is meagre empirical support in other studies, using an approach similar to this, of the hypothesis that increased competition from the South has impaired the situation of the less skilled. Anderton and Brenton (1998) examine the effects of increased Southern import penetration on the skill intensity (share of nonmanual workers) in the UK textiles and nonelectrical machinery sectors, 1970–83. They obtain a large positive impact in textiles, while the effect in nonelectrical machinery is smaller. Desjonquers et al. (1999) estimate bivariate regressions between changes in skill intensities (share of non-production workers) and increases in South-

ern import penetration in 16 manufacturing industries in ten developed countries between 1970 and 1990 and find no association. It is noteworthy that if we in specification (1) in Table 8 above, exclude the technology indicator, $TECH$, the coefficient on $\Delta(M/C)^{Non-OECD}$ is insignificant. Finally, in the study of Machin and Van Reneen (1998) on 15 manufacturing industries in seven OECD countries, the relationship in Sweden between increased competition from the South and changes in skill intensities (share of nonproduction workers) is positive, but insignificant. In fact, they never get a positive and significant effect—rather, in many cases, the coefficient has a perverse negative sign.

38. The difference between the coefficients is 0.085 [1.27], t-value in square brackets.

39. By the textile industry I mean ISIC 32; i.e., the industry contains textile, apparel, footwear, and leather. Remarkably, the coefficient on $\Delta(M/C)^{Non-OECD}$ is insignificant if we exclude the textile industry.

40. In textiles (ISIC 32), the non-OECD import share of consumption increased from 6.5% in 1970 to 37.4% in 1993, while the textile industry share of manufacturing employment dropped from 9.8% in 1970 to 2.7% in 1993. The corresponding figures for the OECD (the same 12 OECD countries as in Table 1) are less dramatic. The import share started out from a lower level, 2.5% in 1970, and increased to 20% in 1993, while the employment share fell from 15.1% in 1970 to 10.6% in 1993.

41. OECD–Europe is Denmark, Finland, France, Germany (West), Italy, the Netherlands, Norway, and the United Kingdom.

42. See Lundberg (1976, Table 4.4).

43. In OECD the employment share fell from 28% in 1970 to 19% in 1994. OECD is the same 12 countries as in Table 1.

44. Wood (1994) and Saeger (1997).

45. Owing to increased relative supply of skilled labor, as a result of the expansion of higher education, we may find rising skill shares both in the manufacturing and nonmanufacturing sectors.

46. This is consistent with the result in Desjonqueres et al. (1999). They find that even within narrowly defined nontrade (nonmanufacturing) sectors there is a shift towards increased skilled-labor employment shares.

47. The shock was a coincidence of, among others things, an international recession, a particularly sharp rise in real interest rates, and a drastic fall in inflated asset prices, combined with an economic policy of nonaccommodation. There was no expansion of domestic demand and the devaluation, at the end of 1992, was resisted to the very last. Higher unemployment in the private sector led to a substantial budget deficit and, to put the budget on a sound basis, the government carried out spending cuts (and tax increases), which in turn reduced employment in the public sector.

48. Assume that a neutral adverse shock reduces employment in each skill group by x percent at given relative wages. The unemployment rates by skill will then increase by an equal percentage. In a second round there may be relative wage changes which push the unemployment effects from equality of percentage-point increases towards equiproportionate increases (Nickell and Bell, 1996).

49. If we regress the difference in unemployment rates on a time trend over the whole period 1971–98 we obtain a positive and highly significant coefficient on the time trend. If we instead exclude the very turbulent period in the Swedish labor market, i.e., the late 1980s (the Swedish economy was overheated and the unemployment rates were extremely low) and the 1990s, we still get a positive and clearly significant coefficient.

50. Nickell and Bell (1996) and OECD (1997).

13
Trade and Wages When the Trade Regime is Determined Endogenously

Robin Naylor

1. Introduction

Within the general literature on the changing nature of international trade and its implications for labor market outcomes, there is no clear consensus on the nature of the link between, on the one hand, trade openness and, on the other, wage determination and labor market outcomes (e.g., Freeman, 1995). One of the crucial areas of work in the discipline of economics in the last ten years or so has concerned this very issue, and much progress has been made in developing empirical methodologies for examining trade and labor market data in order to gain insights into the processes and market mechanisms connecting them. The current chapter attempts to make a theoretical contribution to the development of appropriate methodologies for the empirical analysis of the relationship between international trade and labor markets.

It is surprising that there is little consensus on the impact of trade openness and labor market outcomes. It is often argued that both the fact of—and even the potential threat of—international trade is likely to impose a more competitive product market discipline on wage-setters and that this should lead to a negative relationship between openness and wage levels, for example. There is some support for this view in the work of Stewart (1990) who finds that union–nonunion wage differentials are much lower in the presence of international market competition even when other conditions are favorable to a union wage influence. A number of theoretical models have been developed which are consistent with this result: see, for example, Brander and Spencer (1988), Driffill and van der Ploeg (1993), and Mezzetti and Dinopoulos (1991). On the other hand, there are arguments which suggest that increased trade openness may increase wages. One such argument is advanced in the current paper. Another is based on the idea that protected industries are less efficient, *ceteris paribus*, and this reduces the scope for workers to negotiate wage premia in such industries. There is evidence also in support of this argument (e.g., Gaston and Trefler, 1994). A consequence of all this is that there is no consensus on how increased economic integration within trading regions or, more generally, reduced costs associated with trade, affect wage and employment outcomes. In terms of direct evidence on the impact of transportation costs of trade on wages, there is some evidence that wages are higher when transport costs are lower. This is consistent with the analysis presented in the current paper, which extends the models developed in Naylor (1998, 1999).

I consider a framework in which trade across imperfectly competitive product markets can be either two-way (intraindustry) or one-way (interindustry). See Greenaway et al. (1995) for an industry-level analysis of intraindustry trade for the UK. I consider the case of an international duopoly and assume that the domestic firm confronts a (monopoly) trade union. I am interested primarily in the union's preferences over the level of the wages it will seek to negotiate with the firm. I show that the union has a dichotomous choice between a "high" and a "low" wage strategy. If it selects the low-wage strategy, then its employer will incur labor costs sufficiently low that it will be able to export abroad. Conversely, with a high-wage strategy selected by the union, the firm will incur labor costs such that it is unable to compete in the foreign market. We show how the union's choice of strategy—and its corresponding strategy-contingent wage—and therefore the trade outcome, depend upon a vector of factors. These factors include: the extent of trade costs, the nature of competition between the firms in the product market, the degree of differentiation between the firms' products, the nature of union preferences, the level of reservation wages in the two countries, and the parameters of product market demand.

In particular, I examine how a change in trade costs influences the union's wage strategy choice. Under specified conditions, the union's optimal wage responds differentially to a fall in trade costs according to whether trade is one-way or two-way. I show also that this is an endogenous outcome: there is a critical or "switching" level of trade costs which induces the union to switch between high- and low-wage strategies and therefore causes the firm to switch between export and nonexport behavior. This has important implications for empirical modeling. If trade is one-way, then a fall in the costs of international trade leads the union to reduce its wage demand. If, on the other hand, trade is two-way then a fall in trade costs has the opposite effect. This, of course, is a clear testable proposition which can be addressed with appropriate micro-data. It is also consistent with the current empirical ambiguity concerning the impact of trade protection on wages.

The analysis suggests that the issue of endogeneity between the nature of the trade regime and labor market behavior is crucial. In empirical work, it might be tempting to simply distinguish between one-way and two-way trade regimes and analyse the impact of changing trade costs on wages in each regime. The present analysis suggests that this is not legitimate. One cannot simply partition the data according to whether trade is one-way or two-way as this is itself influenced by union behavior, and thus by the extent of trade costs. Instead, I demonstrate in this chapter that it is important to identify the determinants of the union's choice over its wage strategy and, in particular, the determinants of the critical trade cost which induces the union to switch behavior. This is the main focus of the current paper.

Section 2 outlines the basic model and presents the derivation of particular testable propositions. Section 3 examines the issue of the endogeneity between trade regime and union behavior and draws conclusions for identifying the crucial "switching" function. Section 4 closes the chapter with general conclusions and suggestions for further research.

2. Theoretical Framework

Consider a situation in which a domestic monopoly firm faces potential competition in its home market from a foreign firm. Assume that trade costs are initially so high as to prohibit import penetration from abroad, given other parameters, such as wage costs. If trade costs fall sufficiently, the foreign firm is just able to break into the market, *ceteris paribus*. Suppose that the home firm is unionized and pays a union bargained wage which exceeds the foreign wage. Hence, this unionized domestic firm is not sufficiently cost-competitive to be able to export, even after small reductions in trade costs. It is likely that the falling trade costs will induce the domestic union to moderate its wage demands in order for the domestic firm to maintain domestic market share. Indeed, the union may be prepared, initially at least, to accept wage reductions which are sufficiently great as to prevent import penetration. Thus, a reduction in trade costs which increases imports—or the threat of imports—is likely to lead to pressure on unions to reduce wages: the relationship between trade costs and union wages is positive, in the sense that they move in the same direction. This describes a situation in which trade—or potential trade—is in imports only. I refer to this as one-way trade and present a formal model of this case in the first subsection below.

As trade costs continue to fall, it is likely that there will come a point at which the domestic firm may have the possibility of exporting to the foreign market: in other words, for trade to become two-way. In part, this will depend on how the domestic union responds to the falling trade costs. This is examined in the second subsection below. Subsequently, I show that there is likely to be a critical level of trade costs which induces the domestic union to shift to a low-wage strategy of accommodating exports, and hence induces a switch from one-way to two-way trade. After this switch, further reductions in trade costs induce the union to make small upward adjustments in wages: the relationship between trade costs and union wages is then negative. The crucial question concerns the determinants of the critical level of trade costs. If one wanted to implement an empirical model of the relationship between trade and wages described in the foregoing discussion, one would need to identify this critical trade cost. This is the focus of the current paper.

One-Way Trade

I now consider the formal analysis behind the situation described above. Suppose that in country A product demand facing the home firm (firm 1) and the foreign firm (firm 2) is given by

$$p_{1A} = a - cx_{2A} - x_{1A}, \qquad (1)$$

where x_{1A}, for example, represents supply by firm 1 to market A. Assume a constant marginal product of labor, which is set as a *numéraire*. Consequently, output and employment are equivalent. c represents the extent of product market substitutability, $-1 \leq c \leq 1$. If $c = 1$ then goods are perfect substitutes; if $c = -1$ they are perfect complements; and if $c = 0$ then they are independent. As c tends to unity, I refer to them as becoming more similar. This approach follows Singh and Vives (1984) and has been exploited by Horn and Wolinsky (1988), though not in the context of international trade. Similarly, for firm 2, demand is given by

$$p_{2A} = a - cx_{1A} - x_{2A}. \qquad (2)$$

Now consider the game in two stages. In stage 1, the wage in firm 1 is determined by a monopoly trade union. In stage 2, the two firms choose output levels. I proceed to solve the model by the customary method of backward induction.

Stage 2 From (1) it follows that the profits of firm 1 will be given by

$$\pi_{1A} = (a - cx_{2A} - x_{1A} - w_1)x_{1A}, \qquad (3)$$

where w_1 is the wage paid by firm 1. An analogous expression holds for the profits of firm 2, but with the addition of a cost, t, representing the per-unit trade cost:

$$\pi_{2A} = (a - cx_{1A} - x_{2A} - w_2 - t)x_{2A}. \tag{4}$$

The first-order condition for profit maximization by firm 1 can be derived as

$$\frac{d\pi_{1A}}{dx_{1A}} = a - c(x_{2A} + \mu x_{1A}) - w_1 - 2x_{1A} = 0, \tag{5}$$

with an equivalent expression defining profit maximization by firm 2

$$\frac{d\pi_{2A}}{dx_{2A}} = a - c(x_{1A} + \mu x_{2A}) - w_2 - 2x_{2A} = 0, \tag{6}$$

where $dx_{2A}/dx_{1A} = \mu$ is the product market conjectural variation parameter capturing how firm 1 believes firm 2 will respond to a change in its output. It is assumed to be symmetric across the two firms. If $\mu = 0$, then this represents the usual Cournot assumption. From (5) and (6), we can derive the two firms' best-reply functions in output-space. These are given by

$$x_{1A} = \frac{1}{2 + c\mu}[a - w_1 - cx_{2A}], \tag{7}$$

$$x_{2A} = \frac{1}{2 + c\mu}[a - w_2 - t - cx_{1A}]. \tag{8}$$

From these expressions, it is clear that the slopes of the best-reply functions depend on the degree of substitutability/complementarity between the two firms' products. The best-reply functions are negatively sloped if the goods are gross substitutes and positively-sloped in the case of gross complements.

We can rearrange (7) and (8) in order to derive the labor demand relation facing union 1, the union of workers in firm 1:

$$x_{1A} = \frac{1}{(2 + c\mu)^2 - c^2}\{[2 - c(1 - \mu)]a - (2 + c\mu)w_1 + cw_2 + ct\}. \tag{9}$$

We can now analyze the union's stage 1 choice of the wage level.

Stage 1 Assume that the union objective can be captured by the specific functional form:

$$U_1 = (w_1 - \overline{w})^\theta x_{1A}, \tag{10}$$

where θ represents the relative weight the union attaches to the wage argument in its utility function. If θ equals unity, then this is the special case of rent maximization by the union. Substituting (9) in (10) and solving for the first-order condition for union utility maximization yields a monopoly union wage choice of

$$w_1 = \frac{1}{(2 + c\mu)(1 + \theta)}\{\theta[2 - c(1 - \mu)]a + c\theta w_2 + c\theta t + (2 + c\mu)\overline{w}\}. \tag{11}$$

From (11), it is possible to establish a number of results concerning the union's choice of the wage and how this will depend on particular parameters of the model. These are summarized in Proposition 1.

PROPOSITION 1. *Under one-way trade, the union's chosen wage will be increasing in the reservation wage, in the union's relative weight on wages, and in the degree of product market collusion. The union wage will be decreasing in the degree of product substitutability. If products are gross substitutes (complements), the union's chosen wage will be increasing (decreasing) in the wage paid by the rival firm and will be increasing (decreasing) in trade costs.*

PROOFS

(i) It is readily seen from (11) that $dw_1/d\overline{w} > 0$. This is a well-established result.
(ii) It can be checked from (11) that $dw_1/d\theta > 0$. This result is intuitive.
(iii) It can be checked from (11) that $dw_1/d\mu > 0$.
(iv) It can be checked from (11) that $dw_1/dc < 0$. Thus, the more similar are traded products, the lower will be the union's chosen wage.
(v) It is readily seen from (11) that dw_1/dw_2 takes the same sign as c. This confirms the result established by Horn and Wolinsky (1988) for bilateral monopoly.
(vi) It can be checked from (11) that

$$\text{sign}[dw_1/dt] = \text{sign}[c], \tag{12}$$

and hence that $\text{sign}[dw_1/dt] = \text{sign}[c]$. □

It follows from Proposition 1 that, if goods are gross substitutes, increased economic integration will lead unions to reduce the wage level they try to negotiate. The greater the degree of substitutability between products—the more similar or homogeneous they are—the more sensitive will be wages to a reduction in trade costs. This is potentially an important empirical issue, as the data on trade often distinguish between the degree of similarity in the products traded.

Finally, substituting (11) in (10), we obtain an expression for the union's optimal level of utility under one-way trade:

$$U_1^I = A\{[2 - c(1-\mu)]a + cw_2 + ct - (2 + c\mu)\overline{w}\}^{1+\theta},$$

$$A = \left[\frac{\theta}{(2+c\mu)(1+\theta)}\right]^\theta \left[\frac{1}{(2+c\mu)^2 - c^2}\right]\left[\frac{1}{1+\theta}\right]. \tag{13}$$

I will make use of this result in the next section of the chapter when considering the union's choice between high- and low-wage strategies. First, I turn to consider the case of two-way trade.

Two-Way Trade

Consider the situation in which union 1 adopts a low-wage strategy which enables firm 1 to export to country B, the foreign market. We allow for the possibility that the foreign firm continues to export into firm 1's home market. Assume that the two countries are identical in all respects, other than the wage. An interesting extension to the model developed here would involve allowing for asymmetries in, for example, demand parameters or productivity levels.

Stage 2 The product market in country B is assumed to be identical to that in country A. Thus, by analogy from (7) and (8), it is readily shown that exports by firm 1 are given by

$$x_{1B} = \frac{1}{(2+c\mu)^2 - c^2}\{[2-c(1-\mu)]a - (2+c\mu)w_1 + cw_2 - (2+c\mu)t\}. \tag{14}$$

Hence, the sum of (9) and (14) gives the total labor demand facing union 1. We can now consider the union's wage choice subject to this labor demand, where the union utility function is as before, and employment consists of $x_{1A} + x_{1B}$. Thus:

$$U_1 = (w_1 - \overline{w})^\theta (x_{1A} + x_{1B}). \tag{15}$$

Stage 1 The union will choose the wage to maximize U_1 as given by (15). The first-order condition for a maximum gives an optimal wage of

$$w_1 = \frac{1}{2(2+c\mu)(1+\theta)}\{2\theta[2-c(1-\mu)]a + 2c\theta w_2 - \theta(2-c(1-\mu))t + 2(2+c\mu)\overline{w}\}. \tag{16}$$

From (16), we can derive various important comparative static properties of the model under two-way trade. These are stated in Proposition 2.

PROPOSITION 2. *Under two-way trade, the union's chosen wage will be increasing in the reservation wage, in union's relative weight on wages, in the degree of product market collusion, and in the level of trade costs. The union wage will be decreasing in the degree of product substitutability. If goods are gross substitutes (complements), the union wage will be decreasing (increasing) in the wage paid by the rival foreign firm.*

The proofs are easily established from equation (16). Compared with Proposition 1 for the case of one-way trade, the major difference concerns the fact that there is no longer an ambiguity on the effect of trade costs on union-set wages. Under two-way trade, the union's chosen wage will be decreasing in t. This also follows from (16):

$$\frac{dw_1}{dt} = \frac{-[2-c(1-\mu)]\theta}{2(2+c\mu)(1+\theta)} < 0. \tag{17}$$

This is the key result of this section of the paper. I have shown that for goods which are gross substitutes, the impact on the union's chosen wage level of a rise in trade costs is negative under two-way trade and positive under one-way trade. This generalizes the results of Naylor (1999) for a more general model. The testable hypothesis is clear: in the case of gross substitutes, when firms are engaged in exporting abroad, a fall in trade costs will lead unions to raise wages, whereas if firms are not exporting the opposite response will occur. With gross complements, union wages will be rising as trade costs fall, independent of the trade regime.

It is now necessary to ascertain the conditions under which trade will be one-way or two-way, as this is an endogenous outcome. As indicated previously, when the trade regime is endogenously determined, we cannot simply partition trade data into one-way or two-way regimes and examine the effects of trade costs on wages separately in the two regimes.

In order to determine which trade regime will obtain, we need to compare union utility under the two regimes. Equation (13) gives union utility under a one-way regime induced by a union high-wage strategy. Substituting (16) in (15), we obtain an expression for the union's optimal level of utility under two-way trade:

$$U_1^{II} = B\{2[2-c(1-\mu)]a + 2cw_2 - [2-c(1-\mu)]t - 2(2+c\mu)\overline{w}\}^{1+\theta},$$

$$B = \left[\frac{\theta}{2(2+c\mu)(1+\theta)}\right]^{\theta}\left[\frac{1}{(2+c\mu)^2 - c^2}\right]\left[\frac{1}{1+\theta}\right]. \quad (18)$$

Equations (13) and (18) give the union utility levels under each of the two kinds of trade regime, so we are in a position to examine the union's choice across the two; that is, the union's decision on whether to opt for the high-wage strategy or the low-wage strategy.

3. One-Way or Two-Way Trade?

The union will choose to set a high-wage strategy if $U_1^I > U_1^{II}$, as in this case the high-wage strategy induced one-way trade regime yields to the union greater utility than the two-way trade regime facilitated by a low-wage strategy. The union is indifferent between the two regimes if $U_1^I = U_1^{II}$; that is, if

$$k\{[2-c(1-\mu)]a + cw_2 - (2+c\mu)\overline{w}\}$$
$$= \{2[2-c(1-\mu)]a + 2cw_2 - [2-c(1-\mu)]t - 2(2+c\mu)\overline{w}\}, \quad (19)$$

where $k = 2^{\theta/(1+\theta)}$. We can solve (19) to find the critical value of trade costs for which the union is just indifferent between the high-wage and the low-wage strategies. Call this the "switching" or "prohibitive" level of trade costs under unions, t_p^U, and it is given by

$$t_p^U = \frac{2-k}{2+c(k-1+\mu)}\{[2-c(1-\mu)]a + cw_2 - (2+c\mu)\overline{w}\}. \quad (20)$$

From (20), we can derive a number of comparative static properties concerning this prohibitive level of trade costs under unions. These are summarized in a series of propositions.

PROPOSITION 3. *If $t > t_p^U$, then the union prefers the high-wage strategy: trade costs are sufficiently high as to preclude the possibility of exports from country A, given the parameters of the model and, particularly, the nature of union preferences. If, on the other hand, $t < t_p^U$, then the union prefers the low-wage strategy and hence trade will be two-way.*

PROOF. The proof follows from comparison of (13) and (18). □

PROPOSITION 4. *The switching level of trade costs is increasing in the reservation price, a: rendering two-way trade more likely the higher is a. It is decreasing in the domestic reservation wage, in the degree of product substitutability, and in the degree of product market collusion. It is increasing (decreasing) in the foreign wage if goods are gross substitutes (complements).*

PROOFS

(i) From (20), it follows that, under the assumptions we have made, $dt_p^U/da > 0$. The intuition is that the greater is the reservation price, the greater are the potential gains from trade and hence the more likely is the union to accommodate trade through a low wage strategy.
(ii) From (20), $dt_p^U/d\overline{w} < 0$. The intuition is that the lower is the reservation wage at home, the greater is the potential gain to the union within the home market, and consequently the lower is the incentive to accommodate two-way trade.
(iii) From (20), $dt_p^U/dw_2 = \{(2-k)c\}/\{2 + c(k-1+\mu)\}$ which is positive if c is positive. This result is intuitive. If c is negative, the opposite result obtains.
(iv) From (20), $dt_p^U/dc < 0$. The intuition is that the more highly substitutable are the two firms' products, the lower are the potential capturable gains for the union from a low-wage strategy of accommodating trade.
(v) From (20), $dt_p^U/d\mu < 0$. The intuition is that the more the firms collude in the home market, the greater is the potential rent to the union within the home market, and consequently the lower is the incentive to accommodate two-way trade. □

PROPOSITION 5. *At least under Cournot–Nash equilibria in the product market, the switching level of trade costs in the presence of a union is less than that in a competitive labor market: rendering two-way trade less likely in a unionized labor market.*

PROOF. It is straightforward to show that, in the absence of unions, the prohibitive trade cost is given by

$$t_p^N = \frac{1}{2}\{(2-c)a + cw_2 - 2\overline{w}\}. \tag{21}$$

Comparison of (20) and (21) reveals that $t_p^U < t_p^N$, at least in the case of Cournot equilibrium in the product market ($\mu = 0$). From this it follows that trade is less likely in the presence of unions, which establishes the proposition. □

In this section of the paper, I have shown that whether the trade regime will be characterized by one-way or two-way trade depends on the level of trade costs relative to a critical or "prohibitive" level. This prohibitive level itself depends upon various economic factors relating to the nature of product market competition and to labor market behavior. The analysis carries an important implication for attempts to test empirically the nature of the relationship between trade costs and labor market outcomes. For example, in the case of products which are gross substitutes, the theory predicts that if trade costs exceed the prohibitive level for exporting—so that any trade is one-way—then a marginal fall in trade costs will be likely to provoke a fall in the union-set wage level. Conversely, if trade costs are less than the prohibitive level—so that exports do occur—then a reduction in trade costs will lead to higher wages. In order to test this prediction of the model against, say, firm-level micro-data, one would need to regress firm-level wages against the level of trade costs, with a model of the selection process in which the observed event of exporting or not depends on the level of trade costs relative to a latent variable, t_p^U, the determinants of which have been the focus of this section of the paper. One of the contributions of the current chapter is that I have been able to identify the kinds of economic variables which are likely to determine the critical level of trade costs. This is important as the critical level is not itself observable and will vary across industries according to their structural characteristics, *inter alia*.

4. Conclusions

The chapter has developed a generalization of the models developed in Naylor (1998, 1999) on the (endogenous) relationship between trade and labor markets. A main focus has concerned the implications of the theoretical analysis for the development of empirical models of trade and wages. The central proposition of the theoretical model is that, depending on the nature of product similarity, the direction of the effect of falling trade costs on wages will vary according to whether trade is one-way or two-way. This could represent a possible explanation for ambiguous empirical evidence on the relationship between wages, on the one hand, and indicators of trade openness and protection, on the other.

Furthermore, the partition of firms across the two sectors—one-way trade or two-way trade—is itself an endogenous outcome: with obvious and important implications for the empirical analysis of the relationship between trade and labor markets. The theoretical analysis has suggested that the nature of the trade regime will depend upon the level of trade costs relative to a critical level. Empirically, this critical level is a latent variable, the determinants of which have been the focus of much of the analysis.

The theoretical model developed here extends previous work in a number of important directions. In particular, the implications drawn out for empirical analysis represent novel innovations. With respect to the theoretical model itself, previous work of the kind has not taken account of the importance of product market behavior, product differentiation, or union preferences. There are, however, directions in which the work might be pursued further. In particular, the model as developed so far focuses on the case of a monopoly union. It is possible to demonstrate, using numerical methods, that the central results carry over to the more general case of the right-to-manage model, but no more general results have yet been obtained. A second direction for future work would involve developing a more general framework than that developed here, where I have concentrated on specific functional forms in order to obtain precise algebraic solutions to the particular problems addressed.

References

Brander, J. and B. Spencer, "Unionized Oligopoly and International Trade Policy," *Journal of International Economics* 24 (1988):217–34.

Driffill, J. and F. van der Ploeg, "Monopoly Unions and the Liberalisation of International Trade," *Economic Journal* 103 (1993):379–85.

Freeman, R. B., "Are Your Wages Set in Beijing?" *Journal of Economic Perspectives*, Summer (1995):15–32.

Gaston, N. and D. Trefler, "Protection, Trade and Wages: Evidence from US Manufacturing," *Industrial and Labor Relations Review* (1994):574–93.

Greenaway, D., R. C. Hine, and C. R. Milner, "Horizontal and Vertical Intraindustry Trade: A Cross-Industry Analysis for the UK," *Economic Journal* 105 (1995):1505–18.

Horn, H. and A. Wolinsky, "Bilateral Monopolies and Incentives for Merger," *Rand Journal of Economics* 19 (1988):408–19.

Mezzetti, C. and E. Dinopoulos, "Domestic Unionization and Import Competition," *Journal of International Economics* 31 (1991):79–100.

Naylor, R. A., "International Trade and Economic Integration when Labour Markets are Generally Unionised," *European Economic Review* 42 (1998):1251–67.

———, "Union Wage Strategies and International Trade," *Economic Journal* 109 (1999):102–25.

Singh, N. and X. Vives, "Price and Quantity Competition in a Differentiated Duopoly," *Rand Journal of Economics* 15 (1984):547–53.

Stewart, M. B., "Union Wage Differentials, Product Market Influences and the Division of Rents," *Economic Journal* 100 (1990):1122–37.

14
Structural Change, Competition, and Job Turnover in Swedish Manufacturing, 1964–96

Linda Andersson, Ola Gustafsson, and Lars Lundberg

1. Background

A sufficient degree of mobility of factors of production among firms and industries is often seen as a precondition for maintaining an efficient resource allocation in an economy facing a changing economic environment. Structural change is reflected in the labor market by reallocation of jobs among firms and industries, and shifting demand for different skill groups. Structural change may include not only changes in the industry composition of output and employment, but also redistribution of employment and market shares among firms within the same industry, or even changes within firms. In this paper we use the term "structural change" in the sense of the rate of job turnover, measured by the rates of change of the distribution of employment among industries and plants.

In a closed economy—or in sectors producing nontraded goods and services—the structure of employment and output will be determined by domestic demand and supply. In general, in a growing economy one should expect increasing shares of total employment in sectors where demand is highly elastic with respect to income. A high rate of growth of productivity will work both ways. On the one hand it will decrease costs and prices and thus increase demand; on the other hand, given output, demand for labor will fall.

In the traded-goods and services sectors, the structure of employment is determined not only by the rate of growth of demand but also by changes in international competitiveness of domestic producers. Employment will shift towards industries with a high rate of growth of demand where domestic firms are able to increase their market shares on export markets as well as on the home market. Moreover, jobs are reallocated among firms within the same industry, in response to firm-specific shifts in demand or technology. The frequency of such demand and supply shocks, as well as the response to them, may depend on the characteristics of the market and of the production process, such as the degree of international competition, market power of sellers, and economies of scale.

The scope of this paper is to study the determinants of the rate of structural change, defined as the rate of job turnover; i.e., the rate of change in the distribution of employment among industries as well as among plants within the same industry.[1] In particular, the paper will focus on the role of competition—both national and international—as a driving force behind structural adjustment. Since most markets for services have, until recently, been virtually closed to international trade, the study is limited to employment in the manufacturing industry.

Since data for employment by industry are available for a much longer period than employment by plant, the analysis is separated into two parts. The first deals with interindustry job turnover. Section 2 proposes a measure of job turnover among industries and presents predictions derived from standard trade theory. Section 3 contains a description of the time pattern of interindustry job turnover in Swedish manufacturing for 1964–96. The determinants of this process, and in particular the role of international competition, are discussed in sections 4 and 5.

The second part focuses on the variation across industries with respect to the rate of intraindustry reallocation of employment among plants. Section 6 surveys job turnover among plants for 1986–96 and the role of entry and exit of plants. The theoretical framework is discussed in section 7. Section 8 contains an analysis of the determinants of intraindustry job turnover. The main issue here is whether rates of turnover are influenced by the exposure to international competition and changes in trade flows as well as by characteristics of the product, the production process, and the market.

2. A Framework for Explaining Interindustry Job Turnover

Following Davis et al. (1996), we define job creation and job destruction as changes in employment at the plant level. At the industry level, job creation is defined as the sum of employment changes in expanding plants, including entries, whereas job destruction is the sum of employment changes in contracting (including exits) plants.[2] Dividing by employment gives the rates of job creation and destruction. The rate of intraindustry gross job reallocation among plants is the sum of the rates of job creation and destruction.

In this paper we focus on the rate of *net* job reallocation; i.e., the rate of redistribution of a given total employment among plants and industries.[3] Starting with the process of structural change of employment among industries within manufacturing, we define the rate of net interindustry job turnover as the sum of absolute values of the annual changes in employment shares by industry:

$$\sigma_t = \sum_{i=1}^{n} |a_{it} - a_{it-1}|, \tag{1}$$

where $a_{it} = L_{it}/L_t$ is the share of the ith industry of total employment in manufacturing in year t, and n is the number of industries.

The actual rate of job turnover and structural change is a result of the interaction of adjustment pressure and adjustment resistance. The former works through changes in prices and market growth as well as by changes in international competitiveness of domestic producers, giving an incentive to increase or reduce employment. The latter includes all kinds of barriers to labor mobility. Thus an increase in the actual rate of job turnover could be caused by increased adjustment incentives, or decreased resistance, or both. A comprehensive analysis of the role of factors influencing both adjustment resistance and barriers to labor mobility is, however, outside the scope of this paper.[4]

Focusing on the role of adjustment pressure, this paper attempts to explore the mechanisms of interindustry job turnover in a small open economy. To derive a testable hypothesis, we start from a very simple theoretical framework, the standard textbook specific factor model of a small open economy. Assuming the wage rate to be equalized across sectors, labor demand in each industry is determined by the (given) world market prices and the technology of domestic producers. It can be shown (Andersson et al., 1998) that domestic technological progress will have exactly the same effect on labor demand as a price increase.

Assume that world market prices change as an effect of shifts in world demand or technical progress in the rest of the world. This affects sectoral labor demand. As a consequence the wage rate will change. As shown in Andersson et al. (1998), employment shares will increase in all sectors where prices rise more than the wage rate (i.e., where the price increase is above average), and fall in all other sectors; the share will increase more the more the price has gone up. The more price changes *differ* among industries, the higher will be the rate of structural change and job turnover. If all prices change in the same proportion there will be no structural change. The same holds for technical change: the larger the *dispersion* among industries with respect to the rate of technical progress, the more the job turnover.

In the empirical application we have no data for world prices or the technology parameters. However, there are data for gross profit margins by industry, defined as one minus wages' share of value-added. We therefore proceed to derive the link in our model between the unobservable price changes and technology shifts and the observable changes in gross profit margins, noting that technical progress will have the same effects as a price increase. This leads us to the following equation for the rate of interindustry job turnover, as defined in (1), expressed in terms of changes in gross profit margins:

$$\sigma_t = \sum_{i=1}^{n} |da_{it}| = \sum_{i=1}^{n} a_{it} \left| \frac{d\pi_{it}}{\alpha_{it}^2} - \sum_{i=1}^{n} \frac{a_{it} d\pi_{it}}{\alpha_{it}^2} \right| = \theta_t, \qquad (2)$$

where $d\pi_i$ and α_i are the change of the gross profit margin and the share of wages of value-added in the ith industry. Equation (2) is derived in Andersson et al. (1998). The rate of reallocation of employment among industries is proportional to θ_t, a weighted measure of the dispersion of changes in gross profit margins among industries. Thus, the larger the differences among industries with respect to price changes and domestic technical progress, the more variation in changes of gross profit rates, and the more job turnover there will be.

3. Interindustry Job Turnover in Swedish Manufacturing, 1964–96

The structure of total employment in Sweden has shifted over the past decades away from industry in favor of services, in particular towards the public sector. The share of manufacturing fell from 30% in 1960–65 to 19% in 1990–95 (OECD, 1997).

Within the manufacturing sector, jobs have mainly been reallocated away from traditional, natural resource-based and export-oriented sectors such as the paper, sawnwood, and steel industries, but also from labor-intensive activities such as production of wearing apparel and shoes. In certain sectors, changes have been dramatic. For shipyards, employment fell to about one-third of the level before the first oil price shock. For clothing, employment gradually decreased by 80% during a 40-year period.

A more comprehensive picture of the time pattern of Swedish industrial restructuring may be obtained from Figure 1, which shows the annual rate of structural change within Swedish manufacturing for 1964–96, defined as the rate of interindustry job turnover, σ_t, calculated according to (1) from data on the most detailed level of the SNI, the Swedish industrial classification system.

The mean of the σ_t series is 5.4%, which means that, on average, 2.7% of the stock of jobs in manufacturing has been reallocated among industries each year.[5] This, of

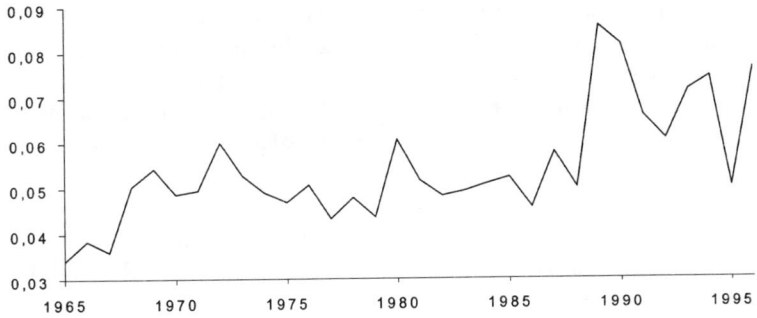

Figure 1. Interindustry Job Turnover in Swedish Manufacturing 1964–96

course, captures only a minor part of total labor mobility, since neither intraindustry turnover of jobs among plants, nor gross flows of workers, are included.

The rate of structural adjustment defined in this way has apparently increased during the last 30 years. The trend is positive and strongly significant. However, this conclusion rests mainly on the first (1965–68) and last (1989–96) years of the period—if these are excluded the trend disappears. Moreover, the volatility of the annual rate of industrial restructuring seems to be higher towards the end of the period.

In the popular debate, the mid-1970s, after the first oil price shock, is usually seen as a period where the pressure for industrial restructuring was particularly intense. This impression seems to be based on the dramatic development in certain industries such as steel mills and shipyards, and was probably reinforced by the fact that the "structural crisis" involved very large plants which dominated local or even regional labor markets. However, this picture is not confirmed by Figure 1. In a historical perspective, the mid-1970s does not seem to be a period of a particularly high rate of interindustry job turnover.

4. Determinants of the Rate of Interindustry Job Turnover

The conclusion from section 2 was that σ, the rate of interindustry job turnover, was determined by θ, a weighted measure of the dispersion of changes in profit margins among industries.[6] In the model the development of θ is driven by industry-specific shifts in international competitiveness caused by domestic technical progress different from that of foreign producers, as well as by shifts in world demand. In addition, the time pattern of σ may be related to a number of macroeconomic variables reflecting the business cycle and/or excess demand and supply in the labor market.

Granted that our variable θ actually measures incentives/pressures to structural change, the response may vary with macroeconomic conditions. *A priori* it is not obvious whether the pattern is pro- or countercyclical. According to Davis et al. (1996), job destruction in the US industry tends to increase strongly in recessions, whereas job creation is more stable, thus leading to a countercyclical pattern of job reallocation. To capture the effects of general labor market conditions we have used two alternative proxies, namely the ratio of unemployment to vacancies, U/V, and the rate of change of industrial employment, $\hat{L}$ (in the terminology of Davis et al. (1996), the rate of total net job creation).

Moreover, it seems likely that industrial policy has affected the rate of interindustry job turnover. After the first oil price shock, the international recession, a steep increase in Swedish relative wage costs and pressure from new producers brought a number of large firms, in particular shipyards and steelmills, close to bankruptcy. To avoid the negative impact on local or regional labor markets (i.e., to preserve jobs in these firms), there was a strong increase in various kinds of selective subsidies (Carlsson, 1983; Eriksson, 1994). To the extent that these subsidies were successful in "saving jobs", they should reduce interindustry job turnover. Thus we include ω, selective industrial subsidies as a proportion of industrial value-added, in the regression.

Since our dependent variable is bounded within the interval $0 \leq \sigma \leq 2$, we use also a logistic functional form (Kmenta, 1971) to ensure that our predicted values fall within this interval:

$$\gamma = \ln\left(\frac{\sigma}{2-\sigma}\right). \tag{3}$$

All variables appear to be stationary except for (U/V) and ω which are $I(1)$; i.e., we obtain stationarity for these two variables by first-differencing each of them. Because of the poor small-sample properties of the augmented Dickey–Fuller test, we use it only as a guideline.

The positive and significant coefficient of θ implies that the larger the dispersion among industries of the change of gross profit margins, the higher was the rate of interindustry job turnover. This confirms the predictions of the model. Furthermore we find a positive and significant effect of $\Delta(U/V)$, or alternatively a negative effect of $\hat{L}$. Thus the rate of interindustry job turnover has been higher in periods with falling employment and increasing excess supply of labor. This countercyclical pattern of job turnover in Swedish manufacturing resembles the results of Davis et al. (1996) from US data.[7]

Our data do not confirm the hypothesis that the expansion of subsidies in the 1970s, the main objective of which was to save firms from going out of business and to reduce or at least postpone layoffs, had an influence on interindustry job turnover in manufacturing. The coefficients of ω and $\Delta\omega$ are negative but never significant. This may be due to errors in estimating the "subsidy equivalent" of different measures.

For the regressions in columns (1), (3), and (4) in Table 1, the Durbin–Watson statistic falls into the inconclusive region. However, according to the Breusch–Godfrey test we cannot find evidence of serial correlation. Plotting the standardized residuals confirms the results of the Breusch–Godfrey test. On the other hand, column (2) shows unanimous sign of autocorrelation.

Re-estimating the linear equation with Huber standard errors, taking account of heteroskedasticity, or estimating a robust regression assessing lower weight to influential observations, does not change the results, nor does re-estimation of the model using the logistic functional form of the dependent variable.

5. International Competition and Interindustry Job Turnover

Changes in international competitiveness of firms and industries may cause both inter- and intraindustry job turnover in an economy. An increase in trade implies increased international specialization. This will result in a reallocation of jobs among industries to the extent that there has been increased interindustry specialization; i.e., increasing

Table 1. Determinants of Interindustry Job Turnover in the Swedish Manufacturing Industry, 1965–96

	1	2	3	4
θ	0.068	0.066	0.070	1.300
	(2.76)	(2.86)	(3.31)	(3.36)
$\Delta(U/V)$	0.001			
	(1.92)			
$\hat{L}$		−0.001	−0.001	−0.024
		(−1.85)	(−2.25)	(−2.35)
$\Delta\omega$	−0.001	−0.002		
	(−0.58)	(−0.78)		
ω			−0.001	−0.019
			(−1.32)	(−1.16)
$\bar{R}^2$	0.188	0.214	0.306	0.311
F	3.32	3.63	5.40	5.52
Durbin–Watson	1.304	1.261	1.326	1.35
Breusch–Godfrey	2.60	3.96	3.37	2.95

Notes: *t*-values in parentheses. The critical values on the 5% significance level for the Breusch–Godfrey test is 3.84, and for the Durbin–Watson test $d_l = 1.244$ and $d_u = 1.650$ (with the null hypothesis no autocorrelation). Dependent variable is σ in columns (1)–(3) and γ in column (4).

exports in some industries and increasing imports in others. If, on the other hand, the increased specialization is mainly of the intraindustry kind (i.e., a parallel increase in exports *and* imports in most industries), it will not necessarily lead to more interindustry turnover of jobs.

Openness to international competition in the Swedish economy has gradually increased. The ratio of exports plus imports to domestic consumption of manufactures doubled from 1969 to 1995. However, as shown by Fuentes–Godoy et al. (1996), almost all of this consisted of increased intraindustry trade. Consequently the effect on interindustry job turnover was probably small.

However, even for a given level of the aggregate trade ratio, job turnover will be directly affected by the actual shifts in relative international competitiveness or comparative advantage among industries. Define revealed international competitiveness in an industry as the ratio of domestic production to domestic consumption. Then it may be shown (Andersson et al., 1998) that the employment share of an industry depends on the budget share of the corresponding good, the international competitiveness of domestic producers, and the amount of labor required per unit of output; i.e., the inverse of labor productivity.

The change in the employment share may be written as the sum of three effects: the competitiveness effect, the demand or market growth effect, and the productivity effect. The rate of interindustry job turnover depends on the *variation* among industries with respect to demand growth, productivity growth, and change of international competitiveness; the larger the differences across industries in these respects, the higher will be the rate of industrial restructuring and job turnover.

The effect of changing relative international competitiveness for job reallocation among industries may then be evaluated by calculating the hypothetical value of the

Figure 2. Effect on the Rate of Interindustry Job Turnover in Swedish Manufacturing of Shifting "Revealed" International Competitiveness, 1970–92

job turnover rate for a given period, obtained by keeping budget shares and productivity constant. The result, shown in Figure 2, measures interindustry job reallocation caused by the competitiveness effect alone. This may be compared with the "true" value of σ according to (1) shown in Figure 1.

The mean value for this variable is 0.046. Comparing this with the mean of the "actual" σ computed for the same period and on the same level of aggregation (4-digit SNI), which is the result of dispersion among industries with respect to all three factors creating turnover (i.e., changes in expenditure shares, labor requirements, and competitiveness), which is 0.041, it would appear that shifting competitiveness alone did account for more than 100% of actual job turnover! It should be remembered, though, that this is the result of a purely mechanical exercise disregarding possible links between the changes. It may well be that industries with large productivity increases (i.e., large negative $\Delta\lambda_i$) tend to improve competitiveness (large positive $\Delta\rho_i$), so that the effects partly cancel out.

It is clear from Figure 2 that σ* tends to grow over time. Our interpretation is that an increasing volatility with respect to shifts in "revealed" competitiveness among industries has contributed to the secular growth in the rate of interindustry job turnover in Swedish manufacturing found in section 3.

6. Intraindustry Job Turnover in Swedish Manufacturing, 1986–96

Next we consider the process of within-industry job reallocation among plants. The rate of intraindustry job turnover may be obtained by summing the absolute value of changes in employment shares across all plants in the industry—expanding as well as contracting. Let a_{ijt}^e be the employment share of a new plant entering the industry (i.e., which exists in year t but not in $t-1$), a_{ijt-1}^x the share of a plant closed down (existing in $t-1$ but not in t), and $a_{ijt}^b - a_{ijt-1}^b$ the change of the employment share for a plant existing in both periods, hereafter called an existing plant. Then the rate of net intraindustry job turnover may be written

$$\sigma_{it} = \sum_{j=1}^{b_i} |a_{ijt}^b - a_{ijt-1}^b| + \sum_{j=1}^{e_i} a_{ijt}^e + \sum_{j=1}^{x_i} a_{ijt-1}^x, \qquad (4)$$

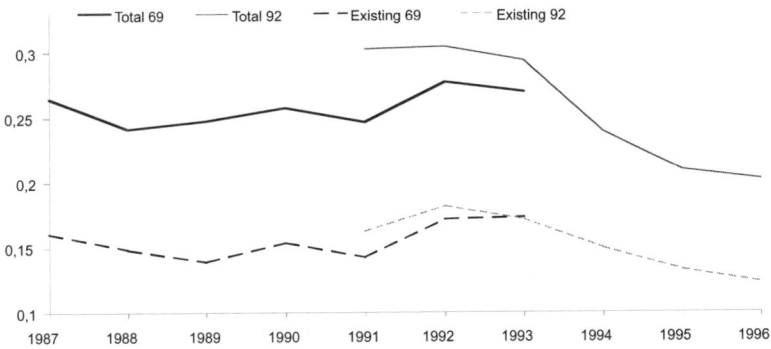

Figure 3. Intraindustry Job Turnover: Total and Within Existing Plants

where b_i, e_i, and x_i are the number of plants existing in both periods, the number of plants entering, and the number of plants exiting from the ith industry. The first term shows the role of reallocation of workers among existing plants, and the second and third the contribution to intraindustry job mobility from entry and exit of plants.

For the period 1986–96 there are data on employment by plant in Swedish manufacturing.[8] Because of the change in the classification system, we work with two (partly overlapping) data panels, the first containing annual changes from 1986 to 1993 for 146 industries on the 5-digit level of SNI69, the second annual changes from 1990 to 1996 for 276 industries on the 5-digit level of SNI92.

On average, 13% of the jobs were reallocated annually among plants within the same industry. Of this, more than half was accounted for by turnover among existing firms, while entry and exit of plants contributed about one-fifth each. The mean rate of total turnover and its components were almost the same in both subperiods, but their variability was higher in the 1990s.[9] Obviously, the mean rate of intraindustry turnover among plants is much higher than reallocation among industries[10] which, as shown in section 3, was less than 3% annually.

Unlike the rate of interindustry restructuring of employment, there seems to be no positive trend in the rate of intraindustry turnover of jobs. Figure 3 shows that the rate of within-industry reallocation was roughly constant up to 1991 but increased slightly in 1992, coinciding with a strong decline in total employment. This was accounted for partly by a rising exit rate,[11] which should be expected in a recession, but mainly by a higher rate of job reallocation among existing plants. Thus, both rates of turnover, inter- as well as intraindustry, show a countercyclical pattern (cf. section 4). Turnover due to entry of new plants seems to have been steadily falling since 1989.

The general impression from Figures 3 and 4 is that, since the early 1990s, the rate of intraindustry job turnover has been gradually falling. This holds for each of its components; i.e., turnover within existing plants as well as turnover due to entry or exit. The process of industrial restructuring thus seems to have entered a more stagnant phase.

7. A Framework for Explaining Intraindustry Job Turnover

For the analysis of intraindustry job turnover among firms or plants within the same industry, we need a different theoretical framework from that in section 2. Obviously,

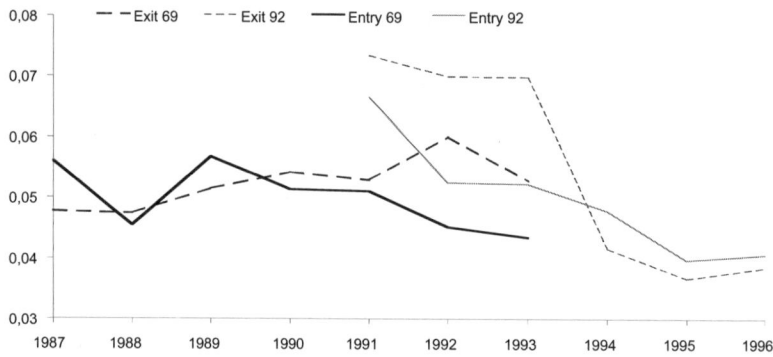

Figure 4. Intraindustry Job Turnover due to Exit and Entry of Plants

models with identical firms and perfect competition cannot contribute much toward the understanding of such job flows.

Assume an industry with monopolistic competition. Firms[12] produce differentiated products but are otherwise identical in the long run, in the sense that the nonstochastic parts of demand and cost functions are identical and constant. In the short run, however, the representative firm is exposed to firm-specific random demand (ε_{ijt}) and supply (t_{ijt}) shocks, with mean equal to one and constant variance, shifting the demand and production functions. Assuming that labor in the short run is the only mobile factor, profit maximization implies that the marginal revenue product of labor equals the wage rate:

$$\varepsilon_{ijt} F_i(q_{ijt}) t_{ijt} f_L(L_{ijt}) = w, \tag{5}$$

where $F_i(\cdot)$ and $f_L(\cdot)$ are the constant, nonstochastic parts of the marginal revenue and marginal productivity of labor functions. The firm adjusts employment and output to these shocks so that (5) is always satisfied.

Obviously, the size of these adjustments for given shocks depends on the slopes of $F_i(\cdot)$ and $f_L(\cdot)$. The more elastic the demand for the output of the representative firm, and the slower the marginal product of labor falls with increasing employment, the higher will be the firm's elasticity of demand for labor, and the more volatility in sales and employment one should expect, given the distribution of supply and demand shocks. This means that if we compare industries exposed to stochastic shocks with the same variance, we should expect the rate of intraindustry job reallocation among firms to be higher, the more elastic the $F_i(\cdot)$ and $f_L(\cdot)$ curves of the representative firm.

Since we cannot measure demand and supply shocks directly, our empirical analysis is more limited in scope. We ask two questions. First, which industries are likely to be exposed to high volatility with respect to demand and supply shocks to the individual firm; i.e., large variance of ε_{ijt} and t_{ijt}? And second, given the patterns of demand and supply shocks, in which kind of industry should we expect to observe the largest effects in terms of reallocation of employment among plants? The answer to that is a matter of the elasticities of marginal revenue and marginal cost. However, since these elasticities cannot be measured directly, what we actually do is to explore the relationship between the rate of intraindustry job turnover and a set of industry characteristics expected to be related to the elasticities of marginal revenue and cost.

One should find a higher volatility for both demand and supply shocks in product groups in the early stages of the life cycle, rather than in more mature industries. Such markets are characterized by high rates of innovation and differentiated demand where fashion and brand images are important, thus making both supply and demand conditions inherently unstable. We expect such industries to show high rates of market growth.

The elasticity of demand for labor of a firm will be higher, the higher is the elasticity of substitution of labor for other factors of production, the higher is the share of wages in total cost, and the more elastic is the demand for the firm's product (Sapsford and Tzannatos, 1993). When the number of firms is large, the price elasticity of demand for the product of the representative firm equals the elasticity of substitution between each pair of products in the industry (Helpman and Krugman, 1985). Thus, $F_i(\cdot)$ is more elastic the closer substitutes (i.e., the less differentiated) products are. However, product differentiation is notoriously difficult to measure (Caves and Williamson, 1985).

If the number of firms is small, the perceived elasticity of demand will reflect the firm's conjectures about the reactions of its competitors to changes in its price and/or sales. In the case of Cournot competition among identical firms, the demand elasticity of the firm will be proportionate to the number of sellers (Richardson, 1989). In general, perceived demand will be inelastic if firms expect competitors to follow their price changes (Helpman and Krugman, 1989). Awareness of such retaliation should be more likely in highly concentrated industries with few sellers. A tendency for higher market share stability in concentrated industries was found for the US by Gort (1963) and Caves and Porter (1978), and for Canada by Baldwin and Gorecki (1994); see also Schmalensee (1989). Lacking an appropriate measure of seller concentration, we use the number of plants in the industry.

Given the patterns of stochastic shocks, the stability of market shares of firms within an industry may be expected to be higher in industries where there is some form of collusive behavior. According to Tirole (1988) and Jaquemin and Slade (1989), tacit collusion will be simpler to enforce, and thus should be more frequent, in strongly concentrated industries.

Intraindustry job reallocation is affected also by entry and exit of firms. High barriers to entry are likely to be found in production with strong economies of scale and high minimum efficient scale (MES), and therefore with high initial investment requirements which may imply high sunk costs and thus more risky projects (Devine et al., 1985; Tirole, 1988). Lacking proper measures of MES of plants, and assuming a market outcome where the actual distribution of plant size in an industry will be concentrated around the MES, we may use average plant size, in terms of output or employment by plant, as a proxy. A negative relationship between plant size and entry of new firms was found for Sweden by Hause and Du Rietz (1984).

Both the *level* and the *change* of trade flows in an industry may have a positive effect on the rate of within-industry job turnover. A parallel increase in exports and imports of a good should give increased intraindustry turnover of jobs among plants, provided that the increase in specialization does not take place within firms and plants. Brülhart (1994) and Brülhart et al. (1998) have argued that the relevant concept for explaining intraindustry adjustment and job turnover is marginal intraindustry trade, defined as[13]

$$A_i = 1 - \frac{|dX_i - dM_i|}{|dX_i| + |dM_i|}. \tag{6}$$

As an alternative we use the changes of the ratios of export to production ($\hat{x}_i$) and imports to consumption ($\hat{m}_i$).

There may be two reasons for expecting higher rates of intraindustry job turnover in industries that are exposed to international competition on the export and/or home market. One is that the demand curve of the representative firm may be more volatile; i.e., that the variance of the stochastic disturbances ε_{ijt} in (5) may be higher than in sheltered sectors. The other reason is that, for a given number of domestic producers and sellers, the market power of the representative firm is inversely related to the market share of imports. This means that the perceived elasticity of demand for the representative firm is positively related to imports, and thus that the effects of given demand and supply shocks on employment will be larger. A negative effect of import competition on mark-up and market power was found for Sweden by Hansson (1992).

8. Determinants of Intraindustry Job Turnover

From the discussion in section 7, we expect the rate of intraindustry job turnover, σ, to behave as follows.

1. It should increase with the number of plants in the industry N, where few plants is supposed to reflect seller concentration and market power of firms, as well as the likelihood of tacit collusion, resulting in inelastic demand curves and a high stability of market shares.
2. It should decrease with average plant size S, implying large minimum efficient scale and high entry barriers.
3. It should decrease with π, the share of nonwage value-added, since the elasticity of demand for labor increases with the share of wages in total costs. π may also reflect a high mark-up of price over marginal cost, and strong market power.
4. It should increase with the rate of growth of employment, $\hat{L}$, reflecting high volatility of demand and supply shocks in early stages of the product cycle.
5. It should increase with the *level* of trade, first because the volatility of shocks may be higher when firms compete in international markets or with imports than for firms in sheltered sectors; and second, because given the number of domestic firms, market power will be eroded by import competition. Trade is measured by m, the import share of consumption, and x, the export share of production.
6. It should increase with an *increase* in trade, in particular intraindustry trade ($\hat{m}, \hat{x}, A$), unless increased specialization takes place within firms.

We work with two (partly overlapping) data panels, 1986–93 and 1990–96.[14] For most of our variables the frequency distributions are strongly positively skewed; i.e., there are a limited number of extreme outliers. Some of the variables, in particular employment growth and the trade ratios, are likely to contain measurement errors that may be especially serious for small industries.

We address this problem by using weighted least-squares regression (WLS) where observations are weighted by employment in order to reduce the noise due to errors concentrated in small industries (Berman et al., 1994). Moreover, we exclude observations with extremely high values of the trade ratios and very large changes in employment (see the notes to Table 2), not because they are outliers *per se* but because the values are unreasonable and hence must be due to measurement errors. However,

Table 2. Determinants of Rates of Intraindustry Job Turnover in Swedish Manufacturing, 1986–93 and 1990–96

	1986–93				1990–96		
	WLS	FEM	BEM	WLS	WLS	FEM	BEM	WLS
No. of plants, N	0.043	−0.570	0.062	0.043	0.096	0.021	0.168	0.099
	(2.54)	(−3.09)	(2.19)	(2.51)	(5.31)	(0.17)	(5.91)	(5.18)
Plant size, $S = L/N$	−0.209	−1.169	−0.231	−0.211	−0.206	−0.542	−0.293	−0.223
	(−9.47)	(−7.16)	(−6.05)	(−9.58)	(−10.01)	(−4.48)	(−7.25)	(−10.46)
Profit margin, π	−0.043	0.370	−0.056	−0.04	−0.106	−0.250	0.185	−0.064
	(−0.39)	(2.68)	(−0.29)	(−0.40)	(−1.60)	(−3.24)	(1.40)	(−0.88)
Growth, $\hat{L}$	−0.771	−0.989	0.224	−0.768	−0.040	−0.395	−1.256	−0.071
	(−4.35)	(−5.86)	(0.43)	(−4.36)	(−0.27)	(−2.83)	(−2.80)	(−0.47)
Export ratio, x	−0.041	0.187	−0.037	−0.040	−0.058	0.066	−0.101	−0.094
	(−1.45)	(1.68)	(−0.76)	(−1.42)	(−2.30)	(0.82)	(−2.00)	(−3.77)
Import ratio, m	0.068	−0.135	0.062	0.065	0.104	−0.172	0.082	0.083
	(2.30)	(−0.88)	(1.08)	(2.18)	(4.14)	(−1.63)	(1.50)	(3.11)
Export change, $\hat{x}$	0.007	−0.072	−0.401		0.049	−0.066	−0.111	
	(0.06)	(−0.63)	(−1.31)		(0.58)	(−0.86)	(−0.39)	
Import change, $\hat{m}$	0.272	0.062	0.946		−0.015	0.122	1.135	
	(1.98)	(0.45)	(2.03)		(−0.18)	(1.46)	(0.53)	
Marginal IIT, A				−0.049				0.089
				(−0.92)				(1.48)
F, period dummies	2.57	0.11		2.32	15.90	13.46		17.67
		(excl.)						
$\bar{R}^2$	0.303			0.300	0.332			0.363
F	25.32	9.08	13.26	27.09	44.94	11.56	26.89	50.53
Observations	785	785	125	791	1,151	1,151	219	1,045
No. of groups								

Notes: All variables except A are in logarithms. The dependent variable is $\gamma = \ln(\sigma/(2 − \sigma))$. Observations with negative consumption, profit margins outside the interval zero to one, export and import ratios above two, or where employment more than doubled/halved in one year, have been dropped. WLS, FEM, and BEM are weighted regression (observations weighted by employment size), panel regression with fixed (within-industry) effects and between-industry estimates. t-values in parentheses. Period dummy variables are not significant in column (2) and are excluded, but they are included in the other equations.

the exclusions do not seem to affect the basic results very much. Since the dependent variable is bounded, we use the logistic functional form of equation (3).

For the dependent variable and most of the explanatory variables, the major part of the variation occurs in the cross-sectional dimension. Moreover, the effect—or even the interpretation—of some variables may be different in the short and long run; i.e., in the time- and cross-sectional dimensions. In a comparison across industries, π may reflect capital intensity, while in the short run it shows fluctuations in profits. Whereas $\hat{L}$ in the cross-section may be related to stages in the life cycle of the product, variations over time reflect the business cycle. For this reason we will argue that, as a complement to the fixed-effect estimates, focusing on the within-industry variation of the variables one should also consider the cross-sectional patterns obtained by the pooled regression and the between-industry estimator.

Since we lack data on the ultimate determinants of job turnover (i.e., the demand and supply shocks), as well as on the appropriate elasticities, and since our variables are but imperfect proxies of the corresponding theoretical concepts, one should not expect our equations to explain all the variation in σ across industries and over time. The $\bar{R}^2$ in the WLS equations are around 0.3. However, all regressions are strongly significant.

There appears to be a time pattern common to all industries especially in the second panel in Table 2, which is not surprising considering the strong macroeconomic fluctuations in the 1990s. In 1993 the ratio of unemployment to vacancies started to fall after a very high increase in the first couple of years. We pick this up with period dummy variables which are negative and strongly significant for 1993 and onwards. Judging from this, the pattern appears to be countercyclical (see section 6).

Breusch–Pagan tests indicate the presence of industry-specific effects (i.e., cross-sectional effects of omitted variables), potentially creating bias in pooled regressions. On the other hand, the fixed effects (FEM) regressions, focusing on within-industry variation over time, produce estimates widely differing from the rest, which may imply that some of our variables in fact measure different effects across industries and over time. Finally, the Hausman tests imply—strongly for the first period, less clear in the second—that the random effects (REM) equations may be misspecified. The REM results are not presented in Table 2.

Summing up the results from Table 2, we find that the rate of job turnover among plants within an industry, σ, has been higher in the following circumstances:

(a) the higher the number of plants N in the industry—the coefficient is positive and strongly significant except for the FEM estimates;
(b) the lower the average plant size $S = L/N$ measured by employment—the coefficient is negative and strongly significant in all regressions;
(c) the higher the import penetration for the corresponding product group—the coefficient is positive, except for the FEM estimates, and significant in the WLS regressions, especially in the later period.

These results confirm our hypotheses. Our interpretation is that the results reflect the role of market power, based on seller concentration, tacit collusion, entry barriers and lack of import competition, to create stability of market shares. The effects of given supply and demand shocks in the form of structural adjustment and job turnover among firms and plants within an industry seem to be larger the more competition there is in the market. Moreover, high import penetration may not only reduce firms' market power and increase the perceived elasticity of demand, but may also increase the volatility of demand shocks.

Other results are less clear-cut and/or contrary to expectations. The coefficient of the employment growth variable is negative, contrary to the hypothesis, and strongly significant (except for BEM in the first panel and WLS in the second panel). Thus, the product cycle argument in section 7 obtains no support. We believe that the data actually capture the effect of business cycle fluctuations on job creation and destruction over time.[15] Not only interindustry (see section 4) but also intraindustry job turnover seems to follow a countercyclical time pattern.

According to our hypothesis, job turnover should be lower in industries with a high mark-up measured as nonwage share of value-added. However, the coefficient for π is significantly negative only in the FEM equation for 1990–96.

We expected the level, as well as the increase, of trade to be positively related to the rate of intraindustry job turnover. The results are somewhat mixed. The *level* of import penetration (m) appears to increase the rate of intraindustry job turnover. *Increasing* import penetration ($\hat{m}$) seems to cause more job turnover among plants in an industry. The coefficient is positive and significant but only in the first panel. The negative employment effects of an increasing import competition in an industry seem to be disproportionately distributed among firms. The performance of the marginal intraindustry trade variable A does not seem to be superior to that of $\hat{m}$.

Somewhat unexpectedly it turns out that export orientation (x) seems, if anything, to have a negative effect on job reallocation, contrary to the hypothesis. The coefficients are negative and significant though only in the later period. The increase in export share has no effect on job turnover. Why market shares in strongly export-oriented industries should be more stable than in other sectors is not easy to explain in a theoretically satisfactory way.

We may, however, offer a tentative explanation based on the market behavior of certain Swedish export industries. Nordic pulp and paper producers have repeatedly been accused by the European Commission of forming price cartels, carving up the market for their exports to the EU. Moreover, expansion of capacity by investment in the forest products industry tends to be lumpy, in the sense that all the large companies tend to make huge investments at the same time. This may explain why employment shares are relatively stable at least in some strongly export-oriented industries, and why export market growth may benefit all firms to the same extent.

9. Conclusions: Competition and Job Turnover

We have found that the rate of interindustry job turnover in the Swedish manufacturing industry, which in 1964–96 on average corresponded to 2.7% of the stock of jobs in manufacturing annually, did show a positive trend over the period. Thus in a historical perspective, the mid-1970s do not stand out as such an exceptional period of industrial restructuring as was thought at the time. The time pattern of job reallocation seems to be countercyclical.

Actual job turnover is the result of adjustment pressure and resistance. Focusing on the former, we found the rate of interindustry job turnover to be driven by the dispersion across industries in the change of the profit margins; the more profit changes differ, the more turnover. Our results indicate that shifts among industries in international competitiveness, which seem to have been increasing over time, did play a central role for the level, as well as for the trend, of the rate of interindustry job turnover.

The rate of intraindustry job turnover among plants within industries was much higher; the annual average in 1986–96 was around 13% of the stock of jobs in the typical industry. More than half of this was reallocation of jobs among existing plants, while entry and exit of plants contributed about one-fifth each. Unlike the reallocation among industries, it displays no trend. Since the early 1990s, within-industry job turnover has been falling; this is also true for its components; i.e., reallocation among existing plants and turnover due to entry and exit.

The results of the econometric analysis indicate that the rate of intraindustry job turnover among plants tends to be high in industries consisting of many small plants where domestic firms are exposed to import competition. Our interpretation is that this reflects the limited market power of firms in such industries, which means that market shares and the distribution of employment will be highly sensitive to firm-specific demand and supply shocks.

References

Andersson, L., O. Gustafsson, and L. Lundberg, "Structural Change, Competition and Job Turnover in the Swedish Manufacturing Industry, 1964–96," FIEF working paper 148 (1998).

Baldwin, J. and P. Gorecki, "Concentration and Mobility Statistics in Canada's Manufacturing Sector," *Journal of Industrial Economics* XLII (1994):93–103.

Berman, E., J. Bound, and Z. Griliches, "Changes in the Demand for Skilled Labor within US Manufacturing: Evidence from the Annual Survey of Manufacturing," *Quarterly Journal of Economics* CIX (1994):367–97.

Blomskog, S., *Essays on the Functioning of the Swedish Labour Market*, Swedish Institute for Social Research dissertation series 27 (1997).

Brülhart, M., "Marginal Intraindustry Trade: Measurement and Relevance for the Pattern of Industrial Adjustment," *Weltwirtschaftliches Archiv* 130 (1994):600–13.

———, "Marginal Intraindustry Trade and Trade Induced Adjustment: A Survey," in M. Brülhart and R. C. Hine (eds.), *Intra-Industry Trade and Adjustment*, Basingstoke: Macmillan (1999).

Brülhart, M., A. Murphy, and E. Strobl, "Intra-Industry Trade and Job Turnover," *GLM* Research Paper 98/4, University of Nottingham (1998).

Carlsson, B., "Det Svenska Industristödet i Internationell Jämförelse," *Ekonomisk Debatt* 11 (1993):466–77.

Caves, R. E. and M. E. Porter, "Market Structure, Oligopoly and Stability of Market Shares," *Journal of Industrial Economics* 27 (1978):289–312.

Caves, R. E. and P. Williamson, "What Is Product Differentiation, Really?" *Journal of Industrial Economics* 34 (1985):113–32.

Davidsson, P., L. Lindmark, and C. Olofsson, *Dynamiken i Svenskt Näringsliv*, Studentlitteratur, Lund (1994).

———, *Näringslivsdynamik under 90-talet*, NUTEK (Swedish National Board for Industrial and Technical Development), Stockholm (1996).

Davis, S., J. C. Haltiwanger, and S. Schuh, *Job Creation and Destruction*, Cambridge, MA: MIT Press (1996).

Devine P., N. Lee, R. Jones, and W. Tyson, *An Introduction to Industrial Economics*, London: Unwin Hyman (1985).

Eriksson, S. I., "Företags- och Branschspecifikt Stöd till Industrin: Bokslut Över en Epok," *Rapport från Struktursekretariatet*, 4/94. Ministry of Industry, Employment and Communications, Stockholm (1994).

Fuentes-Godoy, C., P. Hansson, and L. Lundberg, "International Specialization and Structural Change in the Swedish Manufacturing Industry, 1969–1992," *Weltwirtschaftliches Archiv* 132 (1996):523–43.

Gort, M., "Analysis of Stability and Change in Market Shares," *Journal of Political Economy* 62 (1963):51–61.
Hansson, P., "The Discipline of Imports: The Case of Sweden," *Scandinavian Journal of Economics* 94 (1992):589–97.
Hause, J. C. and G. Du Rietz, "Entry, Industry Growth and the Microdynamics of Industry Supply," *Journal of Political Economy* 72 (1984):733–57.
Helpman, E. and P. Krugman, *Market Structure and Foreign Trade*, Cambridge, MA: MIT Press (1985).
———, *Trade Policy and Market Structure*, Cambridge, MA: MIT Press (1989).
Holmlund, B., *Labor Mobility: Studies of Labor Turnover and Migration in the Swedish Labor Market*, Stockholm: IUI/Almqvist & Wiksell (1984).
Jaquemin, A. and M. Slade, "Cartels, Collusion and Horizontal Merger," in R. Schmalensee and R. Willig (eds.), *Handbook of Industrial Organization*, Vol I, Amsterdam: North-Holland (1989).
Kmenta, J., *Elements of Econometrics*, New York: Macmillan (1971).
OECD, *Historical Statistics* (1997).
Persson, H., "Job and Worker Flows in Sweden 1986–1995: Who Gets the New Jobs and Who Loses the Old Jobs?" SOFI working paper 6/1998 (1998).
Richardson, D., "Empirical Research on Trade Liberalization with Imperfect Competition: A Survey," *OECD Economic Studies*, no. 12 (1989).
Salvanes, K. G., "Market Rigidities and Labour Market Flexibility: An International Comparison," *Scandinavian Journal of Economics* 99 (1997):315–33.
Sapsford, D. and Z. Tzannatos, *The Economics of the Labor Market*, Basingstoke: Macmillan (1993).
Schmalensee, R., "Interindustry Studies of Structure and Performance," in R. Schmalensee and R. Willig (eds.), *Handbook of Industrial Organization*, Vol. 2, Amsterdam: North-Holland (1989).
Tirole, J., *The Theory of Industrial Organization*, Cambridge, MA: MIT Press (1988).
Zetterberg, J., "Flödesstatistik i Arbetsmarknadsforskningen: Bakgrundsfakta till Arbetsmarknads- och Flödesstatistiken," 1997:2. Statistics Sweden.

Notes

1. This paper studies *job* turnover but not *labor* turnover, the mobility of individual workers (i.e., the gross flows on the labor market). For studies of labor mobility in Sweden—geographical and/or occupational—see e.g., Holmlund (1984) and Blomskog (1997).
2. See also Davidsson et al. (1996) and Zetterberg (1997).
3. The relationship between gross and net job reallocation (turnover) is derived in Andersson et al. (1998).
4. For an international comparison relating rates of job turnover to national market rigidities, see Salvanes (1997).
5. Since, assuming total manufacturing employment constant, a worker moving from one industry to another will be counted twice.
6. Note that the particular form in (2), i.e., the equality $\sigma = \theta$, is a feature of the particular model used. In the empirical application we use the more general formulation $\sigma = a + b\theta$.
7. It may be argued that θ and $\hat{L}$ are actually endogenous which would generate inconsistent OLS estimates. A test for this using lagged values as instruments does not point to serious endogeneity problems.
8. Data for job creation, destruction and reallocation on the plant level for the Swedish economy 1986–93 have been presented by Davidsson et al. (1994, 1996) in a study focusing on the role of small firms, an issue outside the scope of this paper.
9. Note that for overlapping years in Figures 3 and 4, the rate of job turnover and its components are generally higher when computed from data classified according to the SNI92, possibly reflecting a finer disaggregation.

10. This confirms the results from previous studies of job turnover, such as Davis et al. (1996) for the US and Davidsson et al. (1994, 1996) and Persson (1998) for Sweden.
11. According to the 1986–93 panel, but not according to the 1990–96 panel, where the peak was one year earlier.
12. In this model we assume that each firm consists of no more than one plant.
13. As pointed out by Brülhart (1999), $A_i = 0$ in all cases where export and import changes have opposite signs.
14. A description of data and methods may be found in Andersson et al. (1998).
15. For those regressions including period dummies, $\hat{L}$ captures the effects of industry-specific cyclical changes in activity, which need not be perfectly synchronized with the overall business cycle.

Index

Note: "n." after a page reference indicates the number of a note on that page.

A index, intraindustry trade   49, 50, 51, 54, 57–8
Armington hypothesis, labor-demand elasticities   132, 135, 142
Australia, smooth and sticky adjustment   146

Balassa, B.
  intraindustry trade   64, 65
  revealed comparative advantage   5, 21
Belgium, labor-demand elasticities   142
Breusch–Godfrey test, Swedish manufacturing   198
Breusch–Pagan tests, Swedish manufacturing   206

Canada
  market share stability   203
  smooth and sticky adjustment   147
cartels, Swedish manufacturing   207
China, outward orientation   172
communication improvements, trade liberalization and technology change   47n.15
comparative advantage, revealed see revealed comparative advantage (RCA)
competing risk model, smooth and sticky adjustment   150
competition in Swedish manufacturing   207–8
  background   194–5
  interindustry job turnover   195–200
  intraindustry job turnover   200–7
computerization, Swedish manufacturing   163, 176
concentration of industries   52–3

Data Generation Process (DGP)   19
demand levels, intraindustry trade and labor-market adjustment   53

de-skilling hypothesis   163
developing countries, trade and wage inequality debate   92
differential factor effect   128–9, 130
differential industry effect   127, 128, 130
differentiated-goods model, trade and technology decompositions   97–101
Durbin–Watson statistic, Swedish manufacturing   198

educational attainment see skill levels
endogenously-determined trade regimes, trade and wages in   184–5, 192
  one-way v. two-way trade   190–2
  theoretical framework   185–90
Ethier two-country model, intraindustry trade   65–7
  marginal   67–72
European Coal and Steel Community, formation   146
European Union (EU), Single Market and eastwards expansion   145
evolving patterns of international trade   1–2, 20–2
  econometric estimation   15–20
  empirical modeling of trade dynamics   5–6
  preliminary data analysis   6–15
  theoretical modeling of trade dynamics   2–5
exports
  endogenously-determined trade regimes   186, 188–9, 190–2
  labor-demand elasticities   134, 138, 139
  multinational enterprises   76, 79–80, 87
  skill structures   162
  structural model choice in trade–wages decompositions   97–8, 100
  Swedish manufacturing   207

factor accumulation, evolving patterns of
    international trade 18, 20
factor-price insensitivity theorem 124n.10
factor proportions theory 132
factor taxes 111, 113–15, 116, 119
FEM regressions, Swedish manufacturing
    206
foreign direct investment (FDI)
    labor-demand elasticities 144n.4
    multinational enterprises 76, 87
foreign ownership, intraindustry trade and
    labor-market adjustment 53
FPE theorem 124n.10
    labor-demand elasticities 132
fragmentation phenomenon, trade
    liberalization and technology choice
    47n.9
France
    evolving patterns of international trade 8,
    9, 10, 13, 20: econometric estimation
    16, 17–18, 19
    labor-demand elasticities 141–2
frictional unemployment 145

Germany, evolving patterns of international
    trade 8, 9, 13, 20
    econometric estimation 17–18, 19
Grubel–Lloyd (GL/G) index, intraindustry
    trade 48, 49, 50, 54, 58, 64
    marginal 67–9, 71

Hausman tests, Swedish manufacturing
    206
hazard rate, smooth and sticky adjustment
    150, 151–4, 155, 156, 157
Heckscher–Ohlin (H–O) model
    structural model choice in trade–wages
        decompositions 90–1, 100–1: trade
        and wage inequality debate 92,
        104n.8; UK 93–7
    technical progress, price adjustments, and
        wages 125
    trade and wages debate, policy implications
        107, 110, 111
    wage inequality 25, 26, 29, 34: empirical
        analysis 31–3; trade liberalization
        37
hoarding, intraindustry trade and labor-
    market adjustment 51
housing market, smooth and sticky
    adjustment 157
human capital
    intraindustry trade 65
    see also skill levels

imports
    competition 45, 47n.15
    endogenously-determined trade regimes
        185–6
    labor-demand elasticities 134, 138
    multinational enterprises 80–1
    skill structures 162, 172–4, 181n.12
    structural model choice in trade–wage
        decompositions 97–8, 100
    Swedish manufacturing 204, 206–7, 208
    wage inequality 26
income distribution
    technical progress, price adjustments, and
        wages 125
    trade and wages debate, policy implications
        108–10, 111–16, 120, 121–2, 123
income tax, trade and wages debate 108,
    111, 112–13, 116
India, outward orientation 172
industrial policy, Sweden 198
information technology, Swedish
    manufacturing 163
internationalization rate, labor-demand
    elasticities 139
intra-distribution dynamics, evolving patterns
    of international trade 5, 10
intraindustry trade (IIT)
    endogenously-determined trade regimes
        184
    and labor-market adjustment 48, 61, 64:
        conceptual issues 48–51; dynamics
        57–60; smooth-adjustment hypothesis,
        testing 51–6
    marginal see marginal intraindustry trade
        (MIIT)
    measuring 48–9
    smooth and sticky adjustment 145, 146
investment
    foreign direct (FDI): labor-demand
        elasticities 144n.4; multinational
        enterprises 76, 87
    Swedish manufacturing 167, 168, 170, 171,
        175
Ireland, Republic of: intraindustry trade and
    labor-market adjustment 48, 49–50,
    53–6, 61
Irish Agency for Enterprise and Technology
    (Forfás) 53–4
Irish Central Statistical Office, Census of
    Industrial Production (CIP) 54
Italy, labor-demand elasticities 134

Japan, evolving patterns of international
    trade 8, 9, 13–15, 20–1

INDEX

econometric estimation 16, 17–18, 19
job turnover
  and intraindustry trade 51–4, 61
  in Swedish manufacturing 207–8: background 194–5; interindustry 195–200; intraindustry 200–7
Jones magnification effect, wage inequality 36n.8

knowledge capital
  Swedish manufacturing 161–2, 163–7, 168, 169, 170, 176
  see also skill levels
knowledge spillovers, evolving patterns of international trade 3–4, 18, 20

labor demand
  elasticities 132, 142: calculation details 142–3; intermediate approach 134–5; neoclassical theory 132–3; new trade theories 133–4; trade openness and aggregate scale effect 135–42
  multinational enterprises 77, 79, 81
labor-market adjustment
  to intraindustry trade 48, 61, 64: conceptual issues 48–51; dynamics 57–60; smooth-adjustment hypothesis, testing 51–6
  to marginal intraindustry trade 48, 61, 64, 72–3: conceptual issues 49–51; dynamics 57–60; related literature 64–5; smooth adjustment hypothesis, testing 51, 53, 54; two-country model 65–72
labor supply
  trade and wages debate, policy implications 122–3
  wage inequality 29–30
learning-by-doing, evolving patterns of international trade 3, 4, 5
learning rate, evolving patterns of international trade 3
Lerner–Pearce diagram, trade and wage debate 107, 110
liberalization of trade 37–8, 45
  intraindustry trade 64–5: marginal 69, 70, 71–2
  technology change induced by 43–5
  technology change versus 39–42

machine tool industry, adjustment process 146
manufacturing sector

evolving patterns of international trade 7–8, 9, 10, 15
smooth and sticky adjustment 158
Sweden – relative demand for skills 161–2, 176: analytical framework 162–5; definitions and data sources 177–8; empirical results 165–76
Sweden – structural change, competition and job turnover 207–8: background 194–5; interindustry job turnover 195–200; intraindustry job turnover 200–7
marginal intraindustry trade (MIIT) and labor-market adjustment 48, 61, 64, 72–3
  conceptual issues 49–51
  dynamics 57–60
  related literature 64–5
  smooth adjustment hypothesis, testing 51, 53, 54
  two-country model 65–72
mark-ups
  labor-demand elasticities 133, 142
  Swedish manufacturing 204, 207
Menon–Dixon (C) index, marginal intraindustry trade 68–9, 71
mobility of labor
  smooth and sticky adjustment 145, 146–7, 154, 156, 157–8
  Swedish manufacturing 163, 195
multinational enterprises (MNEs), Sweden: competition from high- and low-wage locations 76–7, 87
  data 81–2
  estimation 82–3
  results 83–7
  theoretical framework 78–81

neoclassical trade theory
  intraindustry trade 48
  labor-demand elasticities 132, 134, 135, 142
Netherlands, labor-demand elasticities 142
nonelectrical machinery sector, UK 182n.37

openness to trade
  endogenously-determined trade regimes 184, 192
  intraindustry trade 53, 61
  labor-demand elasticities 132–3, 134, 135–42, 143
  Swedish manufacturing 199

Organization of Economic Cooperation and Development (OECD), *Bilateral Trade Database* (BTD)   6–7, 21
outsourcing
  labor-demand elasticities   133
  by multinationals   77
  and skill levels   161: Swedish manufacturing   172
  trade and wage inequality debate   92

paper and pulp sector   207
prices
  labor-demand elasticities   133
  marginal intraindustry trade and labor adjustment   66–7
  structural model choice in trade–wage decompositions   95–6
  Swedish manufacturing   196
  technical progress and wages   125–30
  trade liberalization and technology change   37, 38–40, 43, 47n.16
  wage inequality   27, 30–1, 32, 33
production taxes, trade and wages debate   111–12, 115, 116
productivity
  evolving patterns of international trade   2, 4–5
  multinational enterprises   83, 86
  Swedish manufacturing   200
  trade liberalization and technology change   42
profitability
  endogenously-determined trade regimes   186–7
  multinational enterprises   78
  Swedish manufacturing   196, 197, 202, 207
  technical progress, price adjustments, and wages   125–6
  trade liberalization and technology change   40, 41, 43
protectionism
  endogenously-determined trade regimes   184, 185, 192
  trade and wage inequality debate   92
pulp and paper sector   207

Quah, Danny: TSRF econometrics package   15
qualifications *see* skill levels

research and development (R&D)
  expenditure, and skill levels   161–2, 163–5, 167, 170–1, 176

revealed comparative advantage (*RCA*)
  evolving patterns of international trade   1, 20: econometric estimation   15–16, 17, 18–20; empirical modeling of trade dynamics   5–6; preliminary data analysis   6, 7–14
  measuring   21–2
Rybczysnki effect
  Swedish manufacturing   168
  wage inequality   29

scale effect, labor-demand elasticities   133, 134, 135–42
sectoral shift hypothesis, smooth and sticky adjustment   146, 154
service sector, Sweden   194, 196
shift-share analyses   161
skill-based technological change (SBTC)   161
  trade and wage inequality debate   92
  trade liberalization   42, 43
  wage inequality   25, 26–8, 30–1, 32–3, 34, 37
skill levels
  labor-demand elasticities   133, 134–5, 137–40
  smooth and sticky adjustment   156–7
  in Swedish manufacturing, relative demand for   161–2, 176: analytical framework   162–5; definitions and data sources   177–8; empirical results   165–76
  trade and wages debate, policy implications   107–10, 111, 121–3
  trade liberalization and technology change   37, 40–1, 42, 45, 47n.15
smooth-adjustment hypothesis
  intraindustry trade and labor-market adjustment   48, 51–6, 60, 61, 74n.1
  US and UK, comparative analysis   145–6, 157–8: data and basic statistics   147–50; earlier work   146–7; modeling unemployment durations with multiple outcomes   150–2; results   152–7
Soviet Union, former: outward orientation   172
specialization
  evolving patterns of international trade   1, 20–1, 22: econometric estimation   16, 18, 19; empirical modeling of trade dynamics   5–6; preliminary data analysis   6, 8, 10–15; theoretical modeling of trade dynamics   4–5

labor-demand elasticities 133
  structural model choice in trade–wages decompositions 91, 95
  Swedish manufacturing 198–9
  trade and wages debate, policy implications 120–2
steel sector, and ECSC formation 146
Stolper–Samuelson theorem 36n.8
  correlation version 36n.14
  marginal intraindustry trade and labor adjustment 75n.13
  technical progress, price adjustments, and wages 125
  trade liberalization 37
structural change in Swedish manufacturing 207–8
  background 194–5
  interindustry job turnover 195–200
  intraindustry job turnover 200–7
structural model choice in trade–wages decompositions 90–1, 101–2
  differentiated-goods model 97–101
  Heckscher–Ohlin model for inequality decomposition in the UK 93–4
  trade and wage inequality debate 91–3
subsidies
  Sweden 198
  trade and wages debate, policy implications 122–3
substitution effect, labor-demand elasticities 133, 134
Sweden
  intraindustry trade 53
  multinationals, and competition from high- and low-wage locations 76–7, 87: data 81–2; estimation 82–3; results 83–7; theoretical framework 78–81
  skills, relative demand in manufacturing 161–2, 176: analytical framework 162–5; definitions and data sources 177–8; empirical results 165–76
  structural change, competition and job turnover in manufacturing 207–8: background 194–5; interindustry job turnover 195–200; intraindustry job turnover 200–7

tariffs
  marginal intraindustry trade and labor adjustment 65, 67, 69–72
  trade and wage debate, policy implications 118–20, 121
taxation, trade and wages debate 111–16

technical change (TC) 37–8, 45
  evolving patterns of international trade 1, 3, 20
  price adjustments and wages 125–30
  skill-biased see skill-biased technical change (SBTC)
  structural model choice in trade–wages decompositions 91, 96, 99
  Swedish manufacturing 163, 164, 165–7, 175, 195–6
  trade and wages debate, policy implications 106
  trade-induced 38–9
  trade liberalization 39–42: induced 43–5; and technology change 41–2
  wage inequality 27, 30–1
technicians, proportion in workforce 164, 171, 172, 181n.20
technology intensity 53
technology shocks
  structural model choice in trade–wages decompositions 90, 91: Heckscher–Ohlin model for the UK 93, 95, 97
  trade and wages debate, policy implications 119–20
technology transfers, evolving patterns of international trade 3–4, 18
temporary layoffs, USA 150, 154
tenure with previous employer, effect on re-employment 156
textile industry
  Sweden 162, 172–3, 176
  UK 182n.37
trade and wages debate, policy implications 106–7, 123
  model 107–11
  redistribution 111–16
  response to change 116–20
  skilled labor supply, changing the 122–3
  specialization and multiple cones 120–2
trade in endogenously-determined trade regimes 184–5, 192
  one-way v. two-way trade 190–2
  theoretical framework 185–90
trade liberalization see liberalization of trade
trade shocks
  structural model choice in trade–wages decompositions 90, 91: Heckscher–Ohlin model for the UK 93, 95
  trade and wages debate, policy implications 116–19

trades unions, endogenously-determined trade regimes 184–6, 187–8, 189–91, 192
trade taxes, trade and wage debate 112, 115–16, 119
trade–wages decompositions, structural model choice in 90–1, 101–2
  differentiated-goods model 97–101
  Heckscher–Ohlin model for inequality decomposition in the UK 93–7
  trade and wages inequality debate 91–3
transport costs, and wages 184

unemployment
  intraindustry trade 52
  labor-demand elasticities 133
  smooth and sticky adjustment 145–6, 147: US and UK, comparative analysis 147–58
  Sweden 162, 175–6, 197, 206
  trade and wage inequality debate 92
unemployment benefits, smooth and sticky adjustment 154–6
unions, endogenously-determined trade regimes 184–6, 187–8, 189–91, 192
United Kingdom
  evolving patterns of international trade 7–8, 9–10, 11–13, 20: econometric estimation 16, 17–18, 19
  intraindustry trade and labor-market adjustment 52, 184
  smooth and sticky adjustment 145–6, 157–8: data and basic statistics 147–50; earlier work 146–7; modeling unemployment duration with multiple outcomes 150–2; results 152–7
  structural model choice in trade–wages decompositions, 90, 91: differentiated-goods model 99; Heckscher–Ohlin model 93–7; trade and wage inequality debate 92
  textiles and nonelectrical machinery sectors 182n.37
  wage inequality 32–3, 34
United States of America
  evolving patterns of international trade 7–8, 13, 20: econometric estimation 16, 17–18, 19
  import competition 173, 174
  intraindustry trade and labor-market adjustment 52
  job turnover 197
  market share stability 203
  multinational enterprises 77, 84, 87
  smooth and sticky adjustment 145–6, 157–8: data and basic statistics 147–50; earlier work 146–7; modeling unemployment duration with multiple outcomes 150–2; results 152–7
  structural model choice in trade–wages decompositions 92
  trade and wages debate, policy implications 106, 123
  wage inequality 32, 33, 34
unit labor cost (ULC), multinational enterprises 86–7

wage inequality, trade and labor approaches to 25, 34
  empirical analysis of H–O model 31–3
  simple framework 25–31
wage levels
  in endogenously-determined trade regimes 184–5, 192: one-way v. two-way trade 190–2; theoretical framework 185–90
  evolving patterns of international trade 2
  intraindustry trade and labor-market adjustment 53, 65: marginal 72
  labor-demand elasticities 132–3, 134, 137–40, 143
  multinational enterprises 76–7, 87: data 81–2; estimation 82–3; results 83–7; theoretical framework 78–81
  smooth and sticky adjustment 146–7, 158
  Swedish manufacturing 163, 168, 169, 176: job turnover 196
  technical progress and price adjustments 125–30
  trade liberalization and technology change 37, 45, 47n.16
wages and trade debate, policy implications 106–7, 123
  model 107–11
  redistribution 111–16
  response to change 116–20
  skilled labor supply, changing the 122–3
  specialization and multiple cones 120–2
wages–trade decompositions, structural model choice in 90–1, 101–2
  differentiated-goods model 97–101
  Heckscher–Ohlin model for inequality decomposition in the UK 93–7
  trade and wages inequality debate 91–3
Walras' law, structural model choice in trade–wages decompositions 99
Weibull distribution, smooth and sticky adjustment 151, 152